Economics Broadly Considered

This work is designed to give the reader a sense of the breadth and possibilities of economics. The essays, all published here for the first time, cover the areas of economics to which Warren J. Samuels has made significant contributions: the history of economic thought, economic methodology, law and economics, and institutional and Post Keynesian economics. Issues investigated include:

*   The institutional structures that shape economic activity and performance.
*   The variety of approaches to economic analysis.
*   The importance of the history of the discipline both inherently and for the study of economics in the modern age.

Economics Broadly Considered offers scholars fresh perspectives on the areas of economics explored by Samuels. With essays from leading scholars, collected and introduced by some of the most eminent authorities in the field, the work is a formidable volume, and one fit to honor one of the most renowned economists of our age.

Jeff E. Biddle is Professor of Economics at Michigan State University. His research in labor economics and the history of economic thought has been published in such journals as the *American Economic Review*, the *Journal of Political Economy*, the *Journal of Labor Economics*, and *History of Political Economy*. He serves as co-editor of *Research in the History of Economic Thought and Methodology*, and his current research concerns the development of the economics profession in the United States during the twentieth century.

John B. Davis is Professor of Economics, Marquette University and editor of the *Review of Social Economy* and the Routledge series, "Advances in Social Economics." He is the author of *Keynes's Philosophical Development* (Cambridge, 1994) and co-editor of *The Handbook of Economic Methodology* (Elgar, 1998). He is also a past President of the History of Economics Society.

Steven G. Medema is Professor of Economics at the University of Colorado at Denver. His research interests include law and economics, public economics, and the economic role of government in the history of economic thought. He serves as editor of the *Journal of the History of Economic Thought*. His most recent books include *Economics and the Law: From Posner to Post Modernism* (with Nicholas Mercuro) and *Lionel Robbins, A History of Economic Thought: The LSE Lectures* (edited with Warren J. Samuels).

Routledge Studies in the History of Economics

Economics Broadly Considered
Essays in honor of Warren J. Samuels

Edited by Jeff E. Biddle, John B. Davis and Steven G. Medema

London and New York

For Warren J. Samuels

First published 2001
by Routledge
11 New Fetter Lane, London EC4P 4EE

Simultaneously published in the USA and Canada
by Routledge
29 West 35th Street, New York, NY 10001

Routledge is an imprint of the Taylor & Francis Group

© 2001 editorial material and selection, Jeff E. Biddle, John B. Davis
and Steven G. Medema, individual chapters, the authors.

Typeset in Times by
M Rules
Printed and bound in Great Britain by
Biddles Ltd, Guildford and King's Lynn

British Library Cataloguing in Publication Data
A catalogue record for this book is available from the British Library

Library of Congress Cataloging in Publication Data
Economics broadly considered: essays in honor of Warren J.
Samuels/edited by Jeff E. Biddle, John B. Davis, and
Steven G. Medema
    p.   cm.
Includes bibliographical references and index.
1. Economics. I. Samuels, Warren J., 1933– II. Biddle, Jeff.
III. Davis, John Bryan. IV. Medema, Steven G.
HB71.E2684 2001
330–dc21   00–045837

ISBN 0 415 23672-X

Contents

Figures and Tables

[†] Figures 11, 12 and 13 on pages 119 and 121 are part of the appendix to Chamberlin's thesis and the original figure notation has been retained.

Contributors

Roger E. Backhouse, Department of Economics, University of Birmingham, Birmingham, United Kingdom

William J. Barber, Department of Economics, Wesleyan University, Middletown, Connecticut, USA

Peter J. Boettke, Department of Economics, George Mason University, Fairfax, Virginia, USA

A. W. Bob Coats, Department of Economics, University of Nottingham, Nottingham, UK

Paul Davidson, Department of Economics, University of Tennessee, Knoxville, Tennessee, USA

Geoffrey M. Hodgson, Business School, University of Hertfordshire, Hertford, UK

S. Todd Lowry, Department of Economics, Washington and Lee University, Lexington, Virginia, USA

Thomas Mayer, Department of Economics, University of California-Davis, Davis, California, USA

Nicholas Mercuro, Lyman Briggs School, Michigan State University, East Lansing, Michigan, USA

Philip Mirowski, Department of Economics, University of Notre Dame, South Bend, Indiana, USA

Mark Perlman, Department of Economics, University of Pittsburgh, Pittsburgh, Pennsylvania, USA

Paul A. Samuelson, Department of Economics, Massachusetts Institute of Technology, Cambridge, Massachusetts, USA

A. Allan Schmid, Department of Agricultural Economics, Michigan State University, East Lansing, Michigan, USA

Andrew Skinner, Department of Economics, University of Glasgow, Glasgow, UK

Robert Solo, Department of Economics, Michigan State University, East Lansing, Michigan, USA

Marc R. Tool, Department of Economics, California State University – Sacramento, Sacramento, California, USA

Harry M. Trebing, Department of Economics and Institute of Public Utilities, Michigan State University, East Lansing, Michigan, USA

Introduction

Economics broadly considered: a glance at Warren J. Samuels' contributions to economics

Jeff E. Biddle, John B. Davis, and Steven G. Medema

Warren J. Samuels was born in New York City and grew up in Miami, Florida. He earned his B.A. from the University of Miami in 1954 and his Ph.D. from the University of Wisconsin in 1957. After holding positions at the University of Missouri, Georgia State University, and the University of Miami, Samuels was Professor of Economics at Michigan State University from 1968 until his retirement in 1998 (for biographical details, see Samuels 1995 and Blaug 1999).

Samuels' contributions to economics range widely across the discipline, but his most significant work, and the largest share of his corpus, falls within the history of economic thought, the economic role of government (and particularly law and economics), and economic methodology. All of this work has been undertaken against the backdrop of an institutional approach to economics and economic thought. Samuels was exposed to the institutional approach already during his undergraduate days at Miami, and he pursued the Ph.D. at Wisconsin because of its institutionalist tradition (then drawing to a close), as evidenced in faculty members such as Edwin Witte, Harold Groves, Martin Glaeser, Kenneth Parsons, and Robert Lampman.

Because of his institutionalist training, Samuels has always had a broad conception of what economics is and can be – something reflected in his scholarship in the history of economic thought and economic methodology as well. Unlike many (and perhaps most) contemporary institutionalists – but in common with, for example, John R. Commons – Samuels does not reject neoclassical economics, seeing it instead as useful for addressing certain types of problems but of limited utility in other contexts, in no small part because its a-institutional character begs certain important issues in economic theory and policy. Samuels' broad-based approach to economic theory and policy analysis thus allows one to view the issues on which it is trained at a deeper and more sophisticated level, although, because of its nature, it often does not lend itself to the determination of the types of unique determinate optimal solutions so much in favor within modern economics.

The extent of Samuels' contributions is made clear by the list of his publications reproduced at the end of this introduction. We cannot hope to survey this vast expanse here. Instead, we shall attempt to give the flavor of a handful of his most significant contributions and how the essays contained in this volume are reflective of these ideas.

The history of economic thought

When Warren Samuels was beginning his career, most research in the history of economic thought could be characterized as history of economic analysis. This research worked with a concept of economic analysis that was derivative of a view of the scope of economics that had its roots in the classical era, but that had been the object of increasing consensus within the profession since World War II: that economic analysis was concerned mainly with questions of value and distribution, economic growth, and the determination of aggregate economic income within a market-based economic system. The history of economic analysis, then, was concerned with correctly describing and perhaps evaluating the attempts of economic thinkers of the past – usually "great men" such as Smith, Ricardo, Marx, Keynes, etcetera – to answer these questions.

Samuels, due to training, native intellectual inclinations, or both, had developed a broader view than most of his fellow economists regarding the scope of economics and the range of questions economists should be interested in addressing, and this broader view of what constituted economic thought implied a longer and more varied list of topics and questions that could be explored under the heading "history of economic thought." Further, it seemed that the questions and topics on this list that Samuels found most interesting were also questions that were receiving relatively little attention from the community of historians of economic thought. For example, in Samuels (1972) he argued that historically, economics had been a discipline of two traditions: Economic Theory and Theory of Economic Policy. The former corresponded more or less with what has been called economic analysis above; the latter was concerned with "the problem of the combination of legal, non-legal and private economic decision making participation, ultimately policy (deliberative and non-deliberative) with respect to the structure of economic organization or power" (249). The Theory of Economic Policy had been relatively neglected by historians of economic thought, and Samuels proposed to "demonstrate the fact of historical existence" of this tradition, and to discuss the content of that tradition as it had historically existed (249). This, of course, was a research program he had started some time earlier – for example, his *Classical Theory of Economic Policy* (Samuels 1966) – and continues to pursue to this day. It has led him to explore aspects of the ideas of the great men of economics that were little noted by others, for as he pointed out in Samuels (1972) "every major economist and every major school of economic thought has had elements of the Theory of Economic Policy in their thought and writing" (249). It has also led him to analyze the writings of a large number of thinkers whose work had been neglected by historians of economic thought, thinkers who may not have defined themselves as economists at the time they wrote, or have looked like economists from the point of view of the late twentieth century, but who had insightful things to say about the organization and structure of the economic system, and its place within the larger social system – people from Robert Lee Hale to Edward Bellamy to Thurman Arnold.

Another thing that set Samuels apart from most mid-century historians of economic thought was his interest, as he put it, in "the form rather than the content of the history of economic thought, with characteristics that inform and channel economic inquiry but represent modes of thought rather than *economic* analysis *per se*" (Samuels 1974: 305). While many historians of economic thought looked at the plethora of theories, systems, and schools populating the history of economic thought and tried to trace out the thread of progress towards truth amidst all the error, Samuels set aside the question of error vs. truth and sought instead to better appreciate complexity and diversity of economic thought, past and present, and understand the reasons for its persistence. An extended quote from his influential article on "The History of Economic Thought as Intellectual History" (Samuels 1974) helps to convey the goals he has set for himself in this respect, and also, incidentally, the obvious pleasure he finds in pursuing those goals:

> The fact of and the opportunities accorded by complexity and diversity relate to what is perhaps the most profound objective of the history of economic thought. On the one hand, it is that of broadening the mind, providing . . . an understanding of meaning in terms of fundamental problems and not particular solutions or positions: on the other hand, it is the combination of a critical posture towards all thought and meaning with an ability to think in terms of different intellectual systems and the mastery of a degree of intellectual and emotional distance with regard to one's own mode or system of thought . . . Needless to say, the accomplishment of this objective is both difficult and deceptive, though it is very rewarding. (306–307)

Samuels' attempt in his 1974 intellectual history article to encourage historians of thought to look at a new range of questions from a new historiographical perspective was only one of many similar attempts he has made during his career. As he has stretched the boundaries of the field by dealing with issues and with people that lie outside the traditional canon of the history of economic thought, he has also employed and encouraged others to experiment with alternative research methods and approaches taken from fields such as history, philosophy, sociology or literary theory. This is a symptom of a pluralism and intellectual openness with respect to historiographical method that parallels his pluralism regarding economic method: a belief that any number of historiographical methods, from rational reconstruction to rhetorical analysis, might help to shed light on the wide array of questions that in his view comprise the subject matter of the history of economics.

A perusal of the list of articles, book reviews, and books in the history of thought that Samuels has written, as lengthy as that list is, reveals only a small part of his contribution to the field. He has, for example, devoted an enormous amount of effort to the exhumation, editing, and publication of archival material – previously unpublished letters, lecture notes, essays, and addresses: the work both of those who have long been regarded as important figures in the history of economics and those whose significance has become apparent largely as a result of Samuels' efforts. He has cooperated with publishers in bringing out new editions of potentially interesting works that had long ago passed out of print, making them more available to historians of economic thought around the world. He has edited a dizzying number of volumes on an incredibly wide array of topics in the history of economic thought and methodology. Perhaps Samuels realized early in his career that he would never have the time to pursue on his own all the research topics that interested him, and saw the edited volume as a vehicle for getting others to dig up the answers for him; in any case, through his work as an editor Samuels has encouraged and facilitated a great deal of important research on a wide variety of topics that might otherwise never have been undertaken. And not least of all, Samuels has always been an active member of the history of economic thought community, commenting quickly and perceptively on manuscripts sent his way, serving frequently as a discussant or session chair at professional meetings, and providing encouragement and sometimes publication opportunities for young scholars and for those who have decided to explore topics or employ research methods that might be considered a bit unorthodox.

The contributions in the history of economic thought section of this volume, taken collectively, are a fitting tribute to Samuels' own career in the history of economic thought, as they deal with a wide range of topics and employ a variety of historiographical and interpretive strategies. Todd Lowry's chapter has produced another example of his "archeological" research into the history of economic thought, exploring two examples of the "mirrors for princes" literature. Lowry argues that this literature, with its emphasis on rational authority in an administered economy, formed an important though now largely unrecognized part of the intellectual background of the contributors to economic and political theory of the seventeenth and eighteenth centuries. Paul Samuelson offers an "ahistorical" use of mathematical analysis to explore certain implications of physiocratic and classical economic thought and argues, among other things, that Sraffa's characterization of the wage/profit trade-off in the classical economic model is inaccurate. This is a classic example of the "history of economic analysis" genre that once dominated the field, and its presence in the volume is quite appropriate, because although Samuels has encouraged scholars to tackle new questions with new methods, he has always also had an interest in the traditional questions of the field, and never denigrated the methods traditionally used to address them. Andrew Skinner's chapter is also a contribution to the history of economic analysis, providing a new perspective on what Edward Chamberlain was trying to accomplish with his theory of monopolistic competition by examining Chamberlain's original Ph.D. thesis in the context of his later work. Geoff Hodgson's chapter deals with two of Samuels' favorite subjects: institutionalism and the thought of Frank Knight. Mark Perlman speculates that Simon Kuznets' negative review of Schumpeter's book on business cycles played an important role in limiting the subsequent influence of Schumpeter's cycle theory, and then uses Kuznets' unpublished Master's thesis to provide a richer understanding of the intellectual background of the review. William Barber's chapter on the alliance between Fisher and Commons regarding monetary reform shows the overlap between the ideas of an economist usually considered quite orthodox and one regarded as a founder of institutionalism. It provides a good illustration of a point frequently made by Samuels: that significant heterogeneity typically characterizes the schools of economic thought identified by historians, and even sometimes the work of an individual economist. Samuels has always been supportive of research that is sensitive to the social nature of the production of economic knowledge, often using sociological tools and concepts to understand it; Bob Coats's contribution to the volume shows the fruitfulness of this approach, as it examines the response of the economics profession through its association to the challenge of radical economics, and compares it to the response to the radicalism of the sixties of professional associations in related disciplines.

Economic methodology

As a recognized subdiscipline of economics, economic methodology is a relatively recent addition to the field, dating from the late 1970s and early 1980s. Its emergence was due in good part to the efforts of Warren Samuels, who early on – as evidenced by his editing the two issue, 1979–1980 *Journal of Economic Issues* symposium "Methodology in Economics" (Vol. XIII, No. 4 and Vol. XIV, No. 1) – grasped not only that economic methodology involves distinctive issues and problems in need of their own focused investigation, but that many of these issues were at the heart of debate over the nature of economics itself. Indeed, this concern with the very nature of economics reflects Samuels' own pathway into the field of economics methodology, since a central influence on his original interest in the field was his effort to understand the relationship between institutionalist economics and neoclassical economics. Samuels understood that many of the fundamental differences between institutionalist economics and neoclassical economics are methodological in nature. Thus it was his insight to see that emphasizing this both clarified these differences, helped explain the nature of economics in general, and helped define the field of economic methodology.

Another of his early contributions to the field, a volume edited with Marc Tool also at this same time, *The Methodology of Economic Thought* (1980;

rev. edn., 1989) similarly drew from *JEI* papers to establish the methodological credentials of such topics as culture, ideology, causality, social values, power, and the nature of rationality. Much of economists' thinking about economic methodology since John Neville Keynes had been dominated by traditional philosophy of science concerns usually associated with natural science. A further preoccupation with issues surrounding the rise and fall of logical positivism from the 1930s through the 1970s helped to maintain this relatively restricted focus for the few economists interested in economic methodology. However, the categories and concepts that Samuels emphasized had different origins. The volume with Tool was in fact one of a trilogy of volumes drawn from the *JEI*, the others being *The Economy as a System of Power* and *State, Society, and Corporate Power*. For Samuels, the methodology of economics was and is intimately related to the operation of the economy as a contested terrain, and this in his view implies the need for a distinctively social science – not natural science – approach to the economy. American institutionalism was of course originally influenced by the nineteenth-century German Historical School, which had strongly differentiated the methods appropriate to natural and social science. Thus part of Samuels' impact on economic methodology can be understood to be a matter of his insuring the continuing influence of this tradition.

A second, somewhat distinct influence on Samuels' thinking about economics methodology was the explosion of interest in the late 1980s in the rhetoric and language of economics. Samuels had had a keen interest in the ideas of Popper, Kuhn, Lakatos, and others in the theory appraisal–growth of knowledge movement that dominated early research in economic methodology, but it was the role of language and the discourse of economics that next most strongly captured his attention. His edited collection, *Economics as Discourse: An Analysis of the Language of Economists* (1990) stepped away from the theory appraisal project to ask – note the subtitle – how economists' thinking was implicitly guided by the language they inherited and mobilized. Language, Samuels argued in the introduction to the volume, bears epistemological, ontological, and practical pre-commitments. This means that facts and theories operate within interpretive frameworks. The economy itself is a system of communication, and economic reality is an interpreted reality subject to competing and often contradictory interpretations. Selective perception of the world guides economists in determining what questions they believe important to investigate, and thus there cannot be any independent, transcendently objective standpoint from which to carry out economic investigation.

Philosophically speaking, Samuels accepts the inevitability of the hermeneutic circle. The idea of the hermeneutic circle is that any explanation or elaboration of "new" concepts presupposes previously held concepts that play a role in that explanation or elaboration, such that there are no independent "foundations" upon which the theorist may rely to build up a theory. Samuels was influenced by Richard Rorty in this regard, who introduced many economic methodologists to Gadamer, Wittgenstein, and others from Continental European philosophy. Yet while interest in the language of economics was a relatively new interest for Samuels, it nonetheless resonated with his early interest in methodology via institutionalism, since the economy as a system of power and process of social valuation – hallmarks of his institutionalism – is equally a network of meanings, ideologies, and interpretations. Thus Samuels' vision of the economy and economics was sharpened as his interests in economic methodology broadened. Given the role of pragmatism in American institutionalism, much like Rorty, Samuels' philosophical thinking underlying his methodological views blended pragmatism and hermeneutical reasoning.

These foundations help to explain why Samuels' position is best characterized as a form of methodological pluralism. A variety of economic methodologists advocate methodological pluralism or forms of methodological pluralism, though often for quite different reasons. Samuels' position stems first from a conviction that there are neither epistemological absolutes, incontrovertible meta-criteria, nor independent standpoints for analyzing and explaining economic life. As he argued in his 1997 paper, "The Case for Methodological Pluralism," and in his *Handbook of Economic Methodology* entry, "methodological pluralism," the economy, economic theory, and economic methodology are all socially constructed in an ever on-going, historical process. Others, of course, hold this or similar views. What distinguishes Samuels' position is his senstivity to the paradox that the absence of absolutes, meta-criteria, creates and independent standpoints create for those who speak and write about the economy and economics. Though many appreciate that the social construction of reality is carried out in many voices, few emphasize how uncomfortable most of these voices are with the indeterminacy, contingency, and ambiguity that this implies. For Samuels, this is because those intent on delivering one view or another of economic life, economics, or even economic methodology, are interested parties participating in a process of social valuation, and thus intent upon legitimating certain determinate explanations and outcomes. But it is impossible for competing and contradictory views to all be legitimated. Thus we must, in principle, embrace indeterminacy, contingency, and ambiguity (properties that Samuels had discovered are also intrinsic to language and meaning). His own methodological pluralism flows out of these conclusions. And, as a measure of his consistency and honesty, Samuels does not deny the self-referential, reflexive nature of this position.

The three chapters in this volume in Part II, "Aspects of Economic Method," were written in the spirit of Samuels' thinking about economic methodology. Roger Backhouse, in "On the Credentials of Methodological Pluralism," opens with a discussion of Samuels' own understanding of the view. Backhouse not only carefully sets forth Samuels' thinking about methodological pluralism, and distinguishes it from similar views held by others, but goes on to make a number of observations about the nature and appeal of methodological pluralism. Tom Mayer in his chapter, "Some Practical Aspects of Pluralism in Economics," addresses the objection to methodological pluralism that either it implies "anything goes" or that it is vacuous and platitudinous as a position. Mayer sets forth a "middle way" understanding of pluralism, and then applies it to both economic policy and economic theory and methodology. Philip Mirowski, in "What Econometrics Can and Cannot Tell Us About Historical Actors: Brewing, Betting and Rationality in London, 1822–44," provides a case-study account of how empirical historical research cannot avoid the phenomenon of path-dependence, thus casting doubt on much cliometric practice. Consistent with Samuels' pluralist views, for Mirowski, economic history and the history of ideas are not sharply separable, and historical location influences both the course of history and our understanding of it.

The legal-economic nexus

The analysis of the economic role of government has been a bright thread in Samuels' contributions. His work here has been aimed at creating "an essentially positive, that is, non-normative and non-ideological, alternative to conventional welfare economics as a foundation for analysing the economic role of government" (Samuels 1992: x). Central to Samuels' thinking here is the concept of the "legal-economic nexus" – the idea that the economy is a function of government and government a function of the economy, and that the two are simultaneously and interdependently determined, rather than being in any way independent or self-determining spheres. In standard economic terminology, the legal-economic nexus can be said to encompass scholarship in the areas of public finance, law and economics, and public choice, and Samuels has made significant contributions to each of these literatures – all reflecting a perspective dominated by this nexus-oriented view.

Thus understood, it should be apparent that Samuels' analysis of the legal-economic nexus is much more broad-based than modern law and economics – particularly its Chicago variant. Building upon the work of John R. Commons and Robert Lee Hale, Samuels' work here emphasizes the falsity of the oft-assumed dichotomy between markets and government, understanding (properly) that the allocation of resources and the distribution of opportunity, income, and wealth are functions not simply of market forces, but of law – government – and the use thereof by those who would attempt to make government work for their advantage.

Related to this is the idea that rights are not pre-existent, but rather are created and modified by government. Government is thus an inevitable and ubiquitous part of the economic system, including the market system, since markets and their performance are a function of the structure of rights that give effect to them. Here Samuels' analysis has much in common with that of Ronald Coase, one manifestation of which is the recognition of the dual nature of rights, the reciprocal nature of externalities, and the ubiquity of externalities. For government to assign a right to A (e.g., the right to be free from pollution) is to impose a cost on B (that of reducing pollution), who becomes subject to the exercise of A's right, while to assign the right to B (e.g., the right to pollute) is to impose a cost on A (the damage resulting from B's pollution). Every right thus creates liberties and exposures, benefits and costs, and one cannot say simply that A's action imposes an externality on B and thus ought to be restrained, since to restrain A in favor of B is for B to impose an externality on A. The question for legal-economic policy is to whom the right should be assigned – that is, whose interests are to be made to count here? The legal-economic nexus is the process through which this is worked out, through which benefits and costs are (selectively) perceived and calculated, through which pressures for and against legal change are brought to bear, through which decisions are made and policies enacted and carried out.

Much of the thrust of modern law and economics revolves around the application of the efficiency criterion to resolve these issues. But one of the several important implications of the foregoing analysis is that the attempt to determine rights on the basis of efficiency is circular: efficiency is *a function of* rights, not the other way around. As such, there is no unique efficient result to be determined – only results that are efficient subject to the assumed underlying structure of rights. But this does not leave economics with nothing to offer to the arena of legal-economic policy making, nor does it imply that efficiency analysis is vacuous: "The dependency of Paretian efficiency on the prior definition and assignment of rights does not preclude . . . the making of antecedent assumptions, implicit or explicit, as to whose interests are to count as rights, thereby determining both the desired efficient result and the interests to be given effect in the definition and assignment of rights" (Samuels 1989: 1563). If there is a normative prescription that attends Samuels' analysis, it is that what is required for sound legal-economic policy making is a comparative institutional approach to the questions at issue – an examination of the benefits and costs, their magnitude and upon whom they rest, the consequent distributions of opportunity, income, and wealth, that attend alternative distributions of rights.

For Samuels, the legal-economic nexus "is a continuing, explorative, and emergent process through which are worked out ongoing solutions to legal-economic problems, such as whose economic and other interests are to count, which economic and other performance results are to be pursued, and who is to make these determinations" (Samuels 1989: 1578). One sees in the corpus of his scholarship not only the philosophical elaboration of the case for this broad-based perspective, but the application of this perspective to a host of legal-economic policy issues, including takings and the compensation principle, the analysis of public utilities, rent-seeking behavior, income distribution, and taxing and spending policy.

Three of the chapters in this volume reflect the themes evidenced in Samuels' writings on the legal-economic nexus. Peter Boettke's chapter revisits Samuels' analysis in "Interrelations Between Legal and Economic Processes" (*Journal of Law and Economics,* 1971) and his subsequent exchange of correspondence on these themes with James Buchanan (*Journal of Economic Issues,* 1975). Working from Samuels' conception of the embeddedness of economic relations within the legal and political structure of society, Boettke presents the case for a pragmatic normativism that recognizes the need to begin legal-economic policy analysis with the *status quo* structure of rights and offers the voluntary-consent mimicking prescription of the compensation principle as a guide to assess potential improvements. Nicholas Mercuro's chapter elaborates the distinctive features of American Institutional (as distinguished from New Institutional) law and economics, and, in particular, the importance of a comparative institutional approach to legal-economic policy making and the output categories for making comparative institutional assessments. Finally, Harry Trebing undertakes an analysis of the public-utility concept and attendant regulation that has currently fallen into disfavor in academic and policy circles. Through an analysis of academic and case literature, Trebing elaborates the history (much of which falls within the institutionalist tradition) of the public-utility concept and the effects of its seeming demise on economic activity and performance, based upon which he sets forth an institutionalist model for the analysis of public-utility regulation.

Aspects of institutional and Post Keynesian economics

Samuels' active scholarly involvement in institutional economics ranges well beyond his writings in the field. He served as editor of the *Journal of Economic Issues,* the flagship journal of institutionalism, from 1979–81 and has edited numerous volumes dealing with institutionalist literature and themes, helping to ensure both that the canonical literature of institutionalism is preserved in accessible form and that there are quality publication outlets for scholarship in this area.

Samuels (1995: 343–44) has said that, to him, institutionalism means the following:

1. A willingness to dissent and to proceed differently and perhaps alone.
2. An evolutionary and holistic conception of the economy.
3. A matter-of-fact, rather than a metaphysical, teleological, orthodox, and/or doctrinaire approach to doing economics, while appreciating the socially constructed nature of putative facts.
4. The centrality of the problem of the organization and control of the economic system and therein the crucial importance of the human belief system, selective perception, hypocrisy, and the legal-economic nexus.
5. The recognition of the hermeneutic character of language and belief, including the importance of interpretation in contrast with absolutist claims of fact and truth.

6. Social constructivism and the importance of the complex processes of working things out.
7. The importance of institutions in generating economic performance, especially of legal institutions informing and channeling the operation of markets.
8. The serious limits of the neoclassical strategy of seeking to produce unique determinate optimum equilibrium solutions.
9. The importance of technology concerning substance, consequences, and interrelations with social structure and process.

Certain of these themes are, of course, reflected in Samuels' extensive work on the legal-economic nexus. But his contributions to the institutionalist literature range across virtually the entire span of analysis, including issues of pricing, cost and valuation, technology, macroeconomic structure and policy, agent behavior, power and coercion, social control, and, as noted above, the history of economic thought (including of institutionalism) and economic methodology.

The chapters that we have chosen to group under the heading "Aspects of Institutional and Post Keynesian Economics" in the present volume are reflective of a number of these themes. A. Allan Schmid, a long-time colleague and collaborator on law and economics research with Samuels, argues the case that good economics very often has an institutionalist perspective, taking as evidence the work of a number of Nobel Prize winners, including, for example, Kenneth Arrow, James Buchanan, Ronald Coase, F. A. Hayek, Douglas North, and Herbert Simon, who have used a wide variety of institutionalist concepts in their scholarship. Marc R. Tool elaborates a theory of instrumental value as reflected in the work of J. Fagg Foster – a theory very much in the tradition of John Dewey, Thorstein Veblen, and Clarence Ayres. Given the inevitability of valuation in the assessment of alternative institutional structures within society, the instrumental valuation principle, Tool argues, allows for the identification and resolution of economic problems through the adjustment of institutions in such a way as to enhance their instrumental functioning. Paul Davidson's chapter treats the institution of money, evaluating the monetarist and chartalist conceptions of money and their respective implications for monetary analysis and policy. Finally, Robert Solo, in his chapter, offers a personal account of where economics and economic policy have gone over the past 65 years. At once retrospective and forward-looking, Solo's discussion points to many of the significant issues and problems that continue to face both economic analysis and contemporary society.

This brief overview of Samuels' contributions, and the chapters contributed to this volume, do not do justice to the depth and breadth of his influence on economics scholarship and on the individuals upon whom he has impacted over the course of his career. We consider it a privilege to be able to assemble this volume of essays in his honor, and we are profoundly grateful to all who have contributed to it. It is our hope both that this volume is a fitting tribute, and that it will illustrate for the reader the scope and possibilities of the subject that has been not only Samuels' life's work, but his joy as well.

References

Samuels, Warren (1966) *The Classical Theory of Economic Policy*, Cleveland, OH: World Publishing Company.

—— (1972) "The Scope of Economics Historically Considered," *Land Economics* 48: 248–68.

—— (1974) "The History of Economic Thought as Intellectual History," *History of Political Economy* 6: 305–23.

—— (1989) "The Legal-Economic Nexus," *George Washington Law Review* 57, 6: 1556–78.

—— (1992) "Introduction," in *Essays on the Economic Role of Government, Volume 1: Fundamentals*, New York: New York University Press, x–xiv.

—— (1995) "The Making of a Relativist and Social Constructivist: Remarks upon Receiving the Veblen-Commons Award," *Journal of Economic Issues* 29 (March): 343–58.

APPENDIX: PUBLICATIONS OF WARREN J. SAMUELS

1. Books

a. *Sets of collected works*

Essays in the History of Mainstream Political Economy, London: Macmillan; New York: New York University Press, 1992.

Essays in the History of Heterodox Political Economy, London: Macmillan; New York: New York University Press, 1992.

Essays on the Economic Role of Government, Volume 1: Fundamentals, London: Macmillan; New York: New York University Press, 1992.

Essays on the Economic Role of Government, Volume 2: Applications, London: Macmillan; New York: New York University Press, 1992.

Essays on the Methodology and Discourse of Economics, London: Macmillan; New York: New York University Press, 1992.

b. *Authored volumes*

With Steven G. Medema and A. Allan Schmid, *The Economy as a Process of Valuation*, Lyme, NH: Edward Elgar, 1997.

With Jeff Biddle and Thomas Patchak-Schuster, *Economic Thought and Discourse in the Twentieth Century*, Brookfield, VT: Edward Elgar, 1993.

With Steven G. Medema, *Gardiner C. Means: Institutionalist and Post Keynesian*, Armonk, NY: M. E. Sharpe, 1990.

Pareto on Policy, New York: Elsevier, 1974.
The Classical Theory of Economic Policy, Cleveland, OH: World, 1966.

c. Edited volumes

Ed., with Steven G. Medema, *Historians of Economics and Economic Thought: The Makers of Disciplinary Memory*, London: Routledge, 2001.

Ed., with Nicholas Mercuro, *The Fundamental Interrelationship Between Government and Property*, Stamford, CT: JAI Press, 1999.

Ed., with Malcolm Rutherford, *Classics in Institutional Economics: Succeeding Generations, 1916–1978*, 5 vols., London: Pickering & Chatto, 1998.

Ed., *The Founding of Institutional Economics: The Leisure Class and Sovereignty*, New York: Routledge, 1998.

Ed., with Natalia Makasheva and Vincent Barnett, *The Works of Nikolai D. Kondratiev*, 4 vols., London: Pickering & Chatto, 1998.

Ed., with Steven G. Medema, *Lionel Robbins, A History of Economic Thought: The LSE Lectures*, Princeton, NJ: Princeton University Press, 1998.

General Ed., *European Economists of the Early 20th Century, Volume I: Studies of Neglected Continental Thinkers of Belgium, France, the Netherlands, and Scandinavia*, Northampton, MA: Edward Elgar Publishing, 1998.

Ed., *Law and Economics*, 2 vols., London: Pickering & Chatto, 1998.

Ed., with Malcolm Rutherford, *Classics in Institutional Economics: The Founders, 1890–1945*, 5 vols., London: Pickering & Chatto, 1997.

Ed., with Gilbert Brian Davis, *The Life and Thought of David Ricardo*, by John P. Henderson and John B. Davis, Boston, MA: Kluwer Academic Publishing, 1997.

Ed., with Malcolm Rutherford, *John R. Commons: Selected Essays*, 2 vols., New York: Routledge, 1996.

Ed., with Steven G. Medema, *The Foundations of Research in Economics: How Do Economists Do Economics?* Brookfield, VT: Edward Elgar Publishing, 1996. Paperback edition, 1998.

Ed., *American Economists of the Late Twentieth Century*, Brookfield, VT: Edward Elgar, 1996.

Ed., with Frederic S. Lee, *A Monetary Theory of Employment*, by Gardiner C. Means, Armonk, NY: M. E. Sharpe, 1994.

Ed., with Geoffrey M. Hodgson and Marc R. Tool, *The Elgar Companion to Institutional and Evolutionary Economics*, 2 vols., Brookfield, VT: Edward Elgar, 1994.

Ed., *New Horizons in Economic Thought: Appraisals of Leading Economists*, Aldershot, UK: Edward Elgar, 1992.

Ed., with Frederic S. Lee, *The Heterodox Economics of Gardiner C. Means: A Collection*, Armonk, NY: M. E. Sharpe, 1992.

Ed., *Economics as Discourse: An Analysis of the Language of Economists*, Boston, MA: Kluwer Academic Publishers, 1990.

Ed., with Klaus Hennings, *Neoclassical Economic Theory, 1870–1930*, Boston, MA: Kluwer Academic Publishers, 1990.

Ed., *Fundamentals of the Economic Role of Government*, Westport, CT: Greenwood Press, 1989.

Ed., with Marc R. Tool, *The Methodology of Economic Thought*, 2nd edn., New Brunswick, NJ: Transaction Books, 1989.

Ed., with Marc R. Tool, *The Economy as a System of Power*, 2nd ed., New Brunswick, NJ: Transaction Books, 1989.

Ed., with Marc R. Tool, *State, Society, and Corporate Power*, 2nd ed., New Brunswick, NJ: Transaction Books, 1989.

Ed., *Institutional Economics*, 3 vols., Aldershot: Edward Elgar Publishing, 1988.

Ed., with Arthur S. Miller, *Corporations and Society: Power and Responsibility*, Westport, CT: Greenwood Press, 1987.

Ed., with Henry W. Spiegel, *Contemporary Economists in Perspective*, 2 vols., Greenwich: JAI Press, 1984.

Ed., with Introduction, Friedrich von Wieser, *The Law of Power*, trans. W. E. Kuhn, Lincoln, NE: Bureau of Business Research, University of Nebraska, 1983.

Ed., with A. Allan Schmid, *Law and Economics: An Institutional Perspective*, Boston, MA: Martinus Nijhoff, 1981.

Ed., with Larry L. Wade, *Taxing and Spending Policy*, Lexington, MA: Lexington Books, 1980.

Ed., *The Methodology of Economic Thought*, New Brunswick, NJ: Transaction Books, 1980.

Ed., *The Economy as a System of Power*, 2 vols., New Brunswick, NJ: Transaction Books, 1979.

Ed., *The Chicago School of Political Economy*, East Lansing, MI: Division of Research, Graduate School of Business Administration, Michigan State University, 1976. Reprinted, with a new Introduction, New Brunswick, NJ: Transaction Books, 1993.

Ed., with Harry M. Trebing, *A Critique of Administration Regulation of Public Utilities*, East Lansing, MI: Institute of Public Utilities, Michigan State University, 1972.

2. Articles, pamphlets, book chapters, and introductions

With Steven G. Medema and Nicholas Mercuro, "Institutional Law and Economics," in Boudewijn Bouckaert and Gerrit De Geest (eds) *Encyclopedia of Law and Economics*, Vol. 1, Aldershot: Edward Elgar Publishing, 2000, 418–55.

With Steven G. Medema and Nicholas Mercuro, "Robert Lee Hale – Legal Economist," in Jürgen G. Backhaus (ed.) *The Elgar Companion to Law and Economics*, Aldershot: Edward Elgar Publishing, 2000, 325–38.

"Thorstein Veblen's *The Theory of the Leisure Class*: Eine Einführung," in *Vademecum zu Einem Klassiker des Institutionellen Denkens*, Düsseldorf: Handelblatt, 2000.

"Walter Adams and James W. Brock's *The Tobacco Wars*: The Final Shot of a Warrior for Competitive Markets and Responsible Government," *Review of Social Economy* 58 (March 2000): 125–33.

"Signs, Pragmatism and Abduction: The Tragedy, Irony and Promise of Charles Sanders Peirce," *Journal of Economic Issues* 34 (March 2000): 207–17.

With Steven G. Medema, "The Economic Role of Government As, In Part, A Matter of Selective Perception, Sentiment and Valuation: The Cases of Pigovian and Paretian Welfare Economics," *American Journal of Economics and Sociology* 57 (January 2000): 87–108.

"The Nash of Nash Equilibrium," *History of Economic Ideas* 7 (1999): 257–64.

"An Economist Turned Entrepreneur," in Martin M. G. Fase, Walter Kanning and Donald A. Walker (eds) *Economics, Welfare Policy and the History of Economic*

Thought: Essays in Honour of Arnold Heertje, Northampton, MA: Edward Elgar, 1999, 392–409.

"Lectures by Selig Perlman on American Labor History and on Capitalism and Socialism, 1955–1956," *Research in the History of Economic Thought and Methodology, Archival Supplement* 8 (1999): 3–58, 101–50.

"Introduction" to Selig Perlman's additional chapters for his History of Trade Unionism, *Research in the History of Economic Thought and Methodology, Archival Supplement* 8 (1999): 153–56.

"Hayek from the Perspective of an Institutionalist Historian of Economic Thought: An Interpretive Essay," *Journal des Economistes et des Etudes Humaines* IX (Juin–Septembre 1999): 279–90.

With others, "Dr. Martin Bronfenbrenner (1914–1997)," *American Journal of Economics and Sociology* 58 (July 1999): 491–522.

"The Rehabilitation of Kondratiev and of Kondratiev Studies: Introduction," *History of Political Economy* 31 (Spring 1999): 133–36.

"Herbert Joseph Davenport," in John A. Garraty and Mark C. Carnes (eds) *American National Biography*, Vol. 6, New York: Oxford University Press, 1999, 133–34.

"An Institutionalist Approach to Income Distribution," in Joep T. J. M. van der Linden and Andre J. C. Manders (eds) *The Economics of Income Distribution: Heterodox Approaches*, Northampton, MA: Edward Elgar, 1999, 15–28.

"The Problem of 'Do Not Quote or Cite Without Permission,'" *Journal of the History of Economic Thought* 21 (June 1999): 187–90.

"Alfred Marshall and Neoclassical Economics: Insights from his Correspondence," *Research in the History of Economic Thought and Methodology* 17 (1999): 45–100.

Ed., Victor E. Smith's Notes on William Jaffé's Lectures on Marshallian Theory, Spring 1937, *Research in the History of Economic Thought and Methodology* 17 (1999): 101–78.

"A Note on Deconstruction," *Journal of Economic Issues* 32 (December 1998): 1127–29.

"The Transformation of American Economics: From Interwar Pluralism to Postwar Neoclassicism: An Interpretive Review of a Conference," *Research in the History of Economic Thought and Methodology* 16 (1998): 179–223.

"Murray Rothbard's Austrian Perspective on the History of Economic Thought," *Critical Review* 12 (Winter–Spring 1998): 71–75.

"Introduction" (Zum Geleit) to Jürgen Löwe, *Contextual Economics: The Theory of Karl Knies as a Basis of an Explanation of Modern Economy* (*Kontextuale Theorie Der Volksvirtschaft: Der Ansatz von Karl Als Grundlage Zukunftiger Wirtschaftspolitik*), Amsterdam: Verlag Fakultas, 1998, ix–xi.

"The Historical Quest for Principles of Valuation: An Interpretive Essay," in Sasan Fayazmanesh and Marc R. Tool (eds) *Institutionalist Method and Value*, Northampton, MA: Edward Elgar, 1998, 112–29.

"Comment on 'Postmodernism and Institutionalism,'" *Journal of Economic Issues* 32 (September 1998): 823–32.

"Spiegel's Pioneering Efforts as a Historian," in "Dr. Henry William Spiegel (1911–1995): Emigré Economist, Historian of Economics, Creative Scholar, and Companion," *American Journal of Economics and Sociology* 57 (July 1998): 349–51.

"Methodological Pluralism," in John B. Davis, D. Wade Hands and Uskali Maki (eds) *The Handbook of Economic Methodology*, Northampton, MA: Edward Elgar, 1998, 300–303.

"On the Labor Theory of Value as a Theory of Value," *Review of Political Economy* 10 (April 1998): 227–32.

"Journal Editing in the History of Economic Thought," *History of Economics Review*, no. 27 (Winter 1998): 3–5.

"Comment: Keynes on the Classics: A Revolution Mainly in Definitions?" in James C. W. Ahiakpor (ed.) *Keynes and the Classics Reconsidered*, Boston, MA: Kluwer Academic Publishers, 1998, 33–35.

"Introduction" to Thorstein Veblen, *An Inquiry into the Nature of Peace and the Terms of Its Perpetuation*, New Brunswick, NJ: Transaction Books, 1998, vii–xxx.

With Steven G. Medema, "Ronald Coase on Policy Analysis: Framework and Implications," in Steven G. Medema (ed.) *Coasean Economics: Law and Economics and the New Institutional Economics*, Boston, MA: Kluwer, 1998, 161–83.

Ed., "Victor E. Smith's Notes on William Jaffé's Lectures on the History of Economic Thought from Plato to Adam Smith," *Research in the History of Economic Thought and Methodology, Archival Supplement* 6 (1997): 1–114.

Ed., "Victor E. Smith's Analysis of Rent," *Research in the History of Economic Thought and Methodology, Archival Supplement* 6 (1997): 115–205.

Ed., "Notes from Lectures by Hans H. Gerth on Democratic and Totalitarian Societies," *Research in the History of Economic Thought and Methodology, Archival Supplement* 6 (1997): 229–62.

"Martin Bronfenbrenner, 1914–1997," *Journal of Income Distribution* 7, 1 (1997): 1–3.

"Foreword" to Robert V. Andelson (ed.) *Land-Value Taxation Around the World*, 2nd ed., New York: Robert Schalkenbach Foundation, 1997, x–xiv.

With Allan Schmid, "Costs and Power," in Nahid Ashlenbeigui and Young Back Choi (eds) *Borderlands of Economics: Essays in Honor of Daniel R. Fusfeld*, New York: Routlege, 1997, 153–70.

With Jeff Biddle, "The Historicism of John R. Commons's *Legal Foundations of Capitalism*," in Peter Koslowski (ed.) *Methodology of the Social Sciences, Ethics, and Economics in the Newer Historical School*, Berlin: Springer, 1997, 291–318.

"The Problem of Vision in Economics: A Review Essay," *Advances in Austrian Economics* 4 (1997): 133–46.

"On the Nature and Utility of the Concept of Equilibrium," *Journal of Post Keynesian Economics* 20 (Fall 1997): 77–88.

"The Work of Historians of Economic Thought," *Research in the History of Economic Thought and Methodology* 15 (1997): 181–97.

"John Richard Hicks," in Thomas Cate (ed.) *Encyclopedia of Keynesian Economics*, Brookfield, VT: Edward Elgar, 1997, 241–44.

With Sylvia Samuels, "The University as a Social Economy: Jane Smiley's *Moo*," *Forum for Social Economics* 26 (Spring 1997): 69–78.

"The Case for Methodological Pluralism," in Andrea Salanti and Ernesto Screpanti (eds) *Pluralism in Economics*, Brookfield, VT: Edward Elgar, 1997, 67–79.

"Methodological Pluralism: The Discussion in Retrospect," in Andrea Salanti and Ernesto Screpanti (eds) *Pluralism in Economics*, Brookfield, VT: Edward Elgar, 1997, 308–309.

"Instrumental Valuation," in Warren J. Samuels, Steven G. Medema and A. Allan Schmid, *The Economy as a Process of Valuation*, Lyme, NH: Edward Elgar, 1997, 1–71.

With Steven G. Medema, "Ronald Coase and Coasean Economics: Some Questions, Conjectures and Implications," in Warren J. Samuels, Steven G. Medema and A.

Allan Schmid, *The Economy as a Process of Valuation*, Lyme, NH: Edward Elgar, 1997, 72–128.

"The Concept of Coercion in Economics," in Warren J. Samuels, Steven G. Medema and A. Allan Schmid, *The Economy as a Process of Valuation*, Lyme, NH: Edward Elgar, 1997, 129–207.

With A. Allan Schmid, "The Concept of Cost in Economics," in Warren J. Samuels, Steven G. Medema and A. Allan Schmid, *The Economy as a Process of Valuation*, Lyme, NH: Edward Elgar, 1997, 208–98.

"Kenneth Boulding's The Image and Contemporary Discourse Analysis," in Warren J. Samuels, Steven G. Medema and A. Allan Schmid, *The Economy as a Process of Valuation*, Lyme, NH: Edward Elgar, 1997, 299–327.

"On Distribution and the Invisible Hand," *Journal of Income Distribution* 6, 2 (1996): 145–46.

"Can Neoclassical Economics Be Social Economics?" *Forum for Social Economics*, 26 (Fall 1996): 1–4.

"Joseph J. Spengler's Concept of the 'Problem of Order': A Reconsideration and Extension," in Philip Arestis (ed.) *Employment, Economic Growth and the Tyranny of the Market*, Brookfield, VT: Edward Elgar, 1996, 185–99.

"Foreword" to Fred E. Foldvary (ed.) *Beyond Neoclassical Economics: Heterodox Approaches to Economic Theory*, Brookfield, VT: Edward Elgar, 1996, xx–xix.

With Jouni Paavola, "Natural Images in Economics: A Review Essay," *Review of Social Economy* 54 (Fall 1996): 341–66.

With Usamah Ramadan, "The Treatment of Post Keynesian Economics in the History of Economic Thought Texts," *Journal of Post Keynesian Economics* 18 (Summer 1996): 547–65.

"Postmodernism and Knowledge: A Middlebrow View," *Journal of Economic Methodology* 3 (June 1996): 113–20.

"My Work as an Historian of Economic Thought," *Journal of the History of Economic Thought* 18 (Spring 1996): 37–75.

"On the Structure of the Archeology of Economic Thought in the Eighteenth Century," *Journal of Interdisciplinary Economics* 7 (1996): 291–313.

"Reader's Guide to John R. Commons, Legal Foundation of Capitalism," *Research in the History of Economic Thought and Methodology, Archival Supplement* 5 (1996): 1–61.

"Richard Reeve's Study of the Kennedy Presidency: Implications for Studying Economics and the History of Economic Thought," *History of Economics Review* no. 23 (Winter 1995): 108–16.

"Some Thoughts on Multiplicity," *Journal of Economic Methodology* 2 (December 1995): 287–91.

"Society is a Process of Mutual Coercion and Governance Selectively Perceived," *Critical Review* 9 (Summer 1995): 437–43.

"Preface" to Paul Wells, *Post-Keynesian Economic Theory*, Boston, MA: Kluwer Academic Publishers, 1995.

"Reflections on the Intellectual Context and Significance of Thorstein Veblen," *Journal of Economic Issues* 29 (September 1995): 915–22.

With Jeff E. Biddle, "J. R. Commons' *Legal Foundations* und seine Beitrage zum Institutionalismus," in Bertram Schefold (ed.) *Uber J. R. Commons' "Legal Foundations of Capitalism,"* Düsseldorf: Handelblatt, 1995, 37–67.

"The Present State of Institutional Economics," *Cambridge Journal of Economics* 19 (August 1995): 569–90.

"Power, the Organization of Inquiry and the Achievement of 'Spontaneous Order,'" *Advances in Austrian Economics* 2, Part B (1995): 417–26.

"The Instrumental Value Principle and its Role," in C. M. A. Clark (ed.) *Institutional Economics and the Theory of Social Value: Essays in Honor of Marc R. Tool*, Boston, MA: Kluwer, 1995, 97–112.

"Evolutionary Economics in Russia: Report on a Conference," *Journal of Economic Issues* 29 (June 1995): 651–61. Also published, in Russian, in Proceedings volume. Moscow, 1995, 148–53.

"The Making of a Relativist and Social Constructivist: Remarks upon Receiving the Veblen-Commons Award," *Journal of Economic Issues* 29 (June 1995): 343–58.

"Government, the People, and the Problem of Order," *Challenge* 38 (May–June 1995): 45–49.

"Some Reflections on the Work of Sergius Bulgakov by an Historian of Economic Thought," in J. Diskin and N. Makasheva (eds) *S. N. Bulgakov (1871–1944): Economics and Culture*, Moscow: Russian Academy of Sciences, Institute for Social and Economic Problems of Population, 1995, 155–81.

With Jeff E. Biddle, "Introduction to John R. Commons's *The Legal Foundations of Capitalism*: J. R. Commons's *Legal Foundations* and Its Contribution to Institutionalism," New Brunswick, NJ: Transaction Books, 1995, xxxxiii.

"On 'Shirking' and 'Business Sabotage': A Note," *Journal of Economic Issues* 28 (December 1994): 1249–55.

"Ludwig Lachmann and his Contributions to Economic Science: Comment on Papers by Roger Koppl and David Prychitko," *Advances in Austrian Economics* 1 (1994): 321–24.

"The Institutional Context of the Macroeconomy and Demand Management Policy: Comment on Cunningham and Vilasuso," *Journal of Post Keynesian Economics* 17 (Winter 1994): 279–83.

"The Political Economic Origins of an American Predicament," *The Centenial Review* 38 (Winter 1994): 161–78.

With A. Allan Schmid and James D. Shaffer, "An Evolutionary Approach to Law and Economics," in Richard W. England (ed.) *Evolutionary Concepts in Contemporary Economics*, Ann Arbor, MI: University of Michigan Press, 1994, 93–110.

"On Macroeconomic Politics," *Journal of Post Keynesian Economics* 16 (Summer 1994): 661–70.

"The Roles of Theory in Economics," in Philip A. Klein (ed.) *The Role of Economic Theory*, Boston, MA: Kluwer, 1994, 21–45.

"Need as a Mode of Discourse," in John B. Davis and Edward J. O'Boyle (eds) *The Social Economics of Human Material Need*, Carbondale, IL: Southern Illinois University Press, 1994, 1–21.

"Rights and the Environment: 'Decisions, Decisions' (Fiddler on the Roof)," in Martin O'Connor (ed.) *Justice and the Environment*, Policy Discussion Papers, Auckland, NZ: Department of Economics, University of Auckland, 1994.

With Peter Fisher and Larry L. Wade, "Taxing and Spending Policy," in Stuart S. Nagel (ed.) *Encyclopedia of Policy Studies*, 2nd edn., New York: Marcel Dekker 1994, 483–506.

Entries: "Adam Smith"; "Karl Marx" (with Geoff Hodgson); "Law and Economics"; "Property"; "Part-Whole Relations"; "Gardiner C. Means" (with Frederick S. Lee); "Edwin E. Witte"; "Robert Lee Hale"; "Inflation" (with Geoff Hodgson); "Welfare Economic Theory"; in Geoffrey M. Hodgson, Warren J. Samuels and

Marc R. Tool (eds) *The Elgar Companion to Institutional and Evolutionary Economics*, Brookfield, VT: Edward Elgar, 1994.

"On the Conclusivity of Certain Lines of Reasoning in Economic Policy Analysis," *Journal of Post Keynesian Economics* 16 (Winter 1993–94): 241–49.

"Three Lives and the Control of the Human Labor Force Through the Control of Government," *History of Economic Ideas* 1 (1993): 105–28.

"Editorial: Method, Methodology and Distribution," *Journal of Income Distribution* 3 (Fall 1993): 141–42.

"The Growth of Government," *Critical Review* 7 (1993): 445–60.

"The Status of Marx after the Disintegration of the USSR," *Challenge* 36 (July/August 1993): 45–49.

"Adam Smith as Social Constructivist and Dialectician: Aspects of Intergenerational Intellectual Relations," *History of Economic Ideas* 1 (1993): 171–92.

"John R. Hicks as Historian of Economic Thought" (extended version), in Warren J. Samuels, Jeff Biddle and Thomas Patchak-Schuster, *Economic Thought and Discourse in the Early Twentieth Century*, Aldershot: Edward Elgar (1993), 1–86; condensed version in *History of Political Economy* 25 (Summer 1993): 351–74.

With Jeff Biddle, "Thorstein Veblen on War and National Security" (extended version), in Warren J. Samuels, Jeff Biddle and Thomas Patchak-Schuster, *Economic Thought and Discourse in the Early Twentieth Century*, Aldershot: Edward Elgar, 1993, 87–158.

With Thomas Schuster, "Aspects of the Discursive and Interpretive Structure of Marshall's *Principles*," in Warren J. Samuels, Jeff Biddle and Thomas Patchak-Schuster, *Economic Thought and Discourse in the Early Twentieth Century*, Aldershot: Edward Elgar, 1993, 159–216.

"Law and Economics: Some Early Conceptions," in Warren J. Samuels, Jeff Biddle and Thomas Patchak-Schuster, *Economic Thought and Discourse in the Early Twentieth Century*, Aldershot: Edward Elgar, 1993, 217–86.

"In (Limited but Affirmative) Defence of Nihilism," *Review of Political Economy* 5 (April 1993): 236–44.

"Thorstein Veblen and the Place of Science," *Society* 30 (January/February 1993): 76–82.

"Institutions and Distribution: Ownership and the Identification of Rent," *Journal of Income Distribution* 2 (Winter 1992): 125–40.

"The 'Italian' International Celebration of the Centenary of Marshall's 'Principles,'" *Marshall Studies Bulletin* 2 (1992): 36–53.

"Marxist and Other Thought in Light of the Gorbachev Revolution," *International Journal of Social Economics* 19 (1992): 37–57.

"Bibliography of Taxing and Spending Policy, with an Emphasis on Developing Countries," *Developmental Policy Studies* 1 (Spring/Summer 1992): 36–38.

With Susan Pozo, "Fernandez Florez's *Las Siete Columnas*: Mandeville Rehearsed," *Research in the History of Economic Thought and Methodology* 9 (1992): 171–97.

"Foreword" to Rick Tilman, *Thorstein Veblen and His Critics, 1891–1963: Conservative, Liberal and Radical Perspectives*, Princeton, NJ: Princeton University Press, 1992, ix–xiii.

"The Pervasive Proposition, 'What Is, Is and Ought to Be': A Critique," in William S. Millberg (ed.) *The Megacorp and Macrodynamics: Essays in Memory of Alfred Eichner*, Armonk, NY: M. E. Sharpe, 1992, 273–85.

"Joan Robinson," in *Encyclopedia of World Biography: Supplement*, Vol. 4, New York: McGraw-Hill, 1992, 453–55.

"Introduction" to James Bonar, *Philosophy and Political Economy*, New Brunswick, NJ: Transaction Publishers, 1992, xiv–xxv.

"Warren J. Samuels," in Philip Arestis and Malcolm C. Sawyer (eds) *A Biographical Dictionary of Dissenting Economists*, Brookfield, VT: Edward Elgar, 1992, 478–84.

"Institutional Economics," in David Greenaway, Michael Bleaney and Ian M. Stewart (eds) *Companion to Contemporary Economic Thought*, New York: Routledge, 1991, 105–18.

"A Biographical Puzzle: Why Did Jevons Write The Coal Question? Comment," *Journal of the History of Economic Thought* 13 (Fall 1991): 236–39.

"Dynamics of Cultural Change," *Society* 29 (November/December 1991): 23–26.

With Jeff E. Biddle, "Thorstein Veblen on War, Peace, and National Security," in Craufurd D. Goodwin (ed.) *Economics and National Security: A History of Their Interaction*, Durham, NC: Duke University Press, 1991, 87–117.

"Veblen and Self-Referentiability: Reply to Baldwin Ranson," *Journal of Economic Issues*, 25 (September 1991): 847–50.

"'Truth' and 'Discourse' in the Social Construction of Economic Reality: An Essay on the Relation of Knowledge to Socioeconomic Policy," *Journal of Post Keynesian Economics* 13 (Summer 1991): 511–24.

With Timothy W. Kelsey, "Some Fundamental Considerations on the Positive Theory of Income Distribution," in Joep T. J. M. van der Linden and Willem L. M. Adriaansen (eds) *Post-Keynesian Thought in Perspective*, Groningen: Wolters-Noordhoff, 1991, 119–39.

"Determinate Solutions and the Foreclosure of Process: A Response to Garretsen," *Journal of Post Keynesian Economics* 13 (Spring 1991): 424–30.

With Edward Puro, "The Problem of Price Controls at the Time of Natural Disaster," *Review of Social Economy* 49 (Spring 1991): 62–75.

"The Firing of E. A. Ross from Stanford University: Injustice Compounded by Deception?" *Journal of Economic Education* 22 (Spring 1991): 183–90.

"Introduction: Frank A. Fetter's 'Present State of Economic Theory in the United States of America,'" *Research in the History of Economic Thought and Methodology, Archival Supplement* 2 (1991): 3–8.

"Introduction: Frank H. Knight's 'The Case for Communism,'" *Research in the History of Economic Thought and Methodology, Archival Supplement* 2 (1991): 49–55.

"Introduction: Lewis Zerby's 'You, Yourself, and Society,'" *Research in the History of Economic Thought and Methodology, Archival Supplement* 2 (1991): 131–36.

"An Essay on the Philosophy and Psychodynamics of Income Distribution," *Journal of Income Distribution* 1 (Fall 1991): 210–20.

With Thomas Schuster, "Aspects of the Discursive and Interpretive Structure of Marshall's Arguments Concerning Labor Economics," *Review of Social Economy* 48 (Winter 1990): 436–49.

"On Causation, the Principle of Unforeseen Consequences, and the Matrix of Human Action: The Case of the Iraqi Conquest of Kuwait," *Methodus* 2 (December 1990): 9–15.

"The Reformation of German Economic Discourse, 1750–1840: A Review Article," *Review of Social Economy* 48 (Fall 1990): 321–32.

"The Self-Referentiability of Thorstein Veblen's Theory of the Preconceptions of Economic Science," *Journal of Economic Issues* 24 (September 1990): 695–718.

"Introduction" to William Harold Hutt, *Economists and the Public*, New Brunswick, NJ: Transaction, 1990, 1–6.

"Institutional Economics and the Theory of Cognition," *Cambridge Journal of Economics* 14 (June 1990): 219–27.

"The Old Versus the New Institutionalism: Comment," *Review of Political Economy* 2 (March 1990): 83–86.

"Foreword" to John F. Henry, *The Making of Neoclassical Economics*, Boston, MA: Unwin Hyman, 1990, vii–xii.

"Four Strands of Social Economics: A Comparative Interpretation," in Mark A. Lutz (ed.) *Social Economics: Retrospect and Prospect*, Boston, MA: Kluwer Academic Publishers, 1990: 269–309.

"Introduction," Thorstein Veblen, *The Place of Science in Modern Civilization*, New Brunswick, NJ: Transaction, 1990, vii–xxx.

"Notes from John Dewey's Lectures on Moral and Political Philosophy and their Relevance to the Study of the History of Economic Thought," *Research in the History of Economic Thought and Methodology, Archival Supplement* 1 (1989): 1–18.

"The Legal-Economic Nexus," *George Washington Law Review* 57 (August 1989): 1556–78.

With Jeff Biddle, "On the Attribution of Causality and Responsibility in Macroeconomics," *Methodus* 1 (December 1989): 9–13.

With Steven G. Medema, "Gardiner C. Means's Institutional and Post-Keynesian Economics," *Review of Political Economy* 1 (July 1989): 163–91.

"Diverse Approaches to the Economic Role of Government: An Interpretive Essay," in Warren J. Samuels (ed.) *Fundamentals of the Economic Role of Government*, Westport, CT: Greenwood Press, 1989, 213–49.

"Determinate Solutions and Valuational Processes: Overcoming the Foreclosure of Process," *Journal of Post Keynesian Economics* 11 (Summer 1989): 531–46. Reprinted in Peter J. Boettke (ed.) *Market Process Theories*, Lyme, NH: Edward Elgar, 1997. Also in A. Allan Schmid (ed.) *Beyond Agricultural Economics: Management, Investment, Policy, and Methodology*, East Lansing, MI: Michigan State University Press, 1997, 223–41.

"Foreword," A. Allan Schmid, *Benefit-Cost Analysis: A Political Economy Approach*, Boulder, CO: Westview Press, 1989, xiii–xviii. Reprinted in Indonesian: *Analisis Diaya Manfaat: Pendekatan Ekonomi Politik*, 1995.

"Austrian and Institutional Economics: Some Common Elements," *Research in the History of Economic Thought and Methodology* 6 (1989): 53–71.

"Comparing Austrian and Institutional Economics: Response," *Research in the History of Economic Thought and Methodology* 6 (1989): 203–25.

"The Methodology of Economics and the Case for Policy Diffidence and Restraint," *Review of Social Economy* 47 (Summer 1989): 113–33. Reprinted in David L. Prychitko (ed.) *Why Economists Disagree*, Albany, NY: SUNY Press, 1998, 345–66.

"Some Fundamentals of the Economic Role of Government," *Journal of Economic Issues* 23 (June 1989): 427–33; and *Fundamentals of the Economic Role of Government*, Westport, CT: Greenwood Press, 1989, 167–72.

With John P. Henderson, "Malthus als Theoretiker," in Horst Claus Recktenwald (ed.) *Uber Malthus' "Principles of Political Economy,"* Düsseldorf: Handelblatt, 1989, 35–59.

"Institutional Reform: The Future of Codetermination: Comment," in H. G. Nitzinger and J. Backhaus (eds) *Codetermination*, Berlin: Springer-Verlag, 1989, 223–28.

"In Praise of Joan Robinson: Economics as Social Control," *Society* 26 (January/February 1989): 73–76.

"Introduction," Frank W. Taussig, *Inventors and Moneymakers*, New Brunswick, NJ: Transaction, 1989, xi–xxxiv.

"Of Lookout Cows and the Methodology of Economics," *Journal of Economic Issues* 22 (September 1988): 853–67. Reprinted in Douglas W. Allen and James W. Dean (eds) *Economic Wit*, Brookfield, VT: Edward Elgar, 1993.

"Product Liability," *Science* 241 (August 5, 1988): 639.

"Schumpeter's Treatment of Samuelson," *History of Economics Society Bulletin* 10 (Spring 1988): 25–31.

"An Essay on the Nature and Significance of the Normative Nature of Economics," *Journal of Post Keynesian Economics* 10 (Spring 1988): 347–54.

Contributions to *The New Palgrave: A Dictionary of Economics*, 4 vols., London: Macmillan, 1987: C. E. Ayres, 1:165; J. M. Clark, 1:431–32; J. R. Commons, 1:506–507; H. J. Davenport, 1:749; P. T. Homan, 2:668; Institutional Economics, 2:864–66; A. S. Johnson, 2:1022; W. G. Sumner, 4:548–49; F. W. Taussig, 4:596; and D. A. Wells, 4:897–98.

Contributions to Roland Turner (ed.) *20th Century Thinkers*, Chicago, IL: St. James Press, 1987: Ragnar Frisch, 256–57; John Maynard Keynes, 400–403; Simon Kuznets, 426–27; Wesley C. Mitchell, 539–40; Gunnar Myrdal, 562–64; and Joan Robinson, 658–59.

(And others), "What Aspects of Keynes's Economic Theories Merit Continued or Renewed Interest?," *Research in the History of Economic Thought and Methodology* 5 (1987): 151–93.

"The Idea of the Corporation as a Person: On the Normative Significance of Judicial Language," in Warren J. Samuels and Arthur S. Miller (eds) *Corporations and Society: Power and Responsibility*, Westport, CT: Greenwood Press, 1987, 113–29.

"Religion and Economics: An Historical Perspective," *The Centennial Review* 31 (Winter 1987): 47–57.

With John P. Henderson, *Zu Malthus' "Essay über die Entwicklung der Bevolkerung,"* Dusseldorf: Handelsblatt, 1986, 39.

"What Aspects of Keynes's Economic Theories Merit Continued or Renewed Interest? One Interpretation," *Journal of Post Keynesian Economics* 9 (Fall 1986): 3–16.

With Nicholas Mercuro, "Wealth Maximization and Judicial Decision-Making: The Issues Further Clarified," *International Review of Law and Economics* 6 (1986): 133–37.

"Benjamin Jowett's Connections with Political Economy," *History of Economics Society Bulletin* 7 (Winter 1986): 33–43.

"Machlup on Knowledge: Science, Subjectivism and the Social Nature of Knowledge," *Research in the History of Economic Thought and Methodology* 3 (1985): 243–55.

"The Wage System and the Distribution of Power," *Forum for Social Economics* (Fall 1985): 31–41.

"The Obfuscation of Choice," *International Social Science Review* 60 (Autumn 1985): 147–52.

"Some Considerations Which May Lead Lawmakers to Modify a Policy When Adopting it as Law: Comment," *Zeitschrift für die Gesamte Staatswissenschaft*, 141 (March 1985): 58–61.

"A Critique of Capitalism, Socialism, and Democracy," in Richard D. Coe and Charles K. Wilber (eds) *Capitalism and Democracy: Schumpeter Revisited*, Notre Dame: University of Notre Dame Press, 1985, 60–119.

With Anthony Y. C. Koo, "Marshall on Balanced Growth from the Supply Side: A Note," *History of Economic Thought Society of Australia Newsletter*, no. 5 (Autumn 1985): 17–26.

"The Resignation of Frank A. Fetter from Stanford University," *History of Economics Society Bulletin* 6 (Winter 1985): 17–25.

"A Consumer View of Financing Nuclear Plant Abandonments," *Public Utilities Fortnightly* 115 (January 10, 1985): 24–27.

"On the Nature and Existence of Economic Coercion: The Correspondence of Robert Lee Hale and Thomas Nixon Carver," *Journal of Economic Issues* 18 (December 1984): 1027–48.

"Comments on McCloskey on Methodology and Rhetoric," *Research in the History of Economic Thought and Methodology* 2 (1984): 207–10.

With Nicholas Mercuro, "Posnerian Law and Economics on the Bench," *International Review of Law and Economics* 4 (December 1984): 107–30.

"Galbraith on Economics as a System of Professional Belief," *Journal of Post Keynesian Economics* 7 (Fall 1984): 61–76.

"Policy Option: Samaritan Advertising," *Journal of Economic Issues* 18 (September 1984): 893–94.

"Institutional Economics," *Journal of Economic Education* 15 (Summer 1984): 211–16.

"Economics and Theology: The Fundamental Common Problem," *Economic Forum* 15 (Summer 1984): 1–7.

"A Centenary Reconsideration of Bellamy's Looking Backward," *American Journal of Economics and Sociology* 43 (April 1984): 129–48.

With A. Allan Schmid, James D. Shaffer, Robert A. Solo and Stephen A. Woodbury, "Technology, Labor Interests, and the Law: Some Fundamental Points and Problems," *Nova Law Journal* 8 (Spring 1984): 487–513.

With Nicholas Mercuro, "A Critique of Rent-Seeking Theory," in David C. Colander (ed.) *Neoclassical Political Economy*, Cambridge: Ballinger, 1984, 55–70.

"Introduction," Helmut Arndt, *Economic Theory vs. Economic Reality*, East Lansing, MI: Michigan State University Press, 1984, 11–16.

"Four Journals in Intellectual History," *History of Economics Society Bulletin* 5 (Winter 1984): 19–21.

With Larry L. Wade, "Taxing and Spending Policy," in Stuart S. Nagel (ed.) *Encyclopedia of Policy Studies*, New York: Marcel Dekker, 1983, 483–501. Chinese edition, 1991.

"Whither (Positive) Political Economy? One Reading," in Larry L. Wade (ed.) *Political Economy*, Boston, MA: Kluwer-Nijhoff, 1983, 157–70. Reprinted in Japanese translation, 1993.

"The Progress and Poverty Centenary," *American Journal of Economics and Sociology* 42 (April 1983): 247–54. Reprinted in *Western Tax Review* 4 (Spring 1983): 1–6. Reprinted in *Pioneers in Economics: Neoclassical Economics and Its Critics, vol. 34, Henry George*, Cheltenham: Edward Elgar, 1992. Reprinted in Will Lissner and Dorothy Burnham Lissner (eds) *George and the Scholars*, New York: Robert Schalkenbach Foundation, 1991.

"The Influence of Friedrich von Wieser on Joseph A. Schumpeter," Presidential Address, *History of Economics Society Bulletin* (Winter 1983): 5–19.

"The Distributional Problem in Risk Policy: A Note," *Land Economics* 59 (February 1983): 114–17.

"Kenneth Boulding's Ecodynamics," *International Social Science Review* 58 (Winter 1983): 3–6.

"Henry George's Challenge to the Economics Profession," *American Journal of Economics and Sociology* 42 (January 1983): 63–66. Reprinted in Mark Blaug (ed.) *Pioneers in Economics: Neoclassical Economics and Its Critics, vol. 34, Henry George*, Cheltenham: Edward Elgar, 1992. Reprinted in Will Lissner and Dorothy Burnham Lissner (eds) *George and the Scholars*, New York: Robert Schalkenbach Foundation, 1991.

"A Critique of the Discursive Systems and Foundation Concepts of Distribution Analysis," *Analyse & Kritik* 4 (October 1982): 4–12.

With James D. Shaffer, "Deregulation: The Principal Inconclusive Arguments," *Policy Studies Review* 1 (February 1982): 463–69.

"The Current State of Economics," *Economic Forum* 12 (Winter 1981–82): 1–8.

"Maximization of Wealth as Justice: An Essay on Posnerian Law and Economics as Policy Analysis," *Texas Law Review* 60 (December 1981): 147–72.

"Edgeworth's Mathematical Psychics: A Centennial Notice," *Eastern Economic Journal* 7 (July–October 1981): 193–98.

"The Historical Treatment of the Problem of Value Judgments: An Interpretation," in Robert A. Solo and Charles W. Anderson (eds) *Value Judgment and Income Distribution*, New York: Praeger, 1981, 57–69.

"Consumerism and the Public Utility Institution," in Harry M. Trebing (ed.) *Challenges for Public Utility Regulation in the 1980s*, East Lansing, MI: Division of Research, Graduate School of Business Administration, Michigan State University, 1981, 445–56.

"A Necessary Normative Context of Positive Economics?" *Journal of Economic Issues* 15 (September 1981): 721–27.

"The Pareto Principle: Another View," *Analyse & Kritik* 3 (August 1981): 124–34.

With A. Allan Schmid and James D. Shaffer, "Regulation and Regulatory Reform: Some Fundamental Conceptions," in Warren J. Samuels and A. Allan Schmid, *Law and Economics: An Institutional Perspective*, Boston, MA: Martinus Nijhoff, 1981, 248–66.

With A. Allan Schmid, "Interdependence and Impacts: Toward the Integration of Externality, Public Goods, and Grants Theories," in *Taxing and Spending Policy*, Lexington, MA: Lexington Books, 1980, 159–70.

"Reflections on the Question of a 'Crisis of Authority,'" *Review of Social Economy* (December 1980): 273–76.

"The Evolving Institution of Legal Services," *Nebraska Journal of Economics and Business* 19 (Autumn 1980): 3–15.

"John Bates Clark and A. Piatt Andrew: Some Modest Anticipations of Keynes," *Journal of Post Keynesian Economics* 3 (Fall 1980): 123–25.

"The Usury Issue in Public Utility Late Payment Charges," *University of Miami Law Review* 34 (September 1980): 1159–97.

"Survival and Pareto Optimality in Public Utility Rate Making," *Journal of Post Keynesian Economics* 2 (Summer 1980): 528–40.

With Nicholas Mercuro, "The Role and Resolution of the Compensation Principle in Society: Part Two – The Resolution," *Research in Law and Economics* 2 (1980): 103–28.

"Dunbar's 'Open Secret' and 'Original Instrument' Clarified," *History of Economics Society Bulletin* 2 (Summer 1980): 24–26.

"Two Concepts of 'Politicization,'" *Social Science* 55 (Spring 1980): 67–70.

"Toward Positive Public Choice Theory," *Review of Social Economy* 38 (April 1980): 55–64.

"Economics as a Science and its Relation to Policy: The Example of Free Trade," *Journal of Economic Issues* 14 (March 1980): 163–85. Reprinted in Mark Blaug (ed.) *Pioneers in Economics*, Vol. 22, Brookfield, VT: Edward Elgar, 1991.

"Problems of Marginal Cost Pricing in Public Utilities," *Public Utilities Fortnightly* 105 (January 31, 1980): 21–24.

"The State, Law, and Economic Organization," *Research in Law and Sociology* 2 (1979): 65–99.

"Thorstein Veblen, Heterodox Economist, in Retrospect," *Social Science Quarterly* 60 (December 1979): 454–59.

"Roy Weintraub's Microfoundations: The State of High Theory, A Review Article," *Journal of Economic Issues* 13 (December 1979): 1019–28.

"Aspects of Soviet Economic Planning: Power and the Optimal Use of Planning Techniques: A Review Article," *Review of Social Economy* 37 (October 1979): 231–39.

With James S. Russell, "Corporate and Public Responsibility in Environmental Policy: A Case Study," *MSU Business Topics* 27 (Autumn 1979): 23–32.

"Legal Realism and the Burden of Symbolism: The Correspondence of Thurman Arnold," *Law and Society Review* 13 (Summer 1979): 997–1011.

"Research Query," *History of Economics Society Bulletin* 1 (Summer 1979): 25–26.

"Nonmarket Corporate Control Networks: Comment," *Journal of Economic Issues* 13 (June 1979): 505–506.

With Nicholas Mercuro, "The Role and Resolution of the Compensation Principle in Society: Part One – The Role," *Research in Law and Economics* 1 (1979): 157–94.

"Normative Premises in Regulatory Theory," *Journal of Post Keynesian Economics* 1 (Fall 1978): 100–14.

"Lifeline Rates: Comments," in Harry M. Trebing (ed.) *Assessing New Pricing Concepts in Public Utilities*, East Lansing, MI: Division of Research, Graduate School of Business Administration, Michigan State University, 1978, 507–12.

"Federal Versus State Taxation of Energy Resources: An Interpretation of the Federal Position," *National Tax Association Proceedings*, 1978, 235–36.

"Federal Versus State Taxation of Energy Resources: Discussion," *National Tax Association Proceedings*, 1978, 257–58.

"Decison-Making Theory for Regulatory Agencies," in *Workshop Proceedings: Capital Investment Decisions*, Palo Alto, CA: Electric Power Research Institute, 1978, 157–63.

"Congressional Budget Reform: Comment," in James M. Buchanan and Richard E. Wagner (eds) *Fiscal Responsibility in Constitutional Democracy*, Boston, MA: Martinus Nijhoff, 1978, 151–55.

"Economic Effects of Secrecy: Discussion," in Barlow Burke, Jr., and Gene Wunderlich (eds) *Secrecy and Disclosure of Wealth in Land*, Chicago, IL: Farm Foundation, 1978, 114–17.

"History of Economics Society Sessions, Report," *History of Economic Thought Newsletter* 20 (Spring 1978): 1–7.

"Economics in the Service of All Mankind: A Review Article," *Review of Social Economy* 36 (April 1978): 79–87.

"Information Systems, Preferences, and the Economy in the *JEI*," *Journal of Economic Issues* 12 (March 1978): 23–41.

With Daniel Bronstein, "Medical Malpractice: The Case for Litigation," *Trial* 14 (February 1978): 48–53.

"Reflections on a Social Economics in a Diverse and Open Economics," *Review of Social Economy* 35 (December 1977): 283–91.

"Technology vis-à-vis Institutions in the JEI: A Suggested Interpretation," *Journal of Economic Issues* 11 (December 1977): 871–95.

"The Knight-Ayres Correspondence: The Grounds of Knowledge and Social Action," *Journal of Economic Issues* 11 (September 1977): 485–525. Reprinted in Mark Blaug (ed.) *Pioneers in Economics*, Vol. III, Brookfield, VT: Edward Elgar, 1992.

"Ashley's and Taussig's Lectures on the History of Economic Thought at Harvard, 1896–1897," *History of Political Economy* 9 (Fall 1977): 384–411.

"Ideology in Economics," in Sidney Weintraub (ed.) *Modern Economic Thought*, Philadelphia, PA: University of Pennsylvania Press, 1977, 467–84.

"Introduction: Commons and Clark on Law and Economics," *Journal of Economic Issues* 10 (December 1976): 743–49.

"The Myths of Liberty and Realities of the Corporate State: A Review Article," *Journal of Economic Issues* 10 (December 1976): 923–42.

With Andrew Gray, "The Teaching of Monetary Economics in the Early 1900's: Insight Into the Development of Monetary Theory," *History of Political Economy* 8 (Fall 1976): 324–40.

"The Political Economy of Adam Smith," *Nebraska Journal of Economics and Business* 15 (Summer 1976): 3–24, reprinted in *Ethics* 87 (April 1977): 189–207. Reprinted in J. C. Wood (ed.) *Adam Smith: Critical Assessments*, Kent: Croom Helm, 1984, Vol. 1.

With A. Allan Schmid, "Polluters' Profit and Political Response: The Dynamics of Rights Creation," *Public Choice* 28 (Winter 1976): 99–105.

With Nicholas Mercuro, "Property Rights, Equity, and Public Utility Pricing," in Harry M. Trebing (ed.) *New Dimensions in Public Utility Pricing*, East Lansing, MI: Division of Research, Graduate School of Business Administration, Michigan State University, 1976, 44–82.

"The Independent Judiciary in an Interest-Group Perspective: Comment," *Journal of Law and Economics* 18 (December 1975): 907–11.

"The Chicago School of Political Economy: Introduction," *Journal of Economic Issues* 9 (December 1975): 585–604.

"Regulation: Bankruptcy, Consumerism, and Lifeline Services," *Public Utilities Fortnightly* 96 (November 20, 1975): 32–37.

"Grants and the Theory of Power," *Public Finance Quarterly* 3 (October 1975): 320–45.

"Approaches to Legal-Economic Policy and Related Problems of Research," in Stuart S. Nagel (ed.) *Policy Studies and the Social Sciences*, Lexington, MA: Lexington Books, 1975, 65–73.

"Joseph Henry Beale's Lectures on Jurisprudence, 1909," *University of Miami Law Review* 29 (Winter 1975): 260–80, 281–333.

"Regulation and Valuation," *Public Utilities Fortnightly* 96 (July 17, 1975): 17–20; also in *Market Appraisals of Public Utilities for Ad Valorem Tax Purposes*, Wichita, KS: Center for Management Development, Wichita State University, and National Tax Association, 1975, 103–106.

"The Industrial Reorganization Bill: The Burden of the Future," *Journal of Economic Issues* 9 (June 1975): 381–94.

"The Veblen-Commons Award: Joseph Dorfman," *Journal of Economic Issues* 9 (June 1975): 143–45.

With James M. Buchanan, "On Some Fundamental Issues in Political Economy: An Exchange of Correspondence," *Journal of Economic Issues* 9 (March 1975): 15–38.

"Market, Institutions, and Technology: Introduction," *Journal of Economic Issues* 8 (December 1974): 663–69.

"An Economic Perspective on the Compensation Problem," *Wayne Law Review* 21 (November 1974): 113–34.

"Anarchism and the Theory of Power," in Gordon Tullock (ed.) *Further Explorations in the Theory of Anarchy*, Blacksburg, SC: University Publications, 1974: 33–57.

"The History of Economic Thought as Intellectual History," *History of Political Economy* 6 (Fall 1974): 305–23. Reprinted in Mark Blaug (ed.) *The Historiography of Economics*, Brookfield, VT: Edward Elgar, 1991, 106–24.

"Social Responsibilities of Public Utilities: Discussion," in *New Challenges to Public Utility Management*, East Lansing, MI: Institute of Public Utilities, Michigan State University, 1974, 243–54.

"Public Utility Rate Making and Competitive Structure: Carterfone in Jeopardy," *Wayne Law Review* 20 (March 1974): 819–43; and in The Industrial Reorganization Act, Hearings, Subcommittee on Antitrust and Monopoly, Committee on the Judiciary, United States Senate, 93rd Congress, 1st Session, Part 2 (1973): 978–92.

With Andrew Gray, "'One Great Tragedy': A Vignette," *History of Political Economy* 6 (February 1974): 114–18.

"The Coase Theorem and the Study of Law and Economics," *Natural Resources Journal* 14 (January 1974): 1–33.

"Public Utilities and the Theory of Power," in Milton Russell (ed.) *Perspectives in Public Regulation*, Carbondale, IL: Southern Illinois University Press, 1973: 1–27.

"Law and Economics: Introduction," *Journal of Economic Issues* 7 (December 1973): 535–41.

"Legal-Economic Policy," *Policy Studies Journal* 2 (Autumn 1973): 12–15.

"The Economy as a System of Power and Its Legal Bases: The Legal Economics of Robert Lee Hale," *University of Miami Law Review* 27 (Spring–Summer 1973): 261–371.

"Utility Late Payment Charges," *Wayne Law Review* 19 (July 1973): 1151–66; reprinted in *Law Review Digest* 23 (May–June 1973): 91–102.

"Models of Power in Decisional Organizations," *Proceedings, Midwest American Institute of Decision Sciences* (1973): D3–D6 [8pp.].

"Law and Economics: A Bibliographical Survey, 1965–1972," *Law Library Journal* 66 (February 1973): 96–110.

"You Cannot Derive 'Ought' From 'Is,'" *Ethics* 83 (January 1973): 159–62.

"Adam Smith and the Economy as a System of Power," *Review of Social Economy* 31 (October 1973): 123–37; and *Indian Economic Journal* 20 (January–March 1973): 363–81. Reprinted in J. C. Wood (ed.) *Adam Smith: Critical Assessments*, Kent: Croom Helm, 1984, Vol. 1.

"Externalities, Rate Structure, and the Theory of Public Utility Regulation," in Harry M. Trebing (ed.) *Essays on Public Utility Pricing and Regulation*, East Lansing, MI: Institute of Public Utilities, Michigan State University, 1972, 357–94.

"Welfare Economics, Power and Property," in G. Wunderich and W. L. Gibson, Jr.

(eds) *Perspectives on Property*, University Park: Institute for Research on Land and Water Resources, Pennsylvania State University, 1972: 61–148.

"The Teaching of Business Cycles in 1905–1906: Insight Into the Development of Macroeconomic Theory," *History of Political Economy* 4 (Spring 1972): 140–62. Reprinted in Mark Blaug (ed.) *Pioneers in Economics*, Vol. 40, Aldershot: Edward Elgar, 1992, 33–55.

"Public Utility Holding Companies and Housing," *Public Utilities Fortnightly* 89 (May 25, 1972): 16–24.

"Tax Pyramiding in Relation to Public Utilities: A Note in Clarification and Review," *Proceedings, National Tax Association* (1972): 553–69.

"The Scope of Economics Historically Considered," *Land Economics* 48 (August 1972): 248–68.

"In Defense of a Positive Approach to Government as an Economic Variable," *Journal of Law and Economics* 15 (October 1972): 453–59.

"Macroeconomic Institutional Innovation: Introduction," *Journal of Economic Issues* 6 (December 1972): 1–7.

"Ecosystem Policy and the Problem of Power," *Environmental Affairs* 2 (Winter 1972): 580–96.

"On the Effect of Regulation on Value," *Public Utilities Fortnightly* 88 (September 2, 1971): 21–29; and *National Tax Journal* 25 (June 1972): 311–19.

"Interrelations Between Legal and Economic Processes," *Journal of Law and Economics* 14 (October 1971): 435–50.

"Public Utilities, Social Order, and Housing," *Public Utilities Fortnightly* 85 (May 7, 1970): 32–36.

"Public Utilities and Social Problems," *Public Utilities Fortnightly* 84 (July 31, 1969): 15–21.

"The Tableau Economique as a Simple Leontief Model: A Precursor to Phillips," *Indian Economic Journal* 17 (July–September 1969): 112–17.

"On the Future of Institutional Economics," *Journal of Economic Issues* 3 (September 1969): 67–72; Reprinted in Markus Stadler (ed.) *Institutional-ismus Heute*, New York: Campus Verlag, 1983: 20–28.

"Taussig on the Psychology of Economic Policy," *Indian Economic Journal* 15 (July–September 1967) 1–13.

"Theory of Regulation in Relation to Return, I–III," *Public Utilities Fortnightly* 80 (November 9, November 23, December 7, 1967): 47–60, 34–41, 33–39.

"Edwin E. Witte's Concept of the Role of Government in the Economy," *Land Economics* 43 (May 1967): 131–47.

"The Nature and Scope of Economic Policy," in Warren J. Samuels, *The Classical Theory of Economic Policy* (Appendix), 237–309.

"Alleged Circularity and Fairness Requirement of Comparative Showings," *Public Utilities Fortnightly* 76 (September 29, 1966): 49–53.

"Legal-Economic Policy: A Bibliographical Survey," *Law Library Journal* 58 (August 1965): 230–52.

"History of Economic Thought: Discussion," *American Economic Review, Papers and Proceedings* 55 (May 1965): 145–47.

"The Classical Theory of Economic Policy: Non-Legal Social Control, I–II," *Southern Economic Journal* 31 (July, October 1964): 1–20, 87–100.

"The Problem of Liquidity: Continuity and Change in Structural Monetary Policy," *CLU Journal* 18 (Spring 1964): 145–54.

"The Physiocratic Theory of Economic Policy," *Quarterly Journal of Economics* 76 (February 1962): 145–62.

"The Physiocratic Theory of Property and State," *Quarterly Journal of Economics* 75 (February 1961): 96–111.

"An Overview of the Relationship of Wisconsin State Government to Business," *Wisconsin Blue Book*, Madison, WI: State of Wisconsin (1956): 71–82.

Part I
The history of economic thought

1 The training of the economist in antiquity

"The mirror for princes" tradition in *Alcibiades Major* and Aquinas' *On Kingship*

S. Todd Lowry

As a result of the eighteenth-century emphasis on natural market forces in economics and natural rights in political theory, the basic administrative tradition has been strangely ignored. Its literary genre, ubiquitous in antiquity, has come to be called "mirrors for princes." This literary tradition persisted as a robust form through the Middle Ages and the Renaissance, leaving its stamp on almost all political-economic tracts up to Adam Smith's time. Its characteristic format was to couch an analytic or policy treatise in terms of advice or recommendations to a young prince or new monarch. The custom was institutionalized to the extent that almost all political or mercantilist tracts were dedicated to the king through the seventeenth and eighteenth centuries.

What is even more interesting from the point of view of the discipline of economics is the precise use of the term. "economist," in a bellwether exemplar of the genre, the pseudo-Platonic dialogue, *Alcibiades Major*. Despite the recognition that Xenophon used the term *oeconomicus* to designate his Socratic dialogue on the efficient management of an agricultural estate, the Polanyi thesis has led us to assume that concern for economic problems was *embedded* in broader social institutions. Early indications of the concept of *political economy* before Montchretien in 1615, are suggested in the pseudo-Aristotelian *Oeconomica*, but this treatise has no suggestion of the concept of such a profession as that of an economist (Baloglou 1998). In the *Alcibiades Major*, however, it is specifically stated that a person should recognize the need for training to be successful as an *economist*, defined with commercial as well as administrative connotations. What is even more striking is that this document was considered an important part of basic education for some 900 years in the Greco-Roman pedagogical tradition.

The explanation for its relative oblivion both as a fount for the "mirror for princes" tradition and for the concept of the education of economists can be explained on two counts. First, the dialogue has been classed as pseudo-Platonic, although written in Plato's century. Its use in antiquity as a clear and simple introduction to Platonic thought, therefore, has not been perpetuated in modern classical scholarship. Second, the failure to find a place for the "mirror for princes" genre in modern disciplinary organization has led to the lack of interest in the apparent source of the intellectual imagery for the appellation, "mirror," that has been given to this literary form.

The existence of this tradition of advice tracts goes back to Egyptian "Wisdom literature" in the middle of the third millennium BC with advice to young pharaohs, or pharaohs to be, written by the grand vizier or a savant (Ray 1995). In the Greek tradition, the well-known instructional piece on peasant life by Hesiod from the eighth century BC, *The Works and Days*, was framed as advice from Hesiod to his wayward brother. Xenophon's romanticized work, *Cyropaedia*, on the education and policies of Cyrus the Great of Persia echoes this tradition of instructional literature on the training of effective leaders in a world where elite individualism was still highly touted despite the stirrings of political democracy in the Greek city-states. There is a well-developed line of "mirror" literature from late Roman times up to the Enlightenment documented by Born (1936). Born's interest, however, is in the form of kingship that began with Alexander the Great. He does not speculate on the origin or significance of the term, "mirror," that came to designate the form. Arabic literature also has a medieval tradition of such advice literature, but does not use the imagery of the mirror (Essid 1995: 19). There is also a very significant body of Iranian literature that falls into this tradition.

The dialogue, *Alcibiades Major*

In the dialogue, Socrates initiates a conversation with Alcibiades announcing that he had been a lover from afar for many years, but now that Alcibiades approached maturity, he felt compelled to come forward and contribute to his education. He points out that Alcibiades is the tallest and most attractive young man in Athens, from the most influential families on both his father's and mother's side, and has been raised under the guardianship of Pericles, the most influential leader in Greece. Granted his boundless ambition to take his place as a public leader, Socrates asserts that he needs training and offers to instruct him.

Although Alcibiades depends upon his natural abilities to succeed in political leadership, Socrates points out that when one goes before the people to advise them, they will want an expert on any technical question that requires decision – construction, shipbuilding, and so on. What then is the definition of the general or abstract expertise that a capable leader can offer? Spartan and Persian rulers are subjected to rigorous training, and Alcibiades cannot expect to compete with them unless he learns this art of successfully managing the affairs of the city that transcends the specific technical skills appropriate to specific activities. Alcibiades is asked about such policy issues as: with whom is it better to make war, when is it better, and for how long a time, etcetera? These are issues that require advice, and advice should be given by someone who knows more than those being advised. The issue is also raised as to whether superior knowledge is to be worked out by oneself, or must it be learned from someone else? (107e)

In the discussion, Socrates badgers Alcibiades to come up with a definition of "the better" that is broader than that specific to an applied art such as diet (108e–109a). Alcibiades is led to define "betterment" in general as equivalent to justice. This is a Platonic shift to a concept of justice as ideal order based on an absolute efficient implementation of the true value system. Alcibiades is, therefore, confronted with the incongruity of identifying a relativistic concept such as "betterment" with an absolute concept such as justice. To pursue the standard Platonic gambit that one cannot know the truth until he admits his ignorance, Socrates asks Alcibiades where he first learned what justice was? Alcibiades answers that he learned it from people in general (110e) and this brings forth Socrates' denunciation of the populace as good teachers. When Alcibiades retorts that he learned Greek from people, Socrates qualifies his adamancy by contending that you can only learn from the people things about which they agree. Issues about which people disagree are demonstrably beyond their ability and one must rely on a superior teacher.

The undercurrent here is a sparring between the Periclean principles of a "led democracy" and the Platonic principle of authoritarian administration by a philosopher king who couches his policies in terms of his own sense of personal justice (integrity) and public justice (the attainment of an optimally efficient society). Alcibiades' reply to this insistence on justice is, "Actually, Socrates, I think the Athenians and the other Greeks rarely discuss which course is more just or unjust. They think that sort of thing is obvious, so they skip over it and ask which one would be advantageous to do" (113d, Cooper ed.).

Socrates then runs Alcibiades through the word-association routine leading him to concede that what is just is admirable, what is admirable is good, and what is good is advantageous, therefore Alcibiades should face his ignorance of what is advantageous or just. Socrates subtly shifts the discussion to a question of individual rational moral choice and contends that when people know that they don't know, they defer to experts. "Don't you realize that the errors in our conduct are caused by this kind of ignorance, of thinking that we know what we don't know?" (117d, Cooper ed.) It is conceded that in the local assembly, Alcibiades would be competing with others who are equally ignorant where Alcibiades is confident that his natural wit would prevail. Socrates assures him, however, that in international relations, he would be dealing with well-trained leaders. The wealth and power of Sparta and Persia are then lauded. Sparta is characterized as the richest city in Greece because much gold flows into the city and none flows out.

The individualistic twist in Plato's political orientation is continued, and the hypothetical evaluation of Alcibiades by the queen mothers of Sparta and Persia is suggested by Socrates. The Spartan queen would belittle Alcibiades for not being as rich as the Spartan king. The Persian queen would characterize him as a presumptive upstart and would say, "I don't know what this fellow could be relying on, except diligence and wisdom – the Greeks don't have anything else worth mentioning" (123d, Cooper ed.). The argument that the queens of Athens's primary enemies would ridicule him for failing to dedicate himself to rigorous training apparently brings Alcibiades around and he agrees to accept training from Socrates.

The search for the definition and subject matter of the abstract skill appropriate to advising a city is taken up again. Alcibiades suggests that the objective is that of leading the citizens of Athens that have the intelligence to participate in ruling. The things these citizens need advice in taking care of require definition. Alcibiades suggests this definition of the abstract activity, "It's when they're helping each other and dealing with each other, as we do in our urban way of life" (125c, Cooper ed.).

Socrates leads the discussion away from this expression of an apparent sophistic formulation of the economic mutuality essential to the *polis*. The question of whether Alcibiades means ruling over men who deal with men is raised. Alcibiades reiterates, "I mean ruling over the men in the city who take part in citizenship and who make a mutual contribution (125d, Cooper ed.). Alcibiades defines the knowledge appropriate to this rule as "the knowledge of good advice," and its purpose is the "safety and better management of the city" (126a, Cooper ed.).

Socrates' question follows, "What about a city? What is it that's present or absent when it's in a better condition and getting better management and treatment? (126b, Cooper ed.) Alcibiades' answer is, ". . . mutual friendship will be present and hatred and insurrection will be absent" (126b, Cooper ed.). Friendship is defined as both public and private agreement, and illustrated by the relationship between parent and child, brother and brother, and husband and wife. These are the basic bonds that Aristotle uses (except for brother and brother) to illustrate the mutuality at the core of the family in *Politics I*. For Aristotle, the family is the basic productive unit that participates in the mutually beneficial exchange that supports the village economy.

Alcibiades is not allowed to develop the broader perspective on civic and commercial friendship that includes commercial partnership in Aristotle's *Nicomachean Ethics*, Book VII. The Platonic position is that individuals with different capacities cannot comprehend each other's role and, therefore, cannot agree. Also, an apparent theme of sophistic thought, namely that individuals are concerned with managing their belongings, is twisted and denounced as a sort of moral ignorance since one's own psychic balance – one's soul – is the proper concern of the individual and the cultivation of one's own virtue is the essential object of training for leadership. This is consistent with the Platonic ideal of the absolute virtuous benevolent despot, the philosopher king. This discussion of self-knowledge following the Delphic motto, "Know Thyself," is developed with a backhanded polemic against the concept of knowing how to manage one's belongings. Socrates sums up the argument, "And farmers and other tradesmen are a long way from knowing themselves. They don't even know what belongs to them [their souls]: Their skills are about what's even further away than what belongs to them. They only know what belongs to the body and how to take care of it [material goods]" (131a–b, Cooper ed., brackets mine).

Defining self-control as the proper pursuit of the individual who cares for his own soul, his prime possession, and rejecting the skills associated with caring for belongings as beneath the training of a gentleman, the dialogue sets the tone of an elite individualism justified by the tradition of *noblesse oblige*. Socrates rejects the more mundane concerns; "And isn't someone who takes care of his wealth caring neither for himself nor for what belongs to him, but for something even further away. . . . So the money-earner is not, in fact, doing his own work" (131c, Cooper ed.). This somewhat ascetic inward-turning of the ostensible leader, who is apparently to advise only himself, takes the dialogue well away from the practical line of political economy that Alcibiades appears to take for granted. Nevertheless, the conceptual framework shows through with the repeated discussions of managing one's "belongings" and "the belongings of one's belongings." Clearly, the idea being so translated is awkwardly rendered and requires further investigation of the cultural connotation involved.

The "mirror for princes" imagery

Socrates formulates the "mirror for princes" concept in his own terms, that is, as an elaboration of the Delphic maxim: "Know thyself." He contends that the best way to explain the meaning of the maxim is to use the illustration of vision, "see thyself." While Alcibiades agrees and suggests that this requires a mirror, Socrates argues that looking into the eye of another permits people to see their reflection in the pupil. The Greek word for "pupil" also means "doll" or "little statue" (133a).

In this dialogue, Socrates makes no real use of the "mirror" symbolism which would lead one to believe that it was an older concept that was incorporated in the dialogue out of deference to tradition. Socrates transfers the illustration to the relationship that one person should have with another from whom he wishes to learn, that is, to key his own soul, or mind, into the mind of another, this being the vital process by which we gain true knowledge and self control. "Then if the soul, Alcibiades, is to know itself, it must look at a soul, and especially at that region in which what makes a soul good, wisdom, occurs . . . (133b, Cooper ed.). If the word "mind" is used instead of the theologically habituated word "soul" to render the concept *psyche*, the pedagogic association that is being promoted becomes clearer.

At this point, in the closing lines of the dialogue, Socrates reiterates the primary importance of self-knowledge and self-control that are prerequisites to a leader knowing about "belongings," and so on. He accepts the concept of a general discipline by contending that it is one person's job or art to know how to deal with his own, other people's, and the city's belongings. The back-handed references to the practical tradition that had been repeatedly alluded to in Alcibiades' responses are capped off with a denunciation of the potential leader that did not "know himself." "So, such a man couldn't become a statesman" and, "Nor could he even manage a household estate" (133c, Cooper ed.). What is of importance here is Cooper's use of the phrase, "manage a household estate," which is the standard classical scholar's formulation of the meaning behind Xenophon's work, the *Oikonomicus*. In the more literal Loeb translation, the line runs, "No, nor an economist either." The Greek terms used for "statesman" and "economist" are "politicos" and "oikonomicos." The discussion clearly deals with the administration of the city including civic and commercial friendship or mutuality. We should keep in mind that in the eastern Mediterranean, at this time, the two economic entities that were dominant in daily life were the agricultural estate and the city – the *oikos* and the *polis*. Management of these two entities can best be characterized as micro and macro management of the firm and the economy. The professional economist was associated with the civic entity with the extended administrative challenges that grew out of the Alexandrian empire, even though Xenophon states that a person can make a living as the manager of an agrarian estate – the firm or basic productive entity in the economy.

After the division of Alexander's empire, the sector controlled by the Ptolemies, Egypt, Palestine, and Syria, was organized under the Persian thesis that the king owned the total real estate and controlled all commerce. We are indebted to the Greek historian, Hecataeus of Abdera, for a report on the adaptation by the Greek Ptolemy I Soter (304–283 BC), of the oriental experience in managing extensive empires. Observing that the administrative organization of Egypt came close to approximating the philosophic ideal of the Greek state, an obvious reference to Plato, Hengel comments that, ". . . under the first Ptolemies the oriental idea of the divinely sanctioned omnipotence of the king was put into effect, with Greek logic" (Hengel 1981: 18–19). Under Ptolemy II Philodelphus, a single official, Apollonius, called the *dioiketes* was responsible for "the entire possessions and income of the king, that is, everything connected with the finances, the economy and the administration of the state"(Hengel 1981: 19). This pattern of dividing military and economic power was replicated at the very lowest district level in Egypt with power divided between a *strategos* and an *economicos*, that is, a military commander and an economist (economic administrator) – both traditional Greek terms. This pattern was replicated with a *hyparch* and *economicos* where Persian administrative institutions were adapted in Palestine and Syria (Hengel 1981: 19–21).

The role of the economist as an economic administrator in the political bureaucracy must be understood in terms of the economic realities of antiquity. The city state and the Hellenistic empire functioned as aggregative/distributive structures. However, the thesis that the empire was conceived as "the oikos writ large" is an oversimplification. Agricultural self-sufficiency was the fundamental economic objective of most economies with limited surpluses supporting the political, commercial, and military superstructure. Foreign military adventures were the primary source of public income up to the time of the Roman empire, when advalorum land taxation (a production tax) began to replace special levies on the rich (Vivenza 1998). This pattern may have been borrowed from the exceptionally rich agricultural productivity of the Nile and Euphrates valleys. In Hellenistic times, however, military entrepreneurship was more remunerative and more dramatic than commercial activity and agricultural improvement. There were, nevertheless, some clear demonstrations of the recognized importance of production and trade. In Xenophon's *Hiero* – another example of "advice literature" – Simonides recommends to the head of a city-state that he give prizes for exemplary levels of agricultural production and for technical innovations. The point is made that nothing can be bought as cheaply as through competitive prizes. Obviously, many individuals expend extra effort in competition for the prize, but only one need be paid! (Lowry 1987: 58). Also, in Xenophon's *Ways and Means*, the last section is devoted to administrative techniques for encouraging commercial activity. The enduring relevance of this advice to the city of Athens is indicated by its inclusion as a supplement in such economic writings as Charles Davenant's *Discourses on the Publick Revenues, and on the Trade of England*, 1698, and in the 1751 edition of William Petty's *Political Arithmetick* (Lowry 1987: 49).

While many of the contributions in this advice tradition do not mention the imagery of the mirror, its persistence can be documented and elaborated. The breadth of meanings derived from the Latin word for mirror, "speculum," that have extended into connotations of hypothetical analysis and risky investment (speculation) is worth noting.

Aristotle's elaboration of the mirror concept

Although the formal imagery of looking into someone's eyes as a mirror is set forth in the pseudo-Platonic *Alcibiades Major*, it rings a bit hollow as a significant concept. It is framed in the context of the Socratic goal of "self-knowledge" – the prime requisite for self-sufficient moral authoritarian rule. However, there may well be an undocumented history of the imagery. Also, the suggestion that there is an undercurrent of more widely held democratic thought reflected in Alcibiades' responses is born out by an examination of Aristotle's work.

If the estimates that the *Alcibiades Major* was written shortly after Plato's death in 347 BC are correct, then it was produced about the same time as Aristotle's *Eudemian Ethics* (*EE*). The types of friendship appropriate to a well-led city, to which Alcibiades alluded, are more thoroughly defined by Aristotle as follows:

> Specified sorts of friendship are therefore the friendship of relatives, that of comrades, that of partners and what is termed civic friendship. Really friendship of relatives has more than one species, one as between

brothers, another as of father and son: . . . [discussing degrees of proportionality and near equality].

(*EE* VII, x, 1; 1242a, Loeb edn., brackets mine)

Civic friendship on the other hand is constituted in the fullest degree on the principle of utility, for it seems to be the individual's lack of self-sufficiency that makes these unions permanent – since they would have been formed in any case merely for the sake of society. Only civic friendships . . . [are] also partnerships on a friendly footing; . . . The justice that underlies a friendship of utility is in the highest degree just, because this is the civic principle of justice.

(*EE* VII, x, 2; 1242a, Loeb edn., brackets mine)

This emphasis on associations based on mutuality with justice defined as a sort of natural consensus for common utility marks the basic difference between Plato and Aristotle. This Aristotelian formulation of justice as a natural phenomenon growing out of public decisions was carried into Roman law (Kelley 1990). In the *Alcibiades Major*, Socrates brings out the Platonic view, arguing that individuals with different skills and capacities cannot agree, even husband and wife, where the wife understands working with wool and the husband understands military tactics, but they do not understand each other's roles (126e–127a). Socrates had defined justice as a well-ordered society, but insisted that since it is impossible for people to agree relative to their individual activities, justice cannot be based on friendship. Alcibiades was presented as making one final argument on this score before capitulating; "But it seems to me that friendships arise among them just on that account – that each of the two parties does its own business" (127b, Cooper ed.). Not only is this remark consistent with the position quoted above from the *Eudemean Ethics*, it echoes Aristotle's emphasis on exchange holding the city together in book V.v. of his *Nicomachean Ethics* (*NE*), and the two books, VIII and IX, on friendship in that work where he elaborates friendships based on utility among mature citizens, "Friendship based on utility is for the commercially minded" (*NE* VIII, vi, 4; 1158a20, Ross edn.). The somewhat more theologically oriented Loeb edition renders this line, ". . . whereas the friendship of utility is a thing for sordid souls" (*NE* VIII, vi, 4; 1158a20, Loeb edn.).

Since there is so much dispute over Aristotle's analysis of exchange presented in Book V "On Justice" in his *Nicomachean Ethics*, we should quote his discussion on the utility of exchange in his treatment of types of friendship in Book IX. In a case where an entertainer was promised additional pay for additional performance, the host refused to honor the commitment telling the entertainer that he had "given pleasure for pleasure." Aristotle comments:

Now if this had been what each wanted, all would have been well but if the one wanted enjoyment but the other gain, and the one has what he wants while the other has not, the terms of the association will not have been properly fulfilled: for what each in fact wants is what he attends to, and it is for the sake of that he will give what he has. But who is to fix the worth of the service: he who makes the sacrifice or he who has got the advantage?

(1164a, 15–20; Ross edn.)

It is the grasp of the practical realities of utilitarian association – friendships – reflected in such discussions that provide the background against which we can understand the issues of economic policy that leaders in the assembly would discuss.

The problem is quite clear in the context of Greek political and economic thought in the fourth century BC. As articulated in Book II of his *Republic*, Plato believed that the division of labor was essential to an efficient, well-ordered just society. However, the achievement of this condition was best attained by the intelligent administrator assigning individuals the tasks for which they were, by nature, best fitted. This identification and training was to be done from an early age. This administrative responsibility was the generalized skill for which Alcibiades needed training – as a *politicos* or *economicos*. Since such an individual was superior and above criticism, administering an unquestionable value system with efficiency and order, he must "know himself" and have his own internal moral commitment to truth and psychic responsibility (Lowry 1987: Ch. 4). By contrast, the Aristotelian theory of mutuality and beneficial interaction is developed in his *Politics*, Book I, where specialization and the division of labor are the outgrowth of the family, village, and city. In Xenophon's work, not only is specialization and the division of labor developed (*Cyropaedia*, VIII. 2.5–6), but the importance of voluntary and enthusiastic participation promoted by incentives and good leadership is thoroughly elaborated. He has a well-rounded appreciation of human beings as the primary resource, that is, a perspective that we would characterize today as human capital theory (Lowry 1995). Considering the Greek perspective of the city as a "commonwealth" of its citizens, in the literal sense of the term, with market supervision and responsibility for public food supplies, the role of the *economicos* as leader and advisor in the public assembly would be a mixture of macro and micro economics. The city was treated as an economy that should be developed, on the one hand, and as a firm that should be efficiently managed, on the other.

Aristotle on the "mirror for princes" image

Towards the end of the third surviving record of Aristotle's work on ethics, the *Magna Morelia*, it is pointed out that even the person who has all material needs satisfied still requires friendship. Human beings are not self-sufficient. If nothing else, they require associates on which they can bestow beneficences as expressions of a fully developed character.

Furthermore, to achieve the ideal goal of "self-knowledge" – the objective in the *Alcibiades Major* – one cannot rely on the divine for insight through comparison. On the other hand, "If a man makes himself the object of his own research, we stigmatize him as a dullard" (*Magna Morelia*, II, xv, 4; 1218a, Loeb edn.). The problem being discussed is whether an individual, desiring self-improvement through self-knowledge, can achieve such a goal independently. As we recall, this possibility was rejected in the *Alcibiades Major* and the need for a teacher was asserted. As the issue is developed by Aristotle, the point is made that a friend is

> a kind of second self, . . . Now to know oneself is a very difficult thing – as even philosophers have told us . . . Direct contemplation of ourselves is moreover impossible, as is shown by the censure we inflict on others for the very things we ourselves unwittingly do – favor or passion being the cause which in many of us blind our judgment. And so, just as when wishing to behold our own faces, we have seen them by looking upon a mirror, whenever we wish to know our own character and personalities, we can recognize them by looking upon a friend; since the friend, as we say, is our "second self." If, therefore, it be pleasant to know ourself, and this knowledge is impossible without another who is a friend, it follows that the self-sufficient man will need friendship . . .
> (*Magna Morelia*, II, xv, 4–8; 1218a, Loeb edn.)

This approach to self-improvement through interaction with a friend echoes a Protagorean thesis that truth is approached by argument, back and forth – a social dialectic. The idea is extended to the process for approaching justice by setting up an adversary system and arguing before a judge or a panel of judges. Protagoras' views are presented in Plato's dialogue, *Theaetetus* (Lowry 1987: Ch. VI). In his dialogue, *Greater Hippias*, Plato presents a concept that straddles the view expressed in the *Alcibiades Major* and that developed by Aristotle in the *Magna Morelia*. This is the theory of the "impartial spectator" (*Greater Hippias*, 286c–298a, 304c–d). However, Plato bends this concept of an interpersonal interaction in search of self-knowledge into an intra personal action, an interaction with one's own *alter ego* or conscience. This view is what is specifically rejected by Aristotle in the *Magna Morelia* quoted above where the necessity of an outside party – a friend – is required for effective self-knowledge and self-improvement.

As somewhat of an aside, although relevant to the perpetuation of the imagery of the mirror in self-evaluation, is a passage in the *New Testament*. In "The Letter of James, I," we find an inverted use of the imagery of the mirror, in which it is used to reject the efficacy of the Platonic view of self-sufficiency in knowledge;

23 For if any be a hearer of the word, and not a doer, he is like unto a man beholding his natural face in a glass:

24 For he beholdeth himself, and straightway goeth his way, forgetting what manner of man he was".

(*Bible*, King James Version)

This passage uses the mirror or looking glass as a passive view of oneself devoid of any effective stimulus toward self-improvement or motivation.

The contrast between the use of the image quoted from the New Testament and that expressed in the *Magna Morelia* is brought out forcefully in the final lines of this latter incomplete work as it trails off:

> This inquiry does not concern every kind of friendship, but only that where the friends are most given to finding fault with one another. In the other kinds, they are less inclined thereto; for example, between father and son there is no such fault-finding as that which in some kinds of friendship men think fit to indulge. "As I treat you," they say, "so you must treat me" – and if he does not, a bitter fault-finding ensues. But between friends who are unequal, this equality has no place.
>
> (*Magna Morelia*, II, xvii, 1–2, 1218b; Loeb edn.)

This final observation, associated with commercial friendship, suggests a notion of an interactive dialectic or bargaining process that improves performance in the marketplace. It is not out of order, therefore, to skip ahead 2,000 years to Adam Smith's discussion of this theme.

Adam Smith and the Aristotelian mirror

In the eighteenth century when Smith wrote his *Theory of Moral Sentiments* (1759), the debate was between the social contract thesis built on the premise of rational individualism, on the one hand, and a theory of social cohesion based on human sympathy (friendship), on the other. Consistent with the Protagorean tradition that human beings had an innate sense of justice and "fellow feeling" – often translated as "reverence" for others – Smith offered a theory of society based on "human sympathy." To explain this position as it applied to individual judgment, he used the concept of the "impartial spectator." Therefore, if we look at his explanation of the individual's necessary interaction with others, we can see that he was clearly an heir of the Aristotelian perspective on the meaning of the "mirror" in political and moral thought.

Part III of Smith's *Theory of Moral Sentiments* (*TMS*) is entitled, "Of the Foundation of our Judgment concerning our own Sentiments and Conduct, and of the Sense of Duty." After some introductory remarks on the reliance of the individual on some outside perspective, the "impartial spectator," Smith sums up his position very succinctly:

> Were it possible that a human creature could grow up to manhood in some solitary place, without any communication with his own species, he

could no more think of his own character, of the propriety or demerit of his own sentiments and conduct, of the beauty or deformity of his own mind, than of . . . his own face. All these are objects which he cannot easily see, which naturally he does not look at, and with regard to which he is provided with no mirror which can present them to his view. Bring him into society, and he is immediately provided with the mirror which he wanted before. It is placed in the countenance and behavior of those he lives with, which always mark when they enter into, and when they disapprove of his sentiments; and it is here that he first views the propriety and impropriety of his own passions.

(*TMS* III, 3: 110)

Smith precedes this elaboration with the observation that we can only see ourselves through the eyes of others. Although these passages resonate with the ideas in the *Alcibiades Major* and the *Magna Morelia*, which Smith had undoubtedly read in the course of his classical education in moral philosophy, there were many other examples of the imagery of the mirror in Renaissance and Enlightenment literature.

Jeffrey Young, who quotes the above passage to illustrate Smith's social theory of morality, goes on to show that Smith extends the analysis, pointing out that the individual can add his own appraisal of his motivations for his conduct. This secondary level of self-evaluation is something concerning which the spectator can only guess (Young 1997: 35).

Thomas Aquinas' Speculum, *On Kingship*

The primary purpose of this inquiry is to examine the early frame of reference of "mirror for princes" literature and the administrative context of its economics. However, a brief look at the contribution of St. Thomas Aquinas to this tradition will help to highlight two major issues that have stimulated interest in this literary genre. The first is the administrative sophistication of these writings. The second is the way that Aquinas' formal contribution to political economy has been so completely ignored by historians of economic thought who have been obsessed with early formulations of market and price theory. Historically, the administrative treatment of the market as something to be structured in an arena, framed by laws and rules, dominated public policy up to the time that improved transportation, communications, and a near religious enthrallment with naturalism in the eighteenth century gave general credibility to Adam Smith's liberal commercial program.

The emphasis in the mirrors or specula was on the responsibilities of the monarch, his personal health and education, personnel selection and management, taxation, warfare, and agricultural policy as well as protection of trade and traders. In ancient and medieval times, the sequence in the preceding list probably correlated fairly well with the order of concern of the ruler with his realm. In the famous *Secretum Secretorum*, an alleged letter of advice

from Aristotle to Alexander the Great, produced in Arabic around the eighth
or ninth century AD, advice on personnel selection and management takes up
a major portion of the book. Its detailed association of variations in facial
appearance with character traits influenced English literature after it reached
that country in vernacular translation in the late 1400s.

Although Lester Born does not discuss the origin of the designation of the
genre, he provides an extensive survey of "mirrors for princes" or "*specula
principi*" in his long introduction to his translation of Erasmus's exemplar
addressed to the young prince Charles V of Spain (Born 1936: 44–132). Born
concentrates on the literature from the sixth to the sixteenth century. It would
require a large volume to properly study these contributions to political economy, but a closer examination of one of them should bring out the cultural
problem of evaluating the analytical level of such literature in its own time
and place.

Shortly after the middle of the thirteenth century AD, possibly 1260,
Thomas Aquinas wrote a "speculum" or treatise of advice directed to the
King of Cyprus. The circumstances or motivation that gave rise to this contribution are unknown, as is even the precise date, and therefore the identity
of the particular king to whom it was directed. Such writings were often precursors to tutorships for young princes, or stipends as court savants. In any
event, Aquinas' essay is of considerable interest to those concerned with economic thought, in part because it has been so systematically ignored by
historians of economic ideas who presume to deal with the Middle Ages.
Most of the work focuses on the legitimacy of monarchy and its responsibilities. These were issues that were realistically of primary importance, but the
general theoretical orientation introducing the work is what draws our
attention.

Beginning with the preliminary necessity to define kingship, Aquinas proceeds to explain the basic social process. The flavor of the Aristotelian logic
and its general relevance to any formal analysis, economic or otherwise, justifies extensive quotation.

> In all things which are ordered towards an end, wherein this or that
> course may be adopted, some directive principle is needed through
> which the due end may be reached by the most direct route. [After using
> a ship's pilot as an illustration, he continues] Now, Man has an end to
> which his whole life and all his actions are ordered; for man is an intel-
> ligent agent, and it is clearly the part of an intelligent agent to act in
> view of an end. Men also adopt different methods in proceeding towards
> their proposed end, as the diversity of men's pursuits and actions clearly
> indicates.
>
> (Aquinas, 3, brackets mine)

"The problem is posed, therefore, that men may not all work together,
although . . . the light of reason is placed by nature in every man, to guide

him in his acts towards his end" (Aquinas: 3). This rationality would suffice as guidance, "if man were intended to live alone, . . . Each man would be a king unto himself" (Aquinas: 3).

Following Aristotle's position that man is a gregarious animal, Aquinas points out that human beings, more than other animals, live in groups. Then, following the Islamic philosopher, Avicenna, as indicated by the editor, Aquinas supports this point with the illustration that all other animals have natural means of protection and sustenance except man: "man was endowed with reason, by the use of which he could procure all these things for himself by the work of his hands" (Aquinas: 4). However, since one man cannot provide defense and sustenance alone, it is "natural that man should live in the society of many" (Aquinas: 4). This point is developed in "Protagoras' Myth" explaining the origin of civic life found in Plato's dialogue, *Protagoras*. Avicenna, however, is generally accepted as a follower of Protagorean ideas.

A further analysis is advanced, in the Avicennan tradition, namely that animals have natural skills and knowledge of what foods to eat, and what plants may have medicinal benefits. Man has only a general sense of necessities and

> is able to attain knowledge of the particular things necessary for human life by reasoning from natural principles. But it is not possible for one man to arrive at a knowledge of all these things by his own individual reason. It is therefore necessary for man to live in a multitude so that each one may assist his fellows.
>
> (Aquinas: 5)

The argument goes on to endorse specialization in research, medicine, and other discoveries. This recognition of population concentrations supported by the human capacity for speech is understood as the avenue to the "information highway" that permits the benefits from specialized research to be shared. These benefits of men living together indicate that society is natural, but "where there are many men together and each one is looking after his own interest, the multitude would be broken up and scattered unless there were also an agency to take care of what appertains to the commonweal" (5–6). This, then, is the basic argument for kingship.

We can recognize this argument from the *Alcibiades Major*, namely, that individuals with different specialties cannot reach agreement and therefore require a generalist at rational administration to govern them. The major burden of the rest of the treatise is to elaborate the responsibility of the monarch to apply reason to governing in the common interest of his subjects. One who governs in his own personal interest is a tyrant and the people owe him no allegiance. The final pages of the treatise discuss the proper balance in a city-state between agricultural self-sufficiency and dependence on trade. It is apparent that these things are considered to be within the control of the ruler if the city is well located with ample arable land. While no city is capable of being completely self-sufficient, only a limited amount of trade should be permitted and a militarily stalwart agricultural population, accustomed to hard work and limited pleasures, should be maintained. Too many foreign traders, primarily interested in making money, will debase the community and divert the citizens from accepting their higher roles in public service. This section is basically a partial review of Aristotle's *Politics I* on the desirability of self-sufficiency. This, however, was consistent with the functional political and economic unit in the Mediterranean up to the emergence of nation-states. The city with its hinterland, ethnic, and municipal traditions supported small monarchies and republics in Italy and the eastern Mediterranean despite the hegemonic vagaries of military and religious empires.

Conclusions

The purpose of this essay has been, primarily, to bring out the importance of the genre of literature illustrated here by the *Alcibiades Major* and Aquinas' *On Kingship*. They both reflect an ongoing endorsement of rational authority in an administered economy while indicating a relatively clear grasp of the basic elements of an economy. The fact that the practicians of the administrative art in the urban Greek states and Hellenistic Ptolemaic provincial administrations were designated *economists* was apparently lost as these roles were fused into small-scale monarchies and republics such as the one envisioned by Aquinas. Nevertheless, the tradition behind this type of literature is continuous and was a rich source of political and economic ideas that was part of the European intellectual tradition. Furthermore, the almost systematic ignoring of this literature by social scientists and intellectual historians is a phenomenon that is a matter of concern in its own right. This pattern is most likely attributable to an exaggerated level of specialization in which the "mirrors" do not quite fall into the category of abstract political theory, market oriented economics, or historical treatises. They are, however, a record of the administrative tradition that, in reality, dominated economic thought for 2,000 years before the seventeenth and eighteenth century excursion into proto-religious naturalism that dominated social thought (Lowry 1995). From the time that Sir Edward Coke abandoned his defense of the royal prerogative under Queen Elizabeth I, and brought the prestige of his legal status as Chief Justice of the Court of King's Bench to bear in support of "the natural rights of Englishmen" – from that time on, natural law and natural rights were elevated to a popular political level to counter the claim of divine right by the Stuart kings. When "nature" had to be made more politically forceful than God, the underwriter of "Divine Right," the tradition of rational administrative science lost its luster until rediscovered by the modern large scale corporation.

References

Aquinas, St. Thomas (1979) *ca.* 1260: *De Regno, Ad Regem Cypri*, published as *On Kingship: To the King of Cyprus*, revised translation, introduction and notes by I. Th. Eschmann, Westport, CT: Hyperion Press (revision of the G. B. Phelan translation published in 1935).

Baloglou, C. P. (1998) "Hellenistic Economic Thought," in S. Todd Lowry and Barry Gordon (eds) *Ancient and Medieval Economic Ideas and Concepts of Social Justice*, Leiden, New York and Köln: E. J. Brill, 105–46.

Born, L. K. (1936) *The Education of a Christian Prince* by Desiderius Erasmus, translated with an introduction by Lester K. Born, New York: Columbia University Press.

Cooper, J. M. (ed.) (1997) *Plato: Complete Works*, with introduction and notes, Indianapolis and Cambridge: Hackett Publishing Company.

Essid, Yassine (1995) *A Critique of the Origins of Islamic Economic Thought*, Leiden, New York and Köln: E. J. Brill.

Hengel, Martin (1981) *Judaism and Hellenism: Studies in their Encounter in Palestine in the Early Hellenistic Period*, translation of the 2nd revised German edn. in 1 vol. Philadelphia, PA: Fortress Press.

Kelley, D. R. (1990) *The Human Measure: Social Thought in the Western Legal Tradition*, Cambridge, MA: Harvard University Press.

Lowry, S. T. (1987) *The Archaeology of Economic Ideas: The Classical Greek Tradition*, Durham, NC: Duke University Press.

—— (1995) "The Ancient Greek Administrative Tradition and Human Capital," in *Archives of Economic History* 6, 1: 7–18.

Ray, J. D. (1995) "Egyptian Wisdom Literature," in John Day, Robert P. Gordon and H. G. M. Williamson (eds) *Wisdom in Ancient Israel: Essays in Honour of J. A. Emerton*, Cambridge: Cambridge University Press.

Smith, Adam (1759) *The Theory of Moral Sentiments*, Glasgow edn., ed. by D. D. Raphael and A. L. MacFie, Oxford and New York: Oxford University Press, 1976.

Vivenza, G. (1998) "Roman Thought on Economics and Justice," in S. Todd Lowry and Barry Gordon (eds) *Ancient and Medieval Economic Ideas and Concepts of Social Justice*, Leiden, New York and Köln: Brill, 269–332.

Young, J. T. (1997) *Economics as a Moral Science: The Political Economy of Adam Smith*, Lyme, NH, and Cheltenham: Edward Elgar.

2 A quintessential (ahistorical) *Tableau Économique*

To sum up pre- and post-Smith classical paradigms

Paul A. Samuelson

François Quesnay (1759) and Physiocratic followers invested with magic a *Tableau Économique* by purporting to unveil the secrets of general equilibrium. This was greeted with genial skepticism by Adam Smith (1776) and with constructive respect by Karl Marx (1885, 1894; 1905–10) when investigating his own *Tableaux of (Stationary and Expanding) Reproduction.* Modern commentators on Quesnay's Tableau, aside from Warren Samuels (1969) himself, have related it to the independent input/output workshops of Wassily Leontief and Piero Sraffa – as in Shigeto Tsuru (1942), George Malanos (1946), Almarin Phillips (1955), Warren Samuels (1969), Shlomo Maital (1972), Paul Samuelson (1982), and Walter Eltis (1996).

During my brief months as a boy scout, to win a Second Class Badge I had to pass a test: employing solely the materials of the forest, build a campfire using only two matches. In that spirit, using only the materials of pre-Smith economics (and eschewing all "marginalisms"), I present here an Agriculture and Manufactures Tableau that can serve to summarize the essence of classical economics:

1. It treats "land" as *exogenously* fixed.
2. It treats labor supply as *endogenously* forthcoming in infinitely elastic supply at an exogenously specifiable "subsistence" real wage rate (expressed here in farm produce).
3. It treats goods' production as requiring advanced payments for inputs of: (a) *labor*; (b) *land*; and (3) *produced* inputs of "capital".

   Employed is a parsimonious technology that can vindicate the cogency of (i) Smith's eclectic tripartite anatomical determination of general equilibrium's competitive prices as the sum of wage costs + land-rent costs + interest (or profit) markups. The analysis can demonstrate (ii) the *non-*generality of Ricardo's critique of Smith for denying the primacy of embodied labor-content *à la* Labour Theory of Value: even when time intensities do not differ, and when the interest rate is zero, land-rent costs do alter relative goods' prices, P_i/P_j. Thus the present Tableau can rebut Sraffa's (1926) calculated claim that modern post-Marshallians can be best served by what his readers could interpret him to assert was a constant-cost, invariant natural-price-ratio, standard classical model. Researchers in the Sraffa papers at Cambridge have reported to me in correspondence that Sraffa admitted three years later in his lectures that differences in labor-to-land intensities between goods would indeed imply an *increasing-cost* rise in the P_i/P_j ratio when demand shifted toward a land-intensive Q_i and away from Q_j. Apparently no one has yet discovered a Sraffa publication wherein he explicitly corrects any earlier readers' misapprehension that in the classical system there is an *endogenous constancy* of the rent/wage ratio while shifts occur in consumers' tastes and demands for final goods.

4. My exposition is ahistorical but would be understandable by Petty, Cantillon, and Turgot. Its model can illuminate Turgot's relating of a positive interest rate to, among other things, the existence of permanent rent-fetching land. Confronted with the present model, the young Schumpeter (1912), who authored the classic *Theory of Economic Development*, could hardly have maintained his idiosyncratic thesis that, in the stationary state (*sans* innovation), the natural rate of interest would *have to* become a *zero* rate of interest.

5. The present scenario demonstrates conclusively that, in it, P_i/P_j fails to equal the ratio of total labors *embodied* respectively in goods i and j. Such would be no more true for labor than for *embodied land contents* of the respective goods. Indeed, in Samuelson's (1959) Physiocratic version of the Ricardian model, when we categorize subsistence-labor inputs themselves as in effect the outputs producible (directly *or indirectly*) from homogeneous primary land, then at prescribed interest rates, the P_i/P_j ratios will be invariant to shifts in the composition of property owners' tastes and consumption demands; and always the P_i/P_j's will exactly equal *required land contents embodied directly and indirectly in the productions of the respective goods and their needed produced inputs, but of course calculated to take account of any positive compound interest incurred for all "earlier" outlays on land throughout the time-phased structure of productions.* In Jürg Niehans' (1990) valuable *A History of Economic Theory*, the author traces such a theory already to Richard Cantillon (1755). Far from being a Labour Theory of Value, the correct classical paradigm of Smith, Malthus, Ricardo, Mill, and the rest is more nearly a "(dated) Land Theory of Value!" (When lands of *diverse* quality are present – surely the realistic historical story – then all the subtleties of a Walrasian general equilibrium, involving interaction between "distribution" theory and "value" theory, are unavoidable for a rigorous modern exposition of mid-eighteenth century scenarios.)

Assumptions

Factor supplies

Land is exogenously given in fixed supply, say at $\overline{A} = 300$. Here, for *simplicity*, land is to be homogeneous, unaugmentable, and undepletable, of use only in agriculture (i.e., in "corn" production).

Labor is also homogeneous, but its population size and input quantity is an endogenous variable. People are readily reproducible in terms of a specifiable real *subsistence* wage rate; for simplicity, only agricultural corn is needed here for the *exogenously* specifiable equilibrium subsistence real wage of $W/P_{corn} = W/P_1 = 1/4$, say. Total L is allocated between agriculture and manufactures: $L = L_1 + L_2$, $L_j \geq 0$.

Technology

Agriculture's gross Q_1 is producible out of land as input, A_1; also out of direct labor as input, L_1; and also out of reproducible corn-seed, Q_{11}, as input for corn production. Quantitatively, 1 of Q_1 at the end of a period requires at the period's beginning 1 of land, 1 of labor and 1/2 of corn itself. In a modern notation, $A_1/Q_1 = b_{A1} = 1$, $L_1/Q_1 = b_{L1} = 1$ and $Q_{11}/Q_1 = a_{11} = 1/2$. No manufactured input cloth is needed for corn production: $Q_{21}/Q_1 = a_{21}$ is zero and ignorable.

Manufacture's gross Q_2 is producible out of direct labor, L_2, and out of farm-produced raw material Q_{12}; I ignore land as a further needed input. Quantitatively, 1 of Q_2 needs 1 of L_2 and (say) 1 of corn Q_{12} as inputs a period earlier. Eschewing modern smooth marginalisms and alternative techniques, I have thus specified $b_{L2} = L_2/Q_2 = 1$, $Q_{12}/Q_2 = a_{12} = 1$, $Q_{22} = 0$, $b_{A2} = 0$.

The choice of 1s for the direct labor requirements is an arbitrary dimensional convention; however, the numerical choices for a_{11} and a_{12} are substantive but qualitatively unbiasing happenstances. The same cannot be said of the generous specifications of zeros in the implied input/output technical coefficients. These do simplify, and do sidestep, some well-known Sraffian possibilities. The results are nonetheless remarkably intuitive and insightful for the quality of 1700–1869 classical thought and presuppositions. Nothing is missed by my not having 99 or some other multiplicity number of luxury manufactures.

Consumer demand allocations

Workers are assumed to consume corn only, wherever they may work. Rent-collecting landowners and profit-earning capitalists here (at first) consume (luxury) manufactures only, wherever their assets may be invested. No need then for marginal utilities or other post-Gossen theories of consumption demand. Readers can provide their own scenarios about any saving, dissaving, or changes in capital formation. I here limit my exposition to the *comparative statics* of various possible *stationary* states, involving viable alterations in equilibrium profit rates, wage rates, and rent rates under both invariant technologies and under viable productivity inventions.

Background fundamentals

Pricing unknowns of our equilibrium system will be (real corn wage rate, real corn rent rate, real interest or profit rate; relative goods and factor prices) $\equiv [\bar{w} = W/P_1, R/P_1, r; P_2/P_1, R/W]$. Equilibrium production and input unknowns will be (population size, land acreage, produced raw materials). The "three-ness" of classical economics, which has been so inadequately stressed even among the better modern commentators, comes through beautifully from contemplation of the present quintessential *Tableau Économique* once its microeconomic foundations have been cogently explicated.[1] For nominal prices I shall use dollars or $. However, in my stationary states only *relative* prices have substantive relevance, exactly as in the usual eighteenth- and nineteenth-century expositions of allegedly normal equilibria. Panics, bubbles, crises, war and post-Columbus inflations are not illuminated by the present paradigms.

The technology defined here sets limits on how high the subsistence wage rate $\bar{w}$ could be. If $\bar{w}$ were specified to exceed 1/2 per worker, the system would be incapable of *maintaining* any finite *positive* population level at all. If $\bar{w}$ is set below 1/2, the system is productive enough to provide a positive menu of corn and manufactures for capitalists and landowners to purchase as final consumption goods out of their feasibly positive rent-and-interest incomes. Were capitalists willing to keep making advances to workers and landowners and keep replacing raw materials, and to do all this for naught in the way of interest or profit; and if the *scarce* land could be got for naught in the way of *positive* rent; if pigs could fly – then our initial 300 workers could each enjoy 1/2 corn in wage, twice the stipulated subsistence wage rate of 1/4 corn. Then, so to speak, all the hours of the workday they would then be actually working "for themselves" and not "for capitalists."

But, on pre- and post-Malthus population theories, such a happy short-run egalitarian state would induce a rising population, inducing births in excess of deaths. A population bigger than 300 workers could then leave too little land for farm-workers to cultivate. And hence the zero-ness of rent on now-ultra-scarce lands would self-destruct. So to speak, under ruthless Darwinian auction bidding, it is workers who would then turn redundant and suffer crashes in the corn wage rate.

Thus, bona fide *classical* economists concluded that there would be an *eventual* return of $\bar{w}$ down to the 1/4 subsistence level. And then the system's producible surplus above subsistence would be back on the capitalists' menu, to be spent on manufactures or on corn or on both. As Tableau I will portray, the $L_1 + L_2$ population will settle down with positive L_2^* whenever non-workers permanently spend something on manufactures. (Yes, Virginia, consumers' tastes do change the total L^* population level for Malthus.)

In the present scenario, the specified total of land acreage limits the size of the labor force working in agriculture; and it therefore limits the gross corn output produced in equilibrium. The size of manufacturing labor, and hence of $L_1 + L_2$, is determined by the tastes of landowners and profit receivers: the less they spend on corn, the more is the demand they create for manufacturing labor and the more the corn they release for raw materials in manufacturing. These qualitative classical properties are succinctly summarizeable by the Physiocrats' *Tableaux Économique.*

The aggregated *Tableau Économique*

An omniscient 1750 economist – not easy to find in history – could deduce from my sparse list of assumptions a *Tableau Économique* like the following:

Table 2.1 Tableau Économique 1

		(Nominal Values $)									
		Payments For Produced Inputs		*Payments For Wages*		*Payments For Land Rent*		*Interest or Profit Payment*			
Agriculture		600	+	300	+	100	+	200	=	1,200
Manufactures		240	+	60	+	0	+	60	=	360
Totals		**840**	+	360	+	100	+	260	=	**1,560**
Net Total Income	=	0	+	360	+	100	+	260	=	720
	=	*Gross* Total Product – $P_1(Q_{11}+Q_{12})$		of	Depreciation					
	=	**$1,560**		–	**$840**		= $720 QED				

Let me now spell out Tableau I's specific micro properties in the background. The workers' equilibrium real wage was hypothesized to be

$$\bar{w} = W/P_1 = 1/4, \text{ for } = 300 \text{ workers and for } L_2^*. \tag{1}$$

And therefore the $300 item in Agriculture's first row corresponds to a *nominal* wage rate set arbitrarily at $W = 1. By implication of the stipulated subsistence wage of 1/4 unit of corn, the first row's final item of competitive price must be P_1, adding up in total to $1,200, equalling $300Q_1$ @ $4. The nominal rent rate must be 100/300 times $1 or $0.33 1/3 per acre, as will be shown later. The profit rate in agriculture – earned there on capitalists' outlay of $600 for raw materials plus $100 for rent plus $200 advanced to wage earners – is set in Tableau I to be $200/$1,000 = 2/10 or 20 percent. If that is so, in Tableau I the residual rent must work out to be 33 1/3 cents for each of the 300 acres of land.

The cost of production for P_2 relevant to Q_2 of manufactures is easy to work out now that we know W to be \$1, P_1 to be \$4, and the interest rate to be already set at 20 percent: P_2 must be

$$P_2 = [(1)W + (0)R](1+r^*) + P_1(1)(1+r^*)$$
$$= \$1(1.2) + \$4(1.2) = \$6. \tag{2}$$

Looking back two-and-a-half centuries, from the year 2000 back to 1750, one finds little remarkable about Tableau I's numerical circular flow. Unfortunately, most *tableaux* in history stopped at this *aggregative* numerical level. Few writers before Dmitriev (1898), Bortkiewicz (1907), and Seton (1957) ever provided us with the *microeconomic foundations* for Tableau I's aggregate numbers.

What is not in the Tableau is as significant as what is included. Note the distinct absence of those mysterious *zig-zags*, which won for Quesnay an aura of mysticism and spurious profundity. (Samuelson (1982) has shown that such zig-zags cannot cogently depict Kahn-Keynes-like *multiplier expenditure* processes; and neither can they depict Leontief *back-in-time input requirements*. We can leave the zig-zags to sophomore sophisticates who insist on writing the integer 2 as $1 + \frac{1}{2} + \frac{1}{4} + \ldots + \frac{1}{2^k} + \ldots$)

My version of Quesnay, Tableau I, resembles those in Marx (1884, *Capital*, Vol. 2) – but, of course, with an extra category here for land rent as distinct from interest payments. However, Marx's novelty in *Capital*, which perversely made direct *wage* payments the *only* recipient of a profit (or "surplus") mark-up, has most definitely here been ignored: *all* outlays on inputs – rent of \$100 and \$600 outlays on reproducible raw materials – receive the same 20 percent profit mark-up as are received by the \$300 of wage advances: the interest rate r^*, which is identically the same thing as the profit rate when there are no probabilistic uncertainties and no monopolistic deviations from classical competition, is here 20 percent per period in *both* industries:

$$r^* = 0.20 = 200/(600 + 300 + 100) = 60/(240 + 60 + 0). \tag{3}$$

Competitive arbitrage enforces this intersectoral equalization.

Tableau I is a mere depiction of the aggregative *anatomy* of an economy. It rests on interest rates, wage rates, and rent rates which *it* does *not at all explain*.[2] I and Quesnay are the puppet-masters who mandate its market aggregates, under the constraints of profit arbitrage. Had the farm profit rate been 10 rather than 20 percent, the Tableau would have been different.

Anatomy is not without its informative content. We see in Tableau I how correct Adam Smith was to break down competitive price into the *tri*partite categories of Wages + Rent + Interest. Tableau I can rebut Karl Marx's repetitious criticism of Smith that Total *Net* Income must include an added *fourth* component of Depreciation. Yes, the *gross* output flows of P_1Q_1 + P_2Q_2, being gross, do contain the fourth (depreciation) components of P_1Q_{11} + P_1Q_{12}; but we need to *subtract* these \$840 items from Gross Income of P_1Q_1 + P_2Q_2 = \$1,560, to arrive at correct *Net* Total Income of $P_1(Consumption)_1$ + $P_2(Consumption)_2$ = \$4(90) + \$6(60) = \$1,560 – \$840 = \$720. Smith properly insists that Depreciation as a cost in one current stage is merely a repayment of earlier stages' direct payments of Wages + Rent + Interest. Under Smith's proper "value-added" accounting, leaving Depreciation out of the tripartite direct cost components is precisely what is needed to avoid double counting. In Marx's language, Smith does send us endlessly "from pillar to post;" but the infinite series is rigorously *convergent* and its sum does vindicate Smith.

In Tableau I', I give the *real* micro breakdown of Tableau I's macro flows (see Table 2.2).

Table 2.2 Tableau Économique I'

Real *Variables* of I*	
150 of Q_{12} @ \$4 + 300 of L_1 @ \$1 + 300 of $\bar{A}$@ \$0.33 1/3	
$\quad$ + r^* of $\frac{1}{5} \times (600 + 300 + 100)$	= \$1,200
	= 300 of Q_1 @ \$4
60 of Q_{12} @ \$4 + 60 of L_2 @ \$1 + 0 of A_2 + $\frac{1}{5}(240 + 60)$	= \$360
	= 60 of Q_2 @ \$6

Notes
Listed below in † and †† are the numerical micro data:
†$(r^*, W/P_1, R/P_1; P_2/P_1)$ = (0.20, ¼, ¹⁄₁₂, ⁶⁄₄ or 1.5)
†† $(L_1^*, L_2^*, L^*; Q_1^*, Q_2^*; C_1^*, C_2^*)$ = (300, 60, 300 + 60; 300, 60; 75 + 15 of subsistence corn, 60 of luxury cloth).

Tableau I' is more important than Tableau I itself!

A Marxian interlude and digression

It was Karl Marx, primarily in *Capital*, Volume II's Tableaux of Stationary Reproduction, who resurrected Quesnay's *Tableau Économique* to the attention of Dmitriev (1898, 1904), Bortkiewicz (1907a, 1907b), Schumpeter (1912), Leontief (1939), Sweezy (1942, 1949), Winternitz (1948), Dobb (1955), Meek (1969), Seton (1957), Samuelson (1970, 1971), and Sraffa (1960). Unable to quite cope with the polynomial algebra of profit rate determination, and in a misguided belief that he was gaining new insight into capitalistic exploitation of propertyless wage earners, Karl Marx innovated a paradigm of "rate of surplus value." Unlike the "rate of profit," which equalized intersectorally the yield on *all* cost outlays of capitalists, Marx proposed a system of "(marked-up) values," where only outlays on *direct* wages received a uniform percentage mark-up in the economy's various industries. Produced raw materials to Marx represented only *dead* past labor, and Marx's passages on land rent never got coherently integrated into his model of *Mehrwert* (or equalized rate of surplus value).

Tableau I can be contrasted with Marx's Tableau II of Surplus Value. Tableau II is not "transformed" from I (nor is I "transformable" *from* II). But each of I or of II can be, *alternatively*, autonomously deduced from the hard micro data of Tableau I'! – a point not yet well understood in the vast literature on this subject. See definitive statements in Seton (1957) and Samuelson (1971, 1972).

Here then, in II, is the Marxian counterpart to Tableau I.

Table 2.3 Tableau Économique II (*à la* Marx)

$$c_1 + v_1 + \mathbf{m}(v_1 + 0) = 600 + 300 + 1.00(300) = 1{,}200 = 300 \text{ corn @ } \mathbf{4}$$
$$c_2 + v_2 + \mathbf{m}(v_2 + 0) = 240 + \underline{60} + \underline{1.00(60)} = \underline{360} = 60 \text{ cloth @ } \mathbf{6}$$
$$840 + 360 + 360 = 1{,}560$$

The total of Marx's surplus, 300 + 60, includes, *along* with interest, agriculture's land rent of 100. Marx's "values" – more correctly his *marked-up* values – are written out in bold face as (**4, 6**). His numerical partitions are never observed by a Kuznets on land or sea; they are a thought experiment by Marx in a paradigm where *only* the direct wage items, (300 + 60), get marked up by what, in this instance, has to be a *100* percent rate of surplus value (or *Mehrwert*) – *arbitrarily* said to be equalized as between sectors.

Artfully, I have concocted my technology and factor prices in Tableaux I, I', and II so that the so-called "organic compositions of capital" are the same (wage cost)/(total cost) in both cloth and corn sectors; therefore in Tableau I the bourgeois price ratio, P_2/P_1, accidentally happens to agree with the Marxian Tableau II's **6/4** = [total embodied labor (direct plus indirect) in cloth] ÷ [total embodied labor (direct plus indirect) in corn]. This gives Marx any rope that he can use: in the contemptuous parlance of the great modern physicist Wolfgang Pauli, Marx is "not even wrong" here. But as far as insight into the physiology of labor's exploitation is concerned, the anatomies of *Tableaux I and II are both completely silent.*

Why does Marx happen to be not even wrong here? It is because I singularly counterbalanced the profit share upward bias in roundabout cloth by an *opposite* and equal extra bias in agriculture of land rents. To help understand this singularity, stipulate alternatively that total population had been so thin compared to the 300 acres of land that land had been redundantly free with $R/P_1 = 0$. How large then must the interest rate be in excess of 20 percent so that workers still will receive only the wage rate of 1/4 corn per worker? Note 1's tradeoff algebra between r and R worked out to require a profit rate of 33 1/3 per cent when R is zero. Tableaux IIIA and IIIB are the recalculated respective pictures for Smith-Ricardo-Walras and for Marx in the zero-rent eventuality. Note that no longer is Marx "not even wrong." With organic compositions of capital no longer equal, Marx's **6/4** no longer equals capitalism's prosaic $6\frac{2}{3}/4$!

Table 2.4 Tableau Économique IIIA: capitalism

$$C_1 + V_1 + r(C_1 + V_1) = 600 + 300 + \tfrac{1}{3}(600 + 300) = 1{,}200 = 300 \text{ corn @ } 4$$
$$C_2 + V_2 + r(C_2 + V_2) = 240 + 60 + \tfrac{1}{3}(240 + 60) = 400 = 60 \text{ cloth @ } 6\tfrac{2}{3}$$
$$840 + 360 + \qquad\qquad 400 = 1{,}600$$

Table 2.5 Tableau Économique IIIB: Marx*

$$c_1 + v_1 + mv_1 = 600 + 300 + 1.00\,(300) = 1{,}200 = 300 \text{ corn @ } \mathbf{4}$$
$$c_2 + v_2 + mv_2 = 240 + 60 + 1.00\,(60) = 360 = 60 \text{ cloth @ } \mathbf{6}$$
$$840 + 360 + \qquad\qquad 360 = 1{,}560$$
$$\neq 400 \quad \neq 1{,}600$$

$${}^*P_2/P_1 = 6\tfrac{2}{3}/4 > 6/4,\ S_1 + S_2 = 400 > s_1 + s_2 = 360$$

Notes
††Remark: Marx, in *Capital*, Vol. 3, wrongly worked back from IIIB to IIIA. Instead of the correct $r^* = 0.33\tfrac{1}{3}$, he calculated $r^* = \mathbf{360}/(840 + 360) = \tfrac{3}{10}, < \tfrac{1}{3}$, perpetrating *multiple* errors (as he admitted).

How tastes for luxuries alter L* of total population

It was shown in Samuelson's (1992) contribution to the John Chipman *Festschrift* (1999) what Ricardo's third edition obliquely implied – that population size in a classical scenario is not a hard Malthus constant. Instead, its total L^* is generically an *endogenous* unknown, dependent on the direct land-rent component in the *final* goods consumed by *non*-laborers.

Tableau Économique IV illuminates what are the changes in equilibrium values created by a shift of tastes of landowners and capitalists toward agriculture's corn and away from manufactures (see Table 2.6). Let them now spend their property incomes 100 percent on corn instead of 100 percent on manufactures. This will ultimately wreak genocide on old $L_2^* = 60$, down to new $L_2^* = 0$ and the $L_1^* = 300 < 360$. (It will also, by the time a new stationary state is settled down to, wreak partial genocide on the vector of manufacturing capital raw material and advances.)

Now Tableau I's two-sector, two-line tableau collapses into Tableau IV's one-line tableau. This one line, on the specification that $(W/P_1\ R/P_1\ r)$ remains the same as in Tableau I, becomes identical with Tableau I's first line: 300 of L_1 plus 150 of Q_{11} corn + 300 of land produces 300 of corn – of which 75 gets consumed by labor as subsistence and 75 gets consumed by income-spending property owners (25 by landowners and 50 by rentier interest-earning capitalists).

Table 2.6 Tableau Économique IV: corn only in demand

$600 Q_{11} + $300 L_1 + $100 rent + 0.20($1,000) = $1,200 of Q_1
        = 300 Q_1 @ $4 = 150 Q_{11} @ $4 + L's fodder of 75 corn +
                  (50 + 25) luxury corn for property owners

Napoleonic Wars *à la* simpliste Ricardo

In Ricardo's final new chapter on Machinery, he noticed that the prolonged Napoleonic Wars created a new intensity of direct demand for human soldiery, tending thereby to *raise* population.

Since mid-century, when I introduced Hitler's "Guns vs. Butter" choice into beginners' first day of economics instruction, students learned about trade-offs *within fixed* factor totals of endowments. In the first day of Ricardo's tutorial, his tutees would have had to learn how, say, taxing away *all* rent and profit incomes in order to pay for a maximal permanent wartime army would divert effective tastes from cloth to direct soldiery. This would, in Ricardo's longest run, bring into existence the needed new $L_1^* + 0 + L_3^*$ population of 300 in agriculture plus 300 in the armies – as if teleologically! One more Widow's Cruse for paradox mongers.

Tableau V honors Tableau I's precise technology and its ($\bar{w}$, r*; R*) specifications. Comparing V's new last row with I's now-extinct last row provides the dramatic comparative statics for consumer taste changes – a consideration downplayed by classical writers who mostly ignored any elaborate theories of consumption demand.

*Table 2.7 Tableau Économique V: permanent, total war**

150 cornseed and 300 L_1^* and 100 of A_1 produce 300 corn
                300 L_3^* produce 300 soldiery

$600	+	$300	+	$100	+	⅕($1,000)	=	$1,200	=	300 Q_1 @ $4
0	+	0	+	0	+	0	=	0	=	0 of Q_2
0	+	$300	+	0	+	⅕($300)	=	$ 360	=	300 Q_3 @ $1.2
$600	+	$600	+	$100	+		$260	=	$1,560		

*P_3/P_1 = 1.2/4 = 0.3

Quesnay's archetype of landowners versus workers

To a romantic ethicist who hankers for labor to get all of the social product, usurious interest profit and undeserving land rent are equally bad. Tableau VI will depict the purest Physiocratic scenario when all that does not go to workers as subsistence wages goes solely to the landowners (see Table 2.8). It is this extreme scenario that best rationalizes the Physiocratic denigration of manufactures as "*sterile*" and of land *alone* as being genuinely productive.

In Tableau VI, r^* is zero *à la* Schumpeter (1912). But *à la* Malthus (1798) the subsistence wage $\bar{w}$ is still at 1/4 of corn per capita. As in Tableau I, non-laborers spend all their income on manufactures alone. Ruthless supply and demand will compel (so-called *residual*) rent to rise from 1/12 of corn per acre up to 1/4 of corn per acre. Tableau VI does not "explain" this to us: so much the worse for over-praised Quesnay schematics. However, the technological background to all the alternative Tableaux compels unequivocally this result.

Ricardo, somewhat begrudgingly, admitted that interest rate changes could alter relative prices, P_2/P_1, away from embodied labor ratios. But nowhere did Ricardo accord proper notice to how alterations in the rent/wage ratio would have to systematically vitiate the obsolescent Labour Theory of Value that he vilified Smith for abandoning. Piero Sraffa as editor is culpably silent on this gap. The present Tableaux provide a skeleton key to full understanding of how classicists' own systems *had* to behave. Here is final Tableau VI.

Table 2.8 Tableau Économique VI: undiluted physiocraticism*

Ag.	$600	+	$300	+	$300	+	$0	=	$1,200	=	300 of Q_1 @ $4
Mfg.	$240	+	$60	+	$0	+	$0	=	$300	=	60 of Q_2 @ $5
	$840	+	$360	+	$300	+	$0	=	$1,500		

*$P_2/P_1 = 5/4 \neq 6/4$; $r^* = 0$; $R/W = 1$, $W/P_1 = 1/4$

Note that *all* productions are identical in Tableaux I and VI (see Tables 2.1 and 2.8). Independently of "embodied labor" defined for Q_1 and Q_2, market P_2/P_1 ratios are different in VI and I – as would *not* be possible if a Ricardo-Marx Labour Theory of Value scenario were a correct scenario.

Samuel Hollander has put emphasis – perhaps over-emphasis – on an alleged profit–wage trade-off in the Ricardian system. That (r^*, w) emphasis could overlook the Hamlet of rent R in Denmark. For true classicals, who in the longest run claimed to be able to specify a meaningful invariant subsistence wage level $\bar{w}$, they are left – out of the general three-ness trade-off among $(r, \bar{w}, R/W)$ of Note 1 – with a two-variable $(\bar{w}, R/W)$ trade-off whenever (in the post-Sraffian fashion) r^* is said to be already specified at some arbitrarily prescribed level.

Summing up

I believe the present detailed exposition will demonstrate that there has to be a basic identity between the methodology of 1800, 1900, and 2000. Later scholars tackle harder problems. Theoretical misunderstandings gradually get cleared up, partially or wholly. But steeping oneself in the texts of pioneer scholars, I believe, enhances our admiration for both their efforts and their achievements.

The variety of the presented tableaux confirms that the determinateness of equilibrium, and its quantitative properties, cannot be inferred solely from the anatomy of the technology, of the tastes and of the factor-endowments data. To exemplify this consider a polemical modern literature by neo-Ricardians and plain-vanilla Ricardians concerning a possible lost 1815 manuscript in which David Ricardo described a scenario in which the profit rate and other key distributional parameters got themselves *autonomously* determined in agriculture alone. If at some future date such a manuscript were to turn up, what would have to be its salient features? My *Tableau Économique* I was fabricated to throw light on this question. The presented analysis qualifies any fundamental importance that such an 1815 work could have if it did happen to exist.

Refer to Note 1 with its "three-ness" relationship between: (i) the real wage rate, W/P_1; (ii) the real rent rate, R/P_1; and (iii) the steady-state interest or profit rate r. Denote this three-way trade-off by

$$(*)\ r^* = f(W/P_1, R/P_1), \tag{4}$$

where f is here *singularly convex*, monotone-decreasing in its arguments.

Relation (*), properly understood, does not (repeat *not*) imply that changes in the non-agricultural sectors are powerless to affect the whole system's profit rate. All that (*) gives is the totality of alternative states compatible with the technology of agriculture and the constraints of ruthless competitive arbitrage. (*) leaves solutions with a two-fold infinity of *alternative* equilibrium states; and under a myriad of 1700–2000 notions about the behavior of people and institutions in a pure or mixed capitalism, quantitative empirical patterns *outside* of agriculture are presumptively of the same key importance as those inside it.

Here is an 1817, or a 1740, for instance. Owners of land and of investable capital decide for any reason to shift their consumptions away from manufactured cloth and toward sun-grown corn. As in Tableau IV (see Table 2.6), suppose that from 100 percent spent on cloth, they gradually move permanently to 100 percent of demand expenditure on corn. It is a slow, steady, and discernible process, which takes us from Tableau I to Tableau IV. Involved is an *endogenous* trend, according to classical scenario building, toward a one-sixth reduction in working-class population. If the property-owning class had been content to maintain and sustain, at a 20 percent profit rate, the *previous* total cornseed and wage-fodder advances plus manufacturing investment outlays, then banal supply and demand might now be whittling down the market-clearing interest rate earnable for capitalists. (Smith understood well in 1776 how "competition of more capitals" must, *ceteris paribus*, bid down the interest rate – from the old Britain-like 20 percent to the new Dutch-like 10 percent or less.) Where does this leave neo-Ricardians with their *simpliste* belief that it is *in agriculture alone* that an 1815 model can determine the interest rate? Logic and empiricism compel them to retreat to an unexciting Walrasian paradigm of general equilibrium, in which interdependence of *all* the sectors determines the equilibrium when it is uniquely determinable and/or chooses between the multiple-equilibrium states compatible with all the arbitrage conditions of the economy contemplated.

Years ago, I wrote aphoristically: "Inside a classical economist, you discern a neoclassical economist trying to get in." My archetypical tableaux flesh out this heuristic perception. And, in my considered opinion, these explications cast cogent doubts on that view popular in the 1950s and early 1960s that "going back to the classics" somehow offered a different and better alternative to the post-neoclassical mainstream paradigms.

Notes

1 With real wage frozen at the stipulated subsistence level $\bar{w} = \frac{1}{4}$ corn, real rent R and real profit rates r are in the non-linear trade-off relation, $R = (1 - 3r)/(1 + r)$. More generally, competition defines the *three-ness* trade-off: $(W/P_1)a_L + (R/P_1) = [1 - a_{11}(1 + r)]/(1 + r)$, when (a_L, a_A, a_{11}) are (direct labor input needed, direct land input needed, corn input needed) to produce one of corn.

2 This is a basic insight about Quesnay's Physiocracy, to be gleaned from the present quintessential tableaux économique. Where the real world will land on technology's three-ness menu of feasible (real wage, real rent, profit rate) *cannot* be learned from a tableau's anatomical structure, but rather from supply and demand generated by technology options, psychological taste patterns, and factor endowments.

References

Bortkiewicz, L. von (1907a) "On the Correction of Marx's Fundamental Theoretical Construction in the Third Volume of 'Capital,'" *Jahrbuch Nationalökonomie Statistik*, 34, 3: 370–85. Translated into English as an appendix by Eugen von Böhm-Bawerk, *Karl Marx and the Close of His System*, in Rudolph Hilferding, *Böhm-Bawerk's Criticism of Marx*, P. Sweezy (ed.), New York: Augustus M. Kelley, 1949.

Bortkiewicz, L. von (1907b) "Value and Price in the Marxian System," *Archiv für Sozialwissenschaft und Sozialpolitik* 25, 1: 10–51; 25, 2: 445–88. Reprinted in *International Economic Papers*, 1952, 2: 5–60.

Cantillon, R. (1755, 1931) *Essai sur la Nature du Commerce en Général*, edited with an English translation by Henry Higgs, London: The Royal Economic Society by Macmillan and Company, 1931. Reissued London: The Royal Economic Society by Frank Cass and Company, Ltd., 1959.

Dmitriev, V. (1898, 1902, 1904) *Ekonomicheskie Ocherki*, translated into English by D. Fry and D. M. Nuti (eds) as *V. K. Dmitriev, Economic Essays on Value, Competition and Utility*, Cambridge: Cambridge University Press, 1974.

Dobb, M. (1955) "A Note on the Transformation Problem," in *On Economic Theory and Socialism*, London: Routledge and Kegan Paul, 273–81.

Eltis, W. (1996) "The Grand Tableau of François Quesnay's Economics," *The European Journal of the History of Economic Thought* 3: 21–43.

Hollander, S. (1987) *Classical Economics*, Oxford and New York: Basil Blackwell.

Leontief, W. (1941) *The Structure of American Economy, 1919–1929*, Cambridge, MA: Harvard University Press.

Maital, S. (1972) "The Tableau Economique as a Simple Leontief Model: An Amendment," *Quarterly Journal of Economics* 86: 504–507.

Malanos, G. (1946) "The Evolution of the General Theory," unpublished doctoral dissertation, Harvard University.

Malthus, T. R. (1798) *An Essay on the Principle of Population as it Affects the Future Improvement of Society, with Remarks on the Speculations of Mr. Godwin, M. Condorcet and Other Writers*, London: J. Johnson. Reprinted by Macmillan, London, 1926.

Marx, K. (1867, 1885, 1894) *Capital*, Vols. I, II, III, Chicago, IL: Charles H. Kerr and Company, 1909. Harmondsworth: Penguin Books, 1976, 1978, 1981. See especially Vol. II.

Marx, K. (1905–10) *Theorien über den Mehrwert*, published by Karl Kautsky. Translated into English as *Theories of Surplus Value*, Moscow: Progress Publishers, 1963.

Meek, R. (1956) "Some Notes on the Transformation Problem," *Economic Journal* 66: 94–107. Reprinted in R. Meek 1967, *Economics and ideology and other essays; Studies in the development of economic thought*, London: Chapman and Hall, 143–57.

Niehans, J. (1990) *A History of Economic Theory, Classical Contributions, 1720–1980*, Baltimore, MD, and London: The Johns Hopkins University Press.

Phillips, A. (1955) "The Tableau Économique as a Simple Leontief Model," *Quarterly Journal of Economics* 69: 137–44.

Quesnay, F. (1759) *Tableaux Économique*.

Ricardo, D. (1951–73) *The Works and Correspondence of David Ricardo*, Vols. I–XI, P. Sraffa (ed.) with collaboration of M. H. Dobb, Cambridge: Cambridge University Press.

Samuels, W. (1969) "The Tableau Économique as a Simple Leontief Model: A Precursor to Phillips," *Indian Economic Journal* 17: 112–17.

Samuelson, P. A. (1959) "A Modern Treatment of the Ricardian Economy: I. The Pricing of Goods and Labor and Land Services," *Quarterly Journal of Economics* 73, 1: 1–35. Reproduced as Ch. 31 in *The Collected Scientific Papers of Paul A. Samuelson*, Vol. 1, Cambridge, MA: The MIT Press, 1966.

—— (1970) "The 'Transformation' from Marxian 'Values' to Competitive Prices: A Process of Rejection and Replacement," *Proceedings of the National Academy of Sciences, U.S.A.* 67, 1: 423–25. Reproduced as Ch. 154 in *The Collected Scientific Papers of Paul A. Samuelson*, Vol. 3, Cambridge, Mass.: The MIT Press, 1972.

—— (1971) "Understanding the Marxian Notion of Exploitation: A Summary of the So-Called Transformation Problem Between Marxian Values and Competitive Prices," *Journal of Economic Literature* 9, 2: 399–431. Reproduced as Ch. 153 in *The Collected Scientific Papers of Paul A. Samuelson*, Vol. 3, Cambridge, MA: The MIT Press, 1972.

—— (1982) "Quesnay's 'Tableau Économique' as a Theorist Would Formulate it Today," in I. Bradley and M. Howard (eds) *Classical and Marxian Political Economy: Essays in Honor of Ronald L. Meek*, New York: St. Martin's Press, 45–78. Reproduced as Ch. 343 in *The Collected Scientific Papers of Paul A. Samuelson*, Vol. 5, Cambridge, MA: The MIT Press, 1986.

—— (1999) "A Classical Theorem for John Chipman: Maximal and Minimal Malthusian Population; a Sweeping Non-Substitution Theorem at the Core of the Canonical Classical Model," in J. Moore, R. Riezman and J. Melvin (eds) *Trade,*

Theory and Econometrics: Essays in Honor of John S. Chipman, New York: Routledge.

Schumpeter, J. (1912) *Theorie der wirtschaftlichen Entwicklung*, Leipzig: Duncker and Humblot. Translated into English by R. Opie as *The Theory of Economic Development*, Cambridge, MA: Harvard University Press, 1934. Reprinted 1961, New York: Oxford University Press.

Seton, F. (1957) "The 'Transformation' Problem," *Review of Economic Studies* 24, 3: 149–60.

Smith, A. (1776) *An Inquiry into the Nature and Causes of the Wealth of Nations*, E. Cannan (ed.), New York: The Modern Library, 1937.

Sraffa, P. (1926) "The Laws of Return under Competitive Conditions," *Economic Journal* 36: 535–50.

Sraffa, P. (1960) *Production of Commodities by Means of Commodities: Prelude to a Critique of Economic Theory*, Cambridge: Cambridge University Press.

Sweezy, P. (1942) *The Theory of Capitalist Development*, Oxford: Oxford University Press.

Sweezy, P. (ed.) (1949) *Karl Marx and the Close of his System by Eugen von Böhm-Bawerk and Böhm-Bawerk's criticism of Marx by Rudolf Hilferding with an appendix by L. von Bortkiewicz*, New York: Augustus M. Kelley. See Bortkiewicz 1907a.

Tsuru, S. (1942) "On Reproduction Schemes," an Appendix to Paul M. Sweezy, *The Theory of Capitalist Development*, New York: Oxford University Press. Reproduced in Shigeto Tsuru, *Towards a New Political Economy*, 1976. Tokyo: Kodansha.

Turgot, A. R. J. (1766) *Reflections on the Formation and the Distribution of Riches*. New York: A. M. Kelley, 1963.

Winternitz, J. (1948) "Values and Prices: A Solution of the So-Called Transformation Problem," *Economic Journal* 58: 276–80.

3 Frank Knight as an institutional economist

*Geoffrey M. Hodgson**

The founding and nature of institutional economics

In France, on 11 November 1918, the armistice was signed that ended hostilities in World War I. A few days later, in December, across the Atlantic, at the annual meeting of the American Economic Association, the term "institutional economics" was first used. This was in a paper delivered by Walton Hamilton (1919).

Thorstein Veblen and John Commons had already set out the approach of institutional economics in the late 1890s (Samuels 1998). Works such as Veblen's *Theory of the Leisure Class* had achieved a mass readership. Commons had already become the foremost authority on American labour organization and had advised the US and Wisconsin state governments. Successive leading institutionalists such as Wesley C. Mitchell and John Maurice Clark had also established prominent academic reputations. But until December 1918 the term "institutional economics" had not been widely used to describe their school.

In the next few years, the influence of institutionalism in America reached its zenith. Mitchell became AEA president in 1924. He was followed in that position by several institutionalists and their fellow travellers, such as Allyn A. Young in 1925, Thomas S. Adams in 1927, J. M. Clark in 1935, Frederick C. Mills in 1940, Sumner H. Slichter in 1941, Edwin G. Nourse in 1942, and Albert B. Wolfe in 1943. Hence, from 1924 to 1943, at least eight out of the 20 AEA presidents were either institutionalists or sympathetic to institutionalism.

In contrast to some modern misconceptions of the "old" institutionalism as "atheoretical" or even "anti-theory," Hamilton (1919: 309–11) argued that

* The Business School, University of Hertfordshire, Mangrove Road, Hertford, Hertfordshire SG13 8QF, UK. *Address for correspondence:* Malting House, 1 Burton End, West Wickham, Cambridgeshire CB1 6SD, UK. *g.m.hodgson@herts.ac.uk* The author is very grateful to Ross Emmett, Stephen Nash, Malcolm Rutherford, and Yuval Yonay for inspiration, comments, and discussions. Emmett's internet site has been particularly useful and his forthcoming intellectual biography of Knight is eagerly awaited.

"'institutional economics' is 'economic theory.'" It "alone meets the demand for a generalized description of the economic order. Its claim is to explain the nature and extent of order amid economic phenomena." He claimed that institutional economics alone could unify economic science by showing how parts of the economic system related to the whole. Emphatically, institutional economics was not then defined in terms of any normative stance, even on the urgent issues of the day. Hamilton declared: "It is not the place of economics to pass judgements upon practical proposals" (313). However, part of its genuine appeal as a theory was the claim that it could be used as a basis for economic policies relevant to the time.

For Hamilton, "most important of all" was the neglect of neoclassical theory of "the influence exercised over conduct by the scheme of institutions under which one lives" (318). Hamilton saw institutionalism as filling this gap. This idea that institutions form and change individuals, just as individuals form and change institutions, is arguably the central tenet of institutionalism. Hamilton's "bare outline of the case for institutionalist theory" accepted that "institutional theory is in process" and emphasized the pressing task of relevant, theoretical development. His institutionalist manifesto is important not simply as a historical document, but as an incomplete working definition of the institutionalist approach at the point where it was to become its most influential.[1]

His manifesto is also an important benchmark to help measure the subsequent changes in institutionalism itself. Institutional economics, from Veblen to John Kenneth Galbraith, has consistently emphasised some of Hamilton's themes. It has always been concerned that economic theory should strive for policy relevance. But, more fundamentally, it has also emphasized the role of institutions in economic life, the qualitatively transformative nature of economic activity, and the way in which those institutional and structural changes both affect and reconstitute human purposes, preferences, psychology, and behaviour. Arguably, these features are defining for institutionalism, and can help us to distinguish it from other schools of economic thought.[2]

Institutionalists do not have a very good record in defining and agreeing among themselves upon the essentials of their approach. I submit, however, there is a single core idea in institutionalism that above all others defines its identity. The idea that institutions can be reconstitutive of individuals is arguably the most fundamental characteristic of institutional economics. Obviously, institutions themselves differ, in time and in space. However, individuals themselves are also likely to be radically affected by these differences. Different institutions can act as more than constraints on behaviour: they may actually change the character and beliefs of the individual. Veblen repeatedly emphasized such an idea: "The situation of today shapes the institutions of tomorrow through a selective, coercive process, by acting upon men's habitual view of things, and so altering or fortifying a point of view or a mental attitude handed down from the past" (Veblen 1899: 190–91). Writing in 1899, Commons (1965: 3), too, had expressed a similar view when he wrote of institutions "shaping each individual." This idea that institutions affect individual purposes or preferences, and hence the individual cannot always be taken as given, is the core idea of institutional economics and runs, as a silken thread, through the whole tradition, from Veblen to Galbraith and beyond.

As a result, the "new" institutional economics of Oliver Williamson (1975) and others is not "institutional economics" in the sense identified by Hamilton. This is because the "new" institutionalism clings on to the very conception of the utility-maximizing, rational individual that Veblen, Commons, Mitchell, Hamilton, and others were so keen to replace. The "new" institutionalism sees people behaving as if it were "the result of conscious endeavour by individuals who knew thoroughly their own interests." But this is Hamilton's (1919: 318) own characterization of the very type of economics that institutionalism sought to supersede. There is little notion in the "new" institutional economics of the individual – and her perceptions of her interests and goals – as being fundamentally transformed by her changing institutional environment. For New Institutionalists such as Williamson, people are enduringly and selfishly "opportunistic." Their character and purposes do not change as they move from institution to institution, even from (say) a caring family to a ruthless capitalist firm. In contrast, "old" institutional economists stress that human beings and their institutional environment changes their purposes. This is the key difference between the "new" institutionalism and the "old."

One of the central problems of social science is the relationship between individual actor and social structure. Veblen attempted to resolve this within a Darwinian and evolutionary framework. For Veblen, Darwinism meant explanation in terms of detailed cause and effect. This had two major implications. Although institutions and structures moulded individuals, this was not through the operation of mysterious "social forces", but by the inculcation of new habits at the individual level. Furthermore, individual intentions could not be regarded as a miraculous additional category of causality, nor an "uncaused cause" but emerging and building from individual habits and instincts. Hence Veblen (1919: 238) wrote:

> The modern scheme of knowledge, on the whole, rests, for its definitive ground, on the relation of cause and effect; the relation of sufficient reason being admitted only provisionally and as a proximate factor in that analysis, always with the unambiguous reservation that the analysis must ultimately come to rest in terms of cause and effect.

It is worth emphasizing that although he believed that economic theory could have policy implications, Hamilton did not define institutional economics in terms of any specific policy stance. Although he was very much concerned to develop institutional economics as an instrument for "the problems of control" – by which was meant a degree of planned intervention into the market economy – he did not *define* institutional economics in policy terms. In practice, institutionalism was adopted by policy makers from a variety of policy viewpoints, from radical social democracy to moderate conservatism.

What is also worth noting at this stage is the extent to which Hamilton (1919: 318) emphasized the contributory importance of "modern social psychology" to the understanding of human behaviour. At the founding of institutionalism in the 1890s, "modern psychology" was the instinct psychology of William James, William McDougall and others. This version of psychology had strongly influenced Veblen. But as noted elsewhere, it was not to last (Degler 1991; Hodgson 1999; Ross 1991). Even before 1918, the psychological and philosophical foundations of institutionalism had already come under severe attack from within the American scientific community. Instinct psychology was rapidly being undermined by behaviourism. In philosophy, positivism was rapidly displacing pragmatism. Furthermore, the links between the social sciences and biology were being axed, and even biological metaphors were becoming suspect (Degler 1991; Hodgson 1999; Ross 1991). The erosion of the Darwinian notion of detailed causal explanation had catastrophic implications for the development of Veblen's ideas concerning causality, agency, and social structure.

Accordingly, even in 1918, at the naming ceremony of the new creed of institutionalism, its philosophical and psychological pillars were under attack. Crucially, even among institutionalists, faith had been lost in the Veblenian research programme to place economics and the social sciences within an encompassing Darwinian and evolutionary framework. This early crisis within institutionalism in the interwar period proved catastrophic for its future development.

At its zenith, in the 1920s, institutionalism had vulnerable and incomplete philosophical and theoretical foundations. It was in this context that two leading contemporary figures emerged. Significantly, they were both friends. One, Clarence Ayres (1891–1972), was eventually to lead the surviving remnants of American institutionalism into the post-1945 epoch and to inspire a further generation of postwar institutionalist scholars. Ayres answered the problem of agency and structure by emphasizing the primacy of social structures over the individual. He thus abandoned the emphasis on materialistic causality that was a feature of Veblen's work. Another, Frank Knight (1885–1972), was an intellectual maverick, generally admired but not massively followed. He answered the very same problem of agency and structure by retaining the uncaused "free-will" that Veblen had attempted to surpass. Again, the Veblenian emphasis on materialistic causality was abandoned. Both Ayres and Knight gave unsatisfactory, pre-Veblenian answers to this question. Nevertheless, I shall argue, Knight was an institutionalist as much as Ayres.

The attempt to establish Knight's credentials as an institutionalist is the major theme of this chapter. It also raises more general questions concerning the compatibility or otherwise of neoclassical and institutionalist theory. By examining Knight it is hoped that we can learn more about the materials and pitfalls involved in the building of a modern institutional economics for the twenty-first century.

Frank Knight: neoclassical, Austrian or institutionalist?

Frank Knight was born in 1885 in Illinois. His parents were farmers and evangelical Protestants of Anglo-Irish descent. He reacted against this deeply religious background in his teens, to become a secular humanist. Nevertheless, as John McKinney (1977: 1438) has pointed out, there remain in his teaching some echoes of theological debates, particularly concerning free will and predestination. Knight went to Cornell University in 1913, at first to study philosophy. He particularly admired Immanuel Kant and he acquired a deep and enduring philosophical awareness. He read widely, including texts in the original German. A major and lasting influence upon him was Max Weber (Schweitzer 1975).[3]

A year after the start of his university studies, Knight transferred to economics. Alvin S. Johnson, then an economics professor at Cornell University, suggested to Knight that he write his doctoral dissertation on the problem of explaining the origin of profit.[4] After Johnson left Cornell, "A Theory of Business Profit" was partly supervised by institutionalist sympathiser Allyn Young. This dissertation was submitted in 1916. Subsequently, it was revised for publication as *Risk, Uncertainty and Profit* under the supervision of the leading institutionalist John Maurice Clark (Knight 1921: ix). It became a classic, and one of the most important economics monographs of the twentieth century.

What was Knight's relationship to the three main schools of economic thought at the time, namely neoclassical, Austrian and institutional economics? There have been attempts to describe Knight as an adherent of the neoclassical and Austrian tenet of methodological individualism. For instance, Ludwig Lachmann (1947: 417) wrote: "For all his strictures on it, Professor Knight is himself a paragon of methodological individualism." R. A. Gonce (1972) and John McKinney (1977) also made this particular methodological claim for Knight.[5] David Seckler (1975: 78) saw Knight as "prominently associated" with the Austrian school of Carl Menger and Ludwig von Mises. Warren Samuels (1977: 485) and Yuval Yonay (1998) described Knight as "neoclassical" or "neoclassicist." In fact, in a generally illuminating account of the struggles between institutionalism and its critics, Yonay followed Dorothy Ross (1991: 425) and went so far as to portray Knight as the leading "neoclassical" opponent of institutionalism.[6]

Few have suggested a contrasting view: that Knight was an institutionalist. Many scholars would perhaps regard such a claim as absurd. Some may dismiss this proposition on the basis of a suggestion that Knight's sympathy for "free market" policies would rule him out of the institutionalist camp. But it would be a crude mistake to define institutional economics – or any other *theoretical* approach in social science – simply or mainly in terms of its policy stance, even on the vital question of the market. It must be realised that other leading and self-confessed institutionalists took pro-market or conservative policy positions. For example, Arthur Frank Burns, the institutionalist and close academic collaborator of Mitchell, advised the conservative President Eisenhower in the 1950s.

Others institutionalists perceive Knight as theoretically remote from institutionalism, perhaps on the basis of his alleged methodological individualism. Keen to claim someone of Knight's stature as their own, neoclassical and Austrian economists can readily join in this unholy alliance. Rejected by institutionalists, neoclassical and Austrian economists endorse this rejection, and thereby take Knight for themselves. For different reasons, neither institutionalists nor mainstream economists have been keen to describe Knight as an institutionalist.

Here, I shall take a different view. I accept that there were both neoclassical and Austrian elements in Knight's thinking, and these played no small part. But also, in a strong and theoretically meaningful sense, he was an institutionalist. In order to attempt to establish this argument, I shall examine Knight's attitude on four key theoretical issues, namely:

(a) the place and role of neoclassical utility theory;
(b) the neoclassical assumption of given preference functions and technological possibilities;
(c) the neoclassical and Austrian assumption of methodological individualism;
(d) the possibility or otherwise of a synthesis between neoclassical economics and institutionalism, and the place of institutional economics.

Knight's writings show a deeper immersion in economic theory and philosophy than most of his American colleagues at the time. He probed and dissected the methodology and assumptions of received doctrines, including the neoclassical. While being critical of many assumptions made by neoclassical economists, he also criticized over-hasty dismissals of neoclassical theory. His writings combine theoretical and philosophical depth with distinctive originality. He fits easily into neither institutionalist nor neoclassical stereotypes. However, while evolving, his works show a substantial consistency of standpoint, and on many issues his position remained unaltered throughout his long life.

Knight and utility theory

In an early essay, Knight (1917: 67) criticized "the pernicious concept of utility dragged into economics by Jevons and the Austrians." He elaborated this critical view in later writings. In 1921 the *American Economic Review* published the proceedings of a discussion on the state of economic theory, in which several institutionalists had pressed their case. In this discussion Knight (1921b: 145) supported some of the arguments of the institutionalists: "I fully agree . . . that utility is misleading as an explanation of economic behavior." However, he immediately went on to suggest: "When we come to pass judgement on the workings of the price system, we have to have a theory of utility as a starting point . . . Utility is an ethical category, as indeed is illustrated by the most important conventional application of it, in justifying progressive taxation" (ibid.).

Accordingly, for Knight, the concept of utility was useless as an *explanation* of human behaviour. However, when it came to matters of normative evaluation or judgement, we are obliged to make rankings consistent with the principles of utility theory. Take, for example, the notion of the diminishing marginal utility of money. For Knight, this does not explain human behaviour. But, for him, it was a useful basis for the normative judgement that an extra dollar for a rich person is of less utility than an extra dollar for a pauper. The idea of the diminishing marginal utility of money provides a basis, as Knight recognized, for a policy of progressive taxation. Clearly, alternative and more conservative normative standards exist within neoclassical utility theory, such the Pareto welfare criterion. This allows aid to the poor only if the government does not take from the rich. In policy terms, Knight was more radical and redistributive than the Pareto criterion would allow. Furthermore, his partial rejection of utility theory distanced him from mainstream neoclassicism.

Knight believed that the version of individualist utilitarianism that had gained ground within economics had misled marginalism to focus on 'subjective" utility evaluations, rather than "objective" evaluations of alternative cost. However, for Knight, to consign utility theory to the normative domain was not to underestimate its significance. A strong lifetime theme through Knight's work is his insistence that economics has to be a moral as well as an ethical science (Nash 1998). It was one of his prominent criticisms of mainstream economics that it downplayed the moral and evaluative dimensions of human behaviour and focused instead on the economic actor as an amoral automaton. Knight (1935b: 282–83) thus protested:

> But the "economic man" is not a "social animal," and economic individualism excludes society in the proper human sense. Economic relations are *impersonal*. The social organization dealt with in economic theory is best pictured as a number of Crusoes interacting through the markets exclusively. . . . It is the market, the exchange opportunity, which is functionally real, not the other human beings . . . The relation is neither one of cooperation nor one of mutual exploitation, but is completely non-moral, non-human. Economic theory takes all economic individuals in an organization as *data*, not subject to "influence," and assumes that they view each other in the same way.

For Knight, taking individual preferences as data was an inadequate view. As he was to write near the end of his life: "Theory on the analogy of mechanics, treating motives as forces, and as 'given,' is illuminating and unavoidable; but the analogy has severe limitations and must not be pressed too far" (Knight 1961: 191).

For Knight, all social actors, including economists themselves, acted on the basis of their own judgements and values. He saw this as creating a theoretical problem. Objective investigations into socioeconomic phenomena, with a view to understanding and explaining them, must also deal with the values and judgements that form part of human motivation and behaviour. The fact human action is always laden with ethical evaluations and judgements of all kinds (ranging from the hedonistic to the altruistic) means that social science is distinguished from the natural sciences. The human social sciences cannot be dissolved into the biological or mechanical. This was clearly a criticism of what more recently has been described as the "physics envy" of some neoclassical theorists. Knight also criticized some strains within institutionalism for neglecting the moral dimension of human behaviour, and treating it investigatively as equivalent to the behaviour of other organisms. He wrote:

> the possibility of developing economics along the lines of the natural sciences naturally suggests itself; the possibility, that is, of using objective data exclusively and eschewing all question of motivation as natural science does those of real cause. It is easy to understand the great stir resulting from efforts to rid economics of utility theory and to supplant it by an objective, quantitative science. With the positive part of this program the present analyst is in hearty accord. But it is the purpose of this paper to show that economics must also continue to develop the older type of theory.
>
> (Knight 1931: 62)

On the other hand, on the question of the place of utility theory, Knight saw himself as being in accord with some other institutionalists, notably the British economist John Atkinson Hobson. Hobson was interpreted by Knight as using aspects of marginalist utilitarianism as the apparatus of ethical evaluation, but seeing the rationalist conception of action as highly limited. On this, Knight agreed: "With Hobson's fundamental position, that marginalism is the necessary form of a rational treatment of choice, and that the rational view of life is subject to drastic limitations, the writer is in hearty accord" (Knight 1921a: 113). Clearly, for Knight, a major reason why "the rational view of life is subject to drastic limitations" was that he believed that human decision making was subject to pervasive uncertainty. Especially in the light of Knight's prominent notion of uncertainty, it is strange that Knight is regarded by some as a mainstream or neoclassical economist. Uncertainty in a Knightian sense is an anathema to neoclassicism. Uncertainty refers to situations where there is no calculable probability. This rules out the possibility of formal modelling, neoclassical style (Lawson 1997). Knight's theory of the firm is dynamic and open-ended, focusing on the indeterminate outcomes of entrepreneurial decision in the face of uncertainty (Boudreaux and Holcombe 1989). Faced with its anti-formalist and indeterminate consequences, leading neoclassical Nobel Laureates have thus dismissed uncertainty from economic theory. Kenneth Arrow (1951: 417) remarked that "no theory can be formulated in this case." Robert Lucas (1981: 224) followed with a similar verdict: "In cases of uncertainty, economic reasoning will be of no value." Knight would have disagreed strongly. He did not regard formal modelling as the *sine qua non* of economic theory. In fact, because of the uncertain, complex, and value-driven nature of the human condition, Knight saw formal modelling as having only a little value in economics. Furthermore, he was the pioneer of a theory that had human uncertainty as its centrepiece and was thus distanced from the mechanistic conceptions of behaviour in neoclassicism.

To summarize, Knight rejected utility theory as a basis to explain human behaviour. But he retained it as part of the evaluative apparatus available to the economist. Knight thus distanced himself from the neoclassical economists who typically rely on utility theory to model, explain or predict human action. He also saw severe limits in the general use of formal modelling in economic theory. Having established some significant distance between Knight and neoclassical theory, let us turn to the second proposition, as a result of which the gap can be further enlarged.

Tastes and technology as dependent variables

Did Knight accept as adequate the neoclassical assumption of given preference functions and technological possibilities? The short answer is "no." In the early 1920s, Knight was invited by the institutional economist Rexford Tugwell to contribute to a collection of writings on the way forward for economics.[7] In his contribution, Knight (1924: 262–63) made it clear – using the memorable metaphor of a river – that the assumption of given preference functions or wants has limited applicability, and is not appropriate in long-run theories of economic change:

> Wants are usually treated as *the* fundamental data, the ultimate driving force in economic activity, and in a short-run view of problems this is scientifically legitimate. But in the long run it is just as clear that wants are dependent variables, that they are largely caused and formed by economic activity. The case is somewhat like that of a river and its channel; for the time being the channel locates the river, but in the long run it is the other way round.

Knight (1924: 263–65) emphasized that wants and preferences were subject to change:

The only ultimately independent variables are those features of nature and human nature which are in fact outside the power of economic forces to change, and it would be hard to say what these are. . . . The largest reservation called for in assuming the fixity of the data controlling production and consumption over a period of years relates to the permanence of wants.

The notion that individual tastes were both malleable and socially formed was a theme repeated in his later works. Of course, Knight (1956: 295) was fully aware of the critical consequences of this for mainstream welfare economics: "But both power and wants or tastes come to the individual chiefly through the processes of the society in which he lives, especially by inheritance, biological and cultural, and through the family. Thus social policy cannot possibly treat the individual as a datum in any of these respects, since he is in fact largely the creation of social action." It was in analysing long-period change that Knight (1924: 264) saw the role of "'institutional' economics, [as] studying 'the cumulative changes of institutions.'" The value of this approach lies in its capacity "to predict long-period changes in the factors that applied economics accepts as data." In a later work, Knight stated a similar position. Concerning what he called "price-theory economics," Knight (1933: xii) admitted that to some extent he was "in sympathy with the reaction against it." He explained:

Economic theory based on utilitarian premises . . . is purely abstract and formal, without content. It deals, in general, with certain formal principles of "economy" without reference to what is to be economized, or how; more specifically, price-economics deals with a social system in which every individual treats all others merely as instrumentalities . . . a mechanical system of Crusoe economies. It discusses the use of given resources by given "owners," in accord with a given system of technology, to satisfy given wants, all organized through a system of perfect markets.

(ibid.)

Knight clearly perceived a limitation of neoclassical economics in terms of its assumption of given wants and technology. He continued: "Any question as to what resources, technology, etc., are met with at a given time and place, must be answered in terms of institutional history, since all such things, in common with the impersonal system of market relations itself, are obviously culture-history facts and products" (ibid.). Knight then went on (xii–xiii) to admit that "economic" motivation was also itself a product of culture and history. In a passage which seems to suggest the influence of John Dewey on his thought, Knight (1956: 295–96) even went on to question the complete and final separation of means from ends:

some mention must be made of the limitations of the whole economic view of life and conduct – the view, that is, in terms of the use of means to achieve ends. There really are no "ends" in any final sense – they are rather milestones on the way ahead and these become means as fast as they are achieved – and the qualities of good and bad belong about as much to means as to ends in any right use of the terms.

Clearly, this placed Knight at some distance from the neoclassical mainstream. On this point he is in accord with Dewey (1939: 45) who argued at length that "there is no end which is not in turn a means."

A related feature of Knight's work that put some distance between him and neoclassical economics was his emphasis on disequilibria in socioeconomic systems. Knight (1935b: 184) wrote:

> Our general conclusion must be that in the field of economic progress the notion of tendency toward equilibrium is definitely inapplicable to particular elements of growth and, with reference to progress as a unitary process or system of interconnected changes, is of such limited and partial application as to be misleading rather than useful. This view is emphasized by reference to the phenomena covered by the loose term "institution." All speculative glimpses at trends in connection with price theory relate to a "competitive" or "capitalistic" economic system. But all the human interests and traits involved in this type of economic life are subject to historical change.

Knight's insistence on ongoing changes, including the alteration of human purposes and preferences, all set in a climate of uncertainty, led him to emphasize the limited value of the equilibrium concept and to hint at the value of historical and institutional analysis.

Knight and methodological individualism

Was Knight a methodological individualist? The answer clearly depends upon what is meant by methodological individualism. It is a notion that must be defined carefully. Gonce (1972: 552, emphasis added) identified its Austrian school meaning and stated that: "it signifies that the subjectivity of the self-interested, rational and free individual is to be used to explain *all* human conduct and social and economic phenomena." Gonce's definition of methodological individualism shall be used here. Note that this version of methodological individualism requires that the individual is used as the basis of the explanation of *all* socioeconomic phenomena. It is consistent with Lachmann's (1969: 94) slightly looser definition "that we shall not be satisfied with any type of explanation of social phenomena which does not lead us ultimately to a human plan." It is also consistent with one of the most precise definitions, by Jon Elster (1982: 453, emphasis added), who saw methodological individualism as: "the doctrine that *all* social phenomena (their structure and their change) are in principle explicable *only* in terms of individuals – their properties, goals, and beliefs." With a substantially similar definition of methodological individualism, Gonce (1972: 552 n.) made the questionable claim that Knight "continuously . . . employed this procedure." To claim support for his view he referred to some parts of Knight's work.[8] But, on the contrary, turning to these passages, we find Knight attempting no such method for explaining *all* socioeconomic phenomena.

Others have suggested that Knight was a methodological individualist, but with an implicitly different definition of that term. For instance, McKinney (1977: 1441) referred to one passage (Knight, 1951: 23–24) alone to support the dubious claim that "Knight is a methodological individualist." In this passage Knight argued that "the organization as a whole has no value in itself or purpose of its own." However, this statement is about the alleged location of values and wills in individuals rather than organizations; it is not about the explanation of socioeconomic phenomena in terms of individuals alone. The passage does not give evidence that Knight was a methodological individualist in the sense defined by Gonce or Elster. The claims of Gonce and McKinney to have found evidence of methodological individualism in Knight's works do not stand up to critical scrutiny.

To play the Devil's Advocate, we may address another passage by Knight which, perhaps at first sight, may seem to support the case that he was a methodological individualist. Consider the following:

> "Institutional Economics" . . . is essentially a continuation or revival of the historical standpoint. But if human and social phenomena can be completely explained in terms of their own history, the result is the same as that of a complete mechanical explanation; there is no such thing as purposive action or as practical relevance. . . . The view here adopted . . . treats social institutions as a product of social choice based on social knowledge of patterns between which choice is made, and has meaning only in so far as such choice may be real.
>
> (Knight 1935b: 285 n.)

Here, Knight made two (valid) points. First, he warned against some real tendencies in historical and institutional economics who wished to explain all socioeconomic phenomena in terms of historical trends, omitting human discretion and creativity. Second, he stated that institutions must be seen as the result of real social choices. There is nothing here to suggest that institutions have to be explained *entirely* in individual terms. Although Knight saw human will at the root of all socioeconomic activity, he did not think that human choices alone were a sufficient explanation of all social and economic phenomena. Indeed, Knight (1924: 263) devoted much attention to the fact that "wants are dependent variables . . . largely caused and formed by economic activity."

In fact, his inclination was against this reductionist thrust of methodological individualism. Knight (1924: 247) wrote: "the way to improve our technique is not to attempt to analyse things into their elements, reduce them to measure and determinate functional relations, but to educate and train one's intuitive powers." Furthermore, Knight rejected the individualist view of knowledge emphasized by the Austrian school. He was much closer to Veblen than to (say) Friedrich Hayek when he wrote that: "all knowledge is itself 'social'; it is based on intercommunication between individuals, each of whom is both subject and object, both to himself and to all others in the thinking community in which knowledge has its being" (Knight 1956: 136). Knight saw the forces of institutionalization and of indeterminate individuality as *both* at play. Like the old institutionalists he stressed the role of habit, imitation, and custom. For Knight, the forces that help to mould human society

> belong to an intermediate category, between instinct and intelligence. They are a matter of custom, tradition, or institutions. Such laws are transmitted in society, and acquired by the individual, through relatively effortless and even unconscious imitation, and conformity with them by any mature individual at any time is a matter of "habit."
>
> (Knight 1947: 224)

His emphasis on the role of customs and institutions was repeated elsewhere:

> Human society must always be largely of the original institutional character; custom and habit must rule most of what people feel, think, and do. Institutions, I repeat, are more or less explained historically rather than scientifically and are little subject to control. The ideal type is language, about which we can do so little that we hardly think of trying.
>
> (Knight 1957: 45)

But nowhere here does Knight fall into the determinist trap of suggesting that human behaviour is *entirely* determined by custom or institutions. In fact, throughout his writings, he attempted to reconcile the non-contradictory propositions of individual "free will" with the additional notion that individual behaviour was moulded and constrained by institutions. Such a reconciliation is problematic, but it does not falter on purely logical grounds. No "paradox" is involved. Indeed, the reconciliation of these two different ideas is part of the enduring agenda of social theory. Knight nowhere evades the problem of structure and agency by succumbing to the untenable extremes of either cultural determinism or methodological individualism. The fact that his own solution was incomplete, and even defective, is beyond the point. The point here is to establish that attempts to describe Knight as a methodological individualist do not work.

Knight on neoclassicism and institutionalism as complements

What was Knight's attitude to the possibility of a synthesis between neoclassical economics and institutionalism? Broadly, he assented to this idea. Knight did not believe that neoclassical theory should be entirely replaced. But it had to be supplemented by studies of history and institutions. The role of "institutional economics" was thus seen as a complement to some aspects of neoclassical economics, including ethically directed utility theory and Marshallian-type price theory.

Does this limited acceptance of neoclassical theory disqualify Knight as an institutionalist? If so, then we must also indict others, including leading institutionalists such as J. R. Commons, W. C. Mitchell, J. M. Clark, P. H. Douglas, and A. F. Burns. They all saw institutionalism as compatible with aspects of Marshallian price theory.[9] This passage from Commons is particularly revealing:

> Sometimes anything additional to or critical of the classical or hedonic economics is deemed to be institutional. . . . [However] institutional economics . . . cannot separate itself from the marvellous discoveries and insight of the classical and psychological economists. . . . Institutional economics is not divorced from the classical and psychological schools of economists.
>
> (Commons 1931: 648–56)

Although Commons did not use the word "neoclassical" here, he clearly was referring in part to this tradition when he used terms such as "hedonic economics" and "classical and psychological schools of economists."[10]

Accordingly, when trying to decide whether person X was or was not an institutionalist, it is difficult to disqualify X simply on the grounds that X accepted elements of neoclassical economics in their theory. If such an overly restrictive criterion is invoked, then we are left with very few institutionalists at all. That is one reason why this criterion must be rejected. What is important is whether X accepted neoclassical thinking as *adequate* for economic theory. Those economists who believe that it is adequate can be described as neoclassical economists. I shall follow this convention here. Those who think that it is inadequate may, subject to further conditions, be described as institutionalists, even if they accept parts of neoclassical economics as valid. Hence to point out that X accepted elements of neoclassical economics in their theory does not necessarily disqualify X from being an institutionalist.

As a result, there is an asymmetry between the two definitions. An institutionalist does not cease to be so if she accepts key elements of neoclassical theory. However, a neoclassical economist ceases to be such, once she accepts the core proposition of institutionalism: that economic theory must take account of changing preferences and purposes and not take them as given.

That change of viewpoint is sufficient to remove the "neoclassical" nametag and install the "institutionalist" one instead. (Incidentally, it is also enough to disqualify the economist from gaining any senior position in any major economics department in Britain or North America today.)

To understand Knight's own position here it is important to appreciate his immersion in the work of Weber and the other German historical school economists.[11] Like the German historical school, Knight tried to grapple with the problem of historical specificity in economic analysis. In his *Risk, Uncertainty and Profit*, Knight (1921a: 9) tried to elucidate some economic principles that are specific to "free enterprise" or "the competitive system." The study of this system, according to Knight, should proceed "as a first approximation" from "a *perfectly* competitive system, in which the multitudinous degrees and kinds of divergences are eliminated by abstraction." He went on to discuss a selection of mainstream economists who have followed such an approach.

In subsequent works, Knight tried to answer the more fundamental question, which had been addressed by historical school thinkers such as Weber and Werner Sombart. True, the system of "free enterprise" may have common features from nation to nation, but a more general methodology is required to define the system of "free enterprise" and to demarcate it from other systems. This more general "economic" discourse may itself contain general concepts, principles or laws. Accordingly, which features, assumptions or laws are general to all economic systems, and which are specific to, say, modern capitalism?[12]

One of Knight's most complete attempts to answer these questions is found in his contribution to the 1924 "institutionalist" Tugwell volume. For Knight, the discovery of universal economic principles or laws assured a place for the abstractions of neoclassical economic theory. But these do not take us far enough:

> The problem of life is to utilize resources "economically," to make them go as far as possible in the production of desired results. The general theory of economics is therefore simply the rationale of life. – In so far as it has any rationale! The first question in regard to scientific economics is this question of how far life is rational, how far its problems reduce to the form of using given means to achieve given ends. Now this, we shall contend, is not very far.
>
> (Knight 1924: 229)

Nevertheless, Knight held that universal principles should not be disregarded. He alleged that there were universals such as "the general laws of choice," "general laws of production and consumption." In other words, for Knight, all individuals throughout history, in their economic activities, make choices, and the same "laws" allegedly govern these choices. Although Knight does not elaborate much on the nature of these allegedly universal laws, he gave an example: "in the large the conditions of supply and demand determine the prices of goods" (Knight 1924: 259). He wrote further:

> Institutions may determine the alternatives of choice and fix the limits of freedom of choice, but the general laws of choice among competing motives or goods are not institutional . . . there are general laws of production and consumption which hold good whatever specific things are thought of as wealth and whatever productive factors and processes in use. . . . The laws of economics are never themselves institutional, though they may relate to institutional situations. Some, as we have observed, are as universal as rational behavior, the presence of alternatives of choice between quantitatively variable ends, or between different means of arriving at ends. . . . A large part of the extant body of economic theory would be as valid in a socialistic society as it is in one organized through exchange between individuals.
>
> (Knight 1924: 258–60)

This argument is questionable, partly because it regards choice as an activity which itself is not framed and formed by institutions. Some may dispute Knight's assertion here that the neoclassical "laws of economics are never themselves institutional." It may be the case that "rational behavior" is universal in an empty sense, simply because no possible form of behaviour can be manifestly inconsistent with its axioms (Boland 1981). Notably, in other passages, Knight (1933: xii–xiii) himself accepted that calculative rationality was a historically specific phenomenon, thus seeming to deny its universality. We may go further: if "supply and demand" are to "determine the price of goods", they may require a prior non-universal institutional framework of exchange and a degree of price flexibility so that these forces can move their objects. Knight's "general laws" may not be so general after all.

But the disputable character of this argument is beyond the point. The main point here is that Knight was trying to demarcate universal from non-universal laws. His claim was that the universal "laws of economics" provided the domain for neoclassical theory, and they had to be supplemented by the historically specific study of institutions. Knight clearly pointed out that not all laws are universal, and that different laws had different domains of applicability:

> Other laws relate to behavior in exchange relations, and of course have no practical significance where such relations are not established. Still others cover behavior in situations created by even more special institutional arrangements, as for example the differences in business conduct created by the custom of selling goods subject to cash discount or by the existence of a branch banking system as contrasted with independent banks. An intelligent conception of the meaning of science requires a clear grasp of the meaning of classification and subclassification, of laws of all

degrees of generality. Each law is universal in the field to which it applies, though it may not give a complete description of the cases which it fits. Quite commonly a law has the form "*insofar as* the situation is of such a character, such things will happen."

(Knight 1924: 260)

Knight's notion here that an "intelligent conception of the meaning of science requires a clear grasp of the meaning of classification and subclassification, of laws of all degrees of generality" shows the particular inspiration of Weber and the German historicists. Knight gave this an additional, institutionalist twist. Institutions were seen to "determine the alternatives of choice and fix the limits of freedom of choice." This, for Knight, was the place for institutional economics. Knight thus insisted that the "general theory of economics" is valid but it does not get us "very far." His writings are admirably consistent on this point. "The principles of the established economics are partial statements, but sound as far as they go, and they go about as far as general principles can be carried. . . . General theory is a *first step*, but never a very long step toward the solution of practical problems" (Knight 1921b: 145). In some passages Knight did make it clear that the approach of neoclassical economics is itself dependent on institutionalist insights for any sort of coherent account of "rational economic man." However, he treats institutions primarily as constraints, rather than them being constitutive of choice and behaviour. Nevertheless, for Knight, without institutions, economic man would exist in a vacuum without a history or a future. Hence he saw the relationship between neoclassical and institutional economics as one of "complementarity" (Knight 1952: 46). As Knight (1924: 262) himself put it: "deductive theory and 'institutional' economics" are both relevant: "at one extreme we might have a discussion limited to the abstract theory of markets . . . at the other extreme we should have the philosophy of history . . . and that is what institutional economics practically comes to. It should go without saying that all are useful and necessary." Knight (1924: 265–66) went on to explain the key role of institutional economics:

The study of such long-time changes would seem to be the most conspicuous task of institutional economics . . . No one would belittle the importance of studying these historic movements in the general structure of social standards and relations . . . But neither, we think, can anyone contend that such a study should displace the other branches of economics which either are fairly independent of institutions or take them as they are at a given time and place and use them in explaining the immediate facts of economic life.

For Knight (1924: 229), it was necessary for the economist to examine the role of institutions and to also embark on "an exploration in the field of values." Institutionalists would agree. In a letter to his friend Talcott Parsons, dated 1 May, 1936, Knight wrote: "I came to Chicago expecting this 'institutionalism' to be my main field of work" (Knight, 1936).[13] He complained that other theoretical controversies and teaching had got in the way of this research project. While at Chicago, Knight taught that institutional economics and Marshallian neoclassical economics had complementary roles. In a letter dated 16 February, 1937, to his friend Ayres, Knight reported that he was giving a course on "Economics from an Institutional Perspective" at Chicago. In fact, Knight had started giving this course in the summer quarter of 1932. Knight's Reading List for Economics 305, Winter 1937, says: "The task of institutionalism [is] that of accounting historically for the factors treated as *data* in rationalistic, price-theory economics." He then lists the topics "individualism and utilitarianism, wants, technology, resources, organization, economic institutions as embodied in law" (Samuels 1977: 503). In principle, there was nothing in Knight's qualified acceptance of some neoclassical tenets to debar him from institutionalism. He himself made the place of institutional economics explicit and extensive.

The evaluation of Knight by James Buchanan (1968: 426) is not far from the mark. According to Buchanan, Knight was "that rare theorist who is also an institutionalist, an institutionalist who is not a data collector." Was Knight an institutionalist? He should have the final word on this question. Knight (1957: 43) declared: "I am in fact as 'institutionalist' as anyone, in a positive sense." In a letter to Ayres dated 13 July, 1969, Knight wrote "I've always considered myself an institutionalist . . . as far as possible" (Samuels 1977: 519). His institutionalism was nonconformist, but it was an institutionalism nevertheless.

Knight and his contemporaries

Although always a maverick and an independent, Knight was clearly willing to follow much of the historical school and institutionalist doctrine. Accordingly, Knight respected the well-known institutionalists. Knight (1920: 519–20) reviewed Veblen's collection of essays entitled *The Place of Science in Modern Civilization* and found it "interesting and intellectually stimulating" despite its occasional "obscurity and confusion" on key points. Generally, Knight admired Veblen but found many of his arguments unclear. Commons was also judged to be obscure on key theoretical points. Nevertheless, with over two hundred other leading American economists, Knight signed in 1925 a petition requesting the nominating committee of the AEA to select Veblen as an honorary president.[14]

Leading contemporary institutionalists respected Knight. J. M. Clark gave him strong support and encouragement. Mitchell (1922) reviewed Knight's *Risk, Uncertainty and Profit* very positively. Ayres held Knight in some esteem, but the theoretical distance between them grew to the point where Knight could not place himself in the institutionalist mainstream.

There were other personal links between Knight and institutionalism. One of Knight's mentors was Herbert J. Davenport (1861–1931). Knight made a number of references to Davenport in his work. Davenport was also a close friend and admirer of Veblen. He had been a faculty member with Veblen at two universities: at Chicago for four years and at Missouri for seven years. Subsequently, in 1916, Davenport moved to Cornell and established a close intellectual relationship with Knight. Like Veblen, Davenport objected to the normative and apologetic abuses of economic theory. Like Veblen, Davenport emphasized the tension between finance and industry and denied that the market is an automatic self-righting mechanism: private gain did not necessarily lead to social welfare. Veblen, Knight, and Davenport rejected the neoclassical division of economic resources into "factors of production." For Davenport, the Austrian theory of alternative costs was essentially correct, but – like Veblen and Knight – he saw the marginalist theory of value and distribution as severely flawed. Like Veblen and Knight, Davenport denied that utility theory could be used as a general explanation of human behaviour. Davenport was elected President of the AEA in 1920.[15]

These personal and intellectual connections between Knight and institutionalism have become obscured and forgotten. As economics has moved away from institutionalism, the history of ideas has itself been rewritten, arguably at some violation to the truth.

This forgetting and rewriting of history also occurs in relation to another episode, which indirectly connects to Knight. Although Britain never had a strong institutionalist tradition, significant changes in economics happened in both Britain as well as America in the interwar period. Notably, in the mid-1920s, the leading economist Allyn Young took a chair at the London School of Economics, and became the first American professor in Britain. Although he was critical of institutionalism, Young retained strong institutionalist sympathies and had written of Veblen as "the most gifted man whom I have ever known" (Dorfman 1934: 299). Tragically, Young became a victim of a severe influenza epidemic, and died in London of pneumonia in March 1929. He was 52 years of age.

This death was to be decisive for the fate of British economics, and for the rewriting of a history in which Knight was an actor. After his election in 1929 to the chair at the London School of Economics that had been vacated by Young, Lionel Robbins (1932) made the famous and enduring claim that economics was founded solely on universal principles concerning choice under scarcity. Robbins set about the task of ridding economics of any vestiges of institutionalism and the historical school. In a masterly stroke, he simply redefined economics in terms that would exclude institutionalism and the historicism from within its disciplinary boundaries, but would retain a place for the Austrian school.[16] In former years, Alfred Marshall and other pioneering neoclassical economists would not have subscribed to such a narrow definition of their discipline. The institutionalists, still influential in America in the 1930s, had little sympathy for such academic sectarianism.

To succeed in defining institutionalism out of the discipline of economics, Robbins had to establish a new but noble lineage for his ideas. This, above all, had to draw upon the intellectual powerhouses of Britain, Germany, Austria, and America. In Britain, Marshall could be cited, but only if his admiration for the German historical school could be overlooked. In his crusade to found economics on universal propositions, Robbins conveniently ignored Marshall's attention to the problem of historical specificity. By heaping masses of praise upon Marshall, while ignoring the central issues pursued by the historical school, Robbins managed to rewrite history, and to make Marshall his ally.

Robbins found a suitable emblem in the pioneering neoclassical economist Philip Wicksteed, and he edited his *Commonsense of Political Economy* (1933). Wicksteed defined an "economic transaction" as one in which one party did not consider the welfare or desires of the other, merely the object of the transaction itself. This attempt to narrow the domain of the "economic" served Robbins' purposes.

The choice in Continental Europe was clear. Robbins chose the Austrian side in the German-speaking *Methodenstreit*, and was thereby able to use the work of Menger and others to dismiss the German historical school.

America, with its strong institutionalist tradition, was more of a problem. Robbins had to identify a leading American economist who seemed sufficiently close to him. But the country was populated with institutionalists. Among the well-known American economists the best option was Knight, but only if he could be repackaged as a neoclassical economist and his institutionalist sympathies could be obscured or forgotten.

Robbins thus contrived an Austro-neoclassical tradition, from Carl Menger through Philip Wicksteed to Frank Knight. This created a splendid Germanic-English-American triad for Robbins' project. However, it ignored Knight's views on the place of utility theory, rationality, historical specificity, institutionalism, and the historical school. Furthermore, Knight was very uneasy about being given this role. He rejected Robbins' insinuation that he had built upon the work of Wicksteed. He insisted in 1934: "I never read the 'Common Sense' until recently" (Knight 1956: 104). Despite this, Robbins eventually won the battle of ideas, and economics today follows more closely his methodological guidelines than those of Knight. The irony is that much of Knight's work would be excluded from the narrow definition of economics that Robbins established in the 1930s. Yet the myth of Knight as an Austro-neoclassical economist, who was opposed to institutionalism, still survives.

Although I do not believe that it is strictly relevant to the establishment of the proposition that Knight was an institutionalist, we can also dwell briefly on his ethical and policy stance. (As we shall see below, this is relevant to an understanding of Knight's relationship with Keynesianism.) Knight was very much concerned about policy. But his recognition of ubiquitous uncertainty in economic life made him cautious about all excessive predictive or policy claims by economists. Nevertheless, Knight was an advocate of progressive taxation and the welfare state. He was sceptical of the view that the amassing of an inheritance was an effective spur to the generation of more wealth, and suggested the imposition of an inheritance tax, following "the Saint-Simonian school of socialists and others" (Knight 1921a: 373–74).

Knight (1956: 170) argued that "a really thoroughgoing laisser-faire individualism, accepting individual preferences as absolutely final" had to be ruled out because individuals "are necessarily reared and educated in the society in which they are to live and function as members." Against neoclassical welfare theory, Knight held that it is "absurd to treat the individual as a datum for purposes of decisions regarding social policy." For Knight, the market was "no agency for improving tastes (wants) or manners or especially for conferring productive capacity to meet wants or needs" (ibid.: 271). He similarly rejected the notion that prices measured values in an ethical sense (Knight 1935b: 55–56; 1951: 36, 46).

However, Knight (1956: 252) was highly critical of the "fallacious doctrine and pernicious consequences" of the work of John Maynard Keynes, "who for a decade succeeded in carrying economic thinking well back to the dark age." Nevertheless, Knight shared Keynes' view that economic recovery from a recession was not automatic, and Knight was in favour of increased public expenditure to alleviate the depression. In a memorandum of 26 April 1932 to Congressman Samuel B. Pettengill (Indiana), 12 Chicago economists, including F. H. Knight, H. Simons, and J. Viner, dismissed faith in the self-righting abilities of the economy. Their advice was that injecting enough new purchasing power through "generous Federal expenditures" could bring about recovery. On 8 May, 1932, Knight himself wrote to Senator Robert F. Wagner in favour of such a strategy: "As far as I know, economists are completely agreed that the Government should spend as much and tax as little as possible, at a time such as this" (J. R. Davis 1968: 479).

There is another example of Knight's readiness to recommend intervention. In the case of the McNary-Haugen bill, Knight was prepared to run against the bulk of professional opinion by arguing that the farmer subsidy was required to counterbalance the protective tariffs placed on industrial goods. In addition, Knight recommended that a government agency, rather than the private banking sector, should deliver additional credit (Dorfman 1959: 476–77).

Some discussion of Knight's relationship with the Department of Economics at the University of Chicago is also relevant. Incidentally, Veblen had been at the Department from its foundation in 1892 until his departure in 1906. Knight was at Chicago from 1917 to 1919. After a spell at the University of Iowa in 1927, Knight returned to the Windy City to take up the chair left vacant by J. M. Clark's departure for Columbia University. Knight remained at Chicago for the remainder of his life, attracting followers and admirers such as Henry Simons, Paul Samuelson, Milton Friedman, and George Stigler. Intellectually, he dominated the department until the outbreak of World War II. However, Knight's view on the limitations of mathematics within economics and his hostility to Keynesianism created opposition from the rising new technocratic wing of neoclassical economics. Samuelson was at Chicago from 1932 to 1935. He suggested in an interview how his admiration for Knight was later challenged: "Mathematics, which I was beginning to get interested in, was laughed at by the Knight wing" (Colander and Landreth 1996: 148). Leading mathematical economists such as Samuelson went on to place a formalized "Keynesian" theory into a neo-classical straitjacket. This awkward combination of mathematics with a bowdlerized Keynesianism was nevertheless deadly for Knight's reputation. As Samuelson pointed out: "By the end of the war the entire academic profession was Keynesian" (ibid.: 158).

Within Chicago itself, some additional and distinctive forces were at play. The first was the arrival of the Cowles Commission in October 1939. Having escaped the effects of the 1929 Great Crash by accident, one Alfred Cowles offered to finance the new Econometrics Society out of his fortune. His original concern was to develop methods of predicting movements of prices on the stock exchange. Set up in 1932, the Cowles Commission was in the vanguard of the resurgence of neoclassical, mathematical economics in the 1930s and 1940s. It stayed at Chicago until the 1950s, and despite Knight's opposition, it helped to transform the entire department (Epstein 1987; Morgan 1990).

Melvin Reder (1982: 10) has argued that the installation of the Cowles Commission in 1939 was one of "three shocks" that hit Chicago economics in the years 1938–39.[17] The second was the early death in a car accident of Henry Schultz in November 1938, and the third was the election of Schultz's friend, the institutionalist Paul Douglas, to the public office of Alderman in November 1939. These three shocks, including the departure of two key personnel, radically changed the balance of opinion within the department against Knight. In addition, in 1938, the young mathematical economist Oskar Lange arrived from Poland as an assistant professor: "Lange was an up-to-the-minute young theorist, in the vanguard of the Keynesian Revolution who had acquired a considerable reputation as a mathematical economist" (Reder 1982: 4). Lange's economic theory was neoclassical, his style mathematical, and his politics Marxist. Even in Chicago, it was his theory and its mathematical style that mattered most. Until his return to Poland in 1945, Lange waged a war against the surviving remnants of Chicago institutionalism and anti-formalism. Ironically, this "Marxist" played a leading role in transforming the Chicago department and defeating institutionalism in America. The immediate outcome was that: "By 1944, a fairly intense struggle was underway between Knight and his former students on one side, and the Cowles Commission and its adherents on the other. . . . It continued for almost 10 years" (Reder 1982: 10). The result was that Knight, along with his remaining followers, plus the institutionalists, were all the losers. "After 1945, if not earlier, Knight's outspoken disdain for empirical, especially quantitative, research set him completely apart from the main body of Chicago economists – including his own former students" (Reder 1982: 6).

Furthermore: "The institutionalist wing of the department was greatly reduced by the retirement of Millis (in 1940) and the departure of Leland for Northwestern in 1946." Friedman was appointed to Chicago in 1946 and Stigler in 1958. It was not until after Friedman's appointment that the distinctive, modern, anti-Keynesian "Chicago school" emerged (Reder 1982: 10). However, Knight (1966: 117) saw it as erroneous to take "the vastly simplified postulates that are legitimate and necessary for the first stage of economic analysis – but which should never be taken as describing reality and still less as normative – and treat them as universal ideals." He could have been criticizing the postwar Chicago school. In Chicago, Knight had become a revered but isolated figure. His marginalization paralleled the decline of institutionalism as a whole. His decline in influence was a result of the same forces that defeated American institutionalism.

While Robbins had simply defined historical and institutional "economics" out of existence in the realm of ideas, the Nazis and World War II did much of the job of destruction in the real world. Fascism and its opponents pulverized German social science. Remnants emerged after 1945, often with a spirit of emulation of their conquerors and with little desire to remember their great, historical school past. The US fought World War II with a faith in the powers of technology and quantitative formalism that radically changed the nature of postwar social science. Both Knight and the institutionalists were the casualties. Within economics, the victors after 1945 were the rising generation of mathematical economists and econometricians, including Kenneth Arrow and Paul Samuelson.

As Samuels (1977) has revealed, Knight was a close friend and contemporary of the leading American institutionalist Ayres. Their published correspondence tells a very interesting story. I have argued elsewhere that Ayres' work was in crucial respects at variance to the preceding tradition of American institutionalism from the 1890s to the 1930s, dominated by Veblen, Commons, and Mitchell (Hodgson 1998, 1999). Ayres' work was very much a reaction to institutionalism's crisis and decline of the 1930s and 1940s.

Although Knight and Ayres were close friends, intellectually, in some crucial respects, they took very different positions.[18] Despite its important insights and innovations, institutionalism under the leadership of Veblen, Commons, and Mitchell had failed to develop a systematic and adequate, theoretical and philosophical base. Knight responded by making individual agency and uncertainty central, in a context where he accepted the role of institutions. Ayres (1935, 1944) took the opposite position, almost forgot the individual, and made institutions barriers in the way of the holistic forces of technological and cultural advance.

In one of their critical engagements, Knight (1935a) responded to Ayres (1935) by noting that Ayres assumed "some kind of inner law of progress of an absolute and inscrutable character" for technology and implied that "there is some equally absolute and inscrutable type of 'causality' by which technology drags behind it and 'determines' other phases of social change" (Knight 1935a: 208). For Knight, the ultimate source of causality in the social realm had to be the choosing individual, not technological or historical "forces" (Knight 1933: xxviii).

What was common to both positions is that they recognized but still underestimated the constitutive role of institutions for individual agency. Both Knight and Ayres failed to emphasize, as Veblen had seen and explained earlier, that institutions involved shared habits of thought and provided the necessary cognitive frameworks of human action. Institutions moulded human action and were not simply barriers on its path.

If all "facts of observation are necessarily seen in the light of the observer's habits of thought" (Veblen 1914: 53) and if "institutions are, in substance, prevalent habits of thought with respect to particular relations and particular functions of the individual and of the community" (Veblen 1899: 190), then human agency is constituted by institutions just as much as institutions are constituted by human agency. From a strictly Veblenian perspective, neither Knight's free-standing, undetermined individual, nor Ayres' institution-free conception of culture and technology, will do. The failure to develop a Veblenian or other suitable perspective led to bifurcation of institutionalism along the diverging Ayresian and Knightian paths of development. From a viewpoint I have developed elsewhere, it can be argued that both paths led to unsatisfactory destinations (Hodgson 1988, 1997, 1998). That is part of the tragedy of the story.

Conclusion

Whatever the rights and wrongs of this debate between Ayres and Knight, the outcome by 1950 was that Knight was isolated from mainstream neoclassicism, Chicago orthodoxy, and the surviving remnants of American institutionalism. Knight's opposition to the rising psychology of behaviourism also isolated him from many psychologists and social scientists. Knight was an isolated figure, but it is important not to overlook his significant affinities with institutionalism. After all, his work shared the same fate as institutionalism as a whole. As institutionalism declined in influence in the post-1945 period so too did the prestige of Knight.

I have argued here that two factors, above all others, place Knight in the institutionalist camp. First, he accepted the importance of social and institutional factors in human preferences and purposes. In this respect, Knight's ideas are remote from those of the overwhelming majority of economists today. Second, he repeatedly described himself as an institutionalist.

In fact, Knight may bequeath as much, if not more, of enduring value for institutionalism as Ayres. Not only was Knight an institutionalist, he was one of the greatest of all institutional economists after Veblen. He differed from mainstream American institutionalism on key points, but he brought to that tradition great insight and rigour. Without reaching a complete solution to the most fundamental and pressing methodological and theoretical problems, he developed an innovative type of economics which, today at least, is far from the mainstream. He grappled with central problems such as the problem of agency and structure. Inspired by Veblen, Weber, and the German historical school, he engaged likewise with the problem of historical specificity in economic theory. He thus addressed two of the most pressing theoretical problems for a revived institutional economics today.

Furthermore, Knight's work is relevant to that still-open question of the relationship between – and compatibility or otherwise of – neoclassical and institutional theory. Is a marriage possible between institutionalism and some kind of post-Marshallian economics? For those who understand that neoclassical economics is not defined by its policy conclusions, and thereby focus on policy rather than theory, this theoretical question is far from closed.[19]

Notes

1 Hamilton's subsequent career is an indication of his own prestige and the status of institutionalism at the time. In 1924 he became director of the new Brookings Graduate School. Ten years later he was an influential member of the National Industrial Recovery Board.

2 It must be stressed that the acceptance of the influence of culture or institutions does not necessarily imply a view of human action as being entirely determined by them. The influence works in both directions, acknowledging individual agency and will. For various arguments along these lines, see, for example, Archer (1995), Bhaskar (1979), Giddens (1984), and Hodgson (1988). Although some institutionalists, such as Ayres, have succumbed to a cultural determinism, this does not mean that all institutionalists are compelled to follow.

3 In 1927 Knight published an English translation of Max Weber's *Wirtschaftsgeschichte* (Weber 1927).

4 Johnson had previously taught Hamilton at the University of Texas, and had persuaded him to take up graduate study in economics, thus confirming Johnson's crucial influence over two figures in American economic science in the twentieth century.

5 However, 20 years later, Gonce (1992: 813) admitted that Knight had "professed to be in part an institutional economist." McKinney (1977: 1441–42) went on, somewhat confusingly, to suggest that Knight had shown that the "fundamental assumptions" of methodological individualism "are false. In fact, alongside his methodological individualism, coexisting with it in a state of pluralistic contradiction, is an extreme form of sociological determinism." McKinney claims to identify a paradox in Knight's thought which does not, in fact, exist. Knight was not a sociological determinist. In fact, Knight was attempting to reconcile the causal role of the individual with broader institutional developments that impinged upon the agent, even changing his or her wants or goals. McKinney was unfortunately afflicted with an, alas, still endemic Austrian disorder that wrongly regards any denial of methodological individualism as an automatic endorsement of methodological collectivism or sociological determinism.

6 Subsequently to the publication of his book, Dr. Yonay and myself have corresponded extensively on this question and – judging especially by our emails of 2 March 1999 –

reached a substantial measure of agreement. Yonay has generously admitted the possibility of a view of Knight different from that portrayed in his 1998 book.

7 Other contributors included the institutionalists J. M. Clark, Paul H. Douglas. W. C. Mitchell, S. H. Slichter, and A. B. Wolfe.

8 Namely, Knight (1921a: 73–74, 264) and Knight (1961).

9 I understand that Warren Samuels, to whom this volume is dedicated, also believes that neoclassical and institutional economics can be complementary.

10 Further similarities between the works of Commons and Knight are explored in Schweikhardt (1988).

11 It is important to realize that Weber was both a self-declared and acknowledged member of the German historical school. See Weber (1949: 106; 1978: 3) and Schumpeter (1954: 815–16). Although he is today labelled as a 'sociologist', in fact he was a professor of political economy, from 1894 at the University of Freiburg and in 1896 in the chair previously occupied by Knies at the University of Heidelberg.

12 Weber attempted to deal with the problem with his theory of "ideal types." The theory of ideal types is discussed at length in Commons (1934: 719–48). On the general problem of historical specificity see also Hodgson (forthcoming).

13 For an illuminating discussion of Parsons, including his relationship with Knight, Hamilton, and Ayres, see Camic (1991). See also Hodgson (forthcoming).

14 With apparent bitterness, Veblen declined the honour (Dorfman 1934: 491–92, 553).

15 Davenport accepted the nomination only because Veblen persuaded him to do so (Dorfman, 1934: 452). Davenport was also a pallbearer at Veblen's funeral (Dorfman 1934: 504).

16 In fact, what Robbins retained within economics alongside neoclassicism was just one strain of "Austrian" theory. As Endres (1997) has shown, "Austrians" such as Friedrich von Wieser and Eugen von Böhm-Bawerk saw it legitimate as economists to explore the formation of preferences, using insights from psychology if needed. Furthermore, they included endogenous preference changes precipitated by learning as part of their theory.

17 The formation of the Cowles Commission was decisive in the struggle between American institutionalism as a whole and the rising mathematical neoclassicism. Consider some of the personnel involved. Before Lange resigned from Chicago and Cowles in 1945, he arranged for J. Marschak to resume the Research Directorship at Cowles in place of T. Yntema in 1943. The future Nobel Laureate L. R. Klein was involved from 1944. Notably, Lange, Marschak, and Klein were socialists. At that time, even in Chicago, technocracy flew a red flag. The future Nobel Laureate T. Koopmans joined Cowles in 1944 and became its Research Director from 1948 to 1955. Von Neumann lectured on game theory at Cowles in 1945. L. Hurwicz and the future Nobel Laureate G. Debreu were also at Cowles.

18 Despite their differences, Ayres wrote in a letter to Charner Perry, dated 9 August, 1934: "I rather think that he [Knight] and I have a good deal more in common than my recent references would suggest" (quoted in Samuels 1977: 496).

19 I criticize the notion that neoclassical economics is adequately defined by its (allegedly promarket or other) policy stance in Hodgson (1999).

References

Archer, Margaret S. (1995) *Realist Social Theory: The Morphogenetic Approach,* Cambridge: Cambridge University Press.

Arrow, Kenneth J. (1951) "Alternative Approaches to the Theory of Choice in Risk-Taking Situations," *Econometrica* 19, 4: 404–37.

Ayres, Clarence E. (1935) "Moral Confusion in Economics," *International Journal of Ethics* 45, January: 170–99. Reprinted in Warren J. Samuels (1988) *Institutional Economics,* Vol. 2, Aldershot: Edward Elgar.

—— (1944) *The Theory of Economic Progress*, 1st edn., Chapel Hill, NC: University of North Carolina Press.

Bhaskar, Roy (1979) *The Possibility of Naturalism: A Philosophic Critique of the Contemporary Human Sciences*, Brighton: Harvester.

Boland, Lawrence A. (1981) "On the Futility of Criticizing the Neoclassical Maximization Hypothesis," *American Economic Review* 71: 1031–36. Reprinted in Lawrence A. Boland (1996) *Critical Economic Methodology: A Personal Odyssey*, London and New York: Routledge.

Boudreaux, D. J., and R. G. Holcombe (1989) "The Coasian and Knightian Theories of the Firm," *Managerial and Decision Economics* 10: 147–54.

Buchanan, James M. (1968) "Knight, Frank H.," *International Encyclopaedia of the Social Sciences,* Vol. 8: 424–28.

Camic, Charles (ed.) (1991) *Talcott Parsons: The Early Essays*, Chicago, IL: University of Chicago Press.

Colander, David C., and Harry Landreth (eds) (1996) *The Coming of Keynesianism to America: Conversations with the Founders of Keynesian Economics*, Aldershot: Edward Elgar.

Commons, John R. (1899–1900) "A Sociological View of Sovereignty," *American Journal of Sociology* 5, 1–3, 1899: 1–15, 155–71, 347–66; 5, 4–6, 1900: 544–52, 683–95, 814–25; 6, 1, 1900: 67–98. Reprinted as John R. Commons (1965) *A Sociological View of Sovereignty,* edited with an introduction by Joseph Dorfman, New York: Augustus Kelley.

—— (1931) "Institutional Economics," *American Economic Review* 21, 4: 648–57. Reprinted in Warren J. Samuels (ed.) (1988) *Institutional Economics*, Vol. 1, Aldershot: Edward Elgar.

—— (1934) *Institutional Economics – Its Place in Political Economy*, New York: Macmillan. Reprinted 1990 with a new introduction by M. Rutherford, New Brunswick, NJ: Transaction.

Degler, Carl N. (1991) *In Search of Human Nature: The Decline and Revival of Darwinism in American Social Thought*, Oxford and New York: Oxford University Press.

Dewey, John (1939) *Theory of Valuation*, Chicago, IL: University of Chicago Press.

Davis, J. Ronnie (1968) "Chicago Economists, Deficit Budgets, and the Early 1930s," *American Economic Review* 58, 3, Part 1: 476–82. Reprinted in Mark Blaug (ed.) (1992) *Frank Knight (1885–1972), Henry Simons (1899–1946), Joseph Schumpeter (1883–1950)*, Aldershot: Edward Elgar.

Dorfman, Joseph (1934) *Thorstein Veblen and His America*, New York: Viking Press. Reprinted 1961, New York: Augustus Kelley.

—— (1974) "Walton Hamilton and Industrial Policy" in Walton H. Hamilton (1974) *Industrial Policy and Institutionalism: Selected Essays*, with an introduction by Joseph Dorfman, New York: Augustus Kelley, 5–28.

Elster, Jon (1982) "Marxism, Functionalism and Game Theory," *Theory and Society* 11, 4: 453–82. Reprinted in John E. Roemer (ed.) (1986) *Analytical Marxism*, Cambridge: Cambridge University Press.

Endres, Anthony M. (1997) *Neoclassical Microeconomic Theory: The Founding Austrian Version*, London and New York: Routledge.

Epstein, R. J. (1987) *A History of Econometrics*, Amsterdam: North-Holland.

Giddens, Anthony (1984) *The Constitution of Society: Outline of the Theory of Structuration*, Cambridge: Polity Press.

Gonce, R. A. (1972) "Frank H. Knight on Social Control and the Scope and Method of Economics," *Southern Economic Journal* 38, 4: 547–58. Reprinted in Mark Blaug (ed.) (1992) *Frank Knight (1885–1972), Henry Simons (1899–1946), Joseph Schumpeter (1883–1950)*, Aldershot: Edward Elgar.

—— (1992) "F. H. Knight on Capitalism and Freedom," *Journal of Economic Issues* 26, 3: 813–44.

Hamilton, Walton H. (1919) "The Institutional Approach to Economic Theory," *American Economic Review* 9, Supplement: 309–18. Reprinted in Walton H. Hamilton (1974) *Industrial Policy and Institutionalism: Selected Essays*, with an introduction by Joseph Dorfman, New York: Augustus Kelley.

Hodgson, Geoffrey M. (1988) *Economics and Institutions: A Manifesto for a Modern Institutional Economics*, Cambridge and Philadelphia, PA: Polity Press and University of Pennsylvania Press.

—— (1997) "The Ubiquity of Habits and Rules," *Cambridge Journal of Economics* 21, 6: 663–84.

—— (1998) "Dichotomizing the Dichotomy: Veblen versus Ayres," in S. Fayazmanesh and M. Tool (eds) *Institutionalist Method and Value*, Cheltenham: Edward Elgar, 48–73.

—— (1999) *Evolution and Institutions: On Evolutionary Economics and the Evolution of Economics*, Cheltenham: Edward Elgar.

—— (forthcoming) *How Economics Forgot History: The Problem of Historical Specificity in Social Science*, London and New York: Routledge.

Knight, Frank H. (1917) "The Concept of Normal Price in Value and Distribution," *Quarterly Journal of Economics* 32: 66–100.

—— (1920) "Review of Thorstein Veblen, *The Place of Science in Modern Civilization*," *Journal of Political Economy* 28, 6: 518–20.

—— (1921a) *Risk, Uncertainty and Profit*, New York: Houghton Mifflin.

—— (1921b) "Discussion: Traditional Economic Theory," *American Economic Review* 11, Supplement: 143–46.

—— (1924) "The Limitations of Scientific Method in Economics," in Tugwell, Rexford G. (ed.) *The Trend of Economics*, New York: Alfred Knopf, 229–67. Reprinted in Frank H. Knight (1935b) *The Ethics of Competition and Other Essays*, New York: Harper.

—— (1931) "Relation of Utility Theory to Economic Method in the Work of William Stanley Jevons and Others," in Stuart A. Rice (ed.) *Methods in Social Science*, Chicago, IL: University of Chicago Press, 59–69.

—— (1933) "Preface to the Re-Issue," in *Risk, Uncertainty and Profit*, 2nd edn., London: London School of Economics, xi–xxxvi.

—— (1935a) "Intellectual Confusion on Morals and Economics," *International Journal of Ethics* 45, 1: 200–20.

—— (1935b) *The Ethics of Competition and Other Essays*, New York: Harper. Reprinted 1951, New York: Augustus Kelley.

—— (1936) Letter to Talcott Parsons, dated 1 May, 1936, Talcott Parsons Papers.

—— (1944) "Realism and Relevance in the Theory of Demand," *Journal of Political Economy* 52, 4: 289–318.

—— (1947) *Freedom and Reform: Essays in Economic and Social Philosophy*, New York: Harper and Brothers. Reprinted 1982 with a Foreword by J. M. Buchanan, Indianapolis: Liberty Press.

—— (1951) *The Economic Organization*, New York: Sentry Press. First published privately in 1933. Reprinted 1967, New York: Augustus Kelley.

—— (1952) "Institutionalism and Empiricism in Economics," *American Economic Review (Papers and Proceedings)* 42 (May): 45–55.

—— (1956) *On the History and Method of Economics*, Chicago, IL: University of Chicago Press.

—— (1957) "A New Look at Institutionalism: Discussion," *American Economic Review (Supplement)* 47, 2: 13–27.

—— (1961) "Methodology in Economics" Parts I and II, *Southern Economic Journal* 27, 3–4: 185–93, 273–82.

—— (1966) "Abstract Economics as Absolute Ethics," *Ethics* 76, 3: 163–77.

—— (1967) "Laissez-faire: Pro and Con," *Journal of Political Economy* 85, 6: 782–95.

Lachmann, Ludwig M. (1947) "Review of Knight, F. H. (1947) *Freedom and Reform*," *Economica* (November): 314–17.

—— (1969) "Methodological Individualism and the Market Economy," in Erich W. Streissler (ed.) *Roads to Freedom: Essays in Honour of Friedrich A. von Hayek*, London: Routledge and Kegan Paul, 89–103. Reprinted in Ludwig M. Lachmann (1977) *Capital, Expectations and the Market Process*, edited with an introduction by W. E. Grinder, Kansas City: Sheed Andrews and McMeel.

Lawson, Tony (1997) *Economics and Reality*, London: Routledge.

Lucas, Robert E., Jr (1981) *Studies in Business Cycle Theory*, Cambridge, MA, and Oxford: MIT Press and Basil Blackwell.

Marshall, Alfred (1949) *The Principles of Economics*, 8th (reset) edn. (1st edn. 1890), London: Macmillan.

McKinney, John (1977) "Frank Knight on Uncertainty and Rational Action," *Southern Economic Journal* 43, 4: 1438–52. Reprinted in Mark Blaug (ed.) (1992) *Frank Knight (1885–1972), Henry Simons (1899–1946), Joseph Schumpeter (1883–1950)*, Aldershot: Edward Elgar.

Mitchell, Wesley C. (1922) "Risk, Uncertainty, and Profit. A Review," *American Economic Review* 12: 274–75.

Morgan, Mary S. (1990) *The History of Econometric Ideas*, Cambridge: Cambridge University Press.

Nash, Stephen J. (1998) *Cost, Uncertainty, and Welfare: Frank Knight's Theory of Imperfect Competition*, Aldershot: Ashgate.

Reder, Melvin W. (1982) "Chicago Economics: Permanence and Change," *Journal of Economic Literature* 20, 1: 1–38. Reprinted in Caldwell (1984) and Mark Blaug (ed.) (1992) *Frank Knight (1885–1972), Henry Simons (1899–1946), Joseph Schumpeter (1883–1950)*, Aldershot: Edward Elgar.

Robbins, Lionel (1932) *An Essay on the Nature and Significance of Economic Science*, 1st edn., London: Macmillan.

Ross, Dorothy (1991) *The Origins of American Social Science*, Cambridge: Cambridge University Press.

Samuels, Warren J. (1977) "The Knight–Ayres Correspondence: The Grounds of Knowledge and Social Action," *Journal of Economic Issues* 11, 3: 485–525. Reprinted in Mark Blaug (ed.) (1992) *Wesley Mitchell (1874–1948), John Commons (1862–1945), Clarence Ayres (1891–1972)*, Aldershot: Edward Elgar.

—— (ed.) (1998) *The Founding of Institutional Economics*, London: Routledge.

Schweikhardt, David B. (1988) "The Role of Values in Economic Theory and Policy: A Comparison of Frank Knight and John R. Commons," *Journal of Economic Issues* 22, 2: 407–14. Reprinted in Mark Blaug (ed.) (1992) *Frank Knight*

(1885–1972), *Henry Simons (1899–1946)*, *Joseph Schumpeter (1883–1950)*, Aldershot: Edward Elgar.

Schweitzer, Arthur (1975) "Frank Knight's Social Economics," *History of Political Economy* 7, 3: 279–92. Reprinted in Mark Blaug (ed.) (1992) *Frank Knight (1885–1972)*, *Henry Simons (1899–1946)*, *Joseph Schumpeter (1883–1950)*, Aldershot: Edward Elgar.

Schumpeter, Joseph A. (1954) *History of Economic Analysis*, New York: Oxford University Press.

Seckler, David (1975) *Thorstein Veblen and the Institutionalists: A Study in the Social Philosophy of Economics*, London: Macmillan.

Veblen, Thorstein B. (1899) *The Theory of the Leisure Class: An Economic Study in the Evolution of Institutions*, New York: Macmillan. Republished 1961, New York: Random House.

—— (1914) *The Instinct of Workmanship, and the State of the Industrial Arts*, New York: Macmillan. Reprinted 1990 with a new introduction by Murray G. Murphey and a 1964 introductory note by J. Dorfman, New Brunswick, NJ: Transaction.

—— (1919) *The Place of Science in Modern Civilisation and Other Essays*, New York: Huebsch. Reprinted 1990 with a new introduction by Warren J. Samuels, New Brunswick, NJ: Transaction.

Weber, Max (1927) *General Economic History*, trans. by Frank H. Knight, London: Allen and Unwin.

—— (1949) *Max Weber on the Methodology of the Social Sciences*, trans. and ed. by Edward A. Shils and Henry A. Finch, Glencoe, IL: Free Press.

—— (1978) *Max Weber: Selections in Translation*, edited and introduced by W. G. Runciman, Cambridge: Cambridge University Press.

Wicksteed, Philip H. (1933) *The Commonsense of Political Economy*, ed. Lionel Robbins, 1st edn. 1910, London: George Routledge.

Yonay, Yuval P. (1998) *The Struggle Over the Soul of Economics: Institutionalist and Neoclassical Economists in America Between the Wars*, Princeton, NJ: Princeton University Press.

4 From divergence to convergence

Irving Fisher and John R. Commons as champions of monetary reforms

William J. Barber

Irving Fisher and John R. Commons brought distinctly different perspectives to their treatments of economic issues. Fisher took pride in his pioneering work in mathematical economics, in his contributions to formal theorizing (especially in his formulation of the theory of capital and interest), and in his efforts to promote econometrics. By contrast, Commons's brand of institutionalism was dedicated to hands-on investigations into components of the economic universe set within a particular social and legal context. He eschewed higher mathematics and was more than a little suspicious of the claims advanced by practitioners of abstract theorizing. And yet – despite profound differences in their respective approaches to the discipline – Fisher and Commons were to form a working partnership as advocates of monetary reforms. This chapter is concerned with the conditions permitting that convergence to come about and with what this story tells us about the state of the profession in America in the interwar years.

Aspects of divergent orientations, pre-World War I

In the first decade of the twentieth century, published exchanges between the two men provided ample evidence of conceptual dissonance. These commentaries were prompted by the publication of Fisher's *The Nature of Capital and Income* in 1906. In this work, Fisher had been at pains to demonstrate that the value of capital was established by the discounted value of the income stream that the asset was expected to generate. This proposition might nowadays be accepted as non-controversial. But that was not the case in the early years of the twentieth century. Fisher's concentration on the valuation of an income-yielding asset amounted to saying that the standard categorization of productive factors – that is, the land, labor, and capital triad – was artificial and unhelpful: after all, the same procedure for capitalizing the value of the income stream could be applied to any of them. Fisher was provocative for other reasons as well. His insistence that income should be defined as consumption – thus excluding saving – was at odds with conventional wisdom both then and now.

When reviewing *The Nature of Capital and Income* in the *Quarterly Journal of Economics*, Commons took issue with Fisher on a number of grounds. In the first instance, he maintained that what Fisher had produced should properly be identified as "business economy," not "political economy." Fisher had focused on the mechanisms determining asset valuations through the interplay of private interests and had not addressed their implications for society's welfare. Commons left his readers in no doubt about where his sympathies lay. The older practitioners of "political economy," as he put it, "were working on a serious social problem – that of earned and unearned incomes." But this problem was no longer on the agenda in works of "business economy" such as Fisher's.[1]

Commons conceded that Fisher may have "perfected this theory of capital value" within the framework of business economy, but he detected an oddity in the timing of this achievement. "A system of social philosophy," he wrote, "seems to reach abstract perfection just after society has begun to knock out its props." The prop-smashing he had in mind was observable in the work of legislatures and courts – institutions that were involved with regulatory rate-making for public utilities. For these purposes, conceptions of "reasonable income" and "reasonable value of the property" were pertinent. As Commons saw matters, the "common sense" approach to asset valuation was based on "its cost of reproduction, less depreciation, plus its value 'as a going concern'; that is, the labor, sacrifice and effort required to construct the property and build up the business."[2] This was self-evidently quite different from Fisher's procedure which rested on the capitalization of the income stream anticipated in the future.

Commons had a further difficulty with the conception of property that Fisher had used in his work. He held that Fisher was on solid ground when defining property as the "right" to future services associated with ownership. But this attribute of property – the "inclusive" one, in Commons's terminology – told only part of the story. There was also an "exclusive" attribute: i.e., "the right to withhold services and to prevent them from materializing." In Commons's view, the "exclusive" attribute "was the all-important half of property from the business standpoint." When a property owner exercised this right, it was conceivable that capital value could be increased when outputs were suppressed or prohibited. (Fisher had illustrated this point by citing the case of a paper manufacturer near New Haven who was offered "a round sum if he would close his mills. This he did, to the benefit of both himself and his former rivals, though not of the public. In this case the contract which he made with his rivals constituted a kind of property for them; the wealth by *means* of which his promise was made good was evidently his own person, together with his plant; and the service performed was the inactivity of both.")[3] Commons was discomfited by a line of analysis in which such anti-social behavior was rewarded.[4]

Fisher did not respond directly to all of the criticisms Commons had levelled. He took serious issue, however, with the manner in which Commons had interpreted the distinction between "political economy" and "business economy" and with the suggestion that Fisher was indifferent to the implications of private market behavior for society's welfare. "The truth is," he wrote, "that market valuation seldom, if ever, exactly registers utility to society." Thus, he observed: "The capital invested in a blackmailing newspaper, in a counterfeiting establishment, in a shop for the manufacture of burglar's tools, in a bureau for the corruption of legislatures, in an opium den, or in other enterprises injurious to society, will always be capital so long as it renders its 'services' to the owners who benefit thereby." Fisher did not wish to minimize the importance of divergences between private and social costs and benefits, and the need for public intervention to address them. He had chosen not to focus on these matters initially and had instead assigned priority to analyzing the "causes which actually determine market valuations." Consideration of potential remedies should come later. He set out his view of correct procedure as follows: "The proper place for the study of social pathology and therapeutics seems to me to be at the end and not at the beginning of economic analysis. We shall reach sounder conclusions in regard to the best remedies to be applied to social conditions if first we study these conditions exactly as they are and not as we should prefer to have them."[5]

Fisher and Commons clearly did not have common tastes with regard to the choice of analytic techniques, nor did they share an understanding of the appropriate positioning of positive economics *vis-à-vis* normative economics. At the same time, they had one trait in common: both argued that state intervention, when correctly applied, could enhance economic performance and the general welfare. Commons acted on this conviction as the principal architect of path-breaking initiatives in the regulation of railroads and public utilities, as well as in the creation of a workman's compensation program, in the heyday of Wisconsin Progressivism. For his part, Fisher had laid out his personal credo in an address to the American Association for the Advancement of Science, entitled "Why Has the Doctrine of Laissez Faire Been Abandoned?", which appeared in 1907.[6] He then found two premises underlying the doctrine of laissez-faire to be flawed. In the first instance, the view that individuals were always the best judges of their own interest was mistaken: this was certainly not true, for example, in the case of the drunkard. There was thus a valid rationale for restraint of the liquor traffic. Similar lines of argument justified "restraint of gambling, vice, the suppression of indecent literature, the compulsion upon landlords to make tenements sanitary . . ."[7] Secondly, the proposition that activity benefiting individuals simultaneously benefited society required modification. Negative externalities – Fisher cited air and water pollution as examples – needed to be corrected through governmental intervention. By 1907, Fisher was persuaded that propounding such arguments from the ivory tower was not sufficient. He then became the prime mover in forming a Committee of One Hundred which was to campaign publicly for the creation of a Federal Department of Health that would be charged to establish minimum public health standards and to enforce them. This was only the first of many instances of Fisher's organizational entrepreneurship in the promotion of good causes.

Working in tandem on monetary matters in the 1920s

Despite differences in their primary substantive concerns within economics, the paths of Fisher and Commons intersected at a number of points during the World War I period. Both were active in the work of the American Association for Labor Legislation and in the American Economic Association. (Commons served as the AEA president in 1917, and Fisher succeeded him in 1918.) Their shared reformist temperament brought them even closer in 1921. With Fisher's leadership, the Stable Money League was then formed to campaign for policies to stabilize the general price level. Commons joined this movement and became the League's second president in 1922. He continued to serve this cause through his active participation in successor organizations: Commons was the first and only president of the National Monetary Association which carried the banner for price-level stabilization in 1923–24 and he remained a committed member of its follow-up organization – the Stable Money Association – which came into being in 1925.

Though Fisher and Commons worked to promote the same objective, they came to it from opposite directions. Fisher was no stranger to monetary matters. For virtually his entire professional career, he had assigned major attention to study of connections between changes in the money supply and variations in the price level. In the mid-1890s, he had first addressed this issue in writings about the economics of bimetallism. This line of inquiry was sustained with the publication of his *Purchasing Power of Money* in 1911. That work was initially conceived as an analysis of the quantity theory of money and its empirical validation. Fisher's findings seemingly demonstrated that proportionate changes in the price level followed from changes in the money supply in the state he characterized as "normal": that is, when the volume of transactions and velocity of monetary circulation were given.[8] In addition, he argued that changes in the purchasing power of money – whether brought about by inflationary or deflationary circumstances – were mischievous because of their perverse impacts on the respective well-being of creditors and debtors. To eliminate such distributive injustices, he proposed a scheme for a "compensated dollar": under its terms, any deviation in the general price level would be offset by varying the gold content of the dollar. He was to be an active promoter of this monetary reform for the next decade.

Commons's interest in matters of money and banking came later and was prompted by decidedly different considerations. He spoke to this matter in testimony before the Committee on Banking and Currency of the House of Representatives when he observed that he was "not an expert in banking" and that his "interest was mainly in labor." He had, however, become "acquainted with the evils due to the fluctuation of prices in 1919." Indeed, he had come to regard the fluctuation of prices "as the most serious of the evils that affect labor in this country." Inflation – such as had occurred immediately after World War I – "demoralizes labor" because workers "lose all sense of responsibility for their jobs." What he had in mind here was the situation of a tight labor market, induced by inflationary pressures, in which workers abandoned their employers to take higher-paying jobs elsewhere. But this was an unstable set of circumstances. When inflation was tamed and a deflationary environment followed, the same laborers would find themselves unemployed. Thus, the demoralization of labor would lead to the "pauperization" of labor.[9] Workers thus had an obvious stake in eliminating such a "boom–bust" cycle.

As his thinking matured on this topic, Commons argued that labor had an interest in price stabilization for yet another reason. By the later 1920s, he believed that increased outputs – fed by productivity increases – would grow faster than the increase in the world's supply of monetary gold. Accordingly, downward pressure on the general price level could be expected, unless deliberate measures were taken to prevent it. Commons set out the significance of this matter as follows:

> [L]ook at the employers as a class. Say they, as a class, increase their efficiency by 10 percent. At the same time the price level falls by 10 percent. What reward is there for their efficiency as a class? . . . But, if on the other hand, the price level remains stable, then they get the difference between . . . this constant price level, and the reduction of the cost which they have made. That is their efficiency earnings; that is a real earning, or income, to which they are entitled. It benefits the community. Furthermore, it benefits the wage earner, because his employer is more likely to be willing to advance his wages if he is making more profits.[10]

Throughout his career, Commons was usually disposed to defer to Fisher's expertise on questions of monetary theory and policy. With regard to one important matter, however, Commons could correctly claim priority. He remarked in his autobiography that he had "never had the opportunity to study the money problem in the banks as [he] had studied the labor problem in the factories," but that he "had read Fisher's and Wicksell's theories and plans."[11] He got his chance for an insider's look at central banking in 1922. This came about as a by-product of his presidency of the National Monetary Association. Governor Benjamin Strong then gave him privileged access to the inner workings of the Federal Reserve Bank of New York. This coincided with the discovery – virtually by accident – of the impact of the central bank's purchases and/or sales of government securities on the reserves of member banks. This insight into the potency of open-market operations was genuinely novel. Commons, so to speak, was "present at the creation" and he was the first to direct the attention of economists to this phenomenon.[12]

Fisher was quick to appreciate the significance of open-market operations and to assimilate this finding into his schemes for monetary reform. In the version of a price stabilization bill that he supported in 1926, for example, the

Federal Reserve's ability to alter the lending capacity of commercial banks through the use of this technique was identified as the primary instrument of monetary control. He then noted that "today it is the volume of credit that determines the purchasing power of the dollar – the price level – more than the volume of gold." Even so, he did not abandon altogether the position he had taken when advancing his "compensated dollar" plan. He still insisted that "you have got to have your gold control as well as your credit control, if you are going to prevent the terrible evils of inflation and deflation in the future."[13] He held that the Federal Reserve's stabilizing role might be compromised unless discretionary authority to alter the gold content of the dollar were available. At one extreme, the system's capacity to fight deflation could be immobilized because of its legal obligation to maintain at least a 40 percent gold backing for the Federal Reserve note issue. It was at least conceivable that expansionary policies might be blocked because the entire gold stock was committed to satisfying that requirement. (In the United States in the spring of 1932, this was not just a hypothetical situation – it was real.) Nor, at the other extreme, could success of a counter-inflationary policy be assured when gold reserves were abundant. The Federal Reserve's ability to make the open-market sales called for in that situation presupposed that it had a portfolio to trade with: if it were obliged to sell all its securities, its "ammunition" would be exhausted. (In 1926, Fisher believed that this state of affairs might be in prospect.)

By the mid-1920s, there was a mutation in Fisher's view concerning the evils associated with price level instability. It was no longer primarily a matter of distributive injustices. The analyses that he had produced by this time indicated that changes in the general price-level typically preceded changes in the volume of trade by seven months or so. This insight had a clear implication for policy: that is, that the way to stabilize economic activity was to stabilize the general price level. Monetary policy, properly conducted, could thus eliminate the phenomenon of the business cycle.[14] The evils associated with fluctuations in the volume of production and employment need no longer be tolerated. On this point, Commons and Fisher were on the same wave length.

Fisher and Commons took turns as star witnesses before Congressional committees considering enactment of legislation directing the Federal Reserve to stabilize the general price level in 1926 and 1927. And they brought the same message. Indeed, there was considerable overlap in their use of language when presenting the case for the necessity of this action: in the absence of a specific Congressional directive to guide it, the Federal Reserve would fail to discharge what they saw as its proper duty. These appeals notwithstanding, the legislative stipulation they sought went nowhere. In the public discussion of this issue, considerable skepticism was expressed by central bankers about their ability to reach a specified price-level target. At least when the system was armed with discretionary authority to vary the price of gold, Fisher and Commons entertained no doubts that the Federal Reserve had the tools to do the job. What was needed was the will to use them and instruction from Congress to do so.

Readjusting sights with the onset of depression

Fisher and Commons had nothing to show for their efforts to persuade Congress to mandate the Federal Reserve to stabilize the general price level. Not surprisingly, the stock market crash of late 1929 (and the economic events that followed) produced a radically changed environment for the discussion of monetary issues. The course of events also called for fundamental rethinking of the analytic props that informed recommendations on monetary policy. For Fisher, this was a matter of urgency and embarrassment. His remarks in September and October 1929 – when he had predicted the continuation of "new era" prosperity – had come back to haunt him. The subsequent behavior of the stock market both damaged his professional reputation and destroyed his personal financial solvency.

In late 1932 – in his presidential address to the American Statistical Association – Fisher offered an account of why his prognostications in the late 1920s had been so drastically wrong:

> I did not know then certain scientific laws and I did not know, as well as I should, the historical background of conditions. For instance, I had counted on the continuance of the open market policy of Benjamin Strong of the Federal Reserve Bank of New York, not knowing that these had largely died with Governor Strong the year before. As to the laws governing depressions, I did not then know, what since I have learned and embodied in my book *Booms and Depressions*, the important role of over-indebtedness and its tendency to break down the price level through distress selling, contraction of deposit currency, and slackening of its velocity.[15]

When making these remarks, Fisher was convinced that his newly conceived "debt-deflation theory of Great Depressions" explained the catastrophe that had befallen the American economy. The perspective offered by this line of analysis indicated that deflationary shocks had no built-in self-correcting properties. Deflation simply generated more deflation. Bankruptcies and shrinking profits led to reductions in output and employment. These circumstances bred pessimism, hoarding, and further slowdown in monetary circulation. The remedy was implicit in the diagnosis: "reflating the price level up to the average level at which outstanding debts were contracted by existing debtors and assumed by existing creditors, and then maintaining that level unchanged."[16]

Commons applauded Fisher's *Booms and Depressions*. In his *Institutional Economics* (first published in 1934), he wrote: "This book is the most important yet published on the subject. It enables us greatly to reduce our discussion by referring the reader to it."[17] In 1934 Commons also spoke approvingly of a "transition" in Fisher's perspective that he detected in *Booms and Depressions*. The thought of the Fisher of the "compensated dollar" had been rooted in the tradition of the quantity theory of money. "But in 1932," Commons wrote, "he took account of the interacting network of many causal factors influencing price stabilization policies, such as the magnitude of debts, debt liquidation, distress selling, fall in commodity prices, changes in net worth (bankruptcies), decrease in profits or increase in losses, reductions or increases in stock market speculation or in construction, output, trade or unemployment, pessimism and optimism, hoarding and like phenomena."[18] For his part, Fisher made his high regard for Commons a matter of public record by naming him among a select handful of men who thoroughly understood money.[19]

Collaboration in a time of crisis

By 1932, "stabilization" was no longer the rallying cry – "reflation" had replaced it. Fisher and Commons made no headway in pressing this cause on President Hoover. Matters changed with the election of Franklin D. Roosevelt in November 1932 and with the financial paralysis that gripped the nation in the weeks preceding Roosevelt's inauguration as President on 4 March, 1933.

In an exchange of telegrams on 5 March, 1933, Fisher and Commons agreed that the gravity of the situation required unprecedented interventions. Commons proposed that the two of them – along with George F. Warren of Cornell – should dispatch an open letter to Roosevelt recommending the following emergency actions:

(1) immediate suspension of all gold payments and all gold contracts; (2) government insurance of all bank deposits; (3) immediate full legal tender status of Federal Reserve and Treasury notes; (4) reduction in the gold content of the dollar by one-third; (5) an increase in the appropriation of the Reconstruction Finance Corporation to $10 billion to be released to business and agriculture; (6) declaration of an end to the emergency when the 1926 price level had been restored, or when international agreement had been reached on an international standard.[20]

Fisher replied that he had already made "the same suggestions and others" to Roosevelt and that he was "optimistic about speedy reflation."[21] One of the "other" suggestions Fisher alluded to here was his proposal that the government issue what he called "stamped scrip." This would be a special note issue that would retain its full value only when a 2-cent stamp was affixed to it each week. In Fisher's view, this would stimulate the velocity of monetary circulation and raise revenue to fund relief for the unemployed. Commons did not share Fisher's enthusiasm for the scheme.[22]

Commons and Fisher could draw some satisfaction from policies adopted by the Roosevelt administration during the first year of the New Deal. On 6 March, 1933, Roosevelt – by executive order – suspended internal gold payments when declaring a bank holiday. This was supplemented by an executive order of 5 April, 1933, outlawing private holdings of monetary gold. The administration also acted to rebuild confidence in the banking system by sponsoring legislation to establish a program of Federal insurance for bank deposits. In addition, it raised the dollar price of gold (thus reducing the gold content of the dollar). All of these measures were compatible with the Fisher–Commons script.

Nonetheless, Fisher was disappointed that Roosevelt had not pushed the reflationary program more aggressively and he frequently advised the White House to that effect. (On one such occasion, Fisher recommended the appointment of Commons – "if in vigorous health" – to administer "reflation."[23]) By late 1934, Fisher was convinced that an effective program of reflation of the price level to its mid-1920s elevation – to be followed by stabilization – required a radical overhaul of the nation's banking system. He then endorsed a reform which would oblige commercial banks to hold 100 percent reserves against their demand deposits. It was outrageous, he argued, that the bulk of the country's money supply could be created (or destroyed) through the activities of profit-seeking bankers when deciding to extend (or to call) loans. The analysis he offered at this time tracked the root cause of price instability – and, hence, instability of income and employment – to this structural fault in the banking system. Control of the money supply was properly a public function and should be exclusively in the hands of a public authority. This result could be achieved through a two-step program. Step 1 was the conversion to 100 percent reserves which would strip private bankers of powers to create or destroy money. Step 2 was the establishment of a body – to be designated as a "Currency Commission" or "Monetary Authority" – which would be charged to expand the money supply sufficiently to reach the reflationary target and, subsequently, to vary the money supply as needed to stabilize the general price level.

Fisher did not invent the idea of 100 percent reserves. He did, however, pour abundant activist energies into promoting it. When doing so, he regarded Commons as a partner in the joint enterprise. Both men put their weight behind efforts to win support for this monetary reform among professional economists. They reported the results of this effort in a "Memorial to Congress" in January 1941 (at a time when the Federal Reserve Board was recommending increases in the required reserve ratios of commercial banks):

> Our program for Monetary Reform, endorsed already by 343 economists (with 50 others who approve with reservations) is enclosed. It would give the [Federal Reserve] Board (or other Monetary Authority, as Congress may prefer) full control over the volume of our money (including "check-book money") and, unlike the Board's temporizing plan,

would do so without hardship to the banks. Best of all, it would do so under a definite stabilization mandate prescribed by Congress. It aims at full employment of men, machines, and money, while maintaining our American system of free enterprise.[24]

As with other legislation they had proposed over nearly two decades of lobbying for price stabilization, this proposal was a non-starter.

A closing word

In their approaches to how economic analysis should be done, Fisher and Commons worked on opposite sides of the street. The gap that separated them over the discussion of Fisher's *The Nature of Capital and Income* in 1907–09 was never really bridged. Commons returned to this theme in his *Institutional Economics* in 1934. He continued to cavil over the feature of Fisher's theoretical construct which permitted the market's valuation of capital to increase when services were withheld. The Commons of 1934 attacked this point with some of the same language he had used in 1907.[25] But divergences at this level of theorizing proved not to be impediments to their collaboration as promoters of monetary reform.

The reformers' engagement with the "real world" was the point at which they could converge. This did not mean that they arrived at that destination by the same route. Commons always insisted that his concerns for price stabilization were motivated by the stake he saw in this outcome for the well-being of workers, whereas Fisher had chosen to focus on this problem because of its implications for distributive justice and for the maintenance of income and employment. Nor did it follow that they subscribed jointly to all the details of specific monetary reform proposals. (Commons, for example, was never enamored with Fisher's enthusiasm for the "compensated dollar" or for "stamped scrip.") They did share a view of the goal to be reached and of the ways to get there. For them, economics was not an intellectual exercise that could be justified for its own sake. Economists instead had a moral obligation to advance the community's welfare. For this purpose, life in the ivory tower was not good enough. They should instead feel honor-bound to expose themselves to the rough and tumble of practical policy making.

This sense of social mission was one of the distinctive attributes of many of the leaders of the American economics profession in the interwar years. Temperamental commonality on this point was quite capable of producing combined energies at the practical level and, in turn, overriding differences in preferences with regard to analytic style. There is an indication here as well that the history of this period is not well written if it turns on sharp and irreconcilable distinctions between competing "schools." The reality is far less black and white. Fisher spoke to this feature of the intellectual climate in his Presidential address to the American Economic Association in December

1918. He then called attention to a duality in the heritage of the American economics profession. The AEA, he reminded his audience, had been born in a struggle between two types of economics. The "new schoolers" – most of whom had been exposed to the German historical school – were eager to promote social and economic reforms, but typically held abstract theorizing at arm's length. The "old schoolers," by contrast, identified with theorizing in the British tradition and were suspicious toward governmental intervention in economic affairs. The next generation of American economists, Fisher maintained, should be able to find common ground by recognizing the role of formal analysis in identifying economic problems and their principal attributes, while simultaneously recognizing that economists had a vital social contribution to make in problem solving.[26]

Notes

1 John R. Commons, "Political Economy and Business Economy: Comments on Fisher's Capital and Income," *Quarterly Journal of Economics* (November 1907): 120–25.
2 Ibid., 1.
3 Irving Fisher, *The Nature of Capital and Income*, New York: Macmillan, 1906, 28.
4 Ibid., 122–23.
5 Fisher, "A Reply to Critics," *Quarterly Journal of Economics* (May 1909): 536–41.
6 The text of this address was first published in *Science*, 4 January, 1907. It has been reprinted in *The Works of Irving Fisher*, William J. Barber, General Editor, London: Pickering and Chatto, 1997, Vol. III, 504–13.
7 Ibid., 506.
8 Fisher's choice of terms here was to be a source of much confusion. His conception of the "normal" was that of an equilibrium – a situation which was not all that frequently realized in the real world. The more standard situations were the "transitional" periods when a strict relationship between the money supply and the behavior of the general price level did not hold. Commons, Testimony before the Committee on Banking and Currency, House of Representatives, 4 February, 1927, 1074–75.
9 Commons, Testimony before the Committee on Banking and Currency, House of Representatives, 21 March, 1928, 82.
10 Commons, Testimony before the Committee on Banking and Currency, House of Representatives, 21 March, 1928, 82.
11 Commons, *Myself: The Autobiography of John R. Commons*, Madison, WI: University of Wisconsin Press, 1964, 190.
12 Commons commented as follows about this episode in his autobiography: "Curiously enough, though I was a late comer in the field of banking, I was, in December 1924, the first to expound to economists at the American Economic Association the principles of control of the money market by the central bank through buying and selling securities on the open market at current prices . . . I understood it because Benjamin Strong and his assistants in the bank had explained it to me." (Ibid., 192–93).
13 Fisher, Testimony before the Committee on Banking and Currency, House of Representatives, 26 March, 1926.
14 This was the central message of Fisher, "The Business Cycle Largely a 'Dance of the Dollar,'" *Journal of the American Statistical Association*, December 1923 and Fisher, "Our Unstable Dollar and the So-Called Business Cycle," *Journal of the American Statistical Association*, June 1925.
15 Fisher, "Statistics in the Service of Economics," *Journal of the American Statistical Association* (March 1933): 9–10.

16 Fisher, Testimony before the Committee on Ways and Means, House of Representatives, 19 May 1933.
17 Commons, *Institutional Economics*, Vol. I with a new introduction by Malcolm Rutherford, New Brunswick, NJ: Transaction, 1990, 608.
18 Commons, "Price Stabilization," article in the *Encyclopaedia of Social Sciences*, Vol. 12, Edwin R. A. Seligman (ed.) New York: Macmillan, 1934, 364.
19 Others on Fisher's list of those "who understand the real meaning of money" were: Harry G. Brown (University of Missouri); G. F. Warren and F. A. Pearson (Cornell); James Harvey Rogers (Yale); Willford I. King (New York University); Warren M. Persons (Standard Statistics Co., New York); Edwin W. Kemmerer (Princeton); Cyril James (University of Pennsylvania); John H. Williams (Harvard); and Jacob Viner (University of Chicago). A number of foreigners were added to the list of academic monetary economists: Keynes (England); Cassel (Sweden); Frisch (Norway); and Schulz-Gaevernitz (Germany). Fisher had compiled this list at the invitation of the president of the Consumers Guild of America, who proceeded to publish it. See the discussion of this point in *The Works of Irving Fisher*, Vol. 14, 118–20.
20 Telegram from Commons to Fisher, 5 March, 1933, as reported in *The Works of Irving Fisher*, Vol. 14, 55–56.
21 Telegram from Fisher to Commons, 5 March, 1933, as reported in ibid., 56.
22 The idea of "stamped scrip," it should be noted, was not original to Fisher. He had borrowed it from Silvio Gesell, a German businessman operating in Argentina, who had proposed it in the 1890s.
23 Fisher to Roosevelt, 13 May, 1933, Franklin D. Roosevelt Presidential Library.
24 Joining Fisher and Commons as signatories of this "Memorial to Congress" were Earl J. Hamilton, Frank D. Graham, Willford I. King, and C. R. Whittlesey.
25 It was a contradiction, he argued, to hold that "a paper mill yields the 'services of wealth' when it is making paper and when it is not making paper" (Commons, *Institutional Economics*, 257). He also took note of Fisher's response to this criticism in 1909: i.e., that his analysis was concerned with identifying the causes of market valuation, not with "social pathology and therapeutics." "But," the Commons of 1934 added, "we are here considering the need of therapeutics" (257n.).
26 Fisher, "Economists in Public Service," *American Economic Review* (March 1919) (reprinted in *The Works*, Vol. 13, 5–18).

References

Commons, John R. (1907) "Political Economy and Business Economy: Comments on Irving Fisher's Capital and Income," *Quarterly Journal of Economics* 22: 120–25.
—— (1927) Testimony before the Committee on Banking and Currency, House of Representatives, 69: 2, 4 February.
—— (1928) Testimony before the Committee on Banking and Currency, House of Representatives, 70: 1, 21 March.
—— (1934a) *Institutional Economics*, New York: Macmillan. Reissued with an introduction by Malcolm Rutherford (1990) New Brunswick, NJ: Transaction Publishers.
—— (1934b) *Myself: The Autobiography of John R. Commons*, New York: Macmillan. Reissued (1963) Madison: University of Wisconsin Press.
—— (1934c) "Price Stabilization," *Encyclopedia of the Social Sciences*, Vol. 12, Edwin R. A. Seligman (ed.), New York: Macmillan, 362–65.
Fisher, Irving (1906) *The Nature of Capital and Income*, New York: Macmillan.

—— (1907) "Why has the Doctrine of Laissez Faire Been Abandoned?" *Science* n.s. XXV, 627 (4 January): 18–27.

—— (1909) "A Reply to Critics," *Quarterly Journal of Economics* 23: 536–41.

—— (1919) "Economists in Public Service," *American Economic Review Supplement* IX: 5–21.

—— (1923) "The Business Cycle Largely a 'Dance of the Dollar,'" *Journal of the American Statistical Association* 18: 1024–28.

—— (1925) "Our Unstable Dollar and the So-Called Business Cycle," *Journal of the American Statistical Association* 20: 179–202.

—— (1926) Testimony Before the Committee on Banking and Currency, House of Representatives, 69: 1, 26 March.

—— (1932) *Booms and Depressions*, New York: Adelphi Company.

—— (1997) *The Works of Irving Fisher*, 14 vols., William J. Barber (general ed.), London: Pickering and Chatto.

5 E. H. Chamberlin

Oligopoly and oligopolistic interdependence: the issue of space*

Andrew Skinner

Introduction

The late 1920s and early 1930s saw considerable activity amongst economists concerned with competitive structures and the "firm." Much of this work may be interpreted as an attack on Marshall's treatment of the subject with a view to replacing it by a more "rigorous" and formal analysis. But E. H. Chamberlin to a very large extent stands apart from these developments, as he makes plain in the "Origin and Early Development of Monopolistic Competition Theory" (1961). Serious work on his thesis apparently began in 1924, was largely completed in 1926, and the study filed in the following year. This means, for example, that Chamberlin's "discovery" of the curves of marginal cost and marginal revenue was made quite independently of his English and German colleagues. Further, as Chamberlin himself made clear, "Nor did the Book itself attack Marshall . . . on any of the issues involved" (ibid.: 532). Indeed, he always insisted that his work was an attack "not on Marshall but on the theory of perfect competition" (ibid.: 540). He might have added that *Monopolistic Competition* is essentially Marshallian both in its style of reasoning and in the preoccupation with realism; a preoccupation which led Chamberlin to play down the operational significance of the marginal curves while recognizing their importance in a technical sense (1957: 274–76).

---

* The argument of this chapter is based upon, but does not replace, analyses contained in previous attempts to deal with Chamberlin's *Monopolistic Competition*. They include "Oligopoly and the Theory of the Firm" (with M. C. Maclennan) in *Economic Analysis in Historical Perspective*, ed. D. P. O'Brien and J. Creedy (London: Butterworths, 1984). "The Origins and Development of Monopolistic Competition" and "Edward Chamberlin: The Theory of Monopolistic Competition: A Re-Orientation of the Theory of Value," both in the *Journal of Economic Studies*, ed. F. H. Stephen, Vol. 10 (1983): 52–67 and Vol. 13 (1986): 27–44. The present version of the argument is prompted by a reading of Chamberlin's original thesis, and by an invitation to contribute to a volume in honour of a notable "institutionalist."

The chapter contains an abridgement and rearrangement of the materials published in the *Journal of Economic Studies* with a view to emphasizing Chamberlin's interest in the issue of the spatial distribution of customers and firms, while also serving as an introduction to a section of the original thesis, here reproduced as an appendix.

In contrast to the origins of Joan Robinson's *Imperfect Competition*, Chamberlin cited three empirical sources of inspiration. First, the "Taussig–Pigou controversy as to whether charging what the market will bear in railway rates was to be explained in terms of monopolistic discrimination or in terms of joint costs" (1961: 517). Secondly, he drew attention to the "literature of business" and especially to the stimulus provided by Allyn Young. As Chamberlin recalled, Young had given particular attention to trade marks and patents insofar as they conferred a monopoly power which is also consistent with competition: "Each makes a product unique in certain respects; this is its monopolistic aspect. Each leaves room for other commodities almost but not quite like it; this is its competitive aspect" (quoted by Chamberlin, ibid.: 525). For Chamberlin, this perspective "became the key to the whole analysis" (ibid.: 526); a new "way of looking at the economic process" (1948: 204).

A third source of stimulus was located in "business economics" with special reference to advertising and the operation of retail markets (1961: 529). Here, Chamberlin drew attention to Pigou's perception that advertising was *peculiar* to what was in effect monopolistic competition, and to Marshall's distinction between "constructive" and "combative" advertising.

II

Chamberlin's main interest was in that situation where the pairing of buyers and sellers was no longer random: that is, where goods are differentiated in the mind of the consumer. Here, the firm may control price, product specification, and selling costs where the latter are "incurred to alter the position or shape of the demand curve" (1948: 117). The problems which are exposed by such a perspective are wide ranging so that it is important to note that Chamberlin concerned himself *at the outset* almost solely with *intra-* rather *inter*-industry competition and that he retained something very like the Marshallian industry in so doing. As he put it: "The group contemplated initially is one which has *ordinarily* been regarded as composing one imperfectly competitive market: a number of automobile manufacturers, or producers of pots and pans, magazine publishers, or of retail shoe dealers" (ibid.: 81). Even this restricted perspective, however, meant that the technical apparatus had to be altered as compared to the treatment of pure competition. The firm now has a choice of cost curve arising from the capacity to alter product specification (ibid.: 94–100), while in addition selling costs have to be added to costs of production. Chamberlin thought that it would be difficult to generalize about the curve of selling costs since its shape would be affected by the nature of the product, the level of planned expenditure, and the choice of media, but gave it a "U" shape in both the short and long run (ibid.: 133–35, 138).

Perhaps the most important innovation resulted from Chamberlin's appreciation of the point that: "A monopoly of Lucky Strikes does not constitute a monopoly of cigarettes, for there is no degree of control whatever over the supply of other substitute brands" (ibid.: 65). He thus introduced *two* revenue curves. The DD curve is defined as the fractional part of the Market Demand curve (e.g., for cigarettes) and "shows the demand for the product of any one seller at various prices on the assumption that his competitors' prices are always identical with his" (ibid.: 90). In contrast, the dd curve provides "a rough index of buyers' preferences for the product of one seller over that of another" (ibid.: 93) and indicates the "increase in sales which he could realise by cutting his price *provided* others did not also cut theirs" (ibid.: 90). In the context of the large group, the relatively elastic (as compared to DD) dd curve is relevant since it is legitimate to assume that any adjustment "by a single producer spreads its influence over so many of his competitors that the impact felt by any one of them is negligible" (ibid.: 83) – that is, the *diffusion* effect.

To ease the task of exposition, Chamberlin proceeded under the "heroic" assumption that both demand and cost curves for all products "are uniform throughout the group" (ibid.: 82), thus permitting the use of a single set of revenue and cost functions – and further heightening the misleading impression that the reader confronts a minor variation of the earlier treatment of pure competition.

But methodologically, the technique is classically Marshallian in that Chamberlin assumed price and product, product and selling costs, selling costs and price to be given, before allowing the third element in each case to vary (ibid.: Chs. 5 and 7). In fact, Chamberlin spent a great deal of time in discussing product variation and selling costs although there is little doubt that the analysis of price adjustment *attracted* most attention from later commentators. But the procedure is familiar: if the typical seller faces a dd curve which is consistent with excess profits, new entry will force the curve to a position of tangency with the cost curve (PP), thus yielding an equilibrium under conditions of decreasing costs – a variant of the Sraffa solution (1953). While Chamberlin makes allowance for changes in the position of the cost curve in consequence of new entry, an interesting example is where numbers are assumed constant and excess profits obtain. In this case, the (unintended) consequence for *each* seller seeking to cut price with a view to maximizing profit is a *general* reduction in the market price so that dd "slides" down DD until the position of tangency is reached. Equilibrium is defined by two conditions: "(a) dd' must be tangent to PP', and (b) DD' must intersect both dd' and PP' at the point of tangency" (ibid.: 93). However, the emphasis on tangency obscures the real purpose, and one must sympathize with Chamberlin's repeated complaint that this solution had come to be regarded as "the central principle involved" (ibid.: 195). In fact, Chamberlin recognized that decisions on cost, price, and selling outlay were closely linked, and therefore that the cost and revenue functions facing the firm were interdependent. The reader is, in fact, presented with a market situation where change is endogenous, in part the result of firms seeking positions of advantage for

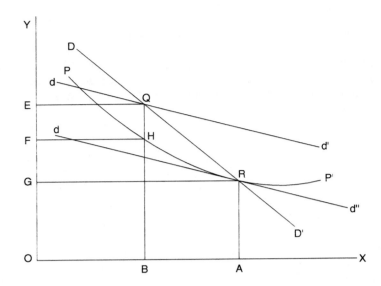

Figure 5.1
Source: Chamberlin (1948: 91).

themselves, so that in practice the "result is heterogeneity of prices, and variation over a wide range of outputs (scales of production) and in profits"
(ibid.: 81) which are unlikely to be completely eliminated even in a competitive environment.

Duopoly

However, to the modern reader as for Chamberlin himself, the third chapter
on "Duopoly and Oligopoly" (which also figured in the thesis, pp. 63–96)
should be among the most interesting. The material was first published in the
Quarterly Journal for 1929. Chamberlin was obliged to strike out the reference
to "oligopoly" at the insistence of F. W. Taussig, the then editor, who
"thought the term a monstrosity" (1957: 33); a decision which must have
cost the author some pain since he was unaware at that time of any prior use
of the term in print.

Chamberlin fared better at the hands of later generations. Romney
Robinson, for example, insisted that the introduction of the analysis of oligopoly was to be regarded as the most important contribution of a writer
who "almost single-handedly introduced the concept . . . and forced it to the
attention of economists" (1971: 63). Bain concurred (1964: 29).

It would be inappropriate here to review the extensive history of *duopoly*
theory or even the treatment which Chamberlin accorded to the subject in his
third chapter (and Appendix A which deals with "Mathematical Theories of

Duopoly and Oligopoly"). However, it *is* appropriate to note that the Cournot model (1838) of two sellers offering an identical product is arguably the most important, at least for didactic purposes.

Basically, Chamberlin reviewed a case where the sellers were interdependent, but pursued policies with regard to price or output on the assumption that their rival's reaction would remain unchanged – the case of *mutual dependence ignored.* In both cases (price and output), Chamberlin confirmed that the outcome would be determinate and accord with the situation which would have obtained under competitive conditions. The case of *mutual dependence recognized* was the more interesting to Chamberlin, and here he drew attention to the use of the chess analogy as used by Pigou (1957: 38) and earlier by Irving Fisher, in "Cournot and Mathematical Economics," in the *Quarterly Journal* for 1898 (1948: 46n.). The dependence recognized case, as Chamberlin reports the matter, was also consistent with a determinate result, namely the monopoly solution, and was associated with Young in his review of Bowley's *Mathematical Groundwork of Economics* published in the *Journal of the American Statistical Association* for 1925 (1948: 47 and n.).

Writing in 1957 Chamberlin was to argue that: "Everyone sought the solution, and I can recall no hint of my own general position that the problem is a manifold one with a large number of different answers depending on which of many possible assumptions are made" (1957: 36). Chamberlin's own results were usefully summarized on pages 53–54 of the original publication and were stated in this form:

1. Duopoly is not one problem, but several. The solution varies, depending upon the conditions assumed. Putting to one side the factor of uncertainty, it is (with minor exceptions) determinate for each set of assumptions made.
2. If sellers have regard to their *total* influence upon price, the price will be the monopoly one.
3. If sellers neglect their indirect influence upon price, each determining his policy as though his competitors were uninfluenced by what he did, the results vary . . .
4. If sellers neglect both their indirect and direct influence upon price, the outcome will be the purely competitive price, *regardless of numbers.*
5. Uncertainty, where present, as to (a) whether other competitors will hold their amounts or their prices constant, (b) whether they are far sighted, (c) the extent of the possible incursions upon their markets, and (d), in the case of a time lag, its length, renders the outcome indeterminate.

In Chamberlin's view, the "real problem" was the development of the dependence recognized case and the exploration of the consequences of uncertainty (1957: 38).

Oligopoly

Seen against this background, Chamberlin's treatment of the small-group case of monopolistic competition was no less dramatic at the time of writing, particularly since the argument brought to the fore a problem which is implicit in the large-group case (with its interdependent functions) – that of determinacy. Building on the analysis of Chapter 3, Chamberlin argued that the particular outcome would depend on the behavioural assumptions made. The *monopoly* (Fig. 5.1) solution will obtain if each seller "sought to maximise his profit with regard to his full influence, direct and indirect, upon the situation" (1948: 100), that is, at point Q in the figure. The *competitive* solution will obtain "if sellers neglect their indirect influence upon the price, each assuming the others to be unaffected by his own actions", but forcing a *reaction* which results in each firm arriving at the point R. The most *probable* solution (dependence recognized) might be expected within these extremes (with dd lying at a point intermediate between Q and R), but with its stability affected by uncertainty:

> The same elements of uncertainty are present here as under the simpler hypothesis of a standardised product . . . Each seller may be in doubt as to his rival's policy, and therefore as to his own, because he does not know (a) whether, if his rival's present policy continues, it will continue with respect to his price or with respect to his output, (b) how intelligent and far-seeing his rival is, and (c) how large would be the incursions made upon him by his own price cut. This last factor is augmented by a new unknown – the extent of the buyer's preferences for his own product over others, expressed by the shape of the demand curves for individual products.
>
> (Ibid.: 101)

But concentration on an *identifiable* range within which a solution may be found (such as RQ in the figure) is itself misleading, depending as it does on the "heroic" assumptions which are not a necessary feature of the model. The material point is that there are as many solutions as there are behavioural assumptions to be made – all in the context of a situation where the demand curves in question are essentially "imagined" ones (since their anticipated shape depends upon judgments as to the future reaction of rivals) and where the cost curves may differ in both location and shape (cf., Sweezy).

However, Chamberlin did offer a number of general conclusions in the context of this market type. He clearly believed that "dependence recognized" was the probable case and that this would tend to be supported by tacit or formal agreements especially as regards price (ibid.: 106). He also considered that price would be relatively stable and based upon an approximation of the full cost principle: "business men may set their prices with reference to costs rather than to demand, aiming at ordinary rather than at maximum profits, and more or less taking it for granted that they will continue to enjoy about their usual share of the total business. They take whatever business comes their way and expect others to do likewise – to live and let live" (ibid.: 105). Further, Chamberlin drew attention in this context to "disguised" price cuts and to non-price competition generally (ibid.: 107ff). Two additional points are deserving of attention.

First, Chamberlin noted that the situation was consistent with conflict; with the attempt by firms to drive rivals from the market. This example makes, in effect, the important point that price-cutting is not always the "irrational" behaviour that the *dependence ignored* case, taken in isolation, might at first sight suggest (1948: 92–93). Secondly, he argued that dependence recognized does not of itself involve collusion (ibid.: 106). As he noted elsewhere, "this is a *legitimate* solution of *oligopoly*, consistent with complete independence of the sellers"; a point which carried with it some important policy implications:

> If a chess player decides against a particular move because the response to it which his rival would make would be damaging to him, he cannot be accused of "spontaneous co-operation"; and he should hardly be *required* by the rules to make the move on the ground that otherwise he would be entering into a "conspiracy in restraint of chess"; or into an agreement with his rival. Why, then, should a businessman who acts with equal (and rather ordinary) intelligence in deciding not to make a price cut, be accused (either by economists or by attorneys general) of collusion, or of *tacitly* co-operating with someone? The point is that the idea of co-operation in *any* sense is *unnecessary* to the result".
>
> (1957: 39)

Oligopoly, as a small-group case, was one thing: oligopolistic interdependence another.

Oligopolistic interdependence: space

Chamberlin always recognized, as Wicksell had done (Schneider, in Kuenne 1967: 139–40) that the issue of location "has been held in undue isolation from the rest of economics" and that "spatial differentiation is the general rule" (1957: 6). The problem of spatial competition was, in fact, central to the analysis contained in Chamberlin's thesis, as submitted to Harvard, featuring as it does (in Ch. 4, Sect. 2) "Spatial Differentiation," pp. 105–109, and again in Chapter 5, Sections 2 and 3 ("Pure Spatial Competition," pp. 167–84; "Spatial Monopoly and Urban Rent," pp. 289–301). But in the published version, the bulk of this material was relegated to two appendices. Appendix C is based upon the second section of Chapter 4, but updated to include a critique of Hotelling's article "Stability in Competition" as published in the *Economic Journal* (31: 1929). Appendix D is an edited version of Section 6 of Chapter 5.

Chamberlin later admitted that the issue of spatial competition had been more marked as a feature of the *thesis* as compared to the *book*, and announced his intention to give the matter more prominence in his "Monopolistic Competition Revisited" (1951, reprinted 1957), and in the article on "The Product as an Economic Variable" (1953; 1957). But the material was not returned to the main text.

Yet Chamberlin did confront the problem which is presented by spatially distributed firms, which may be members of a *large group* operating under conditions of monopolistic competition. For example, retail stores or filling stations may form a network of interwoven markets. A (retail) seller of petrol may cut price to a limited extent, forcing adjacent rivals to make *some* response. A more extensive cut, on the other hand, could force a like response from rivals within the relevant area and hence from those who are on the boundary of *neighbouring areas* – the "chain linking effect," which suggests that even if the numbers selling physically similar (or, indeed, identical) products are large, consideration of indirect influence may enter in when account is taken of location.

To clarify the point, Chamberlin later commented on the phenomenon of the "isolated monopolist" who is not subject to repercussions in that when he cuts price, "he makes his gains from a large number of others, so that no *one* of them is appreciably affected by what he does" (1957: 54) – a condition (isolation) which can also be extended to pure competition *(*ibid.: 56). This case was contrasted with *the non-isolated seller* (ibid.:57), covering "the problem commonly known as oligopoly" and also the *relationships* between firms which are likely to obtain when allowance is made for spatial distribution.

But the specific problem in which Chamberlin became increasingly interested was the one posed by Kaldor, who was concerned with the problem of competition between *quite different* products sold in different places. Kaldor cited the case of demand for cigarettes in a given location being more affected by the price of beer in the same location than by the price of cigarettes in a distant place – thus rendering the demand curves indeterminate (1934: 340; 1953: 40). In noting the problems involved, Chamberlin recognized the possible applications of the model of price discrimination (which had been mentioned in the thesis but not the book (1961: 519; cf., Philips 1983). At the same time, he also came to believe that the "subject needs to be re-written in terms of that extremely useful concept which originated, I believe, with Mr Kaldor, of cross elasticity of demand, rather than in terms of the number of sellers in a market" (1957: 61).

The full implications of this perspective are best summarized by Chamberlin himself. As compared to the original version:

> The present formulation is much simpler. It begins with the individual seller and uses the spatial example to illustrate how the entire economic system may be viewed as an elaborate network of inter-related firms,

each one being able to adjust from the beginning either its price, product, or selling outlay. The uniformity assumption is used only momentarily, and diversity appears at once in the form of concentration of buyers. The individual firm is either isolated or related oligopolistically to others. The group has disappeared from the formulation here given, and with it the concept of large numbers, since the individual seller in this latter instance is again correctly described as isolated, even in the special case of pure competition.

(Ibid.: 68)

Little of the formal structure of *Monopolistic Competition* would appear to survive, even if there had been no change in Chamberlin's understanding of the characteristics of the market as a type.

However, Chamberlin had no compelling reason to drop the concept of the group ("if it had meant an industry, the word industry would have been used" (1957: 68n.)) or subgroup (1948: 102–103) in the context of small numbers. There are, as a matter of fact, "industries" as the term is ordinarily understood (1948: 81) composed of a small number of identifiable firms, such as automobiles, and which provide classic examples of oligopoly as Chamberlin originally defined the term. What Chamberlin did was to generalize the model along the lines suggested in the first edition. He also added a concern with the *oligopolistic relationship* which emerges as soon as the diffusion assumption is dropped; a point which is particularly relevant when spatial considerations are introduced and other forms of differentiation are present.

What Chamberlin had done was gradually to widen his understanding of "sources of influence", notably as a result of introducing the problem of spatial distribution both of customers and firms. This in turn led to an appreciation not just of oligopoly, but of the phenomenon of *oligopolistic interdependence*, thus giving a new meaning to the original claim: "it seems evident to me that oligopolistic elements are very general in the economic system and that economic study must be increasingly concerned with their influence upon prices and other economic categories" (1948: 61). In short, we face an economic *system* (not just a single model) which is characterized by interdependence and thereby by uncertainty and conjecture. The "imagined curves" confronting the oligopolistic firm have implications for the treatment of input analysis (1948: Ch. 8; cf., Skinner 1981), while the situation is further complicated by Chamberlin's belief that in the labour market, the characteristic relationship was that of bilateral monopoly (1957: Ch. 12).

In such situations there is no clearly definable path to equilibrium; indeed, as Brian Loasby has noted, "in this fog of ignorance, there is no equilibrium" (1976: 189). Writing in 1961 Chamberlin noted that he could: "see no escape (and no reason to try to escape) from the conclusion that the ubiquitous forces of oligopoly and of non-price competition (to name only these) must be responsible for many loose ends, multiple optima and indeterminateness in one sense or another in 'groups' and in the system" (1961: 539).

What we have to avoid is the temptation "of formulating problems with the *objective* of assuring a determinate result" (1957: 62).

Conclusion

Chamberlin spent a great deal of time in the 30-plus years after his book was first published in seeking to differentiate his "product" from that of Mrs. Robinson and for good reason. Yet in a sense, his effort was misdirected. It is quite clear from the thesis, from the book, from the appendices which were gradually added, and from the articles published in collected form in 1957, that his thinking in this field had progressively developed in a positive way. The "manifesto" of 1951 and the retrospective review of 1961 amply testify to his intentions. Yet the book was never rewritten in a way which would have reflected the evolving plan with the result that the reader was left to reinterpret the original, in the light of later developments, and to alter the weighting to be attached to its component parts.

In retrospect it is now clear that Chamberlin intended his readers to attach different meanings to his treatment of oligopoly and of oligopolistic interdependence as compared to those which might have been ascribed to them when first perusing the *Theory*.

Chamberlin used the phrase "a re-orientation of the theory of value" when describing the purpose behind his work, but in practice the implications were more profound. In the world described by Chamberlin, we confront a situation where firms effectively compete by changing the conditions which confront their rivals; they compete through the introduction of new products or the manipulation of demand conditions to create positions of advantage for themselves (1948: 213) against a background of imperfect knowledge. Here the causes of change are endogenous so that, in a sense, the argument invites attention to the problem of disequilibrium as a special and essential feature of the economic process. It is hardly surprising that Chamberlin should have likened his own position to that of Schumpeter (1957: 62–63). Elsewhere he observed that "certain features of monopolistic competition would indicate that it is necessarily a theory of change to be associated with dynamics rather than with circular flows" (op. cit.: 225).

The result was not so much the reorientation, as the wreckage of the *theory* of value in the sense that we can no longer work in terms of unambiguous relationships between demand, supply, and price or even identify equilibrium positions (Shackle 1967: 27). Shackle added:

> When economic theory elects to bring in imperfect competition and to recognize uncertainty, there is an end to the meaning of general equilibrium. Economics thereafter is the description, piece by piece, of a

collection of fragments. These fragments may fit together into a brilliant, arrestingly suggestive mosaic, but they do not compose a pattern of unique, inevitable order.

(Op. cit.: 295)

Yet as Shackle recognized, generalization is still possible when based on a study of the market type of the kind offered, for example by Rothschild (1947), who based his argument on analogies drawn from Clausewitz rather than Newton. In a notable article, Rothschild was able to conclude, *inter alia*, that "*price rigidity is an essential aspect of normal oligopolistic price strategy*" (1953: 455) and that "*oligopolistic circumstances lead to a multitude of conditions surrounding the quoted price*" (op. cit.: 456).

This is the direction in which Chamberlin wished to move the discussion so that Georgescu-Roegen was surely correct in emphasizing his concern with "the analysis of the actual" (in Kuenne 1967: 38). The point has been widely made in the literature, notably by Galbraith (1948: 104, 107) and J. S. Bain (in Kuenne 1967: 152ff). In an interesting monograph on Chamberlin, Romney Robinson noted that he had "pushed the whole of price analysis a major step towards that descriptive realism which had been so sadly lacking in post-Marshallian theory" (1971: 42). He added that: "Chamberlin's monopolistic competition theory can fairly be described as an attempt to interpret more fully the world which Marshall discussed" (op. cit.: 10). In the same vein, Denis O'Brien has drawn attention to the Marshallian *style* of the work, notably in connection with Chamberlin's reliance on average, rather than on marginal, curves (1982: 14, 18). In Chamberlin's own words, his book "contains not a technique, but a way of looking at the economic system" (1948: 204); in effect, a return to the perspective supplied by Marshall's *Industry and Trade* but by a circuitous and demanding route. The response, in short, is a reminder of the value of the "institutionalist" approach: and of the importance of *space*.

PURE SPATIAL COMPETITION*

The problem of pure spatial competition is defined very simply, although the full implications of the hypothesis which is required may not be appreciated until actual development of the theory is undertaken. Just as a seller's market

---

* "Pure Spatial Competition" formed part of the text of Chamberlin's thesis, as recorded at pages 167–84. This material was the basis of Appendix C of the published work but is reprinted here in its original form.

   Many years ago, when I hoped to visit the Chamberlin archive, his daughter, Mrs Oakes Spaulding (Monique Chamberlin), gave me permission to use his papers. The appendix is published, courtesy of the Harvard University Press. The numbering of the notes, and the pagination, has been altered.

is large or small depending on the price he sets, so it varies with the location he chooses. People not only buy where prices are cheapest; they also trade at the store which is most conveniently located. The analysis of prices ordinarily assumes that other bases of competition than that of price "remain equal"; it is now proposed to assume that prices and everything else but location "remain equal," while merchants attempt to secure a market for themselves solely by the wise selection of their place of business. The problem is to ascertain by isolating this single factor, its significance in helping to explain the whole complex competitive process.

Spatial competition is a vital type, but one whose effects are worked out slowly. Merchants already in business do not ordinarily (although they do sometimes) shift their locations; as they change their prices or the quality of their goods, in competing with one another. But old stores go out of business and new ones become established. In this way the arrangement of the selling area is gradually changed and we can determine the norm by asking what arrangement would result if the mobility were perfect and frictionless.

The moving force in establishing any arrangement will clearly be the attempt on the part of the sellers to find the location which promises the largest market – the greatest volume of sales. But before examining the outcome of a struggle of this kind, in which locations may be constantly *changing*, let us see how the trade of the entire area would be divided among the sellers at any one time or for any *given* arrangement of stores. The market for any one seller would be perfectly determinate. Those to whom he was most convenient would trade with him, either through deliberate, rational calculation and comparison between the advantages of purchasing there and elsewhere, or simply through their naturally entering the nearest shop without giving any thought to the matter. If two or three stores were of exactly the same convenience for a buyer, he would presumably divide his custom between them, for, under our assumptions, he is uninfluenced by habit, and would not feel its cumulative force in compelling him to continue a customer of the one he happened to patronize first. Even if we permit habit to enter in here, each store would have an equal chance at securing his initial and hence his later business.

The division of the whole area into separate markets is illustrated by Figure 11, a map in which the dots represent stores and the lines delimit the market of each.[1] "X" indicates the location of a new store and the dotted lines the market which it would take away from those already established. The diagram must be taken as symbolic only, for the vagaries of streets make it impossible to measure distance from residence to store in a straight line.[2] Again, strictly speaking, the map allocates buyers to a particular market on the assumption that each buyer can be represented by a dot at one place on the area. This is accurate only where a buyer starts out from his residence for the sole purpose of making purchases. As he goes to and from his work, his amusement or any other pursuits, his "location" changes and many of his purchases may be made at stores more convenient to his travels than to his residence. The

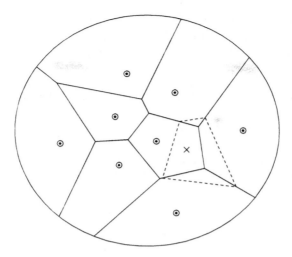

Figure 11

diagram is incapable of showing accurately such forces as these. But it is helpful in indicating that the buyers within the whole area do not patronize sellers at random, but with reference to their proximity.[3]

Now, if the distribution of population and of stores were given, this would be the end of the analysis. Since, other things being equal, buyers will patronize the most convenient seller, it follows at once that for any given arrangement of buyers and sellers every merchant will have a determinate market. But what determines the arrangement? We have still to inquire to what degree and according to what principles there is adaptation of this part of the economic system to the wants of the people – their wants for convenience. If a merchant can increase his sales by changing his location, he will do so. Is there any tendency towards a stable equilibrium in the sense of an arrangement where no one would be able to better his position by a change? How are tendencies towards concentration and towards dispersion to be explained and what is their effect on site rents? In general, the more stores there are, the smaller the volume of business for each one. How many will there be, and is there any tendency for the "most efficient size" or for any other size to be established?

The central problem lies in the adaptation of the distribution of stores and the distribution of population to each other. Little or nothing can be done with the question of size under our assumptions, for it depends on the relation between cost and the uniform price assumed to be charged by all producers. This price depends on the degree of importance buyers attach to convenience – the more they are willing to pay for it, the smaller will be the stores and the more dense will be their distribution. The forces affecting size will be considered below (Sections 3 and 4), where it will be shown that the scale of production is inevitably smaller than that which is most efficient. For the time being, then, we must accept provisionally the idea of a kind of normal size, leaving the question of what determines it until later.

The distribution of buyers to which the location of stores would roughly conform would be quite different if convenience were the *only* factor buyers had to consider in making their purchases. The striking concentration of population in the "shopping district" (not in the sense that people *live* there, of course, but in the sense that they *come* there in large numbers) would not be present, for there would be no shopping district. "Shopping" – inspecting the wares and prices of several stores before purchasing – is necessary only because there are other differences between goods than those pertaining to their accessibility, and because these differences have to be investigated. The existence of a district where "shopping goods" are sold economizes the shoppers' time. But such a district would not exist if standardization made inspection and comparison unnecessary. More conveniently located stores would drive those in the shopping district out of business.

Although due, fundamentally, to the fact that goods are not standardized, this concentration of buyers, once begun, is cumulative for other reasons. To those who go to the district to purchase must be added those who go there to work. Goods which are habitually purchased at the nearest store without "shopping," may be sold in the shopping district or on the way to and from it because the people are there, and once there, want to buy other things conveniently.

If all goods were standardized, buyers would be loath to visit a distant shopping district to secure them. The "population" would then be more dispersed and stores dealing in all kinds of goods would adapt their locations accordingly. Any big department store, now located in the shopping district, could secure for itself a larger market as well as a saving in rent by moving to a spot more remote from its competitors. Here, it would be assured of all the business of the surrounding territory to which it was more convenient. The tendency would be towards dispersion rather than concentration. And just as the concentration of population in the shopping district is cumulative, so its dispersion would be cumulative. As stores became more scattered the routes of the people trading with them and working in them would be more evenly distributed. This would lead in its turn to a still more even distribution of stores.

It is not meant to imply that stores of all kinds would be sprinkled here and there with no concentration whatever. Stores of different types would be grouped, for it would suit the convenience of purchasers if, on one buying trip, they could make all of their purchases in the same vicinity. If we apply the reasoning to a kind of "general merchandise store" which would sell almost everything (and which might easily develop under such conditions), the general conclusion is that such stores would be fairly evenly dispersed. If we apply it to stores dealing in a certain type or class of goods as book stores, or shoe stores, the conclusion is that stores of any type would be fairly

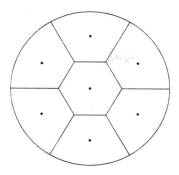

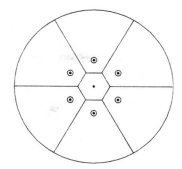

Figure 12   Figure 13

evenly dispersed and that stores of different types would tend to be gathered into groups which would be roughly equi-distant from each other.

Let us examine the adaptation of stores to population more carefully. For a given distribution of population would there be a determinate distribution of stores? With perfect mobility the answer is no. There would exist no arrangement at which it would not be to the advantage of someone to change his location (corresponding to the equilibrium under pure competition where it is to the advantage of no one to change his output).

The indeterminateness of location can be illustrated in a simple case. Suppose the selling area to be as in Figure 12, and divided equally among seven sellers. Any of the six outer sellers could enlarge his market by moving towards the centre and forcing the unfortunate one in that position to share with him. Let us suppose that they were all to follow this policy.

When they had each moved half way, the markets would be arranged as in Figure 13, the encircled dot in each case showing the new location. Each one except the middle one would have his old market plus a part of the middle area. But the movement could not stop until they had all reached the centre, whereupon the seven of them would share the entire area equally as before. There would be no separate markets, to be sure, but the total business would be divided about equally, since there would be no reason for buyers selecting one seller over another. Here, however, any one of them could secure more than one-seventh by moving away from the centre again. And so the oscillation would continue. The sellers might combine at the centre and set up one large store, but, with competition on the basis of location alone, this would be useless. Competitors would appear at once to share in the gains and they could secure markets by simply setting themselves up in appropriate locations.

Of course, the actual stability of store locations, because of the immobility of capital, makes the very idea of continuous oscillation seem absurd. The actual arrangement is highly stable, since the problem of location imposes itself on a merchant, broadly speaking, only when he first sets himself up in business and at rare intervals thereafter. The fundamental instability of the system, however, is significant. It reveals itself in differences of rent and profits (due also, of course, to many other causes) rather than in constant movement which would wipe out these differences as soon as they appeared.

The conclusion of ultimate instability involves that at any one time, although stores as a whole are scattered, they may be scattered very unevenly. The forces pictured in the example by which we have illustrated instability might make for concentration in small groups or for an even distribution or for something in between. There could be no very considerable concentration because of its great inconvenience to buyers compared to a number of smaller scattered centres.

But immobility not only makes the actual situation *stable*, no matter how *arranged*. It also makes for even dispersion where population is fairly evenly distributed. If several sellers are gathered together, any one is in a particularly vulnerable position. In Figure 12, if all seven sellers are in the centre, six newcomers, taking the outer positions, can force them to fail or incur the expense and loss of moving. If seven sellers is the number which can most advantageously serve the district, the newcomers are now in a better position to survive than the original seven. If they had chosen the scattered locations in the first place, there would have been nothing to attract others to compete with them. Immobility will thus lead merchants to seek the locations in the first place which give the greatest protection to the spatial monopoly they seek, and each seller is best protected when they are evenly distributed.

The reaction of other bases of competition on spatial monopoly is another factor making for dispersion. The closer are two competitors, the more nearly are they on a par, and the less secure is the market of each from the encroachments of the other by price cuts or other methods. The slight spatial advantage over a larger number of purchasers, gained, perhaps, by locating closer to a competitor, may be less desirable than a more secure advantage over a smaller number which is to be had by isolating oneself. To be isolated is to be protected to a degree from other means of competition, of course, the final decision as to location must turn on the nature of the good, the various ways in which it can be and is differentiated from others, and the relative importance of convenience as a factor in its purchase. But in general, whereas the arrangement might be indeterminate if location were absolutely the only basis for competition, the introduction of other bases makes it more likely that sellers will be dispersed. For the market of any one is as large in either case, and better protected from other types of competition if spatial differentiation is carried as far as possible.

By contrast, there seem to be no forces making for concentration, under our assumptions, unless there be also a concentration of population. This is especially significant where population is more dense in the sense that particular streets or street intersections are travelled by people in large numbers in their daily goings and comings (other than for purposes of buying). Here the outcome depends on the degree of concentration. If there is room enough, the result will simply be more stores of the same size and rate of profits, and paying the same rent. Any merchant securing a larger volume of business and larger profits would be forced to share his market with competitors who would locate nearby. This competition would force the same volume of business as was secured in less densely populated districts, and there could be no rent above that which the land would yield for residential or other purposes, since the location would yield no greater market than any other.

But the concentration may be very great in an area so small that there is not room for all the competitors who would naturally be attracted. The levelling effect of competition on profits and the resulting tendency towards a uniform scale of production is then restricted by the impossibility of piling stores on top of each other. Competitors would be unable to make incursions upon the larger markets afforded to those who secured locations in the district. But they could prevent them from enjoying the increased profits arising from a larger scale of production and diminished unit costs–profits which are ordinarily eliminated by an increase in the number of stores. Their competitive bidding for the sites would force these gains into the hands of the landowners in the form of rent. It seems unlikely, however, that this tendency would be very important under purely spatial competition because of the fairly even distribution of population.

There would be variations in size, in rents, and in profits from another cause, which is closely allied to concentration – unevenness in the distribution of population, not in the sense of the existence of certain areas where it is on the whole more dense, but in the sense that the markets fit into each other in a highly irregular fashion. It has already been remarked that the arrangement of Figure 11 (page 119) is symbolic only. The vagaries of streets and the fact that a retail store does not occupy an infinitesimally small space characteristically make it impossible to divide a selling area into equal markets. This irregularity reveals itself in several ways. If a particular corner is passed by 8,000 people a day, it gives a better market than the nearest possible location (next door, but not on the corner) where 5,000 people pass daily. *Other things being equal*, its sales will be greater in the proportion of 8 to 5 and profits will be larger. Since competitors will not have the alternative of sharing in this market by setting up for themselves next door or nearby, they will bid for the occupancy of the better site and thus put into the hands of the landowner all of the extra profits it affords. Competition here levels profits by converting a portion of them into rent. And the tendency towards a uniform size is modified by the fact that markets are to a degree concentrated at *one spot* and not spread over an area which can be divided.

Again, it might seem that if a seller's nearest competitor were at a considerable distance, it would be almost a matter of indifference which one of a dozen adjacent sites he chose. And so it might be, if his trade came entirely from those whose *residences* were in the vicinity of his store. But many of those living nearest to him pass other stores in their daily travels. He must choose a site which will be convenient to the goings and comings of as many as possible, and there may be one or two which are markedly superior in this respect. Also, a particular location within the district at a street intersection may bring him a large volume of business from people passing through which he would otherwise miss entirely. Such factors as these give varying importance to different sites, even though they be adjacent, the differences in the advantages they afford being exacted by the owner of the superior site in every case. It is obvious that any location giving an unusually large market will have that market cut into by a competitor if there exists an available site which will allow sufficient incursions to pay the ordinary rate of profits, so that, except in very congested districts, there is a definite limit to the volume of business secured by any single seller. The more "smooth" the distribution of population – that is, the more alike are the opportunities afforded by a number of contiguous sites, the smaller will be the variations from the "normal" site.

These irregularities in markets may bring variations in profits instead of in rents. If a market is so large as to yield exceptional profits to one merchant and yet not large enough to give the ordinary rate to two, the seller who happens to get there first may succeed in keeping the extra profit, providing there are several sites which are about equally attractive. There could be no rent in this case beyond that given to the land for other uses, say residential purposes, for the competition of landowners would reduce to that level. The higher rate of profits could not be diminished by a new competitor, for he, as well as the first seller, would lose by his entrance. The forces tending to give surpluses resulting from irregularities of this kind to landlord or entrepreneur are probably mixed in most cases so that there may be variations in both rent and profits throughout the area on this account. Since those negotiating in regard to a site are characteristically few, there is considerable room for bargaining, and this may divide the gain or throw it one way or the other.

This concludes our analysis of the spatial factor in complete isolation. Some of the tendencies discovered may be observed in real life; others are buried from view by the more powerful forces which have, of necessity, been ignored in order to isolate this one factor. Yet, even though buried, they must be of some significance, if it be granted that location is even a small part of the whole complex competitive process. If the results seems abstract and unreal, they will serve the purpose, at least, of suggesting that the exclusive attention commonly given to *price* competition gives conclusions which may be criticized on the same score. Where product is differentiated, the theory of prices inevitably tells only a part of the story – in some cases perhaps only a small part. The theory of "pure spatial competition" is indicative of the other forces which are at work.

Notes

1 Cf. Fetter's analysis of the spatial factor (*Economic Principles*, p. 392 ff).
2 In this connection, it is often true that certain streets are devoted exclusively to business purposes, others to residential purposes. In a large city, for instance, the north and south streets
   may contain stores, those running east and west, residences or apartment houses.
3 Wherever the phrase "distribution of population" is used hereafter, it will refer not simply
   to the distribution of residences, but to the distribution of routes as well, and will take into
   account all the complex forces here implied. For instance, there is a "concentration of population" in this sense in the "shopping district."

References and authorities

Andrews, P. W. S. (1964) *On Competition in Economic Theory*, London: Macmillan.

Bain, J. S. (1964) "The Impact on Industrial Organisation," *American Economic Association Papers and Proceedings* 74: 28–32.

—— (1967) "Chamberlin's Impact on Microeconomic Theory," in R. E. Kuenne (ed.) *Monopolistic Competition Theory: Studies in Impact*, London: John Wiley.

Bishop, R. L. (1964) "The Impact on General Theory," *American Economic Association Papers and Proceedings* 54: 33–43.

Blitch, C. P. (1983) "Allan A. Young: A Curious Case of Professional Neglect," *History of Political Economy* 15: 1–24.

Boulding, K. (1942) "The Theory of the Firm in the Last Ten Years," *American Economic Review* 32: 791–802.

Boulding, K., and G. J. Stigler (eds) (1953) *Readings in Price Theory*, London: George Allen & Unwin.

Chamberlin, E. H. (1948) *The Theory of Monopolistic Competition*, Cambridge, MA.: Harvard University Press.

—— (1957) *Towards a More General Theory of Value*, Oxford: Oxford University Press.

—— (1961) "The Origin and Early Development of Monopolistic Competition Theory," *Quarterly Journal of Economics* 75: 515–43.

Clapham, J. H. (1953), "Of Empty Boxes," *Economic Journal*, reprinted in K. Boulding and G. J. Stigler (eds) (1953) *Readings in Price Theory*, London: George Allen & Unwin.

Cournot, A. (1838) *Recherches sur les Principes Mathématiques de la Théorie les Richesses*, Paris.

Ellis, H. S. (ed.) (1948) *A Survey of Contemporary Economics*, Homewood, IL: Richard D. Irwin.

Fellner, W. (1949) *Competition Among the Few*, New York: Alfred Knopf.

Galbraith, J. K. (1948) "Monopoly and the Concentration of Economic Power," in H. S. Ellis (ed.) *A Survey of Contemporary Economics*, Homewood, IL: Richard D. Irwin.

Georgescu-Roegen, N. (1967) "Chamberlin's New Economics and the Unit of Production," in R. E. Kuenne (ed.) *Monopolistic Competition Theory: Studies in Impact*, London: John Wiley.

Hall, R. L., and C. J. Hitch (1939) "Price Theory and Business Behaviour," *Oxford Economic Papers* 2.

Hotelling, H. (1953) "Stability in Competition," reprinted in K. Boulding and G. J. Stigler (eds) (1953) *Readings in Price Theory*, London: George Allen & Unwin.

Hutcheson, T. W. (1953) *A Review of Economic Doctrines, 1878–1929*, Oxford: Oxford University Press.

Kaldor, N. (1934) "Mrs. Robinson's Economics of Imperfect Competition," *Econometrica* 1: 335–41.

—— (1935) "Market Imperfection and Excess Capacity," *Economica* 2: 33–50.

Keynes, J. M. (1951) *Essays in Biography*, London: Rupert Hart-Davis.

Kuenne, R. E. (1967) *Monopolistic Competition Theory: Studies in Impact*, London: John Wiley.

Loasby, B. J. (1976) *Choice, Complexity and Ignorance*, Cambridge: Cambridge University Press.

Marshall, A. (1920) *Industry and Trade*, London: Macmillan.

—— (1956) *Principles of Economics*, 8th edn., London: Macmillan.

O'Brien, D. P. (1981) "A. Marshall, 1842–1924," in D. P. O'Brien and J. R. Presley (eds) *Pioneers of Modern Economics in Britain*, London: Macmillan.

—— (1984) "The Evolution of the Theory of the Firm," in E H Stephen (ed.), *Firms, Organization and Labour*, London: Macmillan.

Philips, L. (1983) *The Economics of Price Discrimination*, Cambridge: Cambridge University Press.

Pigou, A. C. (1924) *The Economics of Welfare*, London: Macmillan.

Reid, S. (1981) *The Kinked Demand Curve Analysis of Oliogopoly*, Edinburgh: Edinburgh University Press.

Rheinwald, T. P. (1977) "The Genesis of Chamberlinian Monopolistic Competition Theory," *History of Political Economy* 9: 522–34.

Robinson, J. (1933) *The Economics of Imperfect Competition*, London: Macmillan.

Robinson, R. (1971) *Edward H. Chamberlin*, New York: Columbia University Press.

Rothschild, K., "Price Theory and Oligopoly," *Economic Journal* 57: 299–320. Reprinted in K. Boulding and G. J. Stigler (eds) (1953) *Readings in Price Theory*, London: George Allen & Unwin.

—— (1967) "Chamberlin and German Economics," in R. E. Kuenne (ed.) *Monopolistic Competition Theory: Studies in Impact*, London: John Wiley.

Samuelson, P. A. (1967) "The Monopolistic Competition Revolution," in R. E. Kuenne (ed.) *Monopolistic Competition Theory: Studies in Impact*, London: John Wiley.

Schneider, E. (1967) "Milestones on the Way to Theory of Monopolistic Competition," in R. E. Kuenne (ed.) *Monopolistic Competition Theory: Studies in Impact*, London: John Wiley.

Schumpeter, J. A. (1954) *History of Economic Analysis*, London: George Allen & Unwin.

Shackle, G. L. S. (1967) *The Years of High Theory*, Cambridge: Cambridge University Press.

Skinner, A. S. (1981) "Of Factor and Commodity Markets: A Note on E. H. Chamberlin," *Oxford Economic Papers* 33: 122–34.

—— (1983) "The Origins and Development of Monopolistic Competition," *Journal of Economic Studies* 10: 52–67.

—— (1984) "Oligopoly and the Theory of the Firm" (with M. C. Maclennan), in J. Creedy and D. P. O'Brien (eds) *Economic Analysis in Historical Perspective*, London: Butterworths.

—— (with F. G. Hay and C. Oughton) (1996) *A Perspective on Intermediate Price Theory*, Manchester: Manchester University Press.

Sraffa, P. (1953) "The Laws of Returns under Competitive Conditions," *Economic Journal*. Reprinted in K. Boulding and G. J. Stigler (eds) (1953) *Readings in Price Theory*, London: George Allen & Unwin.

Stigler, G. J. (1950) "Capitalism and Monopolistic Competition," *American Economic Review Papers and Proceedings* 40: 63.

—— (1949) "Monopolistic Competition in Retrospect," in *Five Lectures on Economic Problems*, New York: Macmillan.

Sweezy, P. M. (1953) "Demand Under Conditions of Oligopoly." Reprinted in K. Boulding and G. J. Stigler (eds) (1953) *Readings in Price Theory*, London: George Allen & Unwin.

Triffin, R. (1956) *Monopolistic Competition and General Equilibrium Theory*, Cambridge, MA: Harvard University Press.

6 Two phases of Kuznets's interest in Schumpeter

Mark Perlman

Introduction

Many reasons have been cited for the economic profession's indifference to Schumpeter's 1939 magnum opus, *Business Cycles: A Theoretical, Historical, and Statistical Analysis of the Capitalist Process* (hereafter referred to as *Business Cycles*).[1] For one, by the time that the book came out and was first digested, problems associated with the outbreak of World War II increasingly dominated economic thinking in lieu of the earlier thinking about the ravages of the Great Depression. For another (and this was Schumpeter's view), an unfortunate general professional fascination with just what Keynes's *General Theory of Employment, Interest, and Money* meant in short-run terms reduced interest in Schumpeter's essentially dynamic schema. Even at Harvard, it was Alvin Hansen's seminar, not Schumpeter's, where the brightest students congregated. And while there are many other reasons as well, Simon Kuznets's measuredly respectful, but overwhelmingly devastating review of the book in the *American Economic Review* (Kuznets 1940) dumped ice-cold water on and drenched Schumpeter's hot ideas. *Capitalism, Socialism, and Democracy*, clearly his most popular book, was, in Schumpeter's retrospect, small potatoes in comparison with his hopes for *Business Cycles* (see Swedberg 1991: 151).

Business Cycles was, I think, mistitled. Had the subtitle and the main title been reversed, I believe that the contents of the book would have been perceived differently. For Schumpeter was nowhere the master of precise statistical detail so much as he was an artist sketching panoramic views of the interrelationship of ideas. This is not to say that *Business Cycles* was not a successful description of the Capitalist Process. Quite the contrary, while it was a time-bound perception, Schumpeter succeeded in extending his "vision" of the process. Perhaps he did it better in his subsequent, intentionally less scholarly, *Capitalism, Socialism, and Democracy*, where no small part of his ideas has been shown to be distorted, if not actually wrong. But *Business Cycles* failed because Schumpeter was technically inept in handling the statistical details, because he phrased the problem in alternative static and dynamic terms, and because his analytical method was primarily based on others' theories or generalizations, that were, in turn, only partly developed and occasionally flawed. All of this is highlighted in Kuznets's review. But where Schumpeter's play failed most was that if he really wanted to offer a general description of the stages of capitalism, his data bank was too small, his analytical powers were inadequate, and his faith in the filiation of ideas was suited neither to understanding modern capitalism nor to analyzing the causes of business cycles. Now that the data are more complete and the analytical methods have been much augmented, there is no one around to choose between ideas and fashion the schema that Schumpeter sought.

Yet, although *Business Cycles* is technically not a gem, it is still very much worth examining, all 1,100 plus pages, for it is a careful demonstration of how a very well read and articulate scholar puts together, that is, synthesizes, his own perceptions and the ideas he has picked up from those whom he considered (and were) great scholars. It is exemplar if one is interested in how an imaginative mind creates, digests, and combines. And if the product is flawed, so what? Over time most great syntheses are seen to be flawed. Perfection is extremely rare, and truly good examples of the creative process are valuable. I hold this book to be an excellent example of a creative process, albeit the result in good measure did not stand up to Kuznets's penetrating eye. And it was, as we shall see, not only Kuznets's penetrating eye about business cycle data in all of its forms, but also a long disdain for Schumpeter's perception of theory building that contributed to Kuznets's judgement.

This chapter has three subsequent sections. The first deals with describing the book and Kuznets's criticisms. The second section takes up a much earlier significant, but unpublished, Kuznets essay where he first laid out his criticisms of Schumpeter's earlier works on methodology, the nature of economic development, and the role of the entrepreneur. The third concludes with a discussion of methodological differences between the two men.

Business Cycles, the book, and Kuznets's review

Time permits but the briefest elaboration of the plan of the book, but from the first it is apparent that Schumpeter sought to fuse the themes of his two initial books (*Das Wesen und der Hauptinhalt der theoretischen Nationalökonomie*, 1908[2] and *Theorie der wirtschaftlichen Entwicklung*, 1912[3]) with a broadened methodological position, including also some statistical and derivative intellectual substance. Written in grand and only semi-technical language, *Business Cycles* is pitched somewhat short of the Marshall goal – to be graspable by sober businessmen with some intuition if not schooling in economics and statistics and still be technically correct. Schumpeter's biographers all mention that he hoped that this work would cap his reputation as the preeminent scholar on the subject of both business cycles and the development of capitalism, seen in stages (Allen 1991: Vol. 2, 71–85; Stolper 1994: 375; Swedberg 1991: 128–35).

There are 15 chapters, the first three of which update the ideas in his 1908 and 1911 works.[4] Chapter 1, carefully eschewing any sociological approach, deals with the methodological question within the framework of capitalistic development.[5] Schumpeter thought good theory involved the integration of the best of others' ideas and theories. Chapter 2 develops a static model of a two-stage business cycle – seen as the result of a market-shaking entrepreneur's innovation followed by the dampening effects of too many imitators. The result is a return to an equilibrium situation, albeit usually at a higher level of gross output than had existed prior to the shake-up. In the third chapter Schumpeter moves to what he thought to be the cycle in a dynamic economy, where he takes account of the destabilizing aspects of the roles of the entrepreneur, the innovator, and the availability of credit in the evolution of the cycle. As conventional then and still so, he separated the static model from dynamic conditions, with the latter being too complicated for him to develop a formal model. One interesting point, however, is that his treatment of manufacturers' market response antedates much of what Joan Robinson in the 1950s called "reswitching" – namely using different combinations of labor and capital as their input–output–cost ratios changed.

Chapter 4 focuses on business entrepreneurs, backed by the banking system, as the initial *dei ex machina* and how their initial intervention is complicated by imitators as well as operational flaws in the credit system. If these four chapters are extensions of his 1911 work, they are succinct and illustrate well the greatly increased sophistication of his later views.

Chapter 5 concerns three exemplar cycles he has drawn from the literature: the Kondratieff[6] (approximate 50-year), the Juglar[7] (approximate ten-year), and the Kitchin[8] (approximate three-year) variants. He suggests, with the use of a purely illustrative graph, what the impact of the summing of these three might be.

Chapters 6 and 7 are historical – episodically, not quantitatively (from the methodological standpoint one can compare them to Thorp, 1926). Schumpeter asserts that the dating of the aforementioned cycles can be confirmed. These chapters, covering the German, English [*sic*], and American experiences, are clearly in the tradition of Schmoller's German historical school. Although Chapter 6's title suggests that it handles the period, 1787–1842, about 35 percent of the material deals with the background and definition of capitalism as well as 300 years of events preceding the period of "modern" business cycles. That last part covers the first Kondratieff wave from 1787–1842, with the first Juglar starting (a year of prosperity) in 1787 and inflecting downwards in 1793. Revival occurred in 1795. From Schumpeter's standpoint the *dei ex machina* were the industrial revolutions in production and canal transportation. Kitchin cycles are dismissed because the pertinent data are missing.

Chapter 7 covers 1843–1919, that period being in part a second Kondratieff wave (1843–97). This Kondratieff focuses on the effect of railroadization on what had been an agricultural economy. Analyzed also are the impacts of two Juglar waves. His data are initially American, but careful reference is also made to German and English [*sic*] evolution. The chapter ends with an analysis of the first 16 [*sic*] years of a third Kondratieff cycle, 1898–1913.

Chapter 8 investigates the role of price variations in cycle behavior. Chapter 9 concerns mainly variations in output, but ends with a discussion of English [*sic*] unemployment data. Chapter 10 turns to the examination of a small number of specific industries. Chapters 11, 12, and 13 handle questions relating to money, not only income and wages but also deposits and loans and fluctuations in the rate of interest, with Chapter 13 covering the performances of the bank ("central") market and the equities market (stock exchanges). The remaining two chapters (14 and 15) deal with the problems of the 1920s and 1930s, respectively.

In his 1940 review of *Business Cycles*, Kuznets asserts in the first paragraph that complete theories are essential to causal analysis, and that as such they should be tested quantitatively. About this assertion I will have more to say in the next section of my chapter.

Kuznets identifies Schumpeter's perception of cycles as:

> pulsations of the rate of economic evolution, . . . with [e]conomic change in general . . . attributed to three groups of forces: external factors [like] the growth of government demand for new military weapons; the factor of growth . . . [being] the continuous gradual changes in population, . . . savings, and accumulation; . . . [and the impact of] innovations, which represent material changes . . . in the production functions. It is innovations that are of strategic importance in the capitalist economy, innovations that are usually introduced by new rather than by old firms, by new men rather than by those who already occupy prominent niches in the functioning system.
>
> (Kuznets 1940: 258–59)

Schumpeter judged that the business cycle reflects recurrent fluctuations in the rate at which innovations occur, and they bunch first because of fluctuations in entrepreneurial endeavor and then mostly because the pioneer is soon followed by a flock of imitators. This swarming, whatever were the conditions at the outset, soon affects input prices (as well as goods' prices) and the banking arrangements. The period of business expansion gives way to unforeseen changes, involving uncertainty (and risk, too). The economy's consequent reaction is to pause, to take stock of the new probable equilibrium situation, to stress risk aversion more than had been the immediately prior case, and thus to thwart budding entrepreneurs' immediate plans. His is, as mentioned earlier, a two-phase cycle, really; one phase of entrepreneur-led expansion, followed by a phase of consolidation.

Kuznets notes that Schumpeter thinks that his two-phase cycle is more basic than most business cycle analysts realize – they see only the monetary and goods level produced aspect. He also seeks out evidence that Schumpeter may be onto something, concluding, ". . . it may be said that in the last quarter of the eighteenth century in England there were several major inventions (cotton textiles, iron and steel, steam engine); that thereafter it was not until the 30s of the nineteenth century that another big group of inventions, connected with steam railroad, became accessible to the entrepreneur; and that as a result we have a two-phase cycle of prosperity in the last quarter of the eighteenth century and of recession in the next quarter" (263–64).

Ultimately, however, Kuznets dismisses this two-phase analysis in favor of the traditional four-phase; recovery, prosperity, decline, and depression, largely because the problems of dating points of inflection (which Schumpeter holds to be the normal equilibrium) involve smoothing data series (certainly not a mechanical task) and the handling of second-order differences. Data are more easily interpreted in a four-phase cycle, one eschewing a 'normal' or an "equilibrium" level.

In the end Kuznets's strongest criticism relates to Schumpeter's use of the three-cycle reference scheme. While the idea may be imaginative, upon examination the facts fail to fit, even approximately. Inventions and innovations come along before the Kondratieff is "ready for them" (268). Furthermore while statistical outliers can be handled by statistical smoothing, external episodic events like wars or famines or epidemics are not so easily processed. Schumpeter's handling of the second half of the first Kondratieff cycle by blaming the 1837 American banking crisis for the continued fall in prices after 1842 (when there was supposed to be Kondratieff upturn) seems to vitiate his fundamental hypothesis (168). In short, Schumpeter's statistical analysis is not only too selective and too crude, but the actual examples he uses to corroborate his thesis simply do not demonstrate what he hoped they would. His treatment of Juglar cycles is inadequate (they seem to be misdated), and data do not really exist to confirm his use of the very short Kitchin cycle until close to the immediate past. After pointing out discrepancies within Schumpeter's conclusions about what data on pig iron consumption, 1857–85 for Britain and Germany and for the United States (1857–75 and again from 1875–90), really show, Kuznets concludes:

> the ease of disagreement of which there are many other instances, is an eloquent testimony to the insufficiency of the crude statistical procedures followed in the treatise to provide a basis for establishing cycle types of so decisive a character as the Kondratieffs.

> The Kitchins are too short and perhaps too mild to be discernible with the available qualitative historical evidence, especially for the years before 1919. Hence the distinction between Juglars and the Kitchins is based in the treatise largely upon statistical evidence, *i.e.* again largely upon the impression conveyed by the charts. The series used for the prewar years are almost exclusively annual, and the comments refer to the existence of the Kitchins, rather than their dates.

. . .

> The evidence . . . in the two volumes . . . suggest[s] with some plausibility the desirability of distinguishing more than one type of cycle . . . But whether the distinctions should be drawn in the specific form suggested by Professor Schumpeter is still an unanswered question.
>
> (269–70)

Kuznets, as we shall soon see, was a long-time student of the Schumpeter schema, and his review contains much that many readers of the review may have erroneously thought was mere sympathetic "throat-clearing." In reality those sections were a very serious recalculation of Schumpeter's ideas about the role of economic theory. Yet, whether Kuznets's closing paragraph is or is not meant to be a *coup de grâce*, it probably served that purpose:

> Thus, whatever the shortcomings of the book as an exposition of a systematic and tested theory of business cycles, these shortcomings are relative to a lofty conception of the requirements such theory should meet. It is the cognizance of these requirements that makes the book valuable even to one who may be interested in the author's comments on the various and sundry historical, statistical, and theoretical matters. But these comments are of high suggestive value and should, if given circulation, prove effective stimuli for further theoretical, historical and statistical study of business cycles and economic evolution. It is my sincere hope that Professor Schumpeter's labor embodied in this treatise will be repaid by an extensive utilization of it by students in the field, aware though they may be of the tentative character of his conclusions and of the personal element in some of his comments and evaluations.
>
> (271)

The background of Kuznets's evaluation[9]

Kuznets did not come to his reviewing of Schumpeter's *Business Cycles* without extensive preparation. Obviously, Kuznets was totally familiar with the work the National Bureau and others had done on the definition, measurement, and analyses of cycles. But what is less known is that he had been studying Schumpeter's schemata for more than 20 years. In this 1940 review he intentionally skips over the first part of the book, noting that it is mostly a consolidation and, in a few instances, an emendation of Schumpeter's earlier works on the subject. Presumably, he was referring mostly to Schumpeter's 1908 and 1911 works, mentioned earlier.[10]

Kuznets's MA thesis, submitted to and approved by Wesley Clair Mitchell, dealt precisely with those two books. While the thesis, itself, has disappeared from the Columbia University storage archives, a draft of it containing some of Mitchell's marginal comments is available in the Kuznets papers at the Harvard University Archives.[11] Entitled, "Dr. Schumpeter's System Presented and Criticized," it was drafted in original, and likely less-sophisticated, form as a second-year paper at the University of Kharkhov shortly before the University was closed during the Bolshevik Revolution. That draft was carried by him when he emigrated with his brothers through Turkey to the United States. Translated and likely greatly revised and expanded, it is the document which brought Kuznets to Wesley Clair Mitchell's attention, a very respectful attention as attested in the marginal notes.

Before beginning the review of the essay, one point should be repeated and another one made. First, Kuznets was convinced that economic theory should be in the Bacon tradition of starting with observations, developing hypotheses, testing and redrawing the hypotheses with iterative observations until the hypothesis would square with repeated observations. That was not Schumpeter's view; he favored the selective filiation of fine ideas. Kuznets came to his view after having been a student of Marxism, another system based on a careful selection of ideas, but one which by 1923 he must have cast aside because those ideas were not being confirmed by observation.[12]

The other point is that even though Kuznets concluded that Schumpeter's perception of theory building was flawed, Kuznets repeatedly refers to the brilliance of Schumpeter's insights. Kuznets was a man who could be impressed with insights, and that he thought Schumpeter's concept of theory inadequate did not apparently vitiate his respect for Schumpeter's insights.

This 1924 essay has five parts. The first, "Schumpeter's System Presented," was purportedly intended to be non-evaluative, and in the first paragraph Kuznets asserts that no one seems to be able to explain the workings of the economy sufficiently satisfactorily to carry the profession with him. There are, he writes,

> three possible ways out of this difficulty. First, one may come to the conclusion that all the theories only obstruct the clear view on real economic life. And this must be discarded to make place for . . . much better methods of obtaining knowledge and understanding. Secondly, insisting on the primary importance of statistical measurements and analysis in the acquisition of true knowledge, one may accept the theories as mere suggestions for the interpretation of statistically established facts and routines, as hints for directing the investigation to this or that particular phenomenon. Thirdly, one may make a judicious choice among the different theories and bring them into some sort of agreement without relying on purely quantitative data, but finding help in 'plain, general observation" and "evident facts' of the old schools.

> Dr.[13] Schumpeter's system of economics is supposed to offer a way out of the chaos of different economic theories. In his first volume, "Das Wesen und Das Hauptinhalt der Theoretischen Nationaloekonomie" (Leipsic, 1908) the author tries to present economic life by a scheme built of the most sound parts of the existing theories. As this scheme does not cover many important phenomena, Dr. Schumpeter fills up the gap

in his later volume, "Die Theorie der Wirtschaftlicher Entwicklung" (Leipsic, 1912). These two volumes together with several occasional articles in some German periodicals give us a highly consistent and elegant system of economics.

Kuznets then identifies Schumpeter's choice of analytical method, that is, describing a phenomenon (y) as function of other phenomena which have to be identified. If that criterion can be fully met we have a determinate (*eindeutig*) system. Added to that logical premise is the human factor, seen in the role of private ownership. Thus enters methodological individualism:

> individualism, because it will permit to describe economic phenomena only in categories of private ownership and individual action; methodological, because it is taken not as a statement of fact or of an ethical ideal but only as a working hypothesis. It does not mean that in real life all movements of good could be accounted for by the action of their owners as individuals, and that there is no place for the social categories signifying group actions. But the individual is assumed arbitrarily to be justified only by the ultimate purpose it serves, that of the final efficient description.
>
> (4)

Space does not permit a full treatment of this section. Yet it remains one of the most comprehensive statements of the assumptions of the Austrian tradition that I know, including a full discussion of the differences between Böhm Bawerk's and Wieser's perceptions of marginalism.

All of the analysis, Schumpeter's, of course, and Kuznets's comments as well, is intentionally static. The survey touches production, exchange, and distribution, with land and labor. Capital, if it means the technical equipment and the raw material, can be conceived only as accumulated land and labor services. When one starts from the finished product and goes back to the goods of higher orders, he passes the capital goods as an intermediate stage and comes to two original productive factors; labor and land. The productive process may thus be conceived as an exchange of labor and land services for the finished consumption good. The value of the finished product is thus accounted for by the claims of the labor and land services only. There is no value surplus which could be a source of interest (15).

But Kuznets, even in this early part of the essay where he is supposed to be describing, not analyzing, begins to ask whether there is a difficulty in this reasoning. What, he ponders, is the value and price of labor and land themselves if in a static economy they are assumed to be inexhaustible resources? As there is no regular traffic in labor and land in a static economy, there is no gap in Schumpeter's system – a system which allows for no interest payments and concludes that profits will only be in the wages of management or the result of monopolistic conditions.

Kuznets eventually turns to considering whether there can be evolution in

a static economy. Here, he credits Schumpeter with a useful change of emphasis. And in the new situation there are rewards for making capital available
(interest) and the emergence of a surplus taken by the entrepreneur.

Part II of the essay, "Total Value," turns to the question of how to make the
system seem more accurately descriptive. Here, he reviews carefully the Böhm
Bawerk, the Wieser, and the Schumpeter contrasting views on marginalism.

Part III, "On the Value of Productive Goods," focuses on Schumpeter's
efforts to explain how one gets "value functions of productive goods from the
value functions of consumable ones" (36). Kuznets's evaluative mind steps in,
and he notes that the process becomes non-addable because of double count-
ing. More important, Schumpeter's solution apparently dismisses marginal
analysis, yet tries to combine both the total value approach with adding the
non-addable marginal values. Here Kuznets concludes that albeit
Schumpeter, to some degree, tries to tie in Böhm Bawerk's work, his math is
not up to the solution. Rather he should have considered pursuing Wieser's
handling of the question (there is an appendix on this topic).

Part IV, "The Theory of Price," is an effort to get to general equilbrium
analysis. On this topic Schumpeter is a thorough Walrasian, and Kuznets,
again bringing in his own reasoning, has doubts that the necessary condition,
that an individual could have endless opportunities to consider alternatives,
was realistic and that all individuals would arrive at their transaction points
simultaneously, even going on at great length to suggest some form of path
dependency which makes the solution, were it possible, improbable.[14] In addition, Kuznets then concludes that the Walrasian system will not work because
whereas price ratios can be formalized, anyone working within this system
will have epistemic views about goods at the specified real price. In his words:

> These exchange ratios have not to be actual prices existing on [sic] the
> market when the prices to be determined are formed. They must be definite
> conceptions of the existing or imagined exchange possibilities in the minds
> of our individuals. It is irrelevant for the static exchange scheme whether a
> cow can be really exchanged [sic] for a horse, but it becomes an important
> datum if the economic individual about to exchange his cow for a good he
> wants best believes that the exchange for a horse is quite possible (54).
>
> . . .

In his second [1911] volume, trying to give a vivid picture of a static
society, Pr. Schumpeter showed how in this society, one economic period
will be the repetition of the preceding, and the balance will be struck
every time at the same prices. In such conditions, if you once found the
equilibrium prices, you are able to forecast an interminable time ahead.
The general equilibrium once established will perpetuate itself, the same
quantities of good being exchanged and in the same ration in every
economic period.

A general state of balance takes place when all the individuals who
form the given society had arrived each to this individual equilibrium. It

is easy to see that *one* general equilibrium is possible only if *all* individuals arrive to their points of balance simultaneously, if all of them settle in the maket at one time, so that the resulting price reflects all the individual valuations in existence. If however for some reason or other the individuals form more than one market by settling their exchange at different times, there is not one equilibrium but several. A general state of balance requires one market not only in space but also in time.

(55)

What emerges bothers Kuznets in terms of the consistency of Schumpeter's methodological commitment because what Schumpeter requires is that the parties to market transactions become passive (suppress their epistemic, highly individualistic, evaluations) and that contradicts the earlier presumption of methodological individualism.[15]

Kuznets's lifetime interest in the distribution of incomes is the basis of his critique of Schumpeter's scheme, the subject of Part V, "On the Exchange Scheme Applied to a Distribution of Income." He opens by noting that in Schumpeter's static economy there is no place either for interest or profits. And wages cannot be treated because there is no free competition in the market for labor (the result of social-class distinctions). Only the price of land, derivative from rents, remains.

Kuznets, further, expresses his own doubts about there being no competition in a structured labor market and about the likelihood of labor not producing a surplus. Of course, once this premise is introduced what follows is a line of thinking saying that profits (a return on capital) can exist in a static situation, and there is a place for the study of income distribution. Ultimately, Kuznets returns to the Böhm Bawerk model of the length of the production cycle, favoring it over Schumpeter's views.

The next three parts (VI, VII, and VIII), explicitly designed to be critical, deal with dynamics of interest, business cycles, and economic statics and dynamics. The chapter on interest is purely theoretical, but Kuznets is obviously impressed with some of the emandations Schumpeter has introduced, while at the same time he concludes:

All in all, the theory of interest presents an unfavorable balance of defects over merits. It is one-sided as a description and arbitrary in its assumptions. It is not without merit because the author does not forget facts and thus lays down a foundation for his scheme in data of real life. But the facts might be said to be not of the "mass" character and thus present an inadequate foundation for a theory that is supposed to describe a phenomenon of an essentially "mass" nature. Interest is paid by the masses of independent business men and cannot be covered by a hypothesis that bases its generalizations on data referring to a small group of economic geniuses . . .

This one-sidedness, leaving out nearly the bulk of the phenomena of real life, relates not only to interest but to all other elements which he thinks to be inherent to the dynamical system.

(85–86)

In this section Kuznets also outlines what has later come to be called satisficing.

Kuznets concludes that Schumpeter's theory of dynamic business cycles is simplice because it is presented as the sole cause of cycles. Further, Kuznets asks three questions: (1) does a period of innovation always signal prosperity; (2) does a shrinkage of innovation always signal shrinkage in the level of economic activity; and (3) do periods of innovation and static equlibrium cover the whole of the business cycle? Playing around with these essentially rhetorical questions, Kuznets comes to a negative answer largely by referring to Mitchell's system.

Part VII concerns statics and dynamics. Kuznets believes that Schumpeter sees dynamics as principally the result of imaginative individuals coming forth with new innovations. Innovators want power; those in a static society want only to earn a living. But, asks Kuznets, what about interest rate changes and changes in comparative prices? Can they not trigger dynamic reactions, too?

> The only thing that can be asserted and that is asserted by Pr. Schumpeter is that the introduced changes are to the better and not to the worse, in consequence of which it can be affirmed that the differential gain arise[s] in favor of different individuals. But all the prices, quantitative determinaton of prices, the lone merit of the static system disappears under the ruthless assault of the dynamic elements.
>
> (91)

Schumpeter gives no way to measure the dynamics of change, and consequently his schema becomes unverifiable statistically.

> All in all, what description of economic life is presented by Pr. Schumpeter's system? Certain phenomena are essentially static, others are essentially dynamic. Not speaking to the fact that the clarification as it was presented is in disagreement with facts, what is the joint result of wages and rent static, interest and profits dynamic? How are the prices determined in a period when dynamic changes are taking place? What is the combined influence of static and dynamic uses of money and credit? Nothing can be said, because the dynamic factor is indefinite.
>
> (94)

The section concludes with some Kuznetsian psychological musings (which he gives and then apologizes for) about Schumpeter's long journey to this "dead end." He concludes that the failure can be associated with the method.

Theory building on the basis of the careful selection of the best ideas, integrating them, and then projecting the result is not a fruitful way to construct testable ideas.

A summing up

The point of this exercise is that Kuznets came to his 1940 review of Schumpeter's *Business Cycles* "baited for bear." He had already devoted considerable time to evaluating the Schumpeter system from a methodological standpoint. Why was he so anti-theory of the type that Schumpeter espoused?

Kuznets's training started with some interest in Marxian socialism (see Kapuria and Perlman 1995) and what was offered at the University of Kharkhov. If Marshall's *Principles* was popular fare in the English-reading world, the Austrians and Marxism were selling better in Eastern Europe. Kuznets, in his salad years something of a Marxist, was interested in total systems, never in partial equilibrium analysis. Accordingly, so much for Marshall. Also important was Kuznets's fluency in German, which made surveying Schumpeter's youthful attempts to synthesize economic theory a practical effort. In any event, at a time when those fluent only in English were dominated by British and American economic writers, Kuznets was doing something quite different.

Schumpeter, himself, had also deplored the dominance of Marshall's thinking in the development of economic theory in America. Yet Schumpeter explained Wesley Clair Mitchell's distaste for formal theorizing by noting that Mitchell's professor, J. Laurence Laughlin, was anti-Marshallian with the result that Mitchell was never schooled in any current economic theorizing tradition (Schumpeter 1952/1998: 241–42).

In 1913 Schumpeter, having been invited by Nicholas Murray Butler to a prestigious visiting professorship at Columbia for the academic year, could have (and did explicitly write that he had) known Mitchell well. Yet I infer from the little subsequent correspondence between them that professionally they had little in common (see my comments on the vagaries of the Mitchell–Schumpeter relationships in Schumpeter 1998, "Introduction").[16]

About ten years later along came Kuznets, mathematically and linguistically fluent, who submits a Master's essay describing and criticizing the scientific bases of Schumpeter's system. As one reads Mitchell's annotations on the draft manuscript of the Master's essay it is easy to see his almost gleeful enthusiasm for the paper (and as Kuznets recalled it, for the author) growing. Why? Because at the outset Kuznets notes the difference in perceptions of science between the two men. Again, Schumpeter believed in the power of carefully selected ideas. Mitchell believed almost totally only in the power of observed facts.

And what Kuznets does in his essay is to go well-beyond his assignment of describing and testing the exposition of an "improvement" of marginal analysis. What Kuznets offered was a rejection of economic theory based on "indisputible" (meaning unmeasured) facts and on the using of constructs to get a conclusion which is not justified (tested). Schumpeter, Kuznets avers, failed to test his system by seeing whether his theory served well as a shortcut to predict outcomes, even though that was explicit in his promise.

And that is just what he does in his review of *Business Cycles*. Mitchell's and Kuznets's skepticism about Schumpeter should be seen for what it likely was. They thought Schumpeter the cleverest of the theorists of those four decades. However, they were skeptical of his findings, not only because they found the analysis not useful in predicting economic events, but also because they felt his perception of theory was flawed. They, too, believed that theory ought to offer verifiable factual shortcuts; and if a theory did not meet that test, it was useless.[17]

My own surmise is that the fate of the book was not so much that it was "unlucky" (as Rendigs Fels [Schumpeter 1964: viii] contends), nor simply produced when most ears were listening to the siren call of Maynard Keynes, nor that the vicissitudes of the emerging military situation had come to dominate all economic thinking, but simply that Schumpeter's vision was not realized. Mark Blaug has noted that Schumpeter's magnificent *History of Economic Analysis* promised more than it delivered. And that was the problem of *Business Cycles* as well. What was perhaps "unlucky" is that Kuznets was chosen as the reviewer. And this is almost apparent when one reads the somewhat cloying letter that Schumpeter wrote to Kuznets when he learned who the reviewer was to be (see Swedberg 1991: 226–27).

All the biographers of Schumpeter note his deep depression during the period after the book and the review came out. The depression is usually attributed to his isolation coming from his anti-American war policy.[18] But I suggest that anyone who had worked as hard on an economic system, whose early promise had been so universally recognized as a planting of a significant 'tree of knowledge,' and who had carefully nurtured that tree – only to see in the end that no one, really great or small, wanted to eat its apples would be totally depressed.

One other personal speculation. In 1947 Tjallings Koopmans wrote a bitter review of Arthur Burns and Wesley Clair Mitchell's *Measuring Business Cycles*. The vehemence of the attack (unlike Kuznets's 1940 review, Koopmans' minced no words) has always fascinated me. Why would a gentleman and a scholar write so passionately? My guess is that it was the payback of the theory crowd, that is, particularly the Europeans who liked and respected Schumpeter, for the damage Kuznets had wrought.

Notes

1 Not all reviews, printed or as phrased in letters, were devastating (see Allen 1991: Vol. 2, 82–83).

2 Translated by me as *The Essence and General Contents of Social Economics*.

3 The later one was republished in 1926 with a subtitle, *Eine Untersuchung über*

Unternehmergenwinn, Kapital, Kredit, Zins und den Konjunkturzyklus. The 1926 version was translated by Redvers Opie and appeared in 1934 under the title of *The Theory of Economic Development: An Inquiry into Profits, Capital, Credit, Interest, and the Business Cycle.*

4 The clearest statement of the message of the book is contained in Rendigs Fels's "Summary" in Schumpeter (1964). The other summaries, like mine, lay out the book more than the message. Kuznets's 1940 summary is very compact. Allen's 1991 summary is considerably longer. Swedberg's (1991) is midway.

5 When Schumpeter was writing, the idea of sequential stages of capitalism was very popular (see Gras 1939; Nussbaum 1933; and Sée 1928).

6 Nicholai Dmitrievich Kondratieff (1892–?1931), a quandom Deputy Minister (for Food) during the Kerensky regime, was probably executed by Stalin's order in his devastation of the agricultural sector. Kondratieff's interest was in economic cycles, with some particular attention paid to those longer than the usual seven- to 11-year business cycle. Professor Wolfgang Stolper, while a student at Harvard, translated and condensed a 1926 German article; this translation appeared in the November 1935 issue of the *Review of Economics and Statistics* (Kondratieff 1935).

7 Clément Juglar (1819–1905) was a French statistician-economist originally interested in measuring changes in marriage, birth, and death rates. That interest led him to investigate changes in business conditions. He 'discovered' business cycles of about seven to 11 years duration (see Schumpeter 1939: 63–64, fn. 2).

8 Both Joseph Kitchin (1861–1932) and William Crum (1923) published articles in the same 1923 issue of the *Review of Economic Statistics* [*sic*] (see Schumpeter 1939: 165, fn.2). Kitchin's article precedes Crum's, covers a longer period, is shorter, sounds more confident, and is better presented. Moreover, at the time (1923) Kitchin's was the better-known name. Kitchin was a British statistician who had worked for the *Financial News*. Later he became a businessman in South Africa and a recognized expert on the statistics of precious metals. Kitchin differentiated these approximately 40-month cycles from the major cycles which lasted seven to 11 years.

9 What follows stems from many conversations with Kuznets, whom I first met in 1955 when we were both on the Johns Hopkins Political Economy faculty. Over the years, particularly after 1961 when he went to Harvard, I visited with him several times annually. I was particularly curious about his education (see Perlman, "Jews and Contributions to Economics: A Bicentennial Review," in Perlman 1996). In the course of these talks he told me about having prepared a second-year (undergraduate) paper in 1917–18 on Schumpeter's ideas, wherein he decided that while Schumpeter was full of marvelous insights, he did not have a proper sense of how theory must be developed. The paper was not submitted because the University closed during the 1917 Bolshevik Revolution.

10 It is unlikely that Kuznets could have had access to the 1914 work, *Epochen der Dogmen- und Methodengeschichte*, if only because of the World War I cancellation of all communications between Germany and Russia. I do not recall whether I ever asked Kuznets whether he had read the 1914 book (really a contribution to an encyclopedia that Max Weber was organizing). Yet I rather suspect that he had not read it because in it, Schumpeter backed away from the certainties exhibited in the 1908 book, and Kuznets would have mentioned it.

11 I am much indebted to Professor Richard Swedberg for help in locating this version.

12 The Bolshevik–Menshevik (meaning *majority* and *minority*) split began in 1903. In 1917 it worked out that the *Jewish Bund*, which held Kuznets's sympathies, was outmaneuvered by Lenin. As I have no access to the original paper I cannot say when the idea of testing a theory by outcomes erased Kuznets's earlier Marxism, certainly a belief in the filiation of ideas. That the family emigrated immediately the chance came certainly suggests skepticism about the future of Leninist Marxism.

13 In the draft Schumpeter's prefix is always 'Pr.,' but Professor Mitchell early on writes that the choice must be between 'Prof.' and "Dr.' 'Dr.' won out, but it was corrected only once in this draft.

14 Here Mitchell penned, "Very clever point."
15 This summary of the Kuznets critique does not do justice to the swift and clean quality of Kuznets's fierce analysis.
16 As can be seen in the text and footnotes of *Business Cycles*, he corresponded with Mitchell regarding business cycles, but it was no more than a formal request for Mitchell's data. However, Swedberg (1991: 127) offers an excerpt from a rather pedantic letter to Mitchell.
17 Kuznets always asserted that he believed in theory, but that he had not found very many which met his scientific test.
18 This effort was so demanding, that he never really started a methodological work, designed to reformulate his ideas in the 1908 book, *The Theoretical Apparatus of Economics*. Part 1 of his posthumous *History of Economic Analysis* was not along the lines of this effort, according to Loring Allen (1991: Vol. 2, 52, 89, 111, 227).

References

Allen, Loring (1991) *Opening Doors: The Life and Work of Joseph Schumpeter*, New Brunswick, NJ: Transaction, 1991.

Crum, W. L. (1923) "Cycle of Rates on Commercial Paper," *Review of Economics Statistics and Supplement* 5: 17–27.

Gras, Norman Scott Buchanan (1939) *Business and Capitalism: An Introduction to Business History*, New York: Crofts.

Juglar, Clement (1966) *Des crises commerciales et de leur retour périodique en France, en Angleterre et aux États-Unis*, 2nd (1889) edn., New York: A. M. Kelley, 1967. Also published as *A Brief History of Panics and their Periodical Occurrence in the United States*, 3d edn., trans. and ed., with an introd., and brought down from 1889 to date by DeCourcy W. Thom, New York: A. M. Kelley, 1966.

Kitchin, Joseph (1923) "Cycles and Trends in Economic Factors," *Review of Economic Statistics and Supplement* 5: 10–16.

Kondratieff, N. D. (1925) "The Major Economic Cycles," *Voprosykon'iunktury* 1: 28–79. An abridged English translation appears as "The Long Waves in Economic Life," *Review of Economics and Statistics*, 1935, 16: 105–15. A complete translation can be found in *Review*, 1979, 2: 519–62.

Koopmans, Tjallings Charles (1946) "Facts without Theory," *Review of Economics and Statistics* 29: 161–72.

Kuznets, Simon Smith (1924?) "Dr. Schumpeter's System Presented and Analyzed," draft of an MA essay submitted at Columbia University. This draft is to be found in Professor Kuznets's collected papers. See Harvard University Archives: HUGFP 88.45, Box 1, 1923–24, 107 pp.

—— (1940) "Review of Joseph Alois Schumpeter's *Business Cycles: A Theoretical, Historical, and Statistical Analysis of the Capitalist Process*," *American Economic Review* 30: 257–71.

Nussbaum, Frederick L. (1933) *A History of the Economic Institutions of Modern Europe: An Introduction of Der Moderne kapitalismus of Werner Sombart*, New York: F. S. Crofts.

Perlman, Mark (1996) "Jews and Contributions to Economics" (1976), in *The Character of Economics, Economic Characters and Economic Institutions*, Ann Arbor, MI: University of Michigan Press, 307–17.

Schumpeter, Joseph Alois (1908) *Das Wesen und der Hauptinhalt der theoretischen Nationalökonomie*, Leipzig.

—— (1911) *Theorie der wirtschaftlichen Entwicklung*, Leipzig.

—— (1939) *Business Cycles: A Theoretical, Historical, and Statistical Analysis of the Capitalist Process*, New York: McGraw-Hill.

—— (1943) *Capitalism, Socialism, and Democracy*, New York: Harper & Bros., 2nd ed. 1947, 3rd ed. 1950.

—— (1952/1998) *Ten Great Economists: From Marx to Keynes*, with an introduction by Mark Perlman, London: Routledge.

—— (1964) *Business Cycles: A Theoretical, Historical, and Statistical Analysis of the Capitalist Process*, abridged with an Introduction by Rendigs Fels, Philadelphia, PA: Porcupine Press.

Sée, Henri Eugène (1928) *Modern Capitalism, its Origin and Evolution*, trans. by Homer B. Vanderblue and Georges F. Doriot, London: N. Douglas.

Stolper, Wolfgang F. (1994) *Joseph Alois Schumpeter: The Public Life of a Private Man*, Princeton, NJ: Princeton University Press.

Swedberg, Richard (1991) *Schumpeter: A Biography*, Princeton, NJ: Princeton University Press.

Thorp, Willard (1926) *Business Annals: United States, England, France, Germany, Austria, Russia, Sweden, Netherlands, Italy, Argentina, Brazil, Canada, South Africa, Australia, India, Japan, China*, with an introductory chapter by Wesley C. Mitchell and a foreword by Edwin F. Gay, New York: National Bureau of Economic Research.

7 The AEA and the radical challenge to American social science

A. W. Bob Coats

Introduction

What is the influence of national scholarly organizations on the development of their respective academic disciplines? To the best of my knowledge there is no general "theory" on this subject, and no agreed set of criteria or yardsticks by which to gauge any given organization's success or failure. Admittedly in the case of economics, which is the primary focus here, one prominent member of the relevant community has recently claimed that the American Economic Association (AEA) has "shaped and formed many features of the profession 'Economics'" (Weintraub 1992: 369); but while such a claim appears reasonable enough at first sight, possibly even obvious, it has limited value unless it is backed by adequate documentation and supported by comparative studies of other disciplines. Unfortunately, it would take some years to complete a serious comparative study of a range of American national scholarly organizations in the social sciences and humanities, let alone the international dimension of such research, and one may legitimately question whether the results would justify the effort involved. Nevertheless, a tentative first step in this direction may be taken via an examination of the varied reactions of a number of American national disciplinary organizations, including the AEA, to the crisis period of the late 1960s and early 1970s, a time when their customarily peaceful activities were seriously disrupted by a remarkable and unprecedented radical uprising which directly challenged their established policies and even their *raison d'être*.

As is the case with most broad social movements the reasons for the upsurge of radicalism in 1960s' America are complex. However, the main elements in the explanation are familiar and widely agreed, including: the rediscovery of poverty and inequality, notwithstanding two postwar decades of prosperity and economic growth; serious urban unrest fueled in part, if not mainly, by racial conflict; the civil rights movement; the rise of feminism; and – most prominently and stridently – the anti-Vietnam War protest campaigns.[1] Within the academic community, which had expanded rapidly since 1945 and was already experiencing serious internal tensions, a growing number of students and faculty (usually, but not invariably, among the younger generation)[2] came to believe that American institutions of higher education were too insulated from and indifferent to contemporary economic and social problems. And the constraints on outspoken criticism of the intra and extra mural *status quo* were weakened by the retreat – although not yet the defeat – of McCarthyism; which had inhibited critical analysis and free public discussion.[3]

Professional issues in American economics

The nature and the range of activities deemed appropriate to a national social science organization are largely matters of custom and definition. If it is conceived narrowly as a traditional type of learned society, then its primary concern must needs be scholarly – the pursuit of knowledge for its own sake – and its focus academic. Its members' status and autonomy are dependent on the command of specialist knowledge, rather than on service to "clients." (The students are not the clients; they are ultimately the university's responsibility, not the faculty's.) Yet ever since the late nineteenth century, the American professoriat had recognized the need for protection from outside interference, hence the importance they attached to academic freedom and the American Association of University Professors (AAUP), despite its limited effectiveness.[4]

In practice the demarcation line between learned society and professional association is both variable and unclear.[5] According to the well-known sociologist, Bernard Barber, the essential attributes of professional behavior are:

(i) a higher degree of generalized and systematic knowledge;
(ii) primary orientation to the community interest rather than to individual self-interests;
(iii) a high degree of self control of behavior through codes of ethics internalized in the process of work socialization and through voluntary associations organized and operated by the work specialists themselves; and
(iv) a system of rewards (monetary and honorary) that is primarily a set of symbols of work achievement and thus ends in themselves rather than means to some end of self-interest.

(Adapted from Barber 1965: 18)

The AEA clearly does not fit this profile exactly. Barber's third attribute is inapplicable, and cynics would argue that so, too, is the second. After all, as economics is a discipline postulating the pursuit of self-interest as a primary human motivation, is it to be expected that economists' behavior, whether individually or collectively, will be based on a different, and higher standard?[6] The AEA has never been a purely scholarly body focusing narrowly on the pursuit of truth for its own sake. Admittedly the discipline has relied heavily on its corpus of theory, yet for many decades theory was conceived not primarily as an end in itself, but more often as an essential tool in understanding the functioning of the economy, and a means to policy making designed to relieve poverty and promote prosperity. It is only comparatively recently that economists collectively have been accused of concentrating exclusively on highly abstract theorizing and sophisticated techniques to the neglect of societal concerns and practical problem solving.[7] Most of the AEA Presidential addresses up to 1970 were more concerned with problems in the application of economic theory and the economists' responsibilities to the public, than theoretical developments *per se*, which might conceivably have "shaped and formed" the discipline.[8]

Turning to the third item in Barber's list, it is clear that the AEA has displayed less interest in questions of professional ethics and standards than any of the other national social science organizations. For obvious reasons (e.g., their strong client orientation and their association with medicine), the psychologists have been by far the most concerned with issues of this kind, their efforts extending from the establishment of a special ethics committee in 1938 through to the painstaking formulation of a professional code in 1952, which was substantially revised in the 1960s.[9] The sheer magnitude of the task indicates the importance attached to it, and the difficulties they encountered may conceivably have been a deterrent to the economists, who steered clear of this delicate area.[10] Like the psychologists, members of the social psychology section of the American Sociological Society (ASA) were sensitive to ethical and professional problems because, like the psychologists, their work brought them into direct contact with the medical profession. Consequently, from 1960 they operated under a code that required them to accept and abide by a specific set of standards that included procedures for dealing with violations and, if necessary, expelling offenders. The ASA as a whole did not go this far, despite 25 years of discussion and investigation of professional problems and the eventual establishment of an ASA code of ethics in 1971. However, there was little inclination to enforce such a code, despite the many discussions and committee reports on ethical and professional matters. Within the American Political Science Association (APSA) and the American Anthropological Association (AAA), the activities, rights, and responsibilities of researchers working on government contracts or employed by other non-academic organizations, were of special concern (cf., *infra*: 9–11). The use of social scientists in secret intelligence work by the Central Intelligence Agency (CIA) and the Federal Departments of State and Defense was deeply disturbing to many moderate social science critics as well as radicals; and there was also the shock effect of publicity about the notorious Project Camelot, an army-financed American University's study of counter-insurgency in Chile (cf., Horowitz 1974: *passim*). Even so, despite fears of the politicization of their disciplines, these events did not lead either the APSA or the AAA to adopt a clear-cut and enforceable ethical and professional code.

If economists were also involved in clandestine or otherwise objectionable activities, the problem seems not to have troubled the AEA. Ever since the early 1890s its leading members and appointed officials had endeavored to maintain a determinedly aloof and non-partisan posture towards public affairs, refusing to become involved *as an Association* in policy issues that might be considered controversial either by some of its members or by outside critics.[11] At an early stage the AEA adopted the device of responding to calls for advice and assistance from appropriate governmental, educational, and other bodies by nominating members in their personal capacity, rather than as official AEA representatives. By contrast with the other leading American social science organizations, the published proceedings of the AEA's Executive Committee and the Association's archives display a remarkable lack of official concern with questions of professional ethics and the responsibilities of researchers, provoking one informed critic to refer scathingly to the "somnolent economists'... wondrous repose." However, he added that

> The moribundity of the AEA has not harmed, and may possibly have enhanced, the rewards and powers of economists... Whether by chance or design, the association has remained remarkably oblivious of policy questions, the many influential policy activities being conducted through other channels; thus by fighting elsewhere, the economists have maintained comparative peace at home.[12]

As we shall see, these shrewd observations are borne out when we compare the AEA's reactions to the radical challenge with those of the other leading social science organizations.

The AEA's response to the radical challenge

Like many other American scholarly and scientific societies, the AEA was inevitably caught up in the radical turmoil of the late 1960s and early 1970s, but its experience was untypical. Two episodes stand out: the reaction to the Chicago police department's brutal treatment of students and other demonstrators at the Democratic Convention in the summer of 1968; and the action of a group of radical students in taking over, and making a political statement at, the 1969 annual AEA business meeting.[13] In the former year many AEA members demanded that the annual meeting be moved away from Chicago, an action taken by at least three other national social science bodies. However, after careful and anxious consultations with colleagues on the Executive Committee, President Kenneth Boulding, a highly conscientious man sympathetic to many liberal and radical causes, took the decision not to move the venue or cancel the meeting, as had been suggested. As a result, at the same time as the scheduled Chicago meeting, there was an unprecedented breakaway gathering in Philadelphia at which several hundred sympathizers enrolled in the newly formed Union for Radical Political Economics (URPE).[14]

The following year the return to normalcy was again temporarily disrupted when a young radical economist interrupted the orderly business meeting by managing to read a prepared statement, denouncing the AEA for "perpetuating professionalism, elitism, and petty irrelevance" and also, somewhat inconsistently, for supporting the elite in perpetuating "inequality, alienation, destruction of the environment, imperialism, racism, and the subjugation of women" – none of which could be considered a petty irrelevance! Curiously enough, after making this statement, the radical group of economists walked ostentatiously out of the meeting during the ensuing discussion and the delivery of a response from Gordon Tullock, a well-known anti-radical economist. Both statements were subsequently printed in the *American Economic Review*'s report of the business meeting, and there the matter ended. Evidently the protesters wished to have no truck with the national body, which they evidently considered irredeemably orthodox and pro-capitalist. They never sought its recognition or support, or a share of its resources.[15] The implications for the development of radical or "alternative" economics will be considered later (*infra*: 151–53).

Radicalism in other American social science associations

As the following examples demonstrate, matters were very different in other national associations in the social sciences and humanities. In each case, the organization was much more seriously disrupted than the AEA, and had far greater difficulties in controlling its radical members.

In the APSA the trouble began in 1967, when the press revealed that the Association's Executive Director and Treasurer/Counsel had occupied leading positions in a policy research body funded indirectly by the CIA.[16] In response to this charge the APSA hastily convened an investigative committee of past Presidents, who reported that nothing improper had occurred. Nevertheless, at the next annual business meeting dissident members were convinced that the report was simply an establishment whitewash. They were further discomfited when the Chairman ruled out of order as "political," and irrelevant to the Association's "direct purpose" as a learned society, an amendment condemning the House un-American Committee's attempt to obtain membership lists of radical campus organizations. Needless to say, many moderate members of the academic community, as well as radicals, considered this congressional intrusion deeply offensive.[17]

During the next 36 hours three successive meetings led to the formation of a Caucus for a New Political Science (CNPS), with a membership exceeding 200 and an Executive Committee of 13. The dissidents attacked the APSA's failure "to study in a radically critical spirit either the great crises of the day or the inherent weaknesses of the American political system." It offered no alternative to the political *status quo*, while the currently fashionable behavioral approach to politics – emphasizing empirical research, operational criteria, quantification, and value neutrality – simply provided "a thin veil of scientificity" to relieve political scientists of the moral and ideological responsibility for their research. Thus, through its many links with government at all levels, the discipline was being corrupted by a combination of federal and corporate power.

During the next four years the CNPS made strenuous efforts to *democratize* and politicize the APSA, and in 1971 the radical activists made remarkable gains, securing two-thirds of the seats on the Association's Executive Committee with the aid of a considerable number of sympathetic senior left-liberal members. However, this was a short-lived success, for in the longer run the CNPS failed to have a lasting influence on the APSA's composition and conduct, and its experience demonstrates the formidable obstacles to efforts to change substantially the composition and policies of a major national scholarly association.[18]

The anthropologists' contribution to the radical challenge was deeply influenced, initially at least, by the Project Camelot scandal (cf., *supra*: 146).This was not simply because anthropologists were involved, but also because fieldwork abroad played such a major role in the discipline's research and training programs, for which adequate research funding was essential. At the 1965 annual meeting an official AAA inquiry was initiated into the agencies sponsoring anthropologists' research. Its report was highly critical of some expensive research projects, including Camelot; also it raised problems of censorship, and it lent credence to stories of CIA involvement. However, the report also attacked "loosely, completely unsubstantiated, and often scarcely credible allegations of spying and intelligence activities made by a few anthropologists against their colleagues" (Beals 1967: 11). It provoked an intense debate at the 1967 annual meeting, at which resolutions were passed criticizing the State Department's Bureau of Intelligence and Research and condemning the Vietnam War and certain weapons and methods used in warfare (for example, genocide and what is now termed "ethnic cleansing"). As a proponent of the original, subsequently toned down, anti-war resolution argued, perceptively:

> The question is not whether the Association should be political; it has made itself political. The only question is what kind of political positions it should adopt. [The Association is inescapably tied] unreflectively to the purposes of the US Government . . . those who now urge an apolitical course on us mean that we should be 'apolitical' for the US Government. not against it. The Association is a body that takes political action: it must now decide what its politics are.
>
> (Aberle 1967: 7)

It is significant that this commentator soon became a member of the AAA's Board.

During the next five years questions of AAA principle and policy were extensively and forcefully debated in the Association's *Fellow Newsletter*, which offers clear testimony to the organization's liveliness and contentious-ness. In 1968 the Presidential Address was intentionally abbreviated in order to allow extra time for questions and answers. Students were given limited voting powers; periodic anti-imperialism and anti-war resolutions were passed; and ethical questions were vigorously discussed in the *Newsletter*'s correspondence columns, including issues of professional and scientific free-dom, and a mini Camelot scandal centering on research in Thailand. One cannot help wondering whether the dissemination of a *Newsletter* would not have enlivened the AEA's dreary and 'safe' official publications on the Association's affairs!

In many respects, developments within the ASA resembled those in the APSA and AAA, rather than in the AEA. The sociologists were, collectively speaking, far more professionally self-conscious than the economists. In 1967 the ASA's business meeting voted in favor of an anti-Vietnam war resolution; and two years later the radicals attacked the Association's professed non-partisanship as a political stance serving the powers that be, and claimed the right to adopt oppositional political positions. When the Secretary of Health, Education and Welfare addressed the Association on aspects of his Department's work, protestors circulated leaflets in the audience denouncing his views.[19] They also disrupted the Presidential address (Rhodes 1981: 50, 60). The Association responded sympathetically to the Radical Caucus's resolu-tion, expressing concerns about the sources of research funding, the conduct of research, and the publication of findings. In 1968 the President-elect, Ralph Turner, proposed a ten-point plan to assist the movement towards equalization and democratization within the organization, covering minorities, gays, politi-cal activists, administrators, "gypsy professionals," and the unemployed.

On the whole, the historians had much greater difficulty in containing or suppressing radical dissent than the aforementioned associations.[20] The "twelfth hour decision" to move the AHA's 1968 meeting from Chicago to New York led to a plenary session on "Professional Organizations and Political Issues," and the formulation of a statement that sought to combine members' rights and obligations with the avoidance of commitment by the historical profession unless the issues involved "are directly connected with the promotion of historical scholarship or are necessary to preserve profes-sional integrity." Needless to say this statement was not universally welcomed. In 1969 there was a contested election for the AHA Presidency between Robert A. Palmer and the radical candidate, Staughton C. Lynd of Yale, who "outlined a proposal against the Vietnam war," attacked as inadequate current proposals for reforming the organization's constitution, and recom-mended the establishment of a substantial special fund "to support various urgent proposals seeking to alter professional and social structures." Palmer was in fact elected, partly because of a split between two groups of left-wing voters, and Lynd's Radical Caucus resolution demanding full disclosure of government (including White House, Pentagon, and CIA) archives was rejected. However two radical resolutions by the Professional Caucus, prescribing guidelines for all departments of history and banning new Ph.D. programs "until the current employment crisis is past," were passed by voice vote.

In 1970 and 1971 anti-Vietnam war resolutions were passed (on the first occasion after an exhaustive debate);[21] proposals to democratize the AHA's Council were extensively discussed; approval was given to Lynd's scheme to raise an Emergency Defense fund to assist members suffering from violations of academic freedom (defined as political repression). It was to be financed by a surtax on members. In 1972 the Committee on the Rights of Historians,[22] established by the Council the previous year, circulated 9,000 questionnaires to members enquiring about academic freedom violations.

Why was the AEA's experience so distinctive?

Why were the late 1960s and early 1970s radical economists so much less successful in influencing the AEA's proceedings and in gaining recognition and concessions from the organization than their counterparts in political science, anthropology, sociology, and history?[23] Does the explanation lie in intellectual, technical, or institutional factors such as: the continuity of the central corpus of economic theory; the increasing influence of the positivist (behaviorist) conception of economic science, at least up to the late 1960s; the degree of control exercised by the discipline's ruling elite; or the longevity and stability of the AEA itself, and the strength of its traditional commitment to non-partisanship, especially with respect to political and public policy affairs? According to Dorothy Ross, a leading American social and intellectual historian, already by the end of the 1920s "the neoclassical paradigm had become entrenched in the professional structure" of economics, and the mainstream (or orthodox) economists "were too fundamentally satisfied with the workings of the market and its long-term ameliorative trend" to be willing to seek an alternative theory to provide a counterweight to market theory.[24] Admittedly Ross's statement overstates the dominance of the neoclassical paradigm, especially in the 1930s, a period nowadays seen by specialist historians of economics as an era of doctrinal and methodological pluralism in economics,[25] and loss of professional self-confidence, largely as a result of the depression. Yet it must be acknowledged that Ross spoke from the standpoint of the social sciences as a whole, rather than as a disciplinary specialist; and her claim has much greater validity as applied to the post-1945 period, when American economists became much more complacent about the workings of the market. Certainly radical economists were highly critical of the apparent love-fest between the business and the academic communities, which can be traced back to developments in the 1920s.[26] As Craufurd Goodwin has observed, after World War II American businessmen discovered that "sober mainstream economists could be effective allies in securing sensible public policies that would respect and strengthen the free enterprise system."[27] This is precisely what the radical economists argued.

Obviously many reasons can be suggested, other than the non-partisanship policy, for the AEA's "wondrous repose" by comparison with the other social science organizations. Over many decades, the Executive Committee and/or the Secretary had consistently resisted members' proposals that the Association should undertake additional activities and responsibilities, such as:

(i)   the certification of economists;
(ii)   the accreditation of economics courses;
(iii) improvements in the preparation of economists for the public service;
(iv)   the defense of members suffering from violations of academic freedom or discrimination;
(v)   the regular publication of consensus statements or expert reports on current policy issues;
(vi)   the sponsorship of research projects; efforts to coordinate existing research activities; and fundraising for substantive projects currently being neglected; and
(vii) the movement of the Association's offices to Washington, DC in order to make a greater impact on public thinking and policy.

Whether a more positive response to these proposals would have been either desirable or effective is not the issue here. In practice, as in the case of professional ethics referred to earlier (*supra*: 146, 149), the AEA's Executive Committee found it easier and safer to preserve "comparative peace at home" by citing past precedents, and taking no action.

As for the radical economists, their symbolic walkout from the AEA's 1970 business meeting meant that they had presumably given up hope of any substantial support from that quarter, whether financial or moral. Yet perhaps they misjudged the Association's official attitude, for that same year "A Statement of Concern" issued by the Black Caucus of economists was received sympathetically, even though some of its more outspoken passages were similar in tone and content to those used by the radicals.[28] Doubtless it was the latter's direct methods, rather than the specific terms of their manifesto, that caused offence. But whatever the reasons, by 1971 the AEA had established committees on The Status of Minorities and the Status of Women in the Economics Profession, with financial support from the Association and from outside agencies.[29]

During the 1970s and 1980s radical economics rapidly gained adherents both within and outside URPE, but given the ferment of ideas, it was not long before divisions appeared within the ranks of 'alternative' or dissenting economists, especially the Marxists. Of particular interest are the links between URPE and the Association for Evolutionary Economics (AFEE), an older and longer-established organization which represented the so-called "old" institutionalism in its late twentieth century eclectic form (O'Hara 1995). Yet another, somewhat looser alliance developed between the social economists (the Society for the Advancement of Social Economics) and the radicals, as the latter group shifted away from the economic determinism of traditional Marxism towards a greater emphasis on the social consequences of capitalism.

These divisions among the radical or dissenting economists seem less surprising when viewed against the wider background of the economics community as a whole. Indeed, there was much talk of a "crisis" in the discipline which extended well beyond the shock of the radical challenge. Some of the divisions were technical, policy-oriented, and methodological or philosophical; others, however, were more ideological or political in their implications. For example, on the left were the neo-Ricardians and Sraffians, as well as the Marxists; on the right there was a striking uprising of neo-Austrian and libertarian writings. To a degree that is difficult to assess precisely, the discipline was shaken by the development of stagflation which posed problems that Keynesian macroeconomics seemed unable to handle. The aftermath of the first oil crisis of 1973 contributed directly to the decline of professional self-confidence; and although the rise of Monetarism seemed to some an adequate counter-revolutionary response to Keynesianism, that is but part of a much more complex story.

It would be too easy to argue that the AEA should have been more active in leading the profession, even perhaps binding up its wounds. But as the previous pages demonstrate, even if there had been an effective answer to the crisis, one could not expect it to come from that quarter.

Notes

1 For an effective brief account of the background, see Rudy (1996: Ch. 5); also Lippit (1996: introduction).
2 Rudy (op. cit.: 167–71) provides a valuable summary of studies of the age and institutional affiliations of anti-Vietnam war members of the professoriate.
3 Schrecker (1986) is an excellent study of the subject.
4 Bloland and Bloland (1974: 6–8); Coats (1998, *passim*).
5 For example, the status of "public history" became a controversial issue among American historians from the 1970s, as academic recession forced an increasing number of trained historians to take non-academic posts. This led to a reconsideration of the distinction between scholarship and professionalism, as public historians became employees, and often advocates of government, business or "other organizations with very particularist agendas inconsistent with universalist norms of disinterested objectivity" (Novick 1988: 512–21; the quotation here is from p. 513).

There is an obvious parallel with economics though the terminology was different because economists usually wished to be regarded as scientists, rather than scholars. In 1959 a National Association of Business Economists was founded, to cater for that species of non-academic economists, who considered they had not been accorded proper recognition by the AEA as potential candidates for office, participants in the annual program, or contributors to the *American Economic Review*. The Secretary's response to an earlier complaint had been a refusal to draw professional lines between different categories of members (Bell 1950: 592).

Although many economists are employed as consultants by special interests or act as expert witnesses in large-scale legal disputes, the role of fraud in economics has never been studied systematically. For a recent scathing comment on professional malpractice, see

Weinstein (1993: 73–96). However, the AEA has never held itself responsible for the ethical or unethical conduct of individual members.

6   This skeptical view is most explicitly and forcefully expressed by radical economists. See, for example, du Boff and Herman (1972: 83); Herman (1982: 275–91).

7   For a powerful protest at this state of affairs, see Hutchison (1992).

8   As Samuelson observed (1962) the Presidential Address is not a suitable vehicle for sophisticated theorizing. Of the 53 I have examined in the 1920–70 period, only two (Plehn 1924; Machlup 1967) or perhaps four (add Mitchell 1925; Fellner 1970) can be said to focus exclusively on theoretical questions without reference to public policy implications. At least two (Schumpeter 1949; Knight 1951) can be described as essentially philosophical, whereas many offer reflections – usually unflattering – on the state of the discipline (e.g., Witte 1957; Stocking 1959; Leontief 1971; Galbraith 1973), or sermonizing on the economist's responsibilities to his profession and/or the public (e.g., Viner 1940; Nourse 1943; Wolfe 1944; Boulding 1969). Occasionally, the captive audience has been subjected to a lengthy and detailed presentation of research results (Douglas 1948; Kuznets 1955; Black 1956). Only two addresses seem to have had a lasting impact on the discipline: Hansen (1939), which initiated the "economic maturity" debate, and Friedman (1968), which launched the "monetarist counter-revolution." I do not mean to imply that "applied" work has no influence on the discipline's shape or form.

9   The 1952 code was "a 117 page volume outlining eighty three ethical problems." It was partly based on the responses to letters of inquiry, which had been sent to all members of the American Psychological Association (Orlans 1973: 75). The code was backed by "laborious, protracted and expensive" semi-judicial procedures (ibid.: 78).

10   See Coats (1998, *passim*); also Coats (1993: 446, 450–51).

11   For example, see Coats (1993: 438, 444, 455–56).

12   Orlans (1973: 25, 23, 27, 49). Harold Orlans had conducted a House of Representatives Research and Technical Programs Subcommittee of the Committee on Government Operations, chaired by Representative Henry S. Reuss of Wisconsin. The materials were published in four volumes entitled *The Use of Social Research in Federal Domestic Programs* (Reuss 1967). Orlans' book contains valuable material on the AEA, and the American Political Science, Sociological, and Anthropological Associations.

13   See Coats (1993: 455, 460); and the official reports of the 1968 and 1969 business meetings in the *American Economic Review*.

14   The Executive Committee stated that the decision to hold the meeting in Chicago "in no way constitutes an endorsement, explicit or implicit, of last summer's actions by the city of Chicago, its officials or the demonstrators." The Association's refusal to take a position on political issues "is a precondition for its individual members to express and work for their own political and social beliefs" (*American Economic Review* 59, May 1969: 571.) In his Presidential Address, "Economics as a Moral Science," Boulding concluded on a reassuring note:

> The anxieties, the moral anguish, and the intense dispute which has racked the American Economic Association this year and is symbolized by the question as to whether we should move our meeting from Chicago is symptomatic of the fact that not even the study of economics can turn people into purely economic men. Strangely enough it was the mathematical economists and econometricians who were most heroically moved by a sense of outrage against their personal identity, and who were least affected by the cost–benefit analysis.
>
> (*American Economic Review* 59, March 1969: 11–12)

What would a skilled deconstructionist make of this passage? Quite apart from the imputation that mathematical economists and econometricians are the least likely among economists to be moved by moral outrage, it must be noted that the AEA's economic historian Secretary, Harold F. Williamson, argued strongly against a move from Chicago not least because of the likely pecuniary liabilities consequent upon the breach of contract with

Chicago hotels. Surely this involved at least an implicit cost–benefit analysis? (The AHA moved from Chicago to New York without incurring such costs.)

15 Cf. *AER* 60, May 1970: 488–89. At the 1967 meeting an anti-Vietnam war resolution had been proposed but it was rejected by the Chair without discussion.

16 The following account is based largely on Bloland and Bloland (1974: Ch. 4) and Orlans (1973: Ch. 2). After 1969 the reports of the business meetings, previously published in the *American Political Science Review*, were transferred to another publication, *PS. Political Science and Politics*. I have been unable to obtain copies of the early issues of this publication.

17 As Orlans notes (op. cit.: 29–30), the APSA had on several previous occasions during and since the 1940s exerted an important influence on the organization of Congress; advocated civilian control of atomic energy; and raised objections to the activities of the House of Representatives Special Committee investigating Tax Exempt Foundations. These were hardly examples of political neutrality.

18 Nevertheless the radical episode was profoundly disturbing, especially to the leading members of the discipline, as indicated in various Presidential and other addresses. For example, Harold D. Lasswell's address "The Future of Political Scientists" (1970), in which he complained that "men of the Profession are ideologically split on fundamental questions that make it impossible for them to remain in the same professional association" (quoted in Somit 1974: 250). Also David Easton, "The New Revolution in Political Science" (1969), and Gabriel Almond (1990: Ch. 1).

19 One protestor, speaking with the ASA officers' permission, maintained that the sociologist is "a kind of spy . . . the professional eyes of the sociologist are on the down people, and the professional palm of the sociologist is stretched towards the up people . . . what if that machinery were reversed? What if the habits, problems, actions, and decisions of the wealthy and powerful were daily scrutinized by a thousand systematic researchers?" (Quoted by Orlans, op. cit.: 38).

20 The following account is based largely on the AHA's Annual Reports for 1968–72, and the lengthy discussion of radical history and historians in Novick (1988: 417–45).

21 The more moderate proposal eventually adopted stated: "The American Historical Association in recognition of the damage here and abroad directly attributable to the Southeast Asia war, and also of the damage to American university intellectual life and to the historical profession, hereby calls for immediate withdrawal of all United States troops and material aid" (*AHA Annual Report* 1970: 72). This is exactly the kind of resolution the AEA's Executive and its officers refused to promulgate.

22 This body was formed in 1970 after a debate on academic freedom, and was approved by a resolution of the AHA Council the following year.

23 Of course radicalization was not restricted to the organizations covered in the preceding section. It also affected the American Psychological Association, the Modern Languages Association, the American Medical Association, and some groups of Federal employees.

24 Ross (1991: 407, 412). Ross remarks on the way that "the common training in neoclassical theory, already part of professional certification and socialization, provide a common style of thinking" that would keep a wide variety of practical specialists "broadly within the neoclassical fold" (ibid.: 410). However, Ross also exaggerates the homogeneity of the interwar American economics profession.

25 For a recent corrective, see the essays in Morgan and Rutherford (1998), and especially the editorial introduction.

26 Cf. the powerful study by Clive Barrow (1990, *passim*); also Alchon (1985).

27 Goodwin, "The Patrons of Economics in a Time of Transformation," in Morgan and Rutherford (1998: 53–81 at 79).

28 The Statement included charges of Social and Racial Bias; Professional Bias, and Lack of Social Responsibility. The study of the economics of poverty was neglected. "Form and technique have been favored over substance and values while issues of policy perspective and institutional performance have been disregarded or downgraded in professional terms. In its

political zeal, the Association has remained silent on the crucial questions and decisions regarding resource utilization affecting minorities." The AEA condones injustice under the "illusion of neutrality on social and political questions" whereas "past experience suggests that 'professional neutrality' perpetuates the *status quo*" (*AEA Proceedings* 1970: 527).

29 From the Association's *Proceedings*; and Coats (1993: 460). *The Review of Black Political Economy* was launched in 1970. It should be noted that the radicals who walked out of the AEA business meeting were not representative of the URPE membership as a whole.

References

Aaron, Henry J. (1993) "Symposium on Economists as Policy Advocates," *Journal of Economic Perspectives* 6, 3: 59–97.

Aberle, David (1967) "Letter," *American Anthropological Association Fellow Newsletter* May: 7.

Alchon, Guy (1985) *The Invisible Hand of Planning: Capitalism, Social Science, and the State in the 1920s*, Princeton, NJ: Princeton University Press.

Almond, Gabriel A. (1990) *A Discipline Divided: Schools and Sects in Political Science*, Newbury Park, MA: Sage Publications.

American Anthropological Association [Fellow] Newsletter.

American Economic Review.

American Historical Association, Annual Reports.

American Political Science Review.

American Sociological Review.

Barber, Bernard (1965) "Some Problems in the Sociology of the Professions," in Kenneth S. Lynn (ed.) *The Professions in America*, Boston, MA: Houghton-Mifflin.

Barrow, Clyde (1990) *Universities and the Capitalist State: Corporate Liberalism and the Reconstruction of American Higher Education, 1894–1928*, Madison, WI: University of Wisconsin Press.

Beals, R. L. and Executive Board (1967) "Background Information on Problems of Anthropological Research and Ethics," *American Anthropological Association Fellow Newsletter* January: 2–13.

Bell, J. W. (1950) "Minutes of the Executive Committee," *American Economic Review* 40 (May): 592.

Bloland, Harland G., Sue M. Bloland (1974) *American Learned Societies in Transition: The Impact of Dissent and Recession*, Berkeley, CA: The Carnegie Commission on Higher Education.

Boulding, Kenneth (1969) "Economics as a Moral Science," *American Economic Review* 59 (March): 1–12.

Coats, A. W. (1977) "The Current 'Crisis' in Economics in Historical Perspective," *Nebraska Journal of Economics and Business* 16 (Summer): 3–16. Reprinted in A. W. Coats, *On the History of Economic Thought: British and American Economic Essays*, Vol. I, London and New York: Routledge, 1992, 459–71.

—— (1985) "The American Economic Association and the Economics Profession," Journal of Economic Literature 23, 4: 1697–1727. Reprinted in A.W. Coats, *The Sociology and Professionalization of Economics: British and American Economic Essays*, Vol. II, London and New York: Routledge, 1993, 433–73.

—— (1992) "Economics in the United States, 1920–70," in A. W. Coats, *On the History of Economic Thought: British and American Economic Essays*, Vol. I, London and New York: Routledge, 407–55.

—— (1993) *The Sociology and Professionalization of Economics: British and American Economic Essays*, Vol. II, London and New York: Routledge.

—— (1998) "Economists, the Economics Profession, and Academic Freedom in the United States," in W. Lee Hansen (ed.) *Academic Freedom on Trial: 100 Years of Sifting and Winnowing at the University of Wisconsin-Madison*, Office of University Publications: University of Wisconsin-Madison.

Du Boff, Richard B., and Edward S. Herman (1972) "The New Economics: Handmaiden of Inspired Truth," *Review of Radical Political Economics* IV, 4: 54–84.

Goodwin, Craufurd D. (1998) "The Patrons of Economics in a Time of Transformation," in Mary S. Morgan and Malcolm Rutherford (eds) *From Interwar Pluralism to Postwar Neoclassicism*, Annual Supplement to Vol. 30 of *History of Political Economy*, Durham, NC: Duke University Press.

Hansen, W. Lee (ed.) (1998) *Academic Freedom on Trial: 100 Years of Sifting and Winnowing at the University of Wisconsin-Madison*, Office of University Publications: University of Wisconsin-Madison.

Herman, Edward S. (1982) "The Institutionalization of Bias in Economics," *Media, Culture and Society* 4 (July): 275–91.

Horowitz, Irving L. (ed.) (1974) *The Rise and Fall of Project Camelot: Studies in the Relationship between Social Science and Practical Politics*, Cambridge, MA: MIT Press.

Hutchison, T. W. (1992) *Changing Aims in Economics*, Oxford: Basil Blackwell.

Lippitt, Victor D. (1996) *Radical Political Economics: Explorations in Alternative Economic Analysis*, Armonk, NY: M. E. Sharpe.

Lynn, Kenneth S. (ed.) (1965) *The Professions in America*, Boston, MA: Houghton-Mifflin.

Miles, Michael W. (1971) *The Radical Probe: The Logic of Student Rebellion*, New York: Athenaeum.

Morgan, Mary S., and Malcolm Rutherford (eds) (1998) *From Interwar Pluralism to Postwar Neoclassicism*, Annual Supplement to Vol. 30 of *History of Political Economy*, Durham, NC: Duke University Press.

Novick, Peter (1988) *That Noble Dream: The 'Objectivity Question' and the American Historical Profession*, Cambridge: Cambridge University Press.

O'Hara, P. A. (1995) "The Association for Evolutionary Economics and the Union for Radical Political Economics: General Issues of Continuity and Integration," *Journal of Economic Issues* 29, 1: 137–59.

Orlans, Harold (1973) *Contracting for Knowledge*, San Francisco, CA: Jossey-Bass Publishers.

Ranson, Baldwin (1981) "AFEE or AFIT: Which Represents Institutional Economics?" *Journal of Economic Issues* 15, 2: 521–29.

Reich, Michael (1993) "Radical Economics in Historical Perspective," *Review of Radical Political Economy* 25, 3: 43–50.

Ross, Dorothy (1991) *The Origins of American Social Science*, Cambridge: Cambridge University Press.

Rudy, G. Willis (1996) *The Campus and a Nation in Crisis: From the American Revolution to Vietnam*, Madison and Teaneck, WI: Farleigh Dickinson University Press. London: Associated University Presses.

Rutherford, Malcolm (1994) *Institutions in Economics: The Old and the New Institutionalism*, Cambridge: Cambridge University Press.

Smith, James Allen (1991) *The Idea Brokers: Think Tanks and the Rise of the New Policy Elite*, New York: The Free Press.

Somit, Albert (ed.) (1974) *Political Science and the Study of the Future*, Hinsdale, IL: Dryden Press.

Stanfield, James R. (1995) *Economics, Power and Culture: Essays in the Development of Radical Institutionalism*, London: Macmillan.

Voss, John, and Paul L. Ward (1970) *Confrontation and Learned Societies*, New York: New York University Press.

Weinstein, M. (1993) "Economists and the Media," *Journal of Economic Perspectives* 6, 3: 73–76.

Weintraub, E. Roy (1992) "Commentary," in N. de Marchi (ed.) *Post-Popperian Methodology of Economics: Recovering Practice*, Boston, MA: Kluwer, 369.

Part II
Aspects of economic method

8   On the credentials of methodological pluralism

Roger E. Backhouse

Introduction

The emergence of economic methodology as a field within economics over the past two decades or so owes much to Warren Samuels. He has, as an editor, been responsible for the publication of an enormous range of work and he has contributed to debates himself. The basis for all this work has been an open and tolerant attitude towards the work of others, including those who do not share his own views. This toleration is not simply due to a generous character (though that is certainly true), but arises from methodological convictions that he has articulated under the label of methodological pluralism.[1] Given the centrality of this to his work, it seems appropriate to explore it here.

I start by outlining what I regard as the clearest, and most explicit statement of what Samuels means by methodological pluralism. I then go on to make three observations. (1) Methodological pluralism rests on the assumption, often implicit, that explicit methodological discussion is valuable. (2) Methodological pluralism is not an absolute but a relative notion, the significance of which depends critically on context. (3) Methodological pluralism has a social dimension that is at least as important as its importance for the individual. I then try to draw some conclusions from these brief remarks.

Warren Samuels on methodological pluralism

[M]ethodological pluralism affirms recognition of alternative methodological credentials, with each scholar having to make his or her choice as to which set of credentials to accept and within what limits.

(Samuels 1997: 68)

Methodological pluralism affirms either that there are no methodological/epistemological absolutes or that no such absolutes have been demonstrated unequivocally. It also affirms that there are no meta-criteria by which to choose between alternative methodologies. The position, therefore, affirms the existence *and legitimacy* of multiple methodological positions.

(Samuels 1997: 74)

In these two quotations, Samuels offers the central features of methodological pluralism, as he understands it (he freely concedes that other understandings are possible and does not try to claim to offer a definitive definition). Several features of this are worth pointing out: (1) Methodological pluralism is a position held by individual scholars. (2) Methodological pluralism is presented as a modest position, resting not on any epistemological absolutes but simply on the failure to find any so far. It may be that there are no absolute meta-criteria on which methodological choices can be made but this is not necessary for his argument. (3) Methodological pluralism is concerned with the *legitimacy*, not the correctness, of individual methodologies.

These propositions lead to what might be termed a "weak" methodological pluralism. This rests on the limitations of what we now know. We simply do not know enough to be in a position to make decisive methodological choices and have, therefore, to adopt a pluralistic position. Economists face many different problems and we have no reason to believe that the same methods will be suitable for tackling all of them. The evidence Samuels adduces to support this is largely negative – all methodologies have limitations and prescriptivism (the attempt to prescribe a specific methodology) has failed. We have simply failed to develop a methodology that is completely free of internal contradictions or to demonstrate "unequivocally" any methodological or epistemological absolutes upon which a final choice between methodologies can rest. Given this, it is wrong to foreclose the process of methodological inquiry.

In addition to these arguments, however, Samuels also argues for a stronger methodological pluralism. He contends, for example, that "*no* position can be summarily disregarded, for example on *a priori* grounds" (Samuels 1997: 74; emphasis added). This is an extremely strong claim. It rests on the argument that reality is socially constructed, with the consequence that meaning depends on "sociological situation and context" (1997: 75).[2] Multiplicity of meaning is the norm, theories perform different roles, and, as a result, it is inevitable that a variety of methods needs to be employed. In short, methodological pluralism follows from relativism.

Critics might argue that this amounts to methodological anarchism – that "anything goes." Samuels defends himself against this charge in two ways. The first defence is an interesting negative one. The alternative to methodological pluralism is what he calls "the prescriptivist programme," in which methodological principles are derived from some "conclusive metaprinciple." In this programme, if one fails to find a "conclusive metaprinciple," there are no constraints and hence "anything necessarily goes" (Samuels 1997: 68). It follows that, given the failure to find a conclusive meta-principle on which to base methodological prescriptions, methodological pluralism is no more anarchistic than the alternative. The second defence is a more positive one. It is that, given the credentials of alternative methodologies, the individual scholar has to make a choice and that "this stipulated recognized necessity of choice is the answer to the prescriptivist criticism that pluralism amounts to 'anything goes'" (Samuels 1997: 68).

Given its importance to Samuels's methodological pluralism, this point needs to be considered in detail. His credentialist approach to methodological choice involves four elements (Samuels 1997: 74):

1. It is necessary to identify the "precise nature, grounds and limits" of individual methodologies.
2. The process whereby knowledge is developed is important.
3. The researcher should make "studied determinations" of the credentials of alternative methodologies.
4. Criticism is a part of the process.

This makes it clear that Samuels is far from suggesting that methodological standards should be abandoned. Individuals inevitably have to make methodological commitments – without these, research would be impossible. What they should do, however, is be aware of the choices they have made, the grounds on which these choices rest, and the limitations of these grounds. In doing so, they will become aware of the limitations of their chosen methodologies and be more open to alternatives. This awareness of the limitations inherent in any methodology may even persuade economists that knowledge can be advanced by undertaking research based on opposing, apparently contradictory, positions – for example, induction and deduction, rationalism and empiricism, realism and nominalism (Samuels 1997: 74).

According to this interpretation, methodological pluralism is primarily about methodological awareness and toleration. It can, I suggest, be separated from Samuels's own views concerning how the economy should be conceived and investigated. It is an appeal against using methodology, either explicitly or implicitly, to foreclose certain lines of inquiry. Though infused with arguments that are conventionally thought to be "postmodern," it can equally be seen as in the spirit of the Enlightenment, with its commitment to the virtues of rational argument. Methodological pluralism is, therefore, for anyone who is convinced that methodology is worth discussing explicitly, an attractive position to hold. It accords with democracy, tolerance, and many other virtues. However, whilst Samuels has made a strong case, there are some further issues that are worth considering.

The importance of explicit methodological discussion

As explained above, Samuels clearly believes that informed methodological choices can be made and that they should be made with as full a knowledge as possible of the credentials attached to each methodology. This presumes that explicit discussion of methodology is worthwhile. This belief can be broken down into two parts: (1) that criticism contributes to the growth of knowledge; and that (2) methodology is something worth criticising. On what basis can these claims be made? Several answers are possible.

The simplest answer is simply to assert these as premises, directly related to basic value judgements. They might be seen as following from the Enlightenment vision of knowledge. Alternatively it can be related to value judgements about democracy and how a democratic society should work. This line of argument is, of course, close to McCloskey's (1986) arguments about the importance of *sprachethik* to good conversation. Such arguments are perfectly acceptable, and arguably very strong, credentials for the claim that criticism is fundamental to knowledge. However, to rely on them is to be open to the charge that methodological pluralism is founded on an optimistic view that might be considered naive.

An alternative answer is to argue that criticism works. It could be argued that this is the essence of the Popperian tradition in economic methodology.[3] Naive falsificationism, for example, asserts that criticism contributes to the growth of knowledge by leading to the refutation of false theories. Lakatos's "sophisticated methodological falsificationism" sought to refine this to take account of the structure of science, but had the same broad objective. Alternatively, a much more pragmatic, empirical line could be taken. It is in this vein that Blaug (1992) argues that, whatever the theoretical defects of falsificationism, attempts to test theories empirically have led to a sharpening of the issues and have been beneficial.

None of these answers is decisive (if Samuels is right, we would not expect them to be). Arguments based on explicit value judgements leave open the reasons why one should hold those value judgements; the limitations of Popperian methodological arguments are well known and the history of economic thought is clearly open to different interpretations, making it very difficult to draw clear methodological lessons. However, rather than simply conclude that the arguments are inconclusive, another response to these answers is possible. This is that, instead of asking whether criticism can lead to the growth of knowledge, looking for a "Yes" or "No" answer, we should instead be asking questions such as: Under what circumstances does criticism lead to the growth of knowledge? How far should criticism be pursued? The essence of the Kuhnian picture of science is that scientists typically take certain features of their science for granted. Much scientific activity would be impossible if they were continually questioning foundations. There are thus good reasons why, at least in some contexts, criticism should be suspended. Perpetual criticism and revolution may not be the best way for science (or any other branch of knowledge) to advance.

The question should also be raised about whether, even if it is conceded that criticism is desirable, methodology is a subject about which it is profitable to have explicit discussion. It may be that economists will do their subject better without thinking explicitly about methodology.[4] If there is a tendency for methodological positions to be over-sold (for their limitations to be under-emphasized), it could be the case that the dangers associated with explicit methodological discussion exceed the benefits. It might, for example, be the case that tacit methodological understandings (which may evolve in response to changing circumstances) will always be superior to anything that can be articulated and that explicit discussion does no more than provide a vocabulary in which misleading methodological prescriptions can be made. There are two responses to this. One is to appeal to the Enlightenment faith in reason – there is no reason why reason should be less effective here than in any other branch of inquiry. The other is to argue, on the basis of past experience, that greater awareness of the methodological choices being made by economists would have had a beneficial effect. The persuasive power of economic ideas has often derived from methodological claims that, when made explicit, are unpersuasive. The subject might be less prone to ephemeral fashions.[5]

The relativity of pluralism

To rephrase and simplify the arguments Samuels has put forward, there are two reasons for supporting pluralism: we may be wrong or there may be no right answer to the questions that are being asked. In either case, pluralism – being open to a variety of answers – may save us from rejecting the right answer or right answers. Its cost, of course, is that we may fail to reject answers that should be rejected. When the problem is put in this way, two conclusions suggest themselves. The first is that pluralism is not a matter of "Yes" or "No," but is a matter of degree. The degree to which we are pluralist should depend, to use the language of statistical inference, on the relative costs of making Type I and Type II errors. For different loss functions, we will end up opting for different degrees of pluralism. The second is that pluralism should not be an issue. Decisions about whether to entertain theories have to be made on a case-by-case basis, taking into account the theories themselves, the strength of the evidence for and against them, and the problem-situations the theories are to be used to address. From this perspective, the question of pluralism *in general* does not seem to be worth asking. It may be that under some circumstances the benefits from pluralism are positive, but that at other times they are not.

It is probably no coincidence that Samuels has been advocating methodological pluralism at the time when neoclassical orthodoxy has been at its height. In the interwar period, and arguably before that, economics was pluralistic (see Morgan and Rutherford 1998). Institutionalism and neoclassicism competed openly without either being dominant. Numerous individuals fitted into neither camp and pursued a variety of approaches. In such a context, appealing for methodological pluralism might have appeared as an attempt to maintain the status quo. However, in the context of the postwar situation, where the analysis of formal mathematical models of optimizing behaviour has, for many economists, come to be seen as the only rigorous way to do economics, the call for methodological pluralism has quite different implications. Thus even if, in the interwar period, there was a need for economists to get on with the task of applying economics to various tasks, if necessary ignoring explicit discussions of methodology, it is arguable that a different strategy is appropriate today. Today, it is more important than in the interwar period to argue the case for pluralism. Where one approach is so clearly dominant, even though its success is still open to question, the notion of risk-spreading should alone be sufficient to justify a degree of pluralism. From this perspective, the question is not pluralism itself but its extent: over what range of approaches should it extend and what resources should be devoted to each?

The social dimension

This takes us to the social dimension. Samuels talks of methodological pluralism as relating to the individual scholar. However, knowledge is created by and has significance within communities. This raises the question of what methodological pluralism should mean at the social level.

On one interpretation, methodological pluralism at the level of society is close to free speech. If other economists choose to express views that are opposed to our own, we allow them to do so. The epistemological merits of free speech do not need to be considered because the question is non-negotiable on ethical or other grounds. One is led, therefore, to focus, as Samuels does, on the individual scholar. Here, it is important to note that it not only operates simply at the level of deciding on one's own research, but also concerns the individual's role in the wider community: in making appointments, allocating resources, and in the process of deciding what gets published where. This is the point where pluralism becomes contentious for it is, in practice, impossible to separate it from the question of standards.[6] Methodological pluralism, if it is to mean anything at all, means being open to work that fails to meet certain methodological standards – the point, made so forcefully by Samuels, is that these standards will reflect meta-criteria that cannot be established categorically and that they should not be imposed rigidly. However, standards cannot be abandoned, which means that difficult decisions have to be made.

One might argue that Samuels is right to focus on the individual scholar. Decisions are taken by individuals, even if those decisions influence and are influenced by the broader social context. Methodological pluralism implies the attitude that individuals should have towards their work. However, the decisions taken by individuals depend on social structures – on the organization of the academic community, how individuals operate within it, its relationships to other academic communities and to society at large. The maintenance of methodological pluralism may depend as much on these structures – on the sociology of the profession – as on the attitudes of individuals. It is possible to imagine a situation where most economists, as individuals, adopt a methodologically pluralist position, but act collectively in such a way that pluralism is hard to maintain. It may make an enormous difference, for example, whether there is a large, competitive academic system, in which competing methodological views can survive in different institutions (or even in different types of institution) or whether there is a centralized system in which pluralism depends on the attitudes of a single decision-making body.[7]

Concluding remarks

Methodological pluralism might seem a far cry from the Popperian and Lakatosian methodology that dominated the field of economic methodology during the 1980s. This view is reinforced when Samuels brings in his own views on economic theory – which, though influenced by neoclassical, Austrian, and even Marxian economics, are rooted in the "old" institutionalist tradition – and when he draws out implications of the socially constructed nature of reality. However, as I hope to have shown, the core of his argument for methodological pluralism ought to be persuasive even to someone in the Popperian tradition.[8] Those who should find it unpalatable are those who believe that methodology is a simple, clear-cut matter that raises no difficult issues and does not merit explicit discussion. Such people are, by and large, found amongst the ranks of economists and not methodologists, for the latter are, almost by definition, people who have become convinced that methodological problems are non-trivial and in need of explicit analysis. Few methodologists would use words such as "absolute," "unequivocal," and so on, which Samuels repeatedly uses in summarizing the positions to which methodological pluralism is opposed.

In responding to methodological pluralism it is important to separate it from substantive views about the economy. It is also important to separate what might be termed the positive and the normative. Take, as an example, the following remark:

> Methodological pluralism will tend to appeal to those who are comfortable with indeterminacy, ambiguity (e.g., plurality of meanings) and openness; and not to those who emphasize or seek determinacy and closure.
>
> (Samuels 1997: 77)

This may be true, but so too is the converse. Methodological pluralism may appeal to those who are uncomfortable with indeterminacy, ambiguity, and so on. I may consider (along with Blaug) that economics makes progress through attempts to resolve indeterminacy and ambiguity – through attempts to reduce disputes to testable propositions (if possible about measurable phenomena) – but nonetheless regard it as vitally important to acknowledge that indeterminacy and ambiguity, in practice, are facts of life.[9] In other words, I may be a methodological pluralist because I believe that is how the world is, not because I am comfortable with the situation. I suggest, therefore, that methodological pluralism does not in any way depend on either a particular view of economics or a postmodern view of the world. It is entirely compatible with the values of the Enlightenment.

In the previous two sections I argued that methodological pluralism should not be seen as an absolute, in two senses. The first is that, setting aside extreme cases, the boundaries of what constitutes methodological pluralism are impossible to define with any precision. It is a matter of degree, not an either/or choice. The second is that the significance of methodological pluralism varies according to the context in which it is advocated. At the outset of the paper on which I have drawn most heavily, Samuels (1997: 67) notes that "The subject is so vast, so complex and so laden with nuance" that he can do no more than provide a "middlebrow" treatment. All I can claim to have done in this chapter is to highlight some aspects of the problem that seem particularly important to someone who finds methodological pluralism attractive, but approaches it from a very different starting point.[10]

Notes

1 Two other advocates of methodological pluralism have been Caldwell (1982) and Dow (1985; 1996). I am not concerned with questions of priority in using the term, for each of these three has, in their own way, made it their own.
2 This line of argument is developed in more detail in Samuels (1991). In this chapter I focus on Samuels (1997) as providing the clearest and most succinct statement of his position. It could be supported with references to other publications.
3 This is argued explicitly by Boland (1994). See also Blaug (1992); Hands (1993).
4 Hargreaves Heap (2000) has outlined and responded to a possible defence of this view.
5 See Backhouse (1997: Ch. 2). Hutchison (1977; 1992) has made related arguments.
6 The implications of pluralism for editing journals are discussed in Hausman and McPherson (1988); Hausman (1994); Backhouse (1994); and Davis (1994).
7 British readers will be aware that this is alluding to the implications of the UK's system of research assessment, whereby funding allocations depend primarily on how research is graded by a national committee (one committee covers "Economics and econometrics"). On such national differences, see Coats (1996; 1999).
8 It is entirely compatible with Popper's (1959: 111) argument that "The empirical basis of objective science has nothing 'absolute' about it."
9 This attitude has much in common with the view of science advocated by C. S. Peirce.
10 For a view that approaches substantially the same conclusion (what he terms "principled relativism") but does so from a postmodern standpoint, see Davis (1999).

References

Backhouse, Roger E. (1994) "Pluralism in the Economic Journal," *History of Economic Ideas* 2, 3: 109–17.
—— (1997) *Truth and Progress in Economic Knowledge*, Cheltenham: Edward Elgar.
Blaug, Mark (1992) *The Methodology of Economics*, 2nd edn., Cambridge: Cambridge University Press.
Boland, Lawrence (1994) "Scientific Thinking Without Scientific Method: Two Views of Popper," in Roger E. Backhouse (ed.) *New Directions in Economic Methodology*, London: Routledge.

Caldwell, Bruce (1982) *Beyond Positivism: Economic Methodology in the Twentieth Century*, London: George Allen and Unwin.

Coats, A. W. Bob (1996) *The Post-1945 Internationalization of Economics*, Annual Supplement to *History of Political Economy* 28, Durham, NC: Duke University Press.

—— (1999) *The Development of Economics in Europe since 1945*, London: Routledge.

Davis, John B. (1994) "Pluralism in social economics," *History of Economic Ideas* 2, 3: 119–28.

—— (1999) "Postmodernism and Identity Conditions for Discourses," in Robert Garnett (ed.) *What do Economists Know?* London and New York: Routledge.

Dow, Sheila (1985) *Macroeconomic Thought: A Methodological Approach*, Oxford: Basil Blackwell.

—— (1996) *The Methodology of Macroeconomic Thought: A Conceptual Analysis of Schools of Thought in Economics*, Cheltenham: Edward Elgar.

Hands, D. Wade (1993) *Testing, Rationality and Progress: Essays on the Popperian Tradition in Economic Methodology*, Lanham, MD: Rowman and Littlefield.

Hargreaves Heap, Sean (2000) "Methodology now!" *Journal of Economic Methododology* 7, 1: 95–108.

Hausman, Daniel M. (1994) "Pluralities of Subject, Method, Goals and Visions," *History of Economic Ideas* 2, 3: 99–108.

Hausman, Daniel M., and Michael McPherson (1988) "Standards," *Economics and Philosophy* 4, 1: 1–8.

Hutchison, Terence (1977) *Knowledge and Ignorance in Economics*, Oxford: Basil Blackwell.

—— (1992) *Changing Aims in Economics*, Oxford: Basil Blackwell.

McCloskey, Donald N. (1986) *The Rhetoric of Economics*, Brighton: Harvester Wheatsheaf.

Popper, Karl R. (1959) *The Logic of Scientific Discovery*, London: Unwin Hyman.

Samuels, Warren J. (1991) "'Truth' and 'Discourse' in the Social Construction of Economic Reality: An Essay on the Relation of Knowledge to Socioeconomic Policy," *Journal of Post Keynesian Economics* 13: 511–24. Reprinted in Warren J. Samuels, *Essays on the Methodology and Discourse of Economics*, London: Macmillan, 1992, 11–28.

—— (1992) *Essays on the Methodology and Discourse of Economics*, London: Macmillan.

—— (1997) "The Case for Methodological Pluralism," in Andrea Salanti and Ernesto Screpanti (eds) *Pluralism in Economics: New Perspectives in History and Methodology*, Cheltenham: Edward Elgar, 67–79.

9   Some practical aspects of pluralism in economics

Thomas Mayer

> Truth is so important, however, that it behooves us not to jump to conclusions about it.
>
> (Samuels, 1997)

Warren Samuels' contribution to our thinking about pluralism has been recognized by his selection as the author of the article on methodological pluralism in the *Handbook of Economic Methodology* (Samuels 1998). This chapter supplements his treatment by presenting a version of epistemic pluralism that is not grounded in postmodernism, and is not subject to the objection that in its strong version it amounts to an "anything goes" relativism, while in its weak version it amounts to no more than the platitudinous mandate: "be open to ideas that differ from yours."

I try to counter the above objection to the weak version of pluralism by presenting a version of epistemic pluralism that focuses on our limited knowledge and our uncertainty about many important aspects of the economy, while accepting the tradition in economics of offering answers to most practical questions that come up, even if such answers have to be based on evidence that is far from compelling. As recent discussions of global warming illustrate, natural scientists sometimes do the same.

I do not presume to contribute to the large philosophical literature on methodological pluralism. The argument is localized to economics – and to the current situation in economics – since it does not discuss whether ultimately we may possess sufficient knowledge to pick the one correct theory. Most of it is therefore consistent with an anti-pluralist position as this is understood in philosophy. Hence, it bypasses some of the problems faced by pluralism that Caldwell (1988) discusses, such as its relation to a theory of truth. And unlike Caldwell, it looks at pluralism in economics as a whole, instead of focusing on pluralism in methodology.

On many issues in economics only zealots hold their conclusions with certainty. Most, while they may think that the evidence for their conclusions is strong, admit at least the possibility that they may be wrong. Yet, in practice, they usually ignore this possibility. Thus, some methodologists – following the lead of many philosophers – seem to argue that some particular method, such as methodological individualism, is the only correct way to do economics, so that any results reached by some other method are worthless. Similarly, in welfare economics economists start (implicitly or explicitly) with a particular value judgment, for example, the importance of egalitarianism, and usually proceed from there without, at least explicitly, allowing alternative value judgments any weight at all. Likewise, only rarely do those who offer policy recommendations discuss whether these recommendations are robust with respect to errors in their model, despite the familiar saying that "all models are wrong – but some are useful."

Such a procedure differs sharply from the way economists describe the behavior of agents. In simple models agents are assumed to calculate certainty equivalents rather than to operate just on the basis of the most likely forecast. And even half-way sophisticated models go beyond certainty equivalents and allow for risk aversion. I will therefore explore the implications of assuming that economists should operate with as much sophistication as they ascribe to agents, so that they realize that they, as well as the agents whose behavior they model, have to live with uncertainty.

My target is therefore segmented decision making, that is, the standard practice of first selecting on one's reading of the best – but perhaps far from conclusive – evidence, a certain proposition (that is a value judgment, a methodological rule, a theorem or an empirical finding), and then to use this proposition in further reasoning as though it were definitively established. This procedure and its questionable nature are both most evident in empirical work. Typically, an econometrician presents not only her point estimate, but also its standard error. But in the next step of the argument, she ignores the standard error, and plugs only the point estimate of the coefficient into the subsequent equation. One should therefore not be surprised if the resulting conclusions are not robust.

A more reasonable alternative is often, though not always, not to accept as the truth a particular proposition because the evidence for it seems strongest, but to carry in one's mind two or more conflicting propositions, while attaching unequal weights to them. (In deciding on these weights one should usually take account of the relative losses from accepting the wrong proposition.) As Mäki (1997: 43) has remarked: "it may be that at some point in time, such as now, the epistemic standing of economic theories is such that we had better tolerate a number of strong . . . [substitute theories] at the same time." More generally, Richard Foley (1983) has shown that it is not always irrational to hold at the same time two logically inconsistent theories.[1]

Such a procedure might be called "probabilistic pluralism", since it attaches different weights to various alternatives. It therefore differs sharply from relativism with its notion that all theories are equal. On the contrary, it assumes that we can – and should – distinguish between theories that are more likely to be true and those that are not. Such probabilistic pluralism is hardly new. Thus it seems to describe how the Federal Reserve, and presumably other policy makers often behave. Thus as monetarism obtained more academic respectability in the 1960s and 1970s the Fed shifted towards monetarism – but only part of the way.

I first discuss probabilistic pluralism with respect to economic policy, and then discuss theory, methodology, and value judgments. I then respond to the argument that pluralism on the level of the individual economist is not needed, since truth will emerge from the debate of various economists, each of whom presents just one point of view and disregards the contribution of other views.

Policy

Choosing a policy is analogous to choosing a portfolio of securities. Economic theory tells us that rational investors do not allocate all of their net worth to the asset that they expect to have the highest yield, but diversify in a way that takes into account various expected states of the world and their relative probabilities, as well as risk aversion. Compare that to the typical paper on economic policy. Here, we are told that a certain policy would improve the functioning of the economy, and the risk inherent in the adoption of this policy is either ignored, or the reader is given reasons for thinking that it is minor. But the probability that these reasons are mistaken, and that the risk is substantial, is usually ignored. Moreover, while some specifics of the analysis are often spelled out in excruciatingly detailed mathematical form, we are told little if anything about the loss function implicit in making the policy recommendations, or about the assumed degree of risk aversion.

To be sure, not all policy literature proceeds in this way. Thus there exists a series of models showing that the optimal size of a stabilization policy depends, in part, on the standard error of the GDP forecast (see, for instance, Friedman 1953; Brainard 1967; Mishkin 1998). Moreover, in many cases – though far from all – it would make little sense to diversify the policy "portfolio" by adopting the policy only in part. But even in all-or-nothing cases, it would help to indicate the riskiness of the policy. To be sure, saying that the author should point out all the weaknesses of the analysis he or she knows about may be a counsel of perfection, because it would require pointing out these weaknesses not just to the reader, but also to the editor and referees. But even leaving aside the ethical problem in hiding weaknesses, there are sources of risk that could safely be pointed out.

For an example of how risk is disregarded, consider the debate on whether banks should be allowed to merge with non-financial firms, or to hold stock in them along the lines of the German and Japanese "universal banking" systems. One might agree with the proponents of such a change that it would probably improve the American financial system. But "probable" is not "certain." Hence, one has to look not just at the size of the gain if they are right, but also at the size of the loss if they are wrong, and at the relative probabilities, as well as the appropriate coefficient of risk aversion. Another example is the argument (cf. Calomaris 1990) that the FDIC should be abolished, and that instead banks should insure each other. One can make a plausible case that this would probably make the financial system more efficient by reducing moral hazard, but there are also risks. The obvious one is that without the FDIC, massive bank failures could set off a major recession.[2] It is not irrational for someone to agree with Calomaris that such a contingency is unlikely, and that the reduction in moral hazard that would result from the abolition of the FDIC is highly desirable, and yet to oppose this change because massive bank failures would be so damaging that, when multiplied by even a small probability, the expected loss outweighs the gain from abolishing the FDIC. And even someone who believes that the mathematical value of the benefit from abolishing the FDIC exceeds the mathematical value of the cost might reasonably oppose it due to risk aversion. Disregarding the risk of error could be defended by arguing that the researcher's task is to develop a particular line of reasoning, and it is up to the reader to keep in mind that this reasoning may be wrong, and to evaluate the resulting risk. There is certainly something to this response, but the reader may not be in as good a position as the researcher to evaluate the probability of error. I return to this topic in the penultimate section.

Theory

The choice of a theory presents a similar situation. Accepting a particular theory is often (like adopting a policy) an action that has consequences, such as influencing the views of other people, or changing one's research procedures or research agenda. To be sure, the loss function is often hard to specify because we do not know all the implications that acceptance of the theory will have, but that does not justify ignoring the loss function altogether. One reasonable response is to say, for example, that although I accept theory T, I am aware that there is a significant probability that it is wrong. Consequently, when undertaking some action, such as choosing a research project, I am reluctant to select one that is worth doing only if T is correct. And my reluctance will depend not only on this probability, but also on the costs and potential pay-offs of the research project. It is, of course, not possible to calculate these probabilities precisely, but one can obtain some rough idea, particularly if one is willing to take other economists' opinions seriously. Thus, if I know that someone, who is just as well informed as I am, disagrees with me and thinks that T is false, should I not tell my students that, though I accept it myself, there is considerable doubt that T is true? And if I write an op-ed article predicated on the truth of T, if there is much dispute about it, shouldn't I warn readers who are unaware of this?

Moreover, theories have specific domains. Not only is this so in the formal use of theories as logical systems whose conclusions depend upon the validity of certain assumptions, but also in their informal use relevant to answering empirical questions, where the assumptions are not intended to hold strictly, but only approximately. If the domains of theories are properly specified, then there need be no conflict between different theories. But if, as is usual in economics, the domains of theories are not clearly specified, then there is likely to be an area in which their claimed domains overlap, or at least an area where it is unclear which theory applies. Hence, there is often room for an eclectic theory that combines elements of two or more conflicting theories, or for maintaining both theories. We know that theory A is better for one problem, and theory B for another, but are uncertain for a third problem where we may want to look at the solutions given by both theories, and if they differ, admit our uncertainty.

To a formalist who would like to model economics on geometry such vagueness may seem "unscientific." But not to those who prefer to model economics on the natural sciences. Ian Hacking (1983: 264) reports that:

> Even people in a team, who work on different parts of the same large experiment, may hold different and mutually incompatible accounts of electrons. That is because different parts of the experiment will make different uses of electrons. Models good for calculations on one aspect of the electrons will be poor for others. Occasionally a team actually has to select a member with a quite different theoretical perspective simply . . . to get someone who can solve those experimental problems.

Such conduct is not inconsistent with the belief that there exists only one given reality (i.e., ontological realism) which we may be able to grasp eventually, but for now we have to make do with what Mäki (1997) calls "temporary pluralism."

Methodology

In the 1950s an anti-pluralist view of methodology was much easier to justify than it is now. One could then argue that there is a delineable set of disciplines known as "science," that we know this set's defining characteristics, and that this set is the sole reliable path to genuine knowledge. To be sure, there were disputes even within the mainstream philosophy of science, but by hindsight they were mere family squabbles. The main task of the economic methodologist was therefore to decide which of the prevailing economic methodologies best captures the defining characteristics of science as set out by philosophers, or if none does so, to develop one that does.

But the "received view" is no more; the old certainties are gone. Even if one rejects (as I do) most of the postmodernist turn, the search for the one true methodology seems quixotic. Now, we need to look not for a demarcation criterion, but for heuristics that advance the growth of knowledge. And these heuristics may have features that seem strange. For many years biology made substantial advances even though it used the crutch of teleological argument.

Inconsistency between quantum theory and relativity theory has not prevented physicists from working with both and making progress.

One should therefore be skeptical about statements that economists must do one thing or another, for example that they must not make statements about aggregates unless these can be shown to be necessary implications of rational utility maximization. That claim seems particularly hard to accept when it comes from those who, in defending the unrealism of assumptions, take refuge in Friedmanian instrumentalism and is worth considering in some detail, because it provides a good example of the flaws of such a monistic methodology.[3]

If physicists could get by for so long by taking gravitation as an unexplained "given," why should macroeconomists, too, not be allowed to take observed regularities as given?[4] Even in the case where macrotheory is actually inconsistent with microtheory, instead of just being not derivable from it, we need not, as the example of relativity theory and quantum mechanics illustrates, drop either. If we want to claim complete knowledge, something will have to give and consistency between macro and micro economics may have to be established. But until we reach the point where such a claim is realistic, we can use both theories. It could be that rational choice theory is a sufficiently close approximation to be useful when dealing with most microeconomic problems, but not when dealing with certain macroeconomic problems.

The insistence of new classical economists that we have to reduce all macroeconomics to microeconomics is therefore hard to justify at this stage of our knowledge, as long as one views economics as an empirical science, that is, as an attempt to explain and predict regularities, rather than as a branch of logic. It would be correct only if three conditions held. The first is the claim that we may not tolerate – even for now – contradictions that we hope to resolved in the future. That claim is hard to justify, though many new classical theorists seem to treat it as obviously correct. The second is that we have sufficient grounds to be more confident in rational choice theory than in the relevant macrotheory – and that is by no means obvious. Third, even if these two conditions hold, we would be justified in dropping the macrotheory only if it is inconsistent with the microtheory, not merely if it cannot be derived from the rational choice theory. Biology is consistent with quantum theory, but nobody would try to reduce biological statements to quantum theory statements.

How then can we understand the new classical insistence on rigorously deriving all macrotheory from microtheory? One possibility is to view new classical theory, not primarily as an attempt to explain observed economic phenomena, but as an attempt to derive the logical implications of rational choice theory, thus in effect defining economics in a Robbinsian rather than a Marshallian way.

Maartan Janssen (1998: 308) has made the interesting suggestion that it is a unity-of-science argument that provides the valid justification for the reductionism that the new classicals insist on, writing:

> Two distinctively separate disciplines such as microeconomics and macro-
> economics can only coexist in a fruitful way if they have different
> domains of application. However, as . . . both study aggregate phenom-
> ena, it is not clear when to apply one (and not the other). It is thus
> natural to study the compatibility of the two disciplines, and as micro-
> economics has a better developed analytical structure, the reason for
> investigating the possibilities for microfoundations becomes clear.

Janssen is right in saying that the interrelation of micro and macro economics
is worth studying, and that it would be desirable to relate them more closely.
But that is very different from saying that we must avoid macroeconomic
statements that cannot be derived from microeconomic foundations, even if it
means having no answers to certain questions, or giving answers that have a
much less secure empirical foundation. Moreover, that microeconomics has
"a better developed analytic structure" does not necessarily mean that it is
superior to macroeconomics. Other criteria, such as empirical confirmation
and applicability, matter too, particularly if one thinks of theories as instru-
ments for either prediction or explanation.

Yet, none of this means that being rigorously derivable from microtheory is
not a desirable attribute of a macrotheory. It does add an additional way of testing a macrotheory, and furthermore, if the macrotheory is well confirmed, it
provides a way of testing the microtheory. But there is a distinction between
being a desirable attribute and being a necessary attribute. Hence, it may well be
useful to have two or more macrotheories (or versions of macrotheory). One
version is at least loosely derivable from microtheory (even if it does not meet the
strict conditions of reducability[5]). The other version, though not inconsistent
with microtheory, is not derivable from it, but can solve some problems that the
derivable theory does not, or has better empirical support. Moreover, the consistency of micro and macro theory should be treated as a two-way street.

Another instance where a pluralistic attitude towards methodology is
appropriate is the debate about *Verstehen*. Obviously, *Verstehen* does not provide evidence that meets the criterion of interpersonal knowledge; what
makes you understand why twelfth-century peasants did not revolt may not
necessarily make me understand it. But if good empirical evidence that is
interpersonal is not available, evidence derived from *Verstehen* is preferable to
mere guesses. Moreover, *Verstehen* can add to the usefulness of a theory in
satisfying our intellectual curiosity, and by making the theory easier to work
with on an intuitive level. So, instead of treating *Verstehen* as either totally
useless or as a necessary attribute of any adequate theory, why not treat it as
a desirable but not a necessary feature?

Value judgments

In making policy recommendations economists must make value judgments.
Even the application of the Pareto criterion is a value judgment, though an

unusually vacuous one that might even be called hypocritical.[6] Usually much less restrictive value judgments are needed. Ideally policy makers or philosophers could provide them. But policy makers are often reluctant to be that explicit, and philosophers do not speak with one voice.[7] Thus, some philosophers tell us that individuals have an inherent right to their property, so that a just state will not redistribute income. Others say that the state should redistribute income because equality is the moral default setting and inequality of income can be justified only insofar as it benefits the poor as well as the rich. Both sides present coherent arguments.

So what should the economist do? One alternative is to confine himself to purely positive economics. But that is hard to do, both because value judgments tend to seep unnoticed into positive analysis (the assumption of a quadratic loss function is one example), and also because the economist's clients, that is, the general public and policy makers, want definite answers to questions that combine positive and normative elements. Another alternative is for the economist, despite his lack of training in philosophy, to take the plunge and make the required value judgments. But that adds an arbitrary element to his conclusions.

A third alternative is to study ethics and political philosophy in depth, However, that suggestion not only comes up against a time constraint, but also seems insufficient. To those who have at least some positivistic tendencies, the various resolutions provided by political philosophy, despite their great sophistication and substantial value-added over untutored common sense, often seem tenuous.

Hence, in making value judgments – regardless of whether economists take an untutored plunge, or devote much study to it – they are on insecure grounds. A related and serious problem is that one's value judgments may be inconsistent. I may believe in the importance of property rights, but also in the need to provide more help to the poor than private charity can make available. Should I favor a progressive income tax to finance a welfare program? Such problems suggest a fourth possibility, straddling. Given uncertainty, straddling, that is, going part of the way with each of two or more contradictory principles, is appropriate if there are increasing costs to errors.

Suppose the issue is whether to tax Peter $10 to pay to Paul, and that we believe that this redistribution is appropriate, but are not sure. Hence, we may tax Peter only, say, $5. If we are right in believing that a $10 tax is appropriate, then by imposing only a $5 tax we commit two injustices, depriving Paul of $5 that are due to him, and permitting Peter to retain $5 that should not be his. And if our belief is not justified, then we also commit two injustices. Alternatively, if we impose the $10 tax, then if our belief is correct we commit no injustice, but if it is incorrect we commit an injustice that in dollar terms is twice as large as in the first case.

Obviously, our decision should depend, in part, on how confident we are in our belief, as well as on our degree of risk aversion.[8] But it should also depend on our evaluation of the relation between the magnitude of this injustice and the loss that this injustice creates, that is, on whether there are increasing, constant or decreasing costs to injustice (cf. Johnson and Mayer 1962). And that is not clear. Neither increasing, constant nor decreasing costs can be dismissed out of hand. Some might argue that there are increasing costs to injustice: that imposing a $10 unjustified tax on any one person has more than twice the moral cost of imposing a $5 unjustified tax on two persons, because unjustified suffering should be spread as thinly as possible rather than concentrated on one person. At the other extreme, some might argue that the very existence of an injustice represents an evil whose undesirability has nothing to do with its size – that it is meaningless to quantify injustice. This is the extreme case of decreasing cost to injustice. A more moderate position is that there are both fixed costs and rising variable costs to injustice, in the sense that the very existence of any injustice, however small, is offensive, and hence imposes a fixed cost, but that there is also an additional cost to injustice that varies more than proportionately with its magnitude.

In the first case (increasing cost) there is a role for straddling, while in the second case (decreasing costs) there is not. In the third case the answer depends on whether the variable costs are increasing at a fast enough rate to outweigh the fixed cost component. Thus in at least one, and perhaps two of the three cases, the pluralist's tendency to straddle may be justified. Probabilistic pluralism in value judgments can also be justified in another way. Theories of ethics are grounded in the basic principles that the public perceive to be ethical. In turn, much of the public's perception is based on its evaluation of particular situations (which may be either actual or hypothetical). And since these evaluations do not necessarily form a coherent, logical system, but have a strong emotive element, it would not be surprising if sometimes there are contradictions.

When confronted with a specific situation, I may decide that X's rights have precedence over Y's, and derive a general rule from this. But when confronted with a very different case, I may decide that Y's rights have precedence and derive a rule that conflicts with the previous one.

A pragmatist might well argue that we simply have to make our peace with a world in which certain moral imperatives have domains that are not adequately demarcated. A decent society needs to think of human life as in one sense sacred, not as something whose value is measured in dollar terms. We do not permit someone to sell to another person the right to kill him. At the same time, in making practical decisions, society sometimes has to weigh human life in dollar terms. Few would advocate spending, say, $100 million on a medical procedure that would prolong one person's life by only one day.[9] And we permit risky activities like coal mining.

Individual or collective pluralism

A speech community may act in accordance with pluralism, even if no individual member does so, by allowing an adequate hearing to diverse points of view. Is that all that one should ask for, or is it desirable that on many issues individual scientists keep several divergent views and their probabilities in mind? In other words, should economists follow lawyers and act as advocates, or should they try to resemble as best they can the picture of the dispassionate scientist found in idealistic discussions of science? There is something to be said on both sides.

On the one side, acting as an advocate rather than dispassionately weighing the evidence and admitting weaknesses in one's arguments comes naturally because it avoids the discomforts of cognitive dissonance. Hence, regardless of whether economists (or other scientists) should behave this way or not, in practice, they are likely to do so and, one might argue, it is better to do so openly, and put the audience on notice. Moreover, economists, like other flesh and blood scientists, need the stimulus that comes from motives like status enhancement; perhaps there is some truth to the frequent confusion of disinterested and uninterested. An attitude of "my theory, right or wrong" is likely to motivate them to work harder than is an objective search for the truth. One might therefore argue that the advocacy model of economics represents a useful and almost necessary division of labor.

But there is a stronger case to be made on the other side. Even if full attainment of the ideal of the dispassionate scientist is out of reach, maintaining this ideal points economists in the right direction. Moreover, the advocacy model has its comparative advantage in situations where the public or policy makers can exercise reasoned judgment about who is right, or putting it less positively, where experts can do little better than the lay public. Thus we let juries decide the facts of the case, while judges decide the law. In economics the public and policy makers find it difficult to decide who is right. And not only the public, but also other economists face this difficulty.

Authors of empirical papers often have many opportunities to skew their results by, for example, leaving out observations. If readers are to take such papers seriously, they must have some confidence that the author is motivated, or at least more or less constrained, by the dispassionate-scientist model.[10] Furthermore, the public is less likely to take the views of economists seriously, even on issues on which most economists agree, if on other issues it sees economists occupying immovable positions that concede nothing to the other side. In addition, if economists, because they see themselves as advocates, are in the habit of ignoring the evidence on the other side when they present their case, they are likely to slip into the same habit when deciding which side to choose, and then to stay with it even if strong contrary evidence comes along. Hardly a formula for swift progress.

Conclusion

Theorems are subject to demonstrative reasoning. Theories and the evidence for or against them generally are not. Insofar as economics models itself on empirical science with its focus on theories rather than theorems, the principles about behavior under uncertainty that economists proclaim with regard to agents should apply to economists themselves. This provides an opening for pluralism. Hence, in giving policy advice economists should seek diversification and consider the probability of error, and also the loss function and risk aversion. And since advocacy of a theory is in a relevant way like a policy decision, the same applies to theories. If this means employing several contradictory theories, then that is consistent with rational behavior. In choosing a methodology, too, a sharp dichotomy of right and wrong is not useful, as the example of new classical reductionism illustrates. Similarly, there is a role for probabilistic pluralism in making value judgments.

Notes

1 Foley (1983) gives an example of rational belief in two conflicting propositions. Suppose that a persuasive experiment shows that there is a 99 percent probability that each one of a set of a hundred hypotheses is true, while another, conclusive experiment shows that not all of these hundred hypotheses can be true at the same time. It is then reasonable to accept each of these hypotheses, while also accepting that at least one of them must be false.
2 There is also the problem that banks might use membership in their insurance organization as a tool for collusion.
3 For a powerful and general critique of reductionist claims, see Kincaid (1997).
4 To be sure, macroeconomic regularities are not as reliable as the regularities that physicists deal with. But then economic theory is also not as solidly established as physical theory. It is therefore far from obvious that in economics observed regularities should play a lesser role relative to theory than in physics. And while, in principle, the Lucas critique makes macroeconomic regularities suspect, there is not much empirical evidence to suggest that in most situations it is empirically important.
5 I am using the term "derivable" in a loose, common-sense fashion that does not imply that the strict conditions for reduction (see Kincaid 1997) are fully met.
6 Sheltering behind the Pareto criterion is hypocritical because the probability that any change would make nobody worse off is so small that if economists take the Pareto criterion seriously, they could make virtually no policy recommendations.
7 Presumably policy makers are reluctant to make value judgments in part because they do not want to admit to themselves that they are making some people worse off. Moreover, in democratic countries policy makers are selected in part on the basis of their skill in papering over differences.
8 This assumes that committing an injustice has no further consequences.
9 Along these lines, see Hausman and McPherson's (1996: Chs. 1 and 14) discussion of rich countries exporting pollution to poor countries.
10 For a survey of the extent to which economists do take econometric evidence seriously see Mayer (1995: Ch. 9)

References

Brainard, William (1967) "Uncertainty and the Effectiveness of Monetary Policy," *American Economic Review* 57 (May): 411–25.

Caldwell, Bruce (1988) "The Case for Pluralism", in Neil De Marchi (ed.) *The Popperian Legacy in Economics*, New York: Cambridge University Press, 231–344.

Calomiris, Charles (1990) "Is Deposit Insurance Necessary? A Historical Perspective," *Journal of Economic History* 50 (June): 283–95.

Foley, R. (1983) "Justified Inconsistent Beliefs," *Analysis 1983* 43: 40–43.

Hacking, Ian (1983) *Representing and Intervening*, New York: Cambridge University Press.

Hausman, Daniel, and Michael McPherson (1996) *Economic Analysis and Moral Philosophy*, New York: Cambridge University Press.

Janssen, Maartan (1998) "Microfoundations," in J. B. Davis, D. W. Hands and U. Mäki (eds) *Handbook of Economic Methodology*, Cheltenham: Edward Elgar, 307–10.

Johnson, Shirley, and Thomas Mayer (1962) "An Extension of Sidgewick's Equity Principle," *Quarterly Journal of Economics* 76 (August): 454–63.

Kincaid, Harold (1997) *Individualism and the Unity of Science*, London: Rowman and Littlefield.

Mäki, Uskali (1997) "The One World and the Many Theories," in Andrea Salanti (ed.) *Pluralism in Economics*, Cheltenham: Edward Elgar, 37–47.

Mayer, Thomas (1995) *Doing Economics*, Cheltenham: Edward Elgar.

Mishkin, Frederick (1998) "Rethinking the Role of the NAIRU in Monetary Policy," Federal Reserve Bank of New York, Research Paper # 9806.

Samuels, Warren J. (1997) "The Case for Methodological Pluralism," in Andrea Salanti (ed.) *Pluralism in Economics*, Cheltenham: Edward Elgar.

—— (1998) "Methodological Pluralism," in J. B. Davis, D. W. Hands and U. Mäki (eds.) *Handbook of Economic Methodology*, Cheltenham: Edward Elgar, 300–303.

10 What econometrics can and cannot tell us about historical actors

Brewing, betting, and rationality in London, 1822–44

*Philip Mirowski**

Why beer should interest economic historians as well as Joe Sixpack

It has been inadequately noted just how much the rise and fall of fascination of economic historians with particular industries has been near exclusively an artifact of neoclassical economics (Cannadine 1984). An earlier vintage of economic historian, perhaps more familiar with the practical workaday physics and chemistry of commodity production, and more concerned with the institutional structures of capitalism, had tended to concentrate upon what now might be considered more prosaic industries, such as brewing (Mathias 1959), for hints as to the causes and consequences of British growth.

As it so happens, there are some very good reasons to look to breweries for exemplars of technological and institutional innovations characterizing the British industrial revolution. On the institutional side, it is fairly clear that, under the force of circumstances, breweries were one of the earliest sectors to innovate many of the organizational structures we now associate with the large-scale corporation. Because of the nature of their product and the exigencies of the excise, they were induced to keep track of many far-flung purchases and sales of relatively small magnitudes, as well as to concentrate upon supervision of the network of tied pubs. Hence we find there one of the earliest well-articulated accounting systems, including attempts to systematically attribute desegregated costs to activities, of any British industry in this era. Moreover, we also find there one of the earliest appearances of a centralized hierarchical management structure, often associated with the railroads by Alfred Chandler and other business historians. On the technological front, it would be a mistake to regard breweries as a backward

* Philip Mirowski, Carl Koch Professor of Economics and the History and Philosophy of Science, University of Notre Dame, Notre Dame, Indiana 46556. E-mail address: *Mirowski.1@nd.edu*. The author wishes to thank Martin Stack for research assistance, and Chris Grandy for comments.

or unprogressive industry. As Mathias explains, they were in the forefront of combining the new physics of heat with problems in chemistry and biology; they were also among the earliest to adapt the steam engine to their production requirements. While it has become commonplace to assert that the steam engine owed very little to the science of physics (Cardwell 1971), it is a Mancunian brewer, James Joule, who is often given credit for the founding of thermodynamics upon the "discovery" of the conservation of energy. Indeed, his apparatus was an only slightly modified device in common use in breweries of the time (Mirowski 1989: 40–43). For all of these reasons, British breweries should be considered some of the most forward-looking and rationalized firms in the era of the British industrial revolution.

It should then come as no surprise that, given their track record of early rationalizing innovations in these spheres, the surviving business archives of British breweries are amongst the highest quality of any such records dating from the eighteenth and early nineteenth centuries. And amongst those, one of the most comprehensive and detailed business archives in the whole of British eighteenth- and early nineteenth-century economic history is that of the brewing firm Truman, Hanbury and Buxton, now housed at the Greater London Record Office. It is one symptom of the biases of the Cliometric approach to history (which harbors a muted suspicion towards business records) that this treasure trove has remained largely untouched, with the exception of some few direct comments by Peter Mathias in his magisterial history of eighteenth-century British brewing, the survey history of British brewing by Gourvish and Wilson (1994), and a largely uninformative vanity history published by the firm of Truman's itself (Anonymous 1959).

For our present purposes, a very sketchy outline of this firm's history in the eighteenth and early nineteenth centuries will help set the stage for our subsequent econometric inquiry. The Black Eagle Street brewhouse predated the involvement of the Truman family, which apparently began when Joseph Truman senior acquired it in 1679. His son Benjamin Truman so expanded the brewery that in 1760 it was the third largest in London. After his death in 1780, James Grant (d. 1788) conducted the business, although ownership was held in trust for Benjamin's great-grandsons Henry (1777–1847) and John Truman Villebois. In 1789 Sampson Hanbury (1769–1835) acquired James Grant's share and managed the business until roughly 1827. His nephew, Thomas Fowell Buxton (1786–1845), joined the firm in 1811, only to immediately install their first Boulton and Watt steam engine; while Thomas and Robert Pryor (1778–1839), proprietors of the recently absorbed Proctor's brewhouse, were made partners in 1816. In 1821, Robert Hanbury (1798–1884) was made restricted second-class partner, though he was increasingly responsible for the day-to-day operation of the business. By dint of aggressive acquisitions and expansion, Truman's became London's second-largest brewer by 1820; at which juncture Thomas Butts Aveling (1783–1837), the head clerk of the concern, married a Truman granddaughter and became a restricted partner in 1825. In 1830, the beer duty was abolished, making it much easier to start up a pub; whilst contemporaneous urban tastes also shifted from porter to lighter ales. The other big Victorian breweries – Barclay Perkins, Whitbread, Meaux Read – were slow to adjust to the new circumstances; but Truman's directors were more sure-footed, and so by 1850 managed to become London's (and Britain's) largest integrated conglomerate of breweries, pubs, and extender of small-scale commercial credits. Truman's continued to grow and prosper and absorb other breweries until the twentieth century, beyond our period of interest.

The immediate motivation for our present interest is a fascinating memo book in the Truman archives (B/THB/C/242) at the Greater London Record Office entitled, "Précis of Hops & Barley, 1822–1880."[1] One early custom of the British brewing industry was the periodic formal closing of the account books at what was called a "Rest Dinner" for the partners and head clerks. These were openly festive occasions, where prodigious quantities of the company product were consumed, and talk regularly turned to the agricultural vicissitudes of the two main ingredients of beer, barley (used to make malt) and hops (a flower used to stabilize and preserve the beer).[2] Since in the early nineteenth century, malt and hops alone accounted for more than 60 percent of the cost of production of beer, the fluctuations of hops and barley prices weighed much on the minds of the partners as they closed their books on another year. What sets the Truman partners apart from other breweries is that they decided to attempt to separate out their prediction skills from other skills of management and organization with regard to their primary inputs. On the first quarto sheet of this memo book, their clerk wrote:

At our Rest Dinner in July 1822 whilst we were speculating on the probable prices of Barley & Hops for the coming Season, it was suggested and agreed to that at our future Annual Rest Dinners each of us should put down in writing what we considered would be the price of Barley and Hops on the first Monday in January in the ensuing year . . . [Here the ground rules for the public report of the price were spelled out (PM).] . . . A Sweepstakes of one Sovereign each in Barley and Hops by each individual & those who were nearest the actual prices of the day to be the Winner.

What then follows in this revealing volume is a continuous record of the prices wagered by each partner, the subsequent actual price, and the declared winner or winners, for the years 1822–46. The partners must have understood the principle of extrapolation from prior trends, since inside the front cover, someone in a different hand had inscribed information from newspapers on prices of wheat and barley, along with comments on the state of the weather, for the years 1790–1837 (though the timing of this inscription cannot be discerned). One gets the impression that the competition was keen and spirited, for although the sum wagered was small for people of their estate in life, a loose sheet included in the volume reveals that someone else, in yet a third hand, had drawn up an extensive table of actual and winning prices for the years 1822–40, with remarks on the spread of realized prices about the actual price, and an Abstract of whom amongst the partners had won for each hops and barley a specified number of times. Given that what we have in this book is a time series of consistent bets on a relatively generic input price for a production process of which they all had at least some control and oversight, this is a very remarkable document.

One imagines that an imaginary representative Cliometrician, especially if she be of a rational expectations bent, would already be inwardly relishing the possibilities; and, indeed, since one expects to encounter many such real characters in the economics profession, that is part of the motivation of our exercise. So much of modern Cliometric history, under the tutelage of orthodox neoclassicism, is taken up with questions of the supposed "rationality" of the historical actors or the "efficiency" of the market in a specific setting, that it would seem almost natural to situate this archival treasure in that frame. However, the problem faced by many Cliometricians, be they concerned with the supposed efficiency of medieval open-field agriculture or the rebuttal of widespread impressions of the decline of late-Victorian entrepreneurial capacity, is that the evidence is always at three or four removes from the original construction of the theoretical problem. Much of this work is predicated upon index numbers, often manufactured for other purposes which inadequately capture the controversy at hand; or when the inquiry does deal with prices, there are no assurances that the data are representative of the exact sorts of market information faced by the actors. In particular, quantitative evidence is often cast in modern definitions presuming modern theories with little or no concern shown for the mentalities or capabilities characteristic of the denizens of the historical era in question. Even in the rational expectations literature of the 1970s and 1980s, where data is supposedly so much better than that dealt with by historians, "tests" of the rational expectations hypothesis mostly made use of mean forecasts, and did not track the actual behavior of living breathing individuals facing rational numbers. This persistent recurrence of aggregation over predictors is offered unapologetically, even though one of the supposed attractions of the orthodoxy is its solid grounding in methodological individualism. When recourse to survey data is had, there is generally no way to track the same individual through time or to ascertain who knows what, when, and how much about the presumed identity of the object of prediction or purchase. I myself have never seen a rational expectations test where real individuals have a chance to track two economic variates simultaneously through time (outside the race track or other leisure contexts), except perhaps in the experimental economics literature. So what we have here is an extremely rare bit of evidence indeed.

Therefore, let us turn first to the sort of Cliometric exercise that an historian trained in an economics department might be inclined to construct, patterned upon the practices of orthodox economics journals; and only then, afterwards, return to the real history, the narrative of these people's lives.

Econometrics and rationality

The standard statistical procedure for addressing the question of the "rationality" of actors' expectations in a market where explicit forecasts have been recorded in a timely manner is to begin by comparing the forecasts and the realized values, here of actual prices. The initial low-tech approach, but one which has decided advantages in terms of intuitive appeal, is simply to plot the values of specified wagered price against actual realized price for each participant in the brewery Rest Dinner. These plots, one each for barley and hops for each player, can be found in the appendix to this chapter (see pages 360–67). At this early stage, it becomes apparent that some bettors had a harder time tracking the turns in prices than others; Thomas Buxton seems to have possessed the curiously useless ability to lead price movements of hops by a full year; Richard Pryor appears by contrast to overestimate price swings of hops; Tom Aveling, on the other hand, seems overly sanguine with regard to the smoothness of barley prices. In a quick geometric manner, we come to observe that different actors have distinct "signatures" in their betting behaviors, signatures which may very well be specific to a particular commodity without carrying over to a complementary commodity. Since the subtext of so much orthodox neoclassical theory is the quest to telegraph that people are fundamentally the "same" in their rational economic behavior, while supposedly simultaneously respecting their idiosyncrasies, it is salutary to get some rough empirical feel for the extent to which people have persistent marked differences in behavior which could potentially be turned to profit.

Undoubtedly our representative Cliometrician would be champing at the bit here, suffused with the conviction that these casual eyeball observations lack the one attribute which she has brought to the discipline, namely, its self-consciously scientific approach. Indeed, the point of the entire exercise in her mind should be to quantify and to "test" hypotheses. As one famous Cliometrician has written:

> historians do not really have a choice of using or not using behavioral models . . . The real choice is whether those models will be implicit, vague, incomplete and internally inconsistent, as Cliometricians contend is frequently the case in traditional historical research, or whether the models will be explicit, with all relevant assumptions clearly stated, and formulated in such a manner as to be subject to rigorous empirical verification.[3]

But a contemporary Cliometrician would not rest satisfied with these research guidelines, for just any behavioral "model" wouldn't do in the current climate; in order to be recognized as legitimate "economic history," it would further be necessary to have recourse to a model which is presently sanctioned by the theoretical orthodoxy in economics departments. It is this requirement, rather than any generic numeracy or familiarity with statistical technique, which has frightened off the vast bulk of practicing historians. But let us accept these constraints for the nonce, and see where this species of scientific history will lead us.

"Rationality," while not well and thoroughly documented within departments of economics, has in the recent past come to signify for neoclassicals some convex combination of no-arbitrage conditions, an "efficient markets" hypothesis, rational expectations, and whatever restrictions that might be deemed imposed by the canons of probability and the underlying price theory. This packet of doctrines has given rise to an accompanying set of statistical procedures, which in the 1980s has diffused throughout the applied economics literature to such an extent that one might readily characterize it, with justice, as a *distinct genre* of journal article.[4] Indeed, one can even cite a very nice survey article which covers many of the relevant statistical points (Jeong and Maddala 1991). It would seem we have the makings here of an exemplary Cliometric paper, bringing together a brace of accepted econometric techniques and an orthodox theoretical model with some antiquarian data to pose the inevitable question, "Were the Actors Rational?" We shall, indeed, proceed to do just that in this section, although at a somewhat more leisurely pace relative to the standard journal literature, in order to draw out the implications of this exercise for economic history and for "scientific empiricism" in general. The fruit of being a bit more explicit about the process of Cliometric research is to insist that inductive research, like so much else in human history, is inexorably path-dependent.

The standard initial step in this literature is to calculate the difference between the predicted and actual prices, in order to discern if there are any systematic patterns in errors of prediction. The justification for highlighting this variable is usually traced to either the rational expectations doctrine or efficient markets hypothesis: if errors are persistently made in a context where they can translate into immediate monetary gain or loss, then "rationality" would dictate that the actor either: (a) changes their behavior; or (b) be eliminated from play by market penalties. Sometimes this is further conflated with the postulate that the actors share the same model of the economy with the neoclassical analyst; a postulate to which we shall return shortly. In practice, one begins by examining the divergence of bets from realized prices, with the stipulation that these divergences should exhibit a mean of zero and be roughly uncorrelated through time for rational actors. In Table 10.1, we present means and standard deviations of each actor's "errors" in bets made at the Truman rest dinners.

Once again we note some personal signatures of individual behavior. Some members of the partnership consistently underestimate the level of agricultural prices: the Villebois brothers, Sampson Hanbury, and Thomas Buxton. Others consistently overestimate their movements, like Tom Aveling, while still others show more mixed results. Everyone remains within one standard deviation of zero, which is the expected value at "rationality"; but for many,

Table 10.1

Name	Bet price, hops		Bet price, barley	
	Mean	Stand. dev.	Mean	Stand. dev.
J. Villebois	−11.00	43.31	−2.40	6.83
H. Villebois	−8.62	37.37	−1.81	7.07
S. Hanbury	−18.76	51.12	−2.34	7.22
T. Buxton	−9.09	39.44	−0.79	5.77
T. Aveling	51.42	57.11	1.71	6.11
R. Hanbury	5.48	39.36	−1.88	6.15
R. Pryor	29.88	87.89	−1.79	6.64
E. Buxton	−5.00	17.81	3.45	5.97
A. Pryor	8.33	29.85	2.60	7.08

this is only the case because the spread of their errors is so large in the first place. Looking at the time series plots of the errors (not included here), it seems highly likely that there is some temporal dependence and probably autocorrelation in many cases: for instance, Richard Hanbury's barley bets. Another question, not often broached in the orthodox literature, is whether the divergences of each individual from the actual price are themselves correlated; and, in this instance, it turns out that they are, with positive correlation coefficients in the 0.5–0.7 range. So these men, the proprietors of the most successful brewery in London in their era, were neither spot on target, but nor were they egregiously and wildly wrong; in some ways they acted alike, but in others display a tenacious individuality. The evidence so far is ambiguous. But we still have yet to deploy our formidable econometric armamentarium.

The next step would then be to recast the hypothesis of rationality as one in which there was no systematic error in betting to conform to a regression model of a generic "rational" expectation. The standard practice is to posit a simple linear equation like:

$$\text{Actual Price} = \alpha + \beta \text{ Bet} + \varepsilon, \tag{1}$$

where $\varepsilon \sim N(0,\sigma^2)$ and expected values, in the case of rationality are $\alpha = 0$ and $\beta = 1$. The problem with this seemingly straightforward procedure is that while the null hypothesis is initially portrayed as reasonably sharp, the alternative hypothesis is in practice extremely diffuse. This problem is paradigmatic of what is wrong with the entire rhetoric of "testing" in Neyman–Pearson econometrics, as we shall discuss below. Here, the Cliometrician may opt to assume as their mandate the objective of presenting the "best" simple time series description of error behavior for each individual bettor which is as "close" to the above equation as possible; that is what is most frequently done in the literature, and that is what we present below in Table 10.2.

Table 10.2 Brewer error equations, 1822–46

Barley

J. Villebois
Price = 27.7 + 0.25 JVILL R^2 = .07
(3.09) (1.00)   t = -2.86 n = 15

H. Villebois
Price = 27.5 + 0.27 HVILL R^2 = .09
(4.35) (1.53)   t = -4.13 n = 24

S. Hanbury
Price = 29.79 + 0.20 SHANB
(2.68) (0.62)   t = -2.50 n = 13

T. Buxton
Price = 18.45 + 0.51 TBUXT R^2 = .18
(2.08) (2.12)   t = -2.00 n = 22

T. Aveling
Price = 22.11 + 0.37 TAVEL R^2 = .07
(1.56) (1.01)   t = -1.69 n = 14

R. Hanbury*
Price = 1.04 RHANB R^2 = .07
(30.79)   t = 1.35 n = 25

R. Pryor
Price = 23.57 + 0.38 RPRYO R^2 = .13
(2.60) (1.52)   t = -2.44 n = 17

E. Buxton
Price = 1.09 EBUXT R^2 = .52
(23.62)   t = 2.14 n = 12

A. Pryor*
Price = 1.07 APRYO R^2 = .40
(18.22)   t = 1.20 n = 10

Hops

J. Villebois
Price = 53.17 + 0.71 JVILL R^2 = .71
(2.47) (5.77)   t = -2.25 n = 15

H. Villebois
Price = 29.02 + 0.86 HVILL $- 0.255_{-1}$ R^2 = .77
(1.83) (8.91)   (1.86)   t = -1.36 n = 24

S. Hanbury*
Price = 1.12 SHANB R^2 = .57
(12.53)   t = 1.36 n = 13

T. Buxton
Price = 34.85 + 0.83 TBUXT R^2 = .75
(1.93) (7.83)   t = -1.60 n = 22

T. Aveling
Price = 0.74 TAVEL R^2 = .57
(12.97)   t = -4.35 n = 14

R. Hanbury
Price = 43.37 + 0.70 RHANB R^2 = .84
(3.64) (11.10)   t = -4.68 n = 25

R. Pryor
Price = 75.41 + 0.43 RPRYO R^2 = .79
(5.62) (7.57)   t = -9.82 n = 17

E. Buxton
Price = 24.90 + 0.86 EBUXT $- 0.51_{-1}$ R^2 = .96
(3.64) (19.69)   (2.05)   t = -2.99 n = 12

A. Pryor*
Price = 0.91 APRYO R^2 = .81
(17.40)   t = -1.60 n = 10

Notes
Candidates for "rational expectations" denoted by a (*). The t-statistics in parentheses refer to the estimated coefficients, while the t-statistic under the R^2 reports the results of a test of the null hypothesis that the coefficient on each individual's bet variable =1.0; that is, is unbiased.

The joint restrictions on α and β may seem fairly stringent, and that impression is initially borne out by the results in our table. For the barley bets, only Robert Hanbury and Arthur Pryor pass the test with flying colors; the reason that Edward Buxton does not is simply that the estimated error variance is so low that the t-test indicates it is more likely that his $\beta > 1$. As for the hops betting, only Sampson Hanbury and Arthur Pryor pass the unbiasedness test. One does get a sense from the R^2 and residual diagnostics that barley prices were much harder to track than hop prices in this period. Thus if we halted our exercise right here, we would be left with the rather disconcerting conclusion that there was only one confirmed consistent *homo economicus* at the Truman breweries in this period; and further, as we shall see shortly, he was not a principal owner, nor even a partner in good standing.

But everyone knows that our dogged Cliometrician would not stop there; nor should she. For no econometrician worth their salt takes all the time and trouble to construct a data set, frame a hypothesis, and deploy statistical skills merely to ask a single one-shot yes or no question of the data. At the very least, it would seem reasonable to begin exploring why the result turned out as it did; and it would take superhuman self-denial not to be on the lookout for any auxiliary hypotheses which might readily overturn an unexpected result. In this particular case, since our Cliometrician is also a partisan of the neoclassical model, she would most likely be distressed with the rather poor showing of our brewers, who, after all, were just about as successful in their economic calling as one could be; and, instead, begin to cast about for explanations which would preserve their "rationality."

One standard response of the disappointed econometrician is to look to the residuals for various diagnostic problems. But we have already encompassed that procedure in our local search for the "best" time series representation of equation (1). Indeed that is why both Henry Villebois and Edward Buxton have a first-order autocorrelation correction in their hops bet equations. However, even this description is not ultimately decisive, since no exhaustive search was performed in the time domain. Another option might be to explicitly model the error divergences in the time domain as VAR processes. For instance, if we designate the Divergence of Robert Hanbury by DRH, then his barley bet errors could be modeled by the following vector autoregression, with t-statistics in brackets:

$$DRH = -2.80 \, [1.42] - 0.45 \, DRH_{-1} \, [2.36] + 0.38 \, \varepsilon_{-1} \, [2.08]. \tag{2}$$

Various other individual divergences have similar autoregressive representations. But our Cliometrician would clearly not like the way this "diagnostic" was trending, since it is generally conceded in the rational expectations literature that temporal structure in errors of prediction are not congruent with the efficient markets hypothesis: someone should be punishing these people for their errors by making arbitrage profits from them. Indeed, our Cliometrician would probably choose not to report the above equation, since it contradicts the result reported in Table 10.2 that Robert Hanbury was "rational" in his barley bets. If she instead tried to brush off the incongruity by suggesting that these bets were only a harmless game, whereas real business was business, she would effectively undercut any justification for her paper in the first place. Other possible "corrections" to estimates of equation (1) will be discussed shortly.

There are some other classes of econometric tests which are claimed to have a bearing upon the question of rationality: for instance, the entire "variance bounds" literature, discussed in Mirowski (1988). Very crudely, the idea behind a variance bounds test is that people's predictions of prices and other economic variates should actually be *smoother* than the realized series, predominantly because of random shocks which could in no way be foreseen beforehand. If, conversely, people's anticipations were seen to fluctuate more extremely than the historical realizations, this would call their rationality into question. Thus our Cliometrician might choose to rephrase the question away from the first moments of the bets, as in Table 10.2, and towards their second moments; and the results are reported in Table 10.3.

This brace of results would surely perk up the flagging spirits of our Cliometrician. For here we not only pick up most of the same "rational actors" who were identified in Table 10.2, but we have now also extended the evidence for "rationality" to ten out of 18 cases. Of course, there are still a few blots on the record: just three people – Sampson Hanbury, Edward Buxton, and Arthur Pryor – qualify as fully-fledged consistently rational actors; and then there is the notable regularity that variance bounds seem easier to pass with barley than with hops. We have already commented that barley was apparently a more difficult agricultural price to predict; hence, by definition, its realized variance would tend to be large. Nevertheless, it is a good bet that our Cliometrician would stop here, write up these tabular results, and ship the whole thing off to the *Journal of Economic History*.

Table 10.3 Variance bounds tests

Name	Var (P) > Var (Bet)?	
	Hops	*Barley*
J. Villebois	no	no
H. Villebois	yes	no
S. Hanbury	yes	yes
T. Buxton	no	yes
T. Aveling	no	yes
R. Hanbury	no	yes
R. Pryor	no	no
E. Buxton	yes	yes
A. Pryor	yes	yes

Yet, the further addition of auxiliary hypotheses and the implied criticism of the econometrics need not halt here. The most common reaction amongst those familiar with the variance bounds and unbiasedness literatures would be to recognize that the widespread rejections of rationality found elsewhere have led to a revanchist literature which finally settled upon generic non-stationarity of economic variates as the main reason for doubting all of the above tests. This revisionism has led to a series of techniques for detecting what is now called "cointegration" of time series.[5] The idea behind cointegration is that if the time series which is to be predicted has a unit-root representation (namely $X_t = X_{t-1} + \varepsilon_t$) then standard time series regression results are invalid, with OLS estimators biased downwards. These observations have given rise to a large econometric literature concerning the estimation of presence of unit roots and subsequent estimation of whether two such unit root series are "cointegrated": intuitively, whether the difference of the two time series might itself be represented as a unit root process, such that neither series wanders "too far" from its counterpart. In some of the macro literature, tests for cointegration are often used synonymously with tests for "rationality"; though as some more judicious commentators have noted (Jeong and Maddala 1991: 432), this does not even approach the level of concrete specification found in the unbiasedness tests above.

Notwithstanding these caveats, suppose our Cliometrician wishes to become known as a woman second to none in keeping up with the snazziest developments in econometrics (or at least those thought snazzy by a previous generation). She therefore subjects the actual barley and actual hop prices to the augmented Dickey–Fuller test (Fuller 1976) for the presence of unit roots. What she finds is that if the specification does not include a constant term, then neither price series has a unit root; but if a constant term is appended, then both do now appear to have a unit root representation. Since there is no theory-driven "estimation" going on here, in the sense that she has complete freedom of specification to define the shape of the "rational" representation, we predict she will choose the one most supportive of the non-stationary interpretation. The next step is to apply the same procedure to the time series of bets; but here she encounters the problem that most of the bets series are appreciably shorter than even those of the actual prices. However, since the bets by Robert Hanbury extend throughout the entire sample period, we can apply the Dickey–Fuller test there, and discover much the same results. Finally, the Dickey–Fuller test is run on the difference between the two series, with the curious outcome for hops that, conversely to the above cases, the unit root appears when the constant is absent. Our Cliometrician would probably report these results as supporting the hypothesis of rationality, again, probably without filling in all the details about specification choices made along the way. Or perhaps she does include these in an appendix, but then the editor asks her to remove them from the published version, because they are boring, and as we all know, resources are scarce.

I, myself, have not reported the cointegration "tests" here because they have a very tenuous claim to be sanctioned as legitimate in this context. First, they don't generally meet the standards of an orthodox test for rationality unless the expected values of prices minus bets are zero (unbiasedness) and the forecasting errors $P_t - B_t$ exhibit no serial correlation. In the case of Robert Hanbury, we have already demonstrated previously that neither condition holds for hops, and the latter condition is violated for barley. But there is a more profound econometric objection. The literature on cointegration arose in areas where very long time series were being used to test market efficiency, and the objection was then very legitimately raised that few economists would expect the relevant time series to be stationary over such long stretches of time. Indeed, the question of non-stationarity may only be legitimately posed in a statistical sense when time series data points number in the hundreds, and better yet, the thousands. This problem has also arisen in the chaos literature, where researchers have given up trying to answer whether economic series are chaotic because of a critical conceptual problem specific to economics. There econometricians can get thousands of readings of financial asset prices, but only if they are willing to take them minute-by-minute; or else over very very long time frames, say, monthly prices over centuries. In the former case, the "deterministic" structure which might be discovered there is inherently not very interesting, while in the latter, almost no one is willing to claim the price actually refers to the "same thing." In our humble little example, precisely what makes the data set so ideal for testing "rationality" – it refers to a consistent set of actual individuals making their bets on clearly identified generic commodities in a repeatable manner – also renders it impossible to ask any serious questions about non-stationarity. Therefore I doubt whether the cointegration tests have any meaning at all in this context.

So, that, if I have not overlooked anything, is pretty much what a standard econometric paper based upon these archival materials would look like, should a Cliometrician have actually encountered this unusual source. However, luckily for us, there is one further significant bit of evidence which should be extracted from the archive and brought to bear on the econometric exercise. We know from the rest books who was declared winner of each wager. Now, if we assume that each player had an equal chance of winning in each bet in which they took part, and standardize for their times participating, we can compare the expected number of wins with their actual experience.[6] This information is presented in Table 10.4, with the last column expressing the ratio of actual wins to the expected number, as defined above. The expected value of this ratio should be unity, with excessive losers tending to zero and outstanding winners achieving two or above. The outcome was that Sampson Hanbury was far and away the most successful wagerer on barley, while Robert Hanbury and, to a slightly lesser extent, Robert Pryor were the most successful in wagering on hop prices.

Table 10.4 Brewers' wager status

Name	Barley				Hops			
	N	Wins	Expec. wins	W/E	N	Wins	Expec. wins	W/E
J. Villebois	15	1	2.16	0.46	15	2	2.16	0.92
H. Villebois	24	5	4.0	1.25	24	3	4	0.75
S. Hanbury	13	4	1.85	2.16*	13	2	1.85	1.08
T. Buxton	22	5	3.5	1.42	22	4	3.5	1.14
T. Aveling	14	2	2	1.0	14	2	2	1.0
R. Hanbury	25	8	4.33	1.84	25	9	4.33	2.07*
R. Pryor	17	3	2.5	1.2	17	5	2.5	2.0
E. Buxton	12	2	2.47	0.74	12	4	2.47	1.61
A. Pryor	10	1	2.16	0.46	10	0	2.16	0.0

This final table brings us to the second major thesis of our paper: were the Cliometrician to write the paper we have outlined above, she would have made the elemental mistake of confusing neoclassical notions of rationality with economic success. For the persons who were far and away the best at winning wagers did not show up as "rational" in most of the econometric tests she had deployed: or to put it somewhat differently, the mechanical rationality characteristic of rational expectations has little or no relationship to the strategic rationality of outsmarting your economic competitors. Indeed, the whole point of rational expectations is to render other economic actors faceless and irrelevant, and to deny history (even if only the pale and tepid version of history as the time series of past realizations) any role in the determination of present choice.[7] But Sampson and Robert Hanbury were smarter than that, which is probably why they sequentially served as (in effect) the chief executive officers of the partnership (as revealed by the memo books B/THB/A/129 and B/THB/B/120) during this era. There is the further irony that it is precisely the case when one of this duo is identified as "rational" by the initial regression analysis, it is the other who manages to dominate in cumulative wins. So in this very specific sense, if we had just stuck to the Cliometrics, we would have negated the historical content of this interesting episode, blurring the economically relevant differences of the actors in the name of "testing a well-defined hypothesis."

But there is another deeper lesson to our little exercise. The reason the sequence of tests was spelled out in such detail above was to begin to reveal the sequence of choices faced by the historian along the way when they start out an econometric inquiry. It is now well understood in the philosophy of science community that no one obeys the standard Neyman–Pearson sequence of "posit H_0 and H_A first; get the data; choose the uniformly most powerful procedure; then run the test" because such behavior would be irrational.[8] Instead, one always does "exploratory data analysis" (if one looks upon the practice favorably) or "data mining" (if one frowns upon it) because hypothesis formation and data construction are inextricably linked and contaminated.[9] What our little Cliometric exercise shows is that, in such a world, with enough persistence, I can get any outcome that I want from the econometrics. Depending upon which sequence of results I choose to report, and of how much freedom of auxiliary hypotheses I choose to take advantage, I can make any member of the Truman partnership appear as "rational" or "irrational" as I please. Our Cliometrician, perhaps now sputtering with barely suppressed indignation, would likely interject here: "What about Arthur Pryor? He consistently passed all rationality tests throughout!" I need only remind her, if she has had a reasonable grounding in Neyman–Pearson theory, that none of the t-statistics or other test statistics are legitimate (and indeed are biased upwards) because I have violated the first precept: Thou shalt not alter the specification to fit the data. Indeed, it is well known among statisticians that if one merely reverses which hypothesis is designated the null and which the alternative, then the outcome of Neyman–Pearson hypothesis testing can often be easily reversed.

The point I wish to make is that Cliometricians have foisted a false set of claims upon economic history. Under the banner of "science," they told their colleagues that to quantify history, to subject it to the regimen of neoclassical theory, and to expose all historical narratives to statistical test, they would curtail the flights of fancy of the mere literary historian, affixing attention to the steely discipline of hard facts. But, of course, nothing of the sort has happened. Rather, the hegemony of neoclassicism has tended to recast any interesting economic question in a concertedly a-historical manner, and then the application of econometrics in the hands of a skilled practitioner merely gives us back, in a less accessible but wantonly anachronistic format, whatever the Cliometrician sought to find in the data in the first place. Even so committed a neoclassical as Robert Solow admits this fact (in Parker 1986). If anything, the narrowing of the discourse to an audience of a few souls sufficiently tooled to see the point of the exercise has substantially increased the freedom of flights of fancy, rather than restricted it. That is the plight of Cliometrics at the start of the millennium.

I should now like to bid our imaginary Cliometrician adieu, retell the story of the Truman partners once more in the supposedly antiquated "literary" format, and to suggest that it is much more likely that the hermeneutic and archival skills of the historian, exemplified by the work of Warren Samuels, can serve to restrict the narrative much more effectively than anything the Cliometrician might snatch out of her econometric bag of tricks.

The semiotics of a Truman Rest Dinner

Any time a deal is cut, or an association is formed, it takes place in a rich context of intended meanings and unintended consequences, of tacit knowledge of the players and their peccadilloes. It is the elaboration of that rich context which makes for a good narrative, a good story. This is not to say that quantitative evidence is downgraded: here it is very interesting to use our data to define divergences and look for "signatures" in each of the actors. Indeed, we find the actors themselves drawing up elaborate summaries of winners and losers, commenting upon the spread of bets and actual prices, and speculating upon causal regularities with weather and the like. But the first rule of hermeneutics is to try and put yourself in the historical actors' shoes: What could they have known and intended? What might we possibly find out about it?

From some work in the history of science which straddles intellectual history and economic history (Daston 1989), we learn that it would be a mistake to situate the betting activity of the Truman partners in a framework of formal probability and inductive inference. Much of the mathematics of probability was still in a highly unstable state in the early nineteenth century, to such an extent that even in situations in which it was acknowledged to be relevant, such as in lotteries and insurance, it was not put into computational practice until very late in that century. Therefore, to phrase the question of rationality as one of stochastic unbiasedness or consistency is to start off on the wrong foot. Instead, it would be better to regard the betting activity at the Rest Dinners as a form of vigorous communication by other means. But, in that case, what could this practice of wagering with such insignificant sums have to do with their business? We need to get better acquainted with the actors to answer that question.

We should start with the partnership in 1811. At that juncture the share valuations were divided as follows: Henry and John Villebois, £101,595 apiece; Sampson Hanbury, £88,343; Thomas Fowell Buxton, just brought on board with £26,503 (B/THB/B/5/9). The Villebois brothers were the old inherited money who behaved much as Martin Weiner (and Adam Smith) described it: they cared little about business, preferring fox hunting, gambling, and country life. Sampson Hanbury was the Quaker made good, starting small by running the business for the Villebois brothers, cementing a relationship with the Gurney banking family by marriage, and increasing his fortunes in tandem with those of the brewery. But he had no children, and sought to construct some sort of continuity in passing the baton by bringing in his nephew Buxton. Thomas Buxton is the most famous of our cast of characters, the only one to make it into the Dictionary of National Biography and to have a memoir published.[10]

Buxton was a terribly earnest young Quaker, and initially threw himself assiduously into his work at the brewery from 1808 to roughly 1815. Indeed, some of his exhortations concerning business practices would warm the cockles of the modern orthodox economist.[11] But this unbending moralist was not temperamentally well-suited to the day-to-day running of a brewery; and soon his energies were progressively diverted elsewhere, first to running a Spitalfields Benevolent Society, and then in 1818 successfully running as MP for Weymouth. His claim to fame was as a major campaigner for the abolition of slavery; after 1820 he was no longer able to give much attention to the Brewery, moving from Hempstead to Cromer. The lack of interest in business was apparent to many visitors to the family: for instance, the Baron Rothschild once told his son, Edward Buxton, to stick to brewing (Buxton 1848: 344).

So Truman's was still faced with the dilemma so common to British family firms: how to ensure the smooth continuity of a successful business? In 1816 Robert Pryor was admitted as a partner with the absorption of Proctor's Brewhouse; but he seemed never to be really admitted to the inner circle. His accession may also have been something of a political move, to cement a relationship with a family of maltsters in Hertfordshire (Anon 1959: 31). An obvious replacement for Thomas Buxton was another Hanbury nephew, Robert, admitted to partnership in 1821. Tom Aveling, the head clerk made good, was admitted to second-class partnership in 1825, though he was always the poorest by far of the group, and treated in brewery documents more like a salaried underling than an equal. Thomas Buxton did manage to get his son Edward made a partner by 1836; but Robert Pryor's similar attempt on the part of his brother Arthur was opposed by Robert Hanbury, who thought him constitutionally unsuitable for business.[12]

By 1836, the status of the partnership shares (B/THB/B/519) stood as follows:

J. Villebois	126,500
H. Villebois	126,500
T. Buxton	88,000
R. Pryor	74,250
T. Aveling	24,750
R. Hanbury	55,000
E. Buxton	22,000

By this time Robert Hanbury was effectively running the business, but there were still many unresolved tensions as to the future disposition of the business and its ownership. These broke out into the open with the death of Henry Villebois in 1847; the contempt of the insiders for the outsiders is expressed in a remarkable letter preserved in the Truman archives (B/THB/G/10A/5) from E. Buxton to Robert Hanbury concerning the son of Henry Villebois:

> Many thanks for your letter. I fully acknowledge the great difficulty of dealing with H. V., whether we decide in favour of excluding him or accepting him back. But I earnestly desire that we may all be led by a spirit of wisdom, justice and mercy. Some of your arguments have much force, but there are others, with which I cannot agree . . . Again you say that it has been "the greatest possible blot and disgrace to be connected with the V. Family." This may be true or it may not, but we knew their character when we consented to join them in business. If we "are ashamed of working for such," our *best* remedy is to retire ourselves

from the concern. Being once a partner, H. V. has as much right to spend his gains in fox hunting as I have to spend mine in a contested election, or you yours in beautiful watercolours

Now that we are aware of some of the context, we can begin to reinterpret the meaning of the hops and barley wagers. They were indeed fundamentally about the ability of each individual to predict the costs of the business, but more than that, they were about signaling who should be running the business. The Villebois, with their ineffectual bets, were expressing their preference to relish their status of the wealthy landed gentry, knowing little about agriculture or brewing and caring less. Thomas Buxton, who did have some knowledge, was far too distracted by the momentous political events of the day, and so his wagers wildly overshot actual movements. Tom Aveling, however close he was to the day-to-day purchases, was not trying to prove his mettle as a contender, but instead his timbre as a team player, making relatively safe and unimaginative bets. The real battle of wits was between the Hanburys and the challengers to their position: the younger Edward Buxton and the Pryors. It is crucial to remember that Arthur Pryor – our neoclassical *homo economicus* – was only acknowledged as a full partner on the heels of the death of his brother, achieving by inheritance what he could not attain by talent.

Why couldn't the partners assess the capabilities of hops and barley knowledge more directly, perhaps by letting the rivals speculate on their prices? This probably had to do with the scruples of Sampson Hanbury, who "did not like to be concerned in any speculation in hops, as all such purchasing was on the joint account of the brewery" (in Mathias 1959: 530). How much better for the health of the firm to have a public joust, with negligible stakes, in full view of all the relevant actors, even if some of those actors were not seriously in the running? Hence, it was of utmost significance that the Hanburys came out on top as the most strategically savvy of the bettors; and it must have been doubly satisfying to have Robert Hanbury's poor opinion of Arthur Pryor reinforced by his dismal showing. One final bit of evidence supporting this interpretation is that when the succession degenerated into legal squabbles upon the death of the Villebois after 1847, the practice of betting at Rest Dinners ceased altogether .

Therefore, what might initially seem a simple expression of prowess in projecting input costs was understood by the players as a restrained expression of the competition for control and dominance of the firm. Outside of the orthodox mindset, it is possible to reconceptualize many, perhaps even most, "economic transactions" as forms of communication and/or the exercise of dominance. There may be circumstances when such an interpretation is strained or tendentious, but the only point to be made here is that at the very least, it provides a much more robust narrative for writing history – and is implicitly held much more closely to the sources – than one which proleptically reassures us that the past was never a foreign country and that on no account could rationality have reasons dictated as much by the heart as by the pocketbook.

Notes

1 All subsequent references of the format (B/THB/. . .) are the manuscript call numbers of the Truman archive at the Greater London Record Office.

2 A good description of the beer-making process can be found in Michael Dunn, *The Penguin Guide* (1979). We should also remind the reader that, in the British context, it was extremely unusual for any British firm to have a fixed periodic and consistent closing of their books until the advent of the Company Acts in the mid-nineteenth century.

3 Robert Fogel, in Fogel and Elton (1983: 26).

4 Brown and Maital (1981); Asch and Quandt (1987); Dokko and Edelstein (1989); Pearce (1984); Weiller and Mirowski (1990).

5 The classic anthology of papers on cointegration is Engle and Granger (1991). A survey is provided by Dickey, Janson and Thornton (1991).

6 In some instances, ties were settled by awarding two winners. Also, at the very end of our period, a few new punters were allowed to bet whom we have excluded from our tables. They were included, however, in our calculations of Table 10.4.

7 Now that the top graduate schools in economics have moved on to game theory as their microeconomics of choice, some might read the above comments as simply endorsing that trend. That would be a mistake; but that particular argument is irrelevant to the present intent of this chapter.

8 See Howson and Urbach (1989); Gigerenzer and Murray (1987); and Mirowski (1995).

9 The Bayesian statistician believes that they have the intellectually superior approach to this problem; but there are good arguments against them as well. See Mirowski (1995) and Gigerenzer and Murray (1987).

10 See the *Dictionary of National Biography*, Vol. 3, 559–61; and Buxton (1848). As yet there exists no scholarly biography.

11 In Thomas Fowell Buxton's Observation book (B/THB/G/63) one finds the following comments dated 29 August, 1812:

> But above all the foregoing modes of improving the profits of our trade, there is one which I have not a doubt is more especially in our interest. This great invaluable secret is – making our beer the best in the Town. Compared with this the mode of gaining trade by large allowances to the publicans – To put it in the most favourable point of view for allowances, we will admit that in the latter case you have the publican in your favour, and the public against you – in the former the public in your favour, and the publican against you, but it is clear to my mind that it is the consumer who ultimately decides, & that his approbation is worth twenty times as much as the retailer is.

12 The following comments are excerpted from (B/THB/A/129), which was Robert Hanbury's personal memo book. In an entry dated 25 August, 1831, he wrote, "It is desirable that we should relieve Mr. Pryor in the management of the storehouse & that we should look out for a suitable head Clerk. He would be more the worse if he understood Ale Brewing." On 13 July, 1837, upon Arthur Pryor being made a partner on a trial basis, Hanbury wrote, "We consent to take him only in the hope that his brother being here will be a cheque upon him & lend to his reform & induce him to render himself useful but if we are disappointed in the hope of his reform he will not be allowed to remain here."

References

Anonymous (1959) *Truman the Brewer*, London.

Asch, P., and R. Quandt (1987) "Efficiency and Profitability in Exotic Bets," *Economica* 54: 289–98.

Brown, Byron, and Schlomo Maital (1981) "What Do Economists Know?" *Econometrica* 49: 491–504.

Buxton, Charles (1848) *Memoirs of Sir Thomas Fowell Buxton*, London.

Cannadine, David (1984) "Past and Present in the English Industrial Revolution," *Past and Present* 103: 131–72.

Cardwell, D. (1971) *From Watt to Clausius*, Ithaca, NY: Cornell University Press.

Cohen, Avi (1984) "The Methodological Resolution of the Cambridge Capital Controversies," *Journal of Post Keynesian Economics* 6: 614–29.

Daston, Lorraine (1989) *Classical Probability in the Age of the Enlightenment*, Princeton, NJ: Princeton University Press.

Dickey, David, Dennis Jansen and Daniel Thornton (1991) "A Primer on Cointegration with an Application to Money and Income," *Review of the Federal Reserve Bank of St. Louis*: 58–78.

Dokko, Y., and R. Edelstein (1989) "How Well Do Economists Forecast Stock Market Prices?" *American Economic Review* 79: 865–71.

Dunn, Michael (1979) *The Penguin Guide to Real Draught Beer*, Harmondsworth: Penguin.

Engle, R., and C. Granger (eds.) (1991) *Long-Run Economic Relationships*, Oxford: Oxford University Press.

Fogel, Robert, and G. R. Elton (eds.) (1983) *Which Road to the Past?* New Haven, CT: Yale University Press.

Gigerenzer, Gerd, and David Murray (1987) *Cognition as Intuitive Statistics*, Hillsdale, NJ: Erbaum.

Gourvish, T.J., and R. G. Wilson (1994) *The British Brewing Industry, 1830–1980*, Cambridge: Cambridge University Press.

Howson, Colin, and Peter Urbach (1989) *Scientific Reasoning*, La Salle, IL: Open Court.

Jeong, J., and G. Maddala (1991) "Measurement Errors and Tests for Rationality," *Journal of Business and Economic Statistics* 9: 431–39.

Mathias, Peter (1959) *The Brewing Industry in England*, Cambridge: Cambridge University Press.

Mirowski, Philip (1988) *Against Mechanism*, Totawa, NJ.

—— (1989) *More Heat than Light*, Cambridge: Cambridge University Press.

—— (1995) "Three Ways of Thinking About Testing in Econometrics," *Journal of Econometrics* 76: 25–46.

Parker, William (ed.) (1986) *Economic History and the Modern Economist*, Oxford.

Pearce, Douglas (1984) "An Empirical Analysis of Expected Stock Price Movements," *Journal of Money, Credit and Banking* 16: 317–27.

Richmond, Lesley, and Alison Turton (1990) *The Brewing Industry*, Manchester: Manchester University Press.

Weiller, K., and P. Mirowski (1990) "Rates of Interest in Eighteenth Century England," *Explorations in Economic History* 27: 1–28.

Part III

The legal-economic nexus

11 Putting the "political" back into political economy

Peter J. Boettke

Warren Samuels has spent his scholarly career examining the intellectual history and internal logic of arguments concerned with the economic role of government. He has been quite eclectic in his approach and has studied deeply the thought of the classical economists, and modern economists such as Pareto, Knight, Hayek, Coase and Buchanan, as well as those scholars working within the institutionalist tradition of economic and political economy scholarship. While he has cast a rather wide net for study, his basic message has been rather consistent. Samuels emphasizes the irreducible embeddness of all economic processes in the political and legal nexus. This is a significant point to emphasize, especially when we remember the post-1950s effort by economists to develop an institutional antiseptic theory of the economic process. By emphasizing the framework within which all economic activity takes place, Samuels has sought to put the political back into political economy and as such, he surely deserves to be recognized as one of the foremost scholars responsible for resurrecting political economy in the second half of the twentieth century.

To illustrate the Samuels contribution to the research program of modern political economy I will examine a debate that he engaged in with James M. Buchanan in the 1970s. The debate not only took place in the exchange in *Journal of Law and Economics*, but in private correspondence between these two scholars that was subsequently published in the *Journal of Economic Issues*. I am quite sympathetic to Samuels's position as articulated in the article and correspondence with regard to the embeddedness of economic action within a political and legal nexus, and I appreciate his point about the essential non-neutrality of all state action (including action associated exclusively with pursuing a so-called *laissez-faire* policy). However, I do not go all the way with him in terms of the implications of the argument. Here, I will pick up a point stressed by Buchanan on the relative position of the *status quo* in political economy analysis which I think Samuels does not fully appreciate in the exchange with Buchanan. This is a point of analytical economics that has normative implications, and not a normative endorsement of whatever exists at the beginning of our analysis. After laying out the positions, I will attempt to illustrate this Buchanan-inspired caveat to the Samuels position by reference to a discussion of transitional political economy in the former Soviet Union.

Samuels does not like school labels and I am starting to appreciate his resistance to this intellectual habit more and more as I mature in my own career. I was going to provide a subtitle to this chapter that read: "Lessons from an Old Institutionalist to a New Austrian." This subtitle does convey some vital information, for Samuels's contribution is an *Institutionalist* critique of orthodox political economy. But it goes beyond those earlier argument found in writers such as Commons and Hale, though it has intellectual roots in those arguments. On the other hand, I am most closely associated with work in the Austrian tradition of economics and the Virginia School of Political Economy, though hopefully someday we can just talk about political economy without the labels and still be able to understand each other. The Samuels exchange with Buchanan demonstrates how two honest and reasonable scholars coming at fundamental questions from radically divergent perspectives can nevertheless find common ground. Despite my only according to Samuels two cheers in his exchange with Buchanan, as opposed to the full three cheers, I want this common ground to be recognized. There is much that a student of Hayek and Buchanan can learn from a student of Commons and Hale, and I believe I have tried to take advantage of that opportunity.

Samuels was never my teacher in the formal sense of the term, but I came under his guiding influence in my first year of graduate school, even though I was in Fairfax and he was located in East Lansing. That influence has been with me ever since. We met through a paper I had written as a first-year graduate student on the relationship between the Austrians and the institutionalists, and specifically the common ground between these two often antithetical schools on the importance of evolutionary change for economic understanding. In writing that paper I had read a similar working paper by Samuels on the topic. These papers were eventually published with commentary by others in the annual *Research in the History of Economic Thought and Methodology* (1989a). But our contact was more than those papers: he came to present a paper at GMU, we exchanged letters and met at HES meetings and discussed an entire range of topics over the years. When I took my first teaching job at Oakland University in Rochester, Michigan, Samuels got me involved with his weekly workshop at Michigan State (a rather short drive from Rochester) and he came and gave presentations at Oakland University and then later also at NYU when I moved there after two years in Michigan. Much of my thinking has been shaped by Samuels, in terms of both style (including professional attitude toward those with whom you have intellectual disagreement, the values of scholarship that are required to advance the dialogue in political economy, and, hopefully, the generosity shown to junior colleagues starting out in the professional discourse) and substantive propositions in economic theory, methodology, and political economy. He has not shaken me of some of my cherished beliefs, but he sure has made me aware of how much some of those beliefs are more acts of faith than of reason. The current chapter attempts to provide some good reasons why incorporating the Samuels lesson on embeddedness can nevertheless reinforce some of those cherished beliefs about private property, permanence and predictability in the law, and the contractual nature of realist reform.

Cedar rust and apple orchards

Samuels (1971) chose the case of *Miller et al. v. Schoene* to examine the essential non-neutrality of limited government because it is a simple illustration of the basic principles of the interdependence of the economic, the legal, and the political. The case concerns the constitutionality of legislation enacted in Virginia in 1914 and was heard before the Supreme Court in 1928. The case involves red cedars and apple trees and their respective owners. Red cedars were vulnerable to developing a plant disease called cedar rust. While cedar rust was harmless to the host cedar trees, the fungus was fatal to apple trees. In 1914, the state legislature of Virginia passed a statute which empowered apple-tree owners to employ the state legal apparatus to uphold their rights with respect to the destructive force of the red-cedar fungus. The plaintiffs in the case, *Miller et al.*, argued that the legislature had unconstitutionally "taken" their property to the benefit of the apple orchard owners. Private property, they argued, had been taken without compensation not for public use, but to benefit another group of private owners.

Samuels argues that this case illustrates the necessity of government to make a choice to support one set of rights at the expense of another. If the legislature had not enacted the statute which enabled apple growers to appeal to the state entomologist to investigate red cedars within a two-mile radius of their orchard, then the law would have been favoring the owners of red cedars at the expense of the apple orchard. The court ultimately ruled that when such a choice is of necessity, the state is not overstepping its constitutional powers by deciding to destroy the property of one class of owners in order to save another class of property owners. The outcome of this particular case is not Samuels's concern.

Instead, as he puts it, it is "the ineluctable necessity of choice" that the case highlights that is relevant for exploring the fundamentals of political economy. "The state had to make a choice as to which property owner was to be made not only formally secure but practically viable in his legal rights" (1971: 142). Without state action to protect the apple growers against the lost value of their destroyed trees, the existing property law would have disadvantaged the apple growers in respect to the red-cedar owners. In other words, one group is going to be protected in their rights, the other is not, and the state must choose which. The generalizable proposition that Samuels wants the reader to walk away with is that it is never the case that the choice is between government or no government, intervention or *laissez-faire*. *Laissez-faire*, in a fundamental sense, is conceptually bankrupt. "Market forces emerge and take on shape and slope only within the pattern of, *inter alia*, legal choices as to relative rights, relative exposure to injury and relative coercive advantage or disadvantage" (ibid.: 144). Once we move away from ideologically charged discussion, we can dispassionately recognize that government is omnipresent as the basic framework against which all economic activity takes place. In this particular case, government is present under the older property law which advantaged the red-cedar tree owners, and it is present under the new property law which advantages the apple-tree owners. It is simply "a matter of which interest government will be used to support" (ibid.: 145).

Samuels' point is well taken and his emphasis on the embedded nature of all economic activity with the political and legal setting is an important point which was not always explicitly recognized in the public choice and law and economics literature of that time. Instead, the early days of public choice and law and economics tended to emphasize how the tools of economic reasoning (maximizing and equilibrium) could be used to address questions in the political and legal nexus. The examination from the other direction of how the political and legal shape economic outcomes was not yet part of the research agenda. Political economy at the time was either a term deployed to describe Marxian scholarship, or a nascent (but growing) rational choice approach to political, legal, and sociological scholarship. Thus, Samuels's emphasis on the embeddedness of economic activity within the political and legal nexus represented an important alternative vision of political economy and served as a corrective to the idea of disembodied economic processes.

The Nobel Prize committee has recognized James Buchanan (politics) and Ronald Coase (law) as being pioneers in the development of this rational choice approach to political economy. Ironically, while both men are correctly identified with the founding of both the public choice and law and economics movements, they both had (have) serious reservations about the way the fields have developed. And the reservations of both come from the crowding out of the embeddedness side of the research program that Samuels emphasizes. I will restrict my comments to Buchanan's exchange with Samuels on the *Miller et al. v. Schoene* case, emphasizing their common ground with regard to embeddedness, but readers interested in the case of Coase are recommended to read Steve Medema's intellectual biography, *Ronald Coase* (1994).

Negotiated solutions and the *status quo*

James Buchanan (1972) chose to respond to Samuels's interpretation of the *Miller et al. v. Schoene* case because in Buchanan's mind Samuels's position reflected the "received wisdom" of the early 1970s which resulted in the "omnipresent hand of the state in all our lives" (1972: 109). Whereas Samuels had chosen the case because he thought it was "not a case with which one can get readily emotionally or ideologically involved" (1971: 139), to Buchanan the account of Samuels is grounded in a different vision of the social order.

Buchanan contends that Samuels's account does not adequately account for the exchange opportunities that would arise in the wake of exogenous changes in the environment. Once the interdependence between the red cedars and apple trees became apparent with the introduction of cedar rust, in Buchanan's language, "potential gains from exchange should have existed that would have allowed this new interdependence to be eliminated" (1972: 97). Rather than placing his trust in the exchange process, Buchanan argues that Samuels's story places faith in the legislative/judicial process that can presumably measure the superior benefits of a new arrangement of property rights which is to be imposed without the necessity of compensation. Buchanan's subjectivism does not allow him to follow this argument.

It is important to recognize, however, that Buchanan does not deny that economic processes always take place against the backdrop of some set of property rights. As he says "The principle to be emphasized, however, is that *some* structure, *any* structure, of well-defined rights is a necessary starting point for the potential trades that are required to remove the newly emergent interdependence" (ibid., 97). The necessary embeddedness of economic action within a legal and political setting is a position shared by both Buchanan and Samuels. They diverge on the role accorded to trading behavior in the resolution of conflict between parties. Buchanan follows the general rule that negotiating away conflicts to internalize costs and benefits is preferred to adjudication; adjudication in a way to clarify the property rights arrangement to ease exchange opportunities is to be preferred to legislation; and finally, if legislation is to be pursued, it should be limited to situations where public goods problems persist even after efforts at negotiating a solution have been attempted.[1] But, as Buchanan points out, even in such cases where the public goods situation justifies collective interference, the question of how collective action is to be organized is an open one. Buchanan, as is now well understood, relies on the Wicksellian principle of unanimity, which is the collective choice analog to mutual beneficial exchange in the private choice setting. In other words, the principle of mutual agreement remains the criterion for collective action as it did in private action. Rather than seeing the resolution of conflicting claims as being resolved through the state apparatus and the rule of experts relied upon in the *Miller et al. v. Schoene* case as described by Samuels, Buchanan's analysis invokes mutual agreement. Resolution is not be done through either/or, but through compromise and agreement. Both interests agree to adjust their expectations and behavior after the exogenous change in the social setting which brought about the interdependencies which previously had not been a problem.

By appealing directly to the state, the apple growers truncated the process by which exchange opportunities could have resolved the conflict between the apple orchard and the red cedars. Instead, the state was required to assess the value of the damage to the apple trees from cedar rust infestation relative to the damage to the cedar trees from premature cutting. In the particular case of *Miller et al. v. Schoene*, the state relied on the expert opinion of a Virginia entomologist to make that determination. There are some important points to consider. First, an entomological determination is not necessarily an economic determination, but from the economic point of view we are concerned with approximating a Pareto solution. Second, it should be recognized that the generalizability of the *Miller et al. v. Schoene* case breaks down when the expert is introduced. As Buchanan puts it: "In most economic interdependencies there are no 'experts,' and there are likely to be major errors in any cost–benefit estimates" (ibid.: 98).

Of course, as pointed out above, Buchanan admits that in the face of a genuine public goods problem (e.g., perhaps the removal of cedar rust in large number situations would qualify) or high transaction costs, the collective decision making of the state legislature might have to substitute for the reconciliation of interests through negotiation. Buchanan points out that the Virginia Cedar Rust Act might have, in fact, recognized the large number problem by requiring a petition of at least ten freeholders before the state entomologist was empowered to act.

Buchanan and Samuels both argue that economic activity is inexorably embedded within political and legal settings. But their approach diverges from this fundamental starting point. Descriptively, Samuels challenges the myth of neutrality of the state in liberal thought. The state is necessarily protecting one set of rights against another whether a decision to intervene is made or not. Samuels is not making a normative judgment here; he does not give us reason to believe he favors apple growers or red-cedar growers. It is an exercise in pure description and the analytical implications of such a description of politics, property, and law. To Buchanan this description must be qualified. No doubt the state is invoked to favor one interest over another, but Buchanan wants to ask on what grounds such a decision is made. Since no persuasive metric is offered, Buchanan's suggestion is to circumscribe state action. Neutrality (or non-discriminatory) state action is not a description in Buchanan, but a goal which the institutional design should be set up to accomplish if it is at all possible.

This is where the position of the *status quo* enters into Buchanan's analytical system. "There is an explicit prejudice in favor of previously existing rights, not because this structure possesses some intrinsic ethical attributes, and because change itself is undesirable, but for the much more elementary reason that only such a prejudice offers incentives for the emergence of voluntarily negotiated settlements among the parties themselves" (Buchanan 1972: 109).

It is the relative status of the *status quo* as laid out in this passage that to a large extent became the focus of the exchange of thoughtful letters between Samuels and Buchanan that were eventually published by them as "On Some Fundamental Issues in Political Economy: An Exchange of Correspondence" (1975). Samuels accuses Buchanan of privileging the *status quo* as a normative ideal for conservative purposes, while Buchanan counters that it is actually Samuels who is the defender of the *status quo*. Samuels responds that it is true that both he and Buchanan have subjective perceptions of the world, but Buchanan has a built-in presumption for the *status quo*, while he is only providing a descriptive starting point for the critical discussion of the *status quo*. The correspondence between them on this issue begins in 1972, ends in 1974, and contains 13 letters. There is some inevitable talking past each other, but there is also the further clarification of respective positions that comes with reiteration of an argument. However, to this reader the issue of the *status quo* is never satisfactorily addressed because the positive, the normative, and the pragmatic are conflated in the exchange.

The *status quo* in Buchanan's work has elements of the positive, the normative, and the pragmatic to it. But the normative enters into the analysis not as Samuels suggests. There is no normative weight to be accorded to the *status quo* position. Instead, the *status quo* serves primarily as positive – this is the world in which we find ourselves – and pragmatic – real reform cannot begin but from the existing *status quo*. In other words, Buchanan emphasizes in various writings that realism in political economy (what he terms politics without romance) must begin with the "here and now" and not some imaginary ideal that the analyst would like to impose on the system. In the case of the red-cedar growers and the apple-tree growers, Buchanan's analysis begins with the existing property law prior to the Cedar Rust Act because it is that arrangement that needed to be adjusted. Samuels comes to understand this point in his correspondence with Buchanan, but he insists that "the problem is that there is no agreement on the mechanism of change" (Samuels and Buchanan 1975: 205). But it is on this point that the pragmatic value of the *status quo* is not completely appreciated. Samuels insists, correctly to my mind, that Buchanan often attempts to "simulate with logic what is *in reality* a function of power, knowledge and psychology" (ibid.: 209). This move in Buchanan is most evident in his work on the basic social contract derived behind a veil of ignorance (or uncertainty). But even here, isn't it really the case that Buchanan's point is a pragmatic one rather than a justificatory one? I choose to interpret the Buchanan point as not denying the function of power, knowledge, and psychology, but instead as beginning with that existing reality as the necessary starting point of analysis. Buchanan does not, to go back to the specific case, deny that under older property arrangement the introduction of cedar rust presents us with a conflict between the different owners. The presence of the new interdependency is what drives the exchange opportunity between the two parties to negotiate away their conflict. In other words, Buchanan denies two levels of "either/or" propositions that are contained in Samuels – the either/or choice at the level of the analysis between the two parties to the exchange, and the either/or choice at the level of social theory. Thus, Samuels's claim that "so long as anarchy without social control is repugnant, the problem boils down to what (whose) system of social control" (ibid.) has different implications for Buchanan. Social "control" in terms of the establishment of the rules of the game is a major theme in all of Buchanan's writings, but within that framework of rules the driving force of the analysis from one state of affairs to another state of affairs is the vehicle of mutual agreement – either through the mechanism of economic exchange or democratic consensus building through the unanimity principle.

It is the compensation principle that is at the core of Buchanan's analysis of the transitional path. We begin with existing rights claims and the social arrangement of power, knowledge, and psychology not because that situation is normatively desirable, but because it represents the "here" that must be transformed to get "there" if that is so desired. It is, as I said above, a blend of the positive (to accurately describe the "here"), the normative (to posit why the "there" would be a "better" situation), and the pragmatic (to analyze potential paths from "here" to "there"). Samuels contends that this position is ultimately confusing; as he says in the correspondence, the Buchanan argument is hard to follow because "Part is against change and part is for change and the part that is for change is against all but contractual change thereafter" (ibid.: 213).

In defense of his position, Buchanan responds to Samuels in the following manner:

> But my defense of the *status quo* stems from my unwillingness, indeed inability, to discuss changes other than those that are contractual in nature. I can, of course, lay down my own notions and think about how God might listen to me and impose these changes on me, you and everyone else. This seems to me what most social scientists do all the time. But, to me, this is simply wasted effort. And explains most of the frustration. It seems to me that our task is really quite different, that of trying to find, locate, invent, schemes that change command unanimous or quasi-unanimous consent and propose them. Since persons disagree on so much, these schemes may be a very limited set, and this may suggest to you that few changes are possible. Hence, the *status quo* is defended indirectly. That *status quo* has no propriety at all save for its existence, and it is all that exists. The point I always emphasize is that we start from here and not from somewhere else. And, as an economist, all I can do is try to talk about and explain ways of changing that are conceptually contractual, nothing more. This does allow me to take a limited step toward normative judgements or hypothesis, namely to suggest that the changes seem to be potentially agreeable to everyone. Pareto efficient changes, which must, of course, include compensations. The criterion in my scheme is agreement, and I cannot stress this too much. My approach is strictly Wicksellian here.
>
> (ibid.: 215)

Samuels, in response, correctly points out that while Buchanan's approach might posit that the *status quo* does not have any propriety save its existence, the unanimity criterion does privilege the existing situation. "Change or continuity of the *status quo is* a normative matter and your approach builds in the continuity of the *status quo*" (ibid.: 217). It seems to me that Samuels is right here; there is a "conservativism" built into the analysis as Buchanan develops the approach. But what is the alternative? We have to begin somewhere in our analysis, and realism in political economy demands that we begin with the existing set of arrangements. Furthermore, what exactly would be the alternative to the mutual agreement model in politics, and why would it have any normative weight? A mutual-consent-driven model does not have to deny Samuels's points about either the non-neutrality of affairs or the necessity of choice between rights claims as points of fact, but it does suggest that we can strive to minimize the impact of non-neutrality (a goal rather than a description) and we can provide an environment within which negotiated solutions to conflicts between agents can be pursued as much as is humanly possible.

Implications for transitional political economy

The former Soviet-type economy is often portrayed as a centrally planned economy. This description misses out on the *de facto* organizing principles of that social system of production by focusing exclusively on the *de jure* pronouncements of economic organization. However, we must also be willing to peer underneath given institutions and explore the practices which govern economic life in a society. In a fundamental sense, markets existed throughout the long history of Soviet planning, they just were pushed into a *sub rosa* level of existence. The basic institutions of a Western market society, for example, do not accord well with the lived experience of the Soviet peoples with markets. Within the Soviet underground setting the institutions of pricing and bargaining took concrete form. But they did so within an environment of black (and other colored) markets without well-defined or enforced property rights, and with a shortage of goods and lack of alternative supply networks. If we just look at the simplest depiction of this shortage economy situation, then we can start to see the problem for transitional political economy that must be addressed. See Figure 11.1.

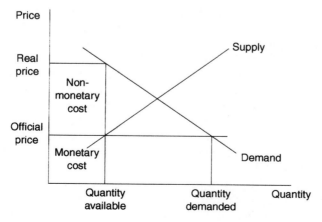

Figure 11.1

This very simple supply and demand configuration brings to the forefront the basic fact that in a shortage situation, the real price of obtaining the good in a shortage economy is higher than the official price. There is a gap between quantity demanded and the quantity supplied which creates a situation where there are non-monetary costs to buyers associated with acquiring the good. Under "normal" market conditions, the costs to buyers are simultaneous benefits to sellers. But in the artificial shortage situation (caused by administered pricing), the non-monetary costs are not immediate benefits to the sellers, so the seller has a strong incentive to transform those non-monetary costs to buyers into benefits (monetary or non-monetary) for themselves. In other words, what this simple diagram reveals is the "rents" that are to be had by those who can exploit the shortage situation – rents that took the form of monetary "bribes," "black market profits," and non-monetary "privileges" to those in special favor with the ruling elite.

Changing this situation is not just a matter of freeing prices so they can adjust to the market clearing level. "Getting the prices right" is not enough. Those who have been in a position to convert the non-monetary costs to buyers into benefits for themselves basically have a "property right" in the existing arrangement. By analogy we can say that the nomenclatura was in a position similar to the red-cedar owners in the *Miller et al. v. Schoene* case discussed by Samuels and Buchanan.

In Samuels's interpretation of the case, the state is required to make a choice either to support the existing arrangement, which benefits the red-cedar growers, or a new property rights system, which supports the apple orchard. The older property rights arrangement was non-problematic until the exogenous shock of cedar rust introduced an interdependency that had not previously existed. In Buchanan's interpretation, the existence of the interdependency provides an opportunity for mutually beneficial exchange, but this option was not pursued because recourse to the state for resolution was pursued rather than negotiation.

Running through these arguments about changing property rights in the post-Soviet context, I believe, highlights the importance for political economy of Buchanan's *status quo*. In the case of *Miller et al. v. Schoene*, the legislative change in property rights is objected to by Buchanan because it didn't follow the compensation principle. Samuels counters that this prejudices Buchanan's position to the *status quo* – in this case, the pre-existing property statutes which favored the red-cedar growers over the apple orchards. In the post-Soviet case, the Buchanan analysis would also suggest the use of the compensation principle as the guide for reform. Begin the analysis by recognizing that some members in that society possess a property right in the rent (the box in Figure 11.1 labelled 'Non-monetary costs'). In other words, they have control over an asset (position) and guard that asset to make sure they receive benefits that accrue from that ownership claim. They will only agree to give up that property right for compensation (in the limit of the present value of the future income stream of their property right).

There is nothing desirable about the pre-existing Soviet situation from the point of view of my analysis, nor am I postulating anything desirable about compensating the nomenclatura for giving up their privileged positions. The point is, and it is the same point suggested by Buchanan, that reform in a manner which does not privilege the will of one over the will of others can only be accomplished following the compensation principle. This move is sometimes quite costly – in fact, if you look at Figure 11.1 closely, you can see that it might cost more to compensate the pre-existing rent-holder for their loss of the future income stream than will be the benefits received by buyers as a result of eliminating the artificial scarcity, depending on the slope of the supply and demand curves. Moreover, high transaction costs may prevent such a deal from being brokered successfully. These concerns are important, but they are secondary to the main point to be stressed – that realism in reform must begin with the existing rights and talk about how to make moves to assure the transition from one set of arrangements to another.

If the compensation principle is not followed in the wake of an exogenous shock (e.g., introduction of the fungus cedar rust, or the collapse of the communist system), then what will the new existing property owners expect when they are confronted with the next exogenous shock? If their expectations are formed on the basis of their previous experience, then they will expect that their property rights could be reassigned without consent or compensation. Accordingly, they will shorten the time horizon of investment and by thwarting the expansion of the market limit the opportunities for specialization and exchange. In short, further opportunities for mutual benefit will be undeveloped and thus unexploited.

This quasi-abstract discussion took on concrete form in the recent privatization debates in the former Soviet Union. The argument I laid out for privatization in my book, *Why Perestroika Failed* (1993), was for privatization by the nomenclatura. The position was influenced by the Buchanan (and Tullock) argument concerning the relative position of the *status quo* and the problems of reforming the rent-seeking society. Given the rather high transactions costs associated with a lump sum transfer to compensate the pre-existing "property owners," I argued that the Russian government should simply formally recognize these *de facto* owners, and then commit to a policy of free entry and zero subsidies. I argued that this would effectively buy out the existing owners by compensating them by formally giving them the cash flow rights to firm assets in addition to their existing control rights over those assets. At the same time, the threat of domestic and foreign entry would ensure that the existing system was not privileged, and instead would lead to a changing structure of rights enacted through mutual agreement and evolutionary adjustment as new opportunities presented themselves along several dimensions.

This argument was too optimistic. The counter-argument at the time took on two forms – either postpone privatization or pursue it without recognizing the pre-existing owners. Neither of these arguments were (are) persuasive in my opinion. The over optimism concerned the desire of the post-Soviet government to create conditions of entry. The compensation principle was followed to some extent during the mass privatization, but the second round of entry and zero subsidies was not. Basically, the same subsidization of the Soviet economy continued in the post-Soviet period (see Ickes and Gaddy 1998). Entry was discouraged with regard to large-scale industry, and discriminatory taxation and burdensome regulation have directed new entry in smaller-scale production into an underground existence. The above ground economy is concerned with restructured (or half-restructured) former state industrial enterprises and the rents that are still possible to garner through political action. As a result, Russia is still a far way from moving along the path toward a private property market economy.

My particular diagnosis of the Russian reform effort is not the point of this detour. Instead, I hoped to highlight the issues that are in the Samuels and Buchanan exchange. Samuels makes much sense when he emphasizes that economic actions are embedded within the political and legal nexus. Moreover, he makes great sense when he insists that the state is an institution which can be, and will be, used by some to exploit others. The state, in this sense, is non-neutral at the core. But, Buchanan's concern that reform must begin here and now also seems right to me. Furthermore, the emphasis on how, beginning in the here and now, the compensation principle must guide the move from here to there unless we want to resort to means beyond mutual agreement is compelling.

Conclusion

Samuels has raised our level of understanding of the political, legal, and social embeddedness of the economy. In fact, he has emphasized not just the interrelations between these separate spheres of social control, but their essential bondedness. They produce and reproduce each other through their operation. The economy takes concrete shape only in relation to the legal and political setting; change the structure of rights and the economy is reconfigured.

Samuels has also raised our awareness of the issue of power within society, including in the economy. In social construction, he has argued, the key policy question is always about whose interests are to count and whose can be ignored. The answer to that question is always defined within the political-legal process and is shaped by existing power relations found in government, in the economy, and in society. Samuels has further advanced our understanding of these issues by highlighting the role of ideology and belief systems in social systems and modes of analysis. As Samuels (1989b) puts it:

> Rights are not produced in a black box called government; and the economy does not operate on its own. A legal-economic nexus is formed

by the process in which both are simultaneously (re)determined. At the heart of society and of social (including legal) change is control and use of the legal-economic nexus, and at the heart thereof is the exercise of government, power and belief system. The fundamentals of the legal-economic nexus are not as simple and obvious as contemplated by views that maintain that the polity and economy are pre-existent, self-subsistent spheres.

(184)

One must appreciate the deep insights that Samuels has given us on the nature of the political economy and the contribution he has made throughout his distinguished career to our discourse on that subject. But I fear that his concern with institutions of mutual coercion has often (though not always) directed his attention away from the institutions of mutual consent. It is not that Samuels does not appreciate the power of the human imagination to realize the mutually advantageous opportunities in the market place, in science, and in cultural transmission. It is just that his work does not emphasize this aspect of human social interaction. In the analysis of legal change, as in the *Miller et al. v. Schoene* case, a blind eye to opportunities for mutually advantageous moves leads to a bias in favor of state action over resolution of conflict through negotiation. But if Samuels is correct in his positive description of the embeddedness of the economy and the power of existing interests, then it seems to me that his analysis must be supplemented with a recognition that the discussion of the transition from one situation to another must begin with the here and now. The *status quo* must be accorded its appropriate place, not because it is anything special, but simply because it *is*. And once that is incorporated into the analysis, the compensation principle becomes the guiding method by which we are able to make whatever improving moves (however small or great) we can make in this world. In short, Samuels's descriptive analysis of social control can be (perhaps must be) the beginning of our analysis, but it is not enough of an analytical framework to address the issue of the political economy of social change. Power, knowledge, and belief systems must be at the core of our analysis, but continuity, predictability, and compensation must be as well. The resulting Buchanan/Samuels hybrid framework provides a blend of the descriptive, the pragmatic, and the normative to forge a political economy worthy of our classical predecessors.

Note

1 Buchanan (1972, 103) argues that the legislative process – an instrument for reconciling separate interests – must be viewed as fundamentally distinct from the judicial process – an instrument for clarifying ambiguities in the existing rights structure. This distinction, Buchanan contends, is absent from the Samuels' discussion.

References

Boettke, P. (1989) "Evolution and Economics: Austrians as Institutionalists," *Research in the History of Economic Thought and Methodology* 6.
—— (1993) *Why Perestroika Failed: The Politics and Economics of Socialist Transformation*, New York: Routledge.
Buchanan, J. (1972) "Politics, Property and the Law," *Journal of Law and Economics*, reprinted in James M. Buchanan, *Freedom in Constitutional Contract*, College Station, TX: Texas A and M University Press, 1979, 94–109.
Ickes, B., and Clifford Gaddy (1998) "The Virtual Economy," *Foreign Affairs* (Fall).
Medema, Steven G. (1994) *Ronald H. Coase*, London: Macmillan.
Samuels, W. (1971) "Interrelations Between Legal and Economic Processes," *Journal of Law and Economics*, reprinted in Warren J. Samuels, *Essays on the Economic Role of Government: Volume 1 – Fundamentals*, New York: New York University Press, 1992, 139–55.
—— (1972) "In Defense of a Positive Approach to Government as an Economic Variable," *Journal of Law and Economics* 15, October: 453–59.
—— (1989a) "Austrians and Institutionalists Compared," *Research in the History of Economic Thought and Methodology* 6.
—— (1989b) "The Legal-Economic Nexus," *George Washington Law Review*, reprinted in Warren J. Samuels, *Essays on the Economic Role of Government: Volume 1 – Fundamentals*, New York: New York University Press, 1992, 162–86.
Samuels, W., and James M. Buchanan (1975) "On Some Fundamental Issues in Political Economy: An Exchange of Correspondence," *Journal of Economic Issues*, reprinted in Warren J. Samuels, *Essays on the Methodology and Discourse of Economics*, New York: New York University Press, 1992, 201–30.

12 Output categories for a comparative institutional approach to law and economics

Nicholas Mercuro[*]

Introduction

Over the last four decades, a variety of legal movements and theories have evolved to make the study of law less autonomous and more open.[1] These several jurisprudential movements advocate different jurisprudential discourses and understandings of modern law. Each movement writes and thinks about law differently; each maintains a different conception of adjudication and practice. These movements include critical legal studies, feminist legal theory, law and literature, critical race theory, and the several schools of thought comprising Law & Economics.[2] The latter of these – Law & Economics – has developed from a small and rather esoteric branch of research within both economics and the law to what is now a substantial movement that has, on the one hand, helped to redefine the study of law and, on the other hand, exposed economics to the important economic implications of the legal environment.[3] Today, almost all American legal scholars, judges, and lawyers hold some instrumental view of the law and recognize, in various degrees, that Law & Economics occupies an important jurisprudential niche in law.

Law & Economics is not a homogeneous movement; it reflects several traditions, sometimes competing and sometimes complementary. It includes Chicago Law and Economics, Public Choice Theory, American Institutional Law and Economics, Neoinstitutional Law and Economics,[4] The New Haven School, and Modern Civic Republicanism. While there is no doubt that today the Chicago School of Law and Economics and Public Choice Theory are the dominant schools of thought, this chapter offers several output categories or performance indicators for a comparative

[*] Lyman Briggs School, Michigan State University. This chapter draws on four previous works (Medema, Mercuro, and Samuels 1997, 2000; Mercuro 1989b; and Mercuro 1997). The earlier work is extended here to suggest six performance indicators for a comparative institutional approach to law and economics consistent with the American Institutional Law and Economics. A special thanks to both Steven G. Medema and David Schweikhardt for comments on earlier drafts of this chapter.

institutional approach within the tradition of American Institutional Law and Economics. The chapter will: (1) briefly review the general contours of American Institutional Law and Economics; (2) describe the comparative institutional approach that is inherent within this school of thought; and (3) suggest six performance indicators that can be used to assess the performance of institutional alternatives.

Institutional economics as a precursor to American Institutional Law and Economics

American Institutional Law and Economics is a direct descendant of institutional economics, the latter essentially an American contribution to economic thought, and one that, like Legal Realism in jurisprudence, is said to have "had its heyday in the 1920s and early 1930s."[5] Institutional economics developed as a heterodox approach to the study of economic society and has often been described as part of "a revolt against formalism," a revolt that took place in law, in history, and in economics at about the same time (Spiegel 1971: 629). The institutionalists focused on inductive analyses of specific institutional aspects of the American economy. While their principal emphasis was on using the inductive method to describe the constituent elements of the economy, the institutionalists never employed the inductive method to extremes and thereby, were still able to make substantive theoretical generalizations. As noted by Walter S. Buckingham (1958: 107–108), the development of generalizations gave institutional economics a greater theoretical content than the largely descriptive [German] historical school was ever able to attain. On the other hand, institutional theory was by no means as refined and exact as orthodox economic theory.

The emergence of institutional economics has been traced to three distinct sources of influence (Whalen 1996). One was the German historical school, which influenced such early institutionalist thinkers as Richard T. Ely. The German historical school, founded by Wilhelm Roscher (1817–1894) and later dominated by Gustav von Schmoller (1838–1917), emerged, at least in part, as a reaction against classical economic thinking in the mid-nineteenth century. It emphasized the dynamics of economic development, the need to use empirical data to ground economic theories (rather than deductions from abstract concepts), and the necessity of paying particular attention to human institutions. The second influence was from American pragmatic philosophy as set forth by, among others, Charles Peirce, William James, and John Dewey. Proponents of American pragmatic philosophy recognized an uncertainty inherent in all forms of knowledge and sought to develop philosophical methods for establishing the meaning of concepts and beliefs. The pragmatists' emphasis on the uncertainty of knowledge served to provide an epistemological foundation and a social philosophy upon which to erect the basic tenets of institutional economic thought. The third influence came through Thorstein Veblen's turn-of-the century writings focusing on the

Darwinian, evolutionary nature of economic change (Veblen 1889, 1904, 1923). Veblen emerged a strong critic of orthodox economic thinking, rejecting the mechanistic view of economic society as reflected in static equilibrium analysis. He believed that the material environment, technology, and propensities of human nature condition the emergence and growth of institutions. Veblen did not seek merely to describe how prevailing institutions worked, but also to understand how the institutions of capitalism evolved.

Modern elements of institutional economics

From the writings of Thorstein Veblen (1889, 1904, 1923), Wesley C. Mitchell (1914, 1928, 1937), Clarence E. Ayres (1944), Robert Lee Hale (1924, 1927, 1952), Walton H. Hamilton (1932), and John R. Commons (1924, 1925, 1934), institutional economics emerged as an alternative approach to analyzing economic society. In its more modern form, as set forth by Robert A. Gordon (1964: 124–25), institutional economics is embodied in a series of propositions defining an approach that is both alternative to and complementary to mainstream economic analysis. These propositions, together with the particular and specific focus contributed by Commons, provide the foundation upon which American Institutional Law and Economics rests:

- Economic behavior is strongly conditioned by the institutional environment within which economic activity takes place, and, simultaneously, economic behavior affects the structure of the institutional environment.
- The mutual interaction between the institutions and the behavior of economic actors is an evolutionary process, requiring an "evolutionary approach" to economics.
- In analyzing the evolutionary processes contained therein, emphasis is directed to the role played by the conditions imposed by modern technology and the monetary institutions of modern, mixed-market capitalism.
- Emphasis is centered upon conflicts within the economic sphere of society as opposed to harmonious order inherent within the cooperative, spontaneous, and unconscious free play of economic actors within the market.
- There is a clear and present need to channel the conflicts inherent in economic relationships by structuring institutions to establish a mechanism of social control over economic activity.
- The complex nature of this evolutionary process requires an interdisciplinary approach calling on psychology, sociology, anthropology, and law to understand the behavior of economic actors in order to generate more accurate assumptions in describing their behavior.

On the one hand, these propositions constitute a partial rejection of the mechanistic price-theoretic approach proffered by the more orthodox neoclassical microeconomics; on the other hand, they are a manifestation of the institutionalist position that continues to assert that the framework of orthodox economic analysis does not allow it to address certain fundamentally important features of economic activity.

American Institutional Law and Economics: the Commons tradition

John R. Commons stands as the central figure in the development of American Institutional Law and Economics. Unlike Thorstein Veblen, who sought a near total rejection of orthodox economic theory, Commons held a much more conciliatory position, believing that institutional economics was a complement to, rather than a substitute for, neoclassical analysis. Commons' institutional economics was conceived as a broad synthesis of law, economics, and ethics; it recognized both conflicts of interest and mutual dependencies as well as the need for security of expectations and order (Spiegel 1971: 638). Commons placed a greater emphasis on the role of collective and corporate activities in the economy and centered his analysis on the conflicts of interest inherent in a modern economy. Human action was seen to be socially, or culturally, determined; that is, human action and cultural determinants were seen as interactive variables. Consequently, the free will of individuals, not only contributed to the cultural environment, but, in turn, was molded by that environment (Buckingham 1958: 104). Commons probed the impact of institutions, particularly the operation of the legal system (including the judiciary, the legislature, and the regulatory commissions) in working out solutions to conflicts, and the impact of those solutions on economic structure and performance.

Virtually all of contemporary American Institutional Law and Economics follows in the tradition of Commons, and much of this emanates from Michigan State University through the work of Warren J. Samuels and A. Allan Schmid, both trained at the University of Wisconsin by students of Commons.[6] Much, though not all, of the work of Schmid and Samuels can be best understood as two complementary modes of analysis in the context of the standard structure-conduct-performance paradigm.[7] For American Institutional Law and Economics, the emphasis is on the interrelations and the mutual interactions between government and the economy.

Both Samuels' and Schmid's practices of Institutional Law and Economics are avowedly positive in nature (Samuels and Schmid 1981: 1). As they describe the thrust of their work in the "Introduction" to their book titled *Law and Economics: An Institutional Perspective*, "Our principal goal is quite simply to understand what is going on – to identify the instrumental variables and fundamental issues and processes – in the operation of legal institutions of economic significance," and to promote "the development of skills with which to analyze and predict the performance consequences of alternative institutional designs" (Samuels and Schmid 1981: 1). Resource allocation and the distribution of income and wealth are explained "in terms of a complex causal chain involving both allocation and distribution as functions of market forces that depend in turn on three critical components (i) power, (ii) rights, and (iii) the use of government" (Samuels and Schmid 1981: 4).

Schmid's analysis takes place within a situation-specific paradigm focusing on the structure-conduct-performance of alternative institutional arrangements, including different definitions and assignments of property rights, together with the (dis)incentives created. From there, the consequences for individuals, firms, and government are identified, and their effects on economic performance and quality of life are assessed. As such, it reflects a "total" approach to policy analysis, one that emphasizes the link between structure and performance (Schmid 1987: 257–58). As posed by Schmid (1987:188) the institutional approach to law and economics must ask: "How do the rules of property structure human relationships and affect participation in decisions when interests conflict or when shared objectives are to be implemented? How do the results affect performance of the economy?"

For Samuels, the organizing concept is that of the legal-economic nexus, wherein "the law is a function of the economy, and the economy (especially its structure) is a function of law . . . [Law and economy] are jointly produced, not independently given and not merely interacting" (Samuels 1989: 1567). Through the legal-economic nexus, the structures of the law and the economic system are worked out, with each serving as both dependent and independent variables in the construction of legal-economic reality. Legal rules govern "the terms of access to and participation in the economy by potential economic actors," and "property and other rights . . . govern whose preferences will be given effect through the market" (Samuels 1975: 66). In all of this, American Institutional Law and Economics is a cumulative undertaking with no sharp dividing line separating the contributions from Commons, Hale, Hamilton . . . etcetera from the works of Samuels, Schmid, and other contemporaries who have contributed to the field.[8]

Central themes of American Institutional Law and Economics

There are five central themes that constitute the core of American Institutional Law and Economics. Each will be briefly outlined here before exploring the central elements of a comparative institutional approach to law and economics that is inherent within this school of thought.

First – the evolutionary nature of law and economy

One of the factors emphasized by the institutionalists, and especially Commons in his discussion of the legal foundations of the capitalist economic system, is the evolutionary nature of the economic system. The import of the evolutionary perspective is that it broadens the frame of analysis beyond the "idea of mechanistic maximization under static constraints" (Hodgson 1994: 223); it widens and deepens the analysis to the longer-run processes of economic development. While not eschewing static analysis or denying its value, the emphasis on historical processes and the role of legal change in affecting the course of economic evolution makes American Institutional Law and Economics inherently evolutionary.

Drawing on the work of Commons, Samuels (1989: 1578) described the legal-economic nexus as "a continuing, explorative, and emergent process through which are worked out ongoing solutions to legal problems." The legal-economic nexus is that sphere of decision making that reflects the working out of whose interests are to count as rights, whose values are to dominate, and who is to make these decisions. The resolution of these issues determines not just rights, but the allocation *and* distribution of resources in society, and hence power, income, and wealth – it positions players for the next "round." The structure of legal-economic institutions, including the firm, the market, and the state (whether the latter is articulated in the context of the executive branch, the legislature, the judiciary, or the bureaucracy), channels legal-economic decision making, with this structure seen as the outcome of an evolutionary process of legal-economic change rather than as movement to a steady-state equilibrium (Schmid 1989: 66). Legal change is both gradual and continuous, and "has led to major transformations of the legal system and of the pattern of rights and, thereby, of the system of economic organization and control" (Samuels and Mercuro 1979: 167). The pervasiveness of legal change and the ongoing process of legal-economic reconstruction through the nexus process thus makes necessary an evolutionary-historical approach that accounts for the array of factors and forces promoting both continuity and change over time.

Second – the tension between continuity versus change

The recognition of the evolutionary nature of legal-economic relations brings to the fore a second fundamental theme within American Institutional Law and Economics – the ever-present tension between continuity and change in legal-economic relations. The evolutionary path of the legal-economic system is derivative of legal-economic policy choices that are made over time. Continuity and change are the outcome of the policy-making process, more specifically, of the interaction between the groups supporting the respective forces of continuity and change and the power that each can bring to bear on this process (Samuels 1966: 267–73). Within this policy-making process (whether in the context of the executive branch, the legislative, the judiciary, or the bureaucracy) arise and operate forces that, through acts of commission or omission, serve to maintain the *status quo* structure of legal-economic institutions and relations – that is, preserve continuity – while other forces promote an alteration in these institutions and relations – that is, promote change. The ongoing choice process within the legal-economic arena determines both the institutional structures that obtain at any given point in time and whether the *status quo* institutional structures, or some other, will prevail in the future, that is, whether there will be change, and if so how much.

Third – *mutual interdependence, conflict, and the problem of order*

American Institutional Law and Economics views the legal-economic system as a system of mutual interdependence rather than one of atomistic independence. The economy, says Schmid (1989: 59), is "a universe of human relations," not merely "a universe of commodities," and within this world each individual has scarcity relationships with others. While it may be that part of life deals with movements from positions off contract curves to positions on contract curves in the process of exhausting gains from trade, American Institutional Law and Economics places strong emphasis on: (1) who gets to play; (2) where one starts in the game; and (3) the rules governing the game.

Society is recognized, at least in part, as a cooperative venture for mutual advantage where there are both identities and conflicts of interests in ongoing human relations. Within this system of mutual interdependence, societal institutions, including the legal system, both enhance the scope of cooperative endeavors and channel political-legal-economic conflict toward resolution (Mercuro 1989b: 2). Given the importance of human interdependence and the emphasis on who plays and what are the starting points, the focus of American Institutional Law and Economics is on conflict rather than harmony, where "[t]he role of the legal system, including both common and constitutional law, is to provide a framework or a process for conflict resolution and the development of legal rights" (Samuels and Mercuro 1979: 166). The resolution of these conflicts, of whose interests government will give effect through law and otherwise, is the resolution of the problem of order in society – a working out of a societal structure that promotes coherence, security, and orderliness in human relations. It is the existence of conflicting interests that necessitates the establishment of processes and methods for deciding between competing interests thereby determining how conflicts are to be resolved. Indeed, the manner by which a society comes to channel conflict says much about its ultimate character. The fundamental problem in fashioning that character is in providing order, that is, in "the reconciling of freedom and control, or autonomy and coordination including hierarchy and equality, with continuity and change" (Samuels 1972: 584). One result is the showing that the unique determinate optimal equilibrium solutions of the neoclassical research protocol are both presumptive and forced, perhaps heuristically useful for analytical exercises, but not representative of actual legal and economic processes in all their evolutionary complexity.

Fourth – *the ongoing reconstruction of rights, power, government, and the economy*

Law is fundamentally a matter of rights creation and re-creation. Consistent with the positive, descriptive nature of American Institutional Law and

Economics, its proponents are concerned with the rights (re)creation process and the impact of this process on legal-economic decision making and activity. From the institutional perspective, the sphere of activities open to individuals and the individual choice process can be recast as an Alpha-Beta conflict. Each individual's ability to determine his or her own choices, and to influence the opportunity sets (and hence choices) of others, is the outcome of a process of mutual coercion, where the ability to coerce is simply the ability of Alpha to impact Beta's opportunity set without B's consent (Samuels 1974).

The ongoing attempts to delineate and redefine opportunity sets, through the machinations of power and mutual coercion in the face of conflicts, give rise to disputes which necessitate resolution. Government is seen to play a central and inevitable role within this process, for property rights, working rules, and legal doctrines are *not* rights, rules, and doctrines because they are pre-existing, but rather because they are protected by government. Rights are thus relative to and contingent upon "the legal limitations inherent in their identification and interpretation, the exercise by others of their rights, and legal and nonlegal change" (Samuels 1974:118). The resolution of Alpha-Beta conflicts comes through the creation and assignment (or reassignment) of property rights, working rules, and the formulation of legal doctrine which define the scope of choices open to each individual and the degree to which each is exposed to the choices of others. The resulting opportunity sets and choices, and hence power, coercion and the ability of individuals to secure rights (or a change therein) through the use and control of government are a function of which rights, rules, and legal doctrines prevail. Contributors to American Institutional Law and Economics thus see terms such as regulation, deregulation, and government intervention as misleading, in that government is omnipresent. This is especially evident in describing the central and inevitable role played by government in institutionalizing the market. As will be explored below (section titled, "A Comparative Institutional Approach to Legal-Economic Analysis"), from the vantage point of American Institutional Law and Economics, to affirm a solution by the market (separate from government) is devoid of meaning in that the market sector is *niched within* legal-economic institutions and thus, cannot have meaning independent of these legal-economic institutions. The question is not, then, one of more versus less government, but rather of whose interests government gives effect to through law – through the process of rights creation and recreation.

The same can be said for externalities. Since virtually every legal change imposes both benefits and costs resulting in the simultaneous enhancement of some opportunity sets and the restriction of others, externalities are thus ubiquitous and reciprocal. The problem for law is to bring order and predictability as to who can create externality for whom, not just how to facilitate trade (Schmid 2000). Any (re)definition, (re)assignment, or change in the degree of enforcement of rights benefits some interests and harms others. The externality remains, in different form; it is merely shifted, as was made clear by Ronald H. Coase in "The Problem of Social Cost" (1960). From the institutionalist perspective, systems of property law, tort law, and contract law – in particular, the legal doctrines that underlie each – then, do not provide solutions to situations of externality (or conflicts generally), but rather only resolutions that rechannel streams of benefit and harm in a particular direction through the legal delimitation of rights, rules, and doctrines.

In the ongoing reconstruction of rights, rules, and legal doctrines there is an inevitable necessity of choice that reveals that law is not something that is given or to be discovered, but is instead a human artifact marked by deliberative and non-deliberative human choice (Samuels 1981: 168). The fact that law is a human choice process means that value judgments will necessarily be introduced in choosing between competing interests. Legal-economic outcomes are thus "an expression of the values of those who have participated and prevailed at each stage of choice in the political-legal-economic arena; that is, those who are able to most effectively use government to further their own ends" (Mercuro 1989b: 10). Justice, then, reflects not some given set of high foundational principles, but rather a normative valuational process that determines the laws, norms, and values that are to govern living (Samuels 1971: 444 ; Samuels and Mercuro 1979: 160–63).

Fifth – the problematic nature of efficiency

One of the hallmarks of American Institutional Law and Economics has been the rejection of the Chicago, Public Choice, and Neoinstitutional *emphasis* on the determination of *the* efficient resolution of legal disputes. Proponents of American Institutional Law and Economics do not reject efficiency as an important variable in legal-economic analysis, but rather maintain that efficiency alone cannot, and should not, determine the assignment of rights (Samuels 1989: 1563).[9]

The starting point for the institutionalist critique of the efficiency criterion is the recognition that economic activity – prices, costs, outputs, risk, income, wealth, etcetera – is not some sort of natural phenomenon, but rather is determined by the extant structure of rights, rules, and doctrines that exist in society, with the levels of and changes in each of these economic variables being, in part, a function of the legal structure and legal change over time.[10] Each particular rights structure will give rise to a particular set of prices, costs, and outputs. Thus, each particular rights structure will give rise to a particular efficient allocation of resources. Hence, there is no unique efficient result.

For proponents of American Institutional Law and Economics, the rhetoric that emanates from the purportedly positivist Chicago-based schools of thought invoking "atomistic industries" or "contestable markets" and the associated concept of "price-taking behavior" is exposed as nothing more than deeply normative "rights-taking behavior."[11] The institutionalists maintain that inasmuch as rights underlie product prices, factors prices, and thus costs, to talk of "price-takers" bypasses virtually all that is (or should be) important in Chicago School of Law and Economics, Public Choice Theory, and Neoinstitutional Law and Economics – "prices takers" are "rights takers." The determination of a particular efficient solution involves a normative and selective choice as to whose interests will be accommodated, who will realize gains, and who will realize losses. Thus, as described by Schmid, "the whole point is that global welfare maximization is meaningless," and "[t]o recommend one rights structure over another, analysts must take their stand as naked normativists without the comfort of the Pareto-better cloak or any other formalism" (Schmid 1989: 69).

Both institutional economics and American Institutional Law and Economics are trying to come to grips with the interrelations between legal and economic processes and the consequences that flow therefrom. Proponents of American Institutional Law and Economics do not feel obliged to identify particular legal arrangements as "optimal." They argue that putatively optimal solutions to problems of policy only give effect to selective preconceptions and assumptions as to whose interests are to count. Whereas some of the more orthodox approaches within Law & Economics seek unique, determinate optimal equilibrium solutions, the five core themes of American Institutional Law and Economics constitute a different approach. Proponents of the latter instead concentrate on identifying and analyzing the processes by which the various legal structures, the conduct, and the economic performance are worked out. In this regard, the need for a comparative institutional approach to law and economics emerges.

A comparative institutional approach to legal-economic analysis

Several undertakings that would be central in establishing a comparative institutional approach to law and economics have been identified: (1) models of legal-political and economic interaction must be developed; (2) objective, positive, empirical studies of government as both a dependent and independent variable must be undertaken; (3) economic activity as both an input and an output of political-legal processes must be explored; and (4) efforts must be made to wed both theoretical and empirical analyses toward an objective, positive comprehension of law and economics (Samuels 1975: 72). Such analysis will serve the twin purposes of deepening the understanding of legal and economic processes and their interrelations, and providing a more sound basis upon which to predict the potential consequences of legal-economic change – hence the need for a comparative institutional approach to legal-economic analysis.[12]

Consistent with the thrust of institutional economics, and American Institutional Law and Economics, institutional structure cannot merely be assumed away or taken as given. Rather, it must be the subject of study involving a comparison of the effects of institutional alternatives focusing on the nexus between the legal-economic decision-making processes and social well-being. The comparative institutional approach outlined here is general rather than partial (Samuels 1972: 582, 585) and consists of describing and analyzing the systematic relationship between: (1) the structure of political-legal-economic institutions, focusing on the property rights, working rules, and legal doctrines by which they operate; (2) the conduct or observed behavior in light of the incentives (penalties and rewards) created by the structure of institutions; and (3) the consequent economic performance as measured by various performance indicators that give meaning to and shape the character of economic life under these institutions.

Within the structure-conduct-performance paradigm, the object, then, is to explain and compare the outcomes that will occur under real, discrete, alternative institutional structures. A comparative institutional approach to law and economics emphasizes the need to explain and analyze the available alternatives and the consequences of choice at three distinct stages: (1) the *constitutional stage of choice*; (2) the *institutional stage of choice*; and (3) the *economic impact stage of choice*.[13] In contemplating the structure of its governing institutions, a nation must be concerned with: (i) those institutional structures that will help promote cooperation among parties of interest; (ii) those that will help channel conflicts; and (iii) those that will help accomplish change. The selection or establishment of a specific set of institutions, and thus the character of life in a society, is the product of choice – choices that are an expression (at the most fundamental level) of the individuals comprising society. The choices may take place at any of the three stages identified above (more fully described below). This is not to suggest that informing choice through a comparative institutional approach is a simple process. Quite to the contrary, the comparative institutional approach is trying to describe what we know to be a very complex choice-making process, an arena where many difficult issues are debated and interests are at stake.

Figure 12.1 depicts the three different levels of choice: (1) the constitutional stage of choice; (2) the institutional stage of choice with its legal doctrines and working rules; and (3) the economic impact stage of choice – included in the latter, the rights structures comprising the *legal relations governing society* defined as the sum of private property rights (within the market sector), status rights (within the public sector), communal property (within the communal sector), and open-access resources. The underlying logic inherent within the figure is that formulating legal-economic policy or altering the law by either: (i) changing the constitution; (ii) altering working rules or legal doctrine; or (iii) refashioning the legal relations governing society will result in systematically altering incentives and behavior, and thus affect economic performance.[14] This logic or line of reasoning can be depicted as follows:

law / working rules / legal doctrines → incentive structure →
institutional behavior → economic performance

Constitutional stage of choice

In order to understand the nature of the choices necessary at the constitutional stage, it is useful to start off thinking about a society in a conceptual state of anarchy (McKenzie and Tullock 1978). In such a state, individuals will contemplate the opportunity costs associated with the protective-defensive resource diversions that are necessary and essential for life under a system of anarchy.[15] Once they recognize the potential prospects for improvement in the character of their economic life made possible by establishing a social contract or constitution, they will enter into some form of social contract or formally adopt a constitution. In establishing their constitution, the individuals will seek to spell out the behavioral limits of what is and what is not mutually acceptable conduct and lay out the so-called *rules for making rules*.

While the established constitution is typically thought to have only a subtle effect on the allocation of resources and distribution of income, however subtle, that impact cannot be ignored. In addition, since constitutions are not immutable, the methods by which constitutional rules can be revised are developed at this level of choice. Once the constitution is framed, it will then provide the basis for the emergence of a broad assemblage of legal-economic-political institutions and the relationships among those institutions. The structuring of these legal-economic institutions through legal doctrines and working rules constitutes the institutional stage of choice and affects the allocation of resources much more directly.

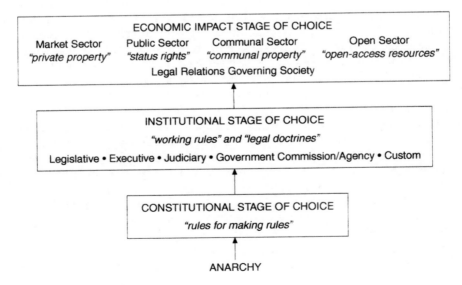

Figure 12.1 Three different levels of choice

Institutional stage of choice

The institutional stage of choice focuses directly on the structure of the political/legal institutions (more commonly referred to as the *State*) as well as the revision of those institutional structures. The two core elements at this stage of choice are the fundamental *legal doctrines* and specific *working rules* of institutional decision-making processes. Legal doctrines evolve over time through legal decision making, whereas working rules (the decision-making processes of an institution) are formally worked out by the institution itself, often in the form of bylaws. Legal doctrines and working rules are partially established by the rules worked out at the constitutional stage of choice; and as well, they are also a partial function of the decisions of other institutions worked out often under complex procedures. Examples of the latter include a court decision which imposes certain restrictions or obligations either upon the decision-making processes of a legislative body or upon the decision-making processes of a government agency.

Individuals may attempt to *establish* or *revise* working rules in the executive, legislative, judicial, and agency branches. From a policy standpoint, the primary difficulty in promulgating working rules lies in trying to design legal-economic institutions that provide decision makers with an incentive structure that channels behavior so as to achieve their stated goals as efficiently as possible. In the simplest of terms, "all bureaucracies are not created equal." With respect to the fashioning or the redesigning of working rules, much work remains to be done identifying which institutional structures go towards enhancing the efficiency of legal institutions. The same can be said for legal doctrines. Legal doctrines evolve over time and as they become institutionalized they ultimately affect economic performance. For example, as controlling doctrines: (i) the criteria as to who may/may not have standing in a court of law; (ii) who is allowed intervene in litigation; and (iii) the standards of admissibility for evidence (e.g., Daubert-type questions) all impact economic performance.

As in the case of constitutions, legal institutions (especially the working rules and legal doctrines that undergird legal institutions) are not set in stone, but rather are themselves a response to economic needs. As such, they can and do undergo structural revisions. Changes in legal doctrines or the working rules of legal institutions will change the decision-making processes of those institutions and may alter the institutional choices that directly impact the extant structure of property rights. A full appreciation of the relationship between legal institutions and the structure of property rights is fundamental to understanding the economic impact stage of choice for it is at this stage of choice we see the most prominent interface between economics and the law.

Economic impact stage of choice

The third stage of choice – the *economic impact stage of choice* – defines the economic impacts of the existing or potentially revised legal-economic relations governing society, be they in the form of private property rights (within the market sector), status rights (within the public sector), communal property (within the communal sector), or open-access resources.[16] Specifically, in formulating legal-economic policy, a nation state can use any of the four property regimes that constitute four different systems of social control: (i) the market sector; (ii) the public sector; (iii) the communal sector; and (iv) the open-access resource sector.

The market sector is structured by private property rights established by the individuals in a society acting through their institutions. It is an arena in which exclusive private property rights are defined and assigned, enforced, and subsequently transferred among the parties so as to exhaust gains from trade. With the market as the system of social control, it is then possible for individuals to enhance their welfare by specializing and engaging in exchange through trade. This process of trade is conventionally viewed as a purely voluntary endeavor. The voluntary nature of this market process is such that no individual will engage in a trade that leaves him worse off. The final allocative outcome will be arrived at once all the gains from trade have been exhausted in both exchange and production. Thus, barring externalities and the problem of public goods, given a defined set of private property rights and given some initial distribution of rights, one can expect, consistent with the duality theorem, the market outcome to provide a Pareto-efficient allocation of resources.

The public sector, an alternative system of social control, is made up of the whole array of status rights across the full range of government institutions. In the public sector, resources are allocated with the establishment of status rights under stipulations set forth by the Federal, state, and/or local governments in pronouncements of eligibility requirements for individuals to use goods, services, or resources. The specific eligibility requirements are set forth by the government – the modern administrative state – in its various capacities including legislative, agency, commissions, and boards. The status rights are taken to be exclusive and non-transferable.[17] Unlike the market sector resource allocations, within the public sector there are no spontaneous mechanisms for ensuring that decision makers in the public sector will formulate public policies that are efficient. This problem is partially offset by the extent to which public sector decisions are based on benefit–cost calculations; in such cases, public sector decisions can be said to approach a Kaldor–Hicks efficient allocation of resources.[18]

The communal sector is comprised of common-property resources, that is, private property owned by a group of co-owners (*res communes*). Under communal ownership, a group of individuals would allocate the rights to use or transfer the resource. Typically, a management group oversees the manner by which a common property resource can be used and reserves the right to exclude non-members. Depending upon the group rules selected to manage the resource, the communal sector can allocate resources in an efficient manner.[19]

And finally, the open-access resource sector is that sector wherein commodities or resources will be owned by no one. In this case there are no property rights to the commodities/resources; since they are equally available to all (*res nullius*), they will belong to the party to first exercise control over the resource. The resulting open-access allocation of the resource will only be allocatively efficient if supply exceeds demand at a zero price. If supply does not exceed demand at a zero price and society nonetheless retains the resource in open access, the resources will be overused.[20]

Typically, Western societies are structured so that the character of life is determined by all four systems of social control: the market sector, the public sector, the communal sector, and the open-access sector. The relative scope and content of each of the systems of social control is the result of a collective determination of those who prevailed in choice-making processes in the political/legal economic arena. Figure 12.1 is intended to integrate the three stages of choice – the constitutional, institutional, and economic impact stage – together with the market, public, communal, and open-access resource sectors. Members of society act both individually and collectively to reshape the ultimate character of economic life within which they live. This is accomplished under the recognition that neither: (i) the constitution; (ii) the legal doctrines and the working rules; nor (iii) the rights structures are given immutably by nature, but are themselves a response to economic needs and flexible in response to changes in those needs. Participants in the political/legal economic arena will (from the bottom up) establish a constitution so as to avoid the pitfalls and inefficiencies of anarchy; set legal doctrines and working rules in place thereby structuring their legal-economic institutions; and define and assign the private property rights, status rights, communal rights and open-access resources – giving rise to the private, public, communal, and open-access resource sectors, respectively.

Consistent with the core themes of American Institutional Law and Economics, it must be emphasized that government is seen to play a central and inevitable role in institutionalizing all four sectors, in particular the market sector (Mercuro and Samuels 1999). Indeed, from the vantage point of the institutionalists, to affirm solution by market (separate from government) is devoid of meaning in that the market sector is *niched within* legal-economic institutions and thus, cannot have meaning independent of these legal-economic institutions. Institutionalized markets are a function of the institutions and power structures which form and operate through them. The market sector exists: (i) within the context of the constitutional laws, existing legal doctrine in the judiciary, and the working rules of the State; and (ii) alongside the other sectors that society has chosen to institutionalize – the public sector, the communal sector, and an open-access resource sector. From this vantage point, the State stands as the essential complement to the market – the latter is not an assumed a superior substitute for the former. In all this government becomes the object of control for those seeking private legal-economic gain or advantage, "a mode through which relative rights and therefore relative market (income securing) status is given effect" (Samuels 1971: 441–42). To arbitrarily affirm solution by a market together with the outcome that obtains and then purported to be optimal, is to give effect to a particular structure of law, certain legal doctrines, working rules, rights, and therefore power and thus begs most of the operative issue(s). The question is not, then, one of more versus less government, but rather of whose interests government gives effect to through law, that is, through the process of rights creation and recreation.

As should be evident, in encompassing the core themes of American Institutional Law and Economics, a comparative institutional approach is inconsistent with some of the other approaches to Law & Economics that tend to begin the formulation of legal-policy options by reciting a long parade of public-sector horribles or by enumerating government imperfections. A comparative institutional approach to law and economics must not fall victim to the tendency toward any "single institutionalism."[21] Given the array of problems confronting a society, again, the issue is not, in the abstract, whether the market sector is *the* solution to an economic issue, or whether the public sector – government – is *the* solution. Indeed, as we have all learned from Coase, little is learned by looking at instances of market failure and deciding that the market is *the* solution because it conforms to one's ideology. Society bears high opportunity costs by engaging in any form of "single-institution-alist" based policy. As Coase (1960: 18–19) has stated:

> Satisfactory views on policy can only come from a patient study of how, in practice, the market, firms, and governments handle the problem of harmful effects . . . . It is my belief that economists, and policy makers generally, have tended to over-estimate the advantages that come from governmental regulation. But this belief, even if justified, does not do more than suggest that government regulation should be curtailed. It does not tell us where the boundary line should be drawn. This, it seems to me, has to come from a detailed investigation of the actual results of handling the problem in different ways.

Not unlike Coase, Neil Komesar (1994: 6) has observed: "The correct question is whether, in any given setting, the market is better or worse than its available alternatives or the political process is better or worse than its available alternatives." Advocates of the market sector as the preferred system of social control must come to recognize that singular solutions to legal-economic issues reflect only one particular set of value premises and one particular conception of the facts, benefits, and costs at issue. In a like manner, advocates of channeling resources through the public sector must be equally attuned to the underlying value judgments inherent in the policies they advocate and the potential costs in implementing those policies. Whatever the public policy goal, institutional alternatives are available and the choice among alternatives is always a choice of highly imperfect alternatives (Komesar 1994: 3–5). Institutional choice reflects the reality that the decision of who decides is really a decision of what institution decides and for whom. The array of alternatives to be considered includes: (i) the potential for constitutional change; (ii) altering legal doctrines in the judiciary or replacing old institutional working rules for new ones within the executive branch, the legislature, and throughout government agencies and commissions; or (iii) altering property rights be they private property rights, status rights, communal rights, or open-access resources in the market, public, communal, or open-access resource sectors, respectively.

Performance indicators /output categories – criteria for assessment

The analysis of law and public policy may be undertaken at any one of three levels of choice. By describing the interrelationships between economics and the law, the comparative institutional approach within the American Institutional approach to Law and Economics attempts to make known the full array of impacts of alternative institutions, different legal arrangements, and alternative public policies together with an articulation of whose interests will be served and at whose expense. To fully inform choice, evaluation of alternatives ought not to be done solely in terms of economic efficiency, but rather should include other performance indicators that, in the aggregate, tell us something of the total character of economic life. The goal, to the extent possible, is not normative judgment, but rather description. By articulating the outcomes of the alternative institutional arrangements available to society, the comparative institutional approach fleshes out what is going on in the legal-economic nexus and identifies the factors and forces at work in the ongoing social construction and reconstruction of the legal-economic reality. From this vantage point, it constitutes a reaffirmation of, and staying within, the positive, descriptive domain of American Institutional Law and Economics.

To more fully assess the outcomes of alternative institutional arrangements, six performance indicators are set forth below. The author is well aware that many of these performance indicators are difficult to quantify and also notes that while some may complement each other, others involve making difficult trade-offs. In addition, the reader is forewarned that no single performance indicator is useful in the abstract – each one is built upon certain antecedent normative premises that at a very deep level, determine whose preferences count (Schmid 1987: 242–43). Consequently, *any* suggested set of performance indicators (including those offered here) constitute the antecedent normative premises of the author's assertion as to what is important in assessing legal change and its impact on the character of economic life. Given these caveats, the six performance indicators identified below are offered as being consistent with the ideas and ideals that emanate from both institutional economics and American Institutional Law and Economics as they endeavor to inform choice.

Efficiency

There is no doubt that within Chicago Law and Economics, Public Choice, Neoinstitutional Law and Economics and, as well, for a comparative institutional approach to law and economics, allocative efficiency and Kaldor–Hicks efficiency can be useful in providing a partial guide to determining the appropriateness of a proposed legal change (be it a new law, an emerging legal doctrine, or a proposed policy). But one must be careful in the application. Frank I. Michelman (1980: 433–34) described the standard approach to conducting an efficiency analysis within Law & Economics as follows:

(i)   a piece of law is selected out for appraisal and, for that purpose, is marked off from the rest;

(ii) the appraisal of the focal piece proceeds on the assumption that the rest of the law is held constant;

(iii) the piece is appraised by comparing it with one or more specific (historically proposed or plausible) alternatives having congruent ranges;

(iv) the piece is called efficient, *vis-à-vis* the alternative(s), if its anticipated resource-allocation outcomes represent greater total "wealth" as measured by total (estimated) willingness to pay for those outcomes.

Thus, in efficiency analysis the strategy is to isolate and focus on a single law, legal doctrine, or policy, and place it against a selected legal relief or background law for analysis. Such an approach inevitably involves making antecedent normative premises concerning both the level of analysis and the appropriate background law. In addition, the entire process is subject to the circularity problem of using rights to define wealth maximizing rights. Further questions arise when an efficiency analysis is attempted across four sectors of the political economy. Each of these is explored below.

Level of analysis/background law

Within Chicago Law and Economics, Public Choice, and Neoinstitutional Law and Economics, the preferred performance indicator to inform choice is economic efficiency; concomitantly, there is a stated willingness to take that legal relief – the *status quo* structure of rights – as given without further discussion. With respect to the former, as stated by Judge Richard A. Posner (1973: 221), "since the efficient use of resources is an important, although not always paramount social value, the burden, I suggest, is on the authors to present reasons why a standard that appears to impose avoidable costs on society should nonetheless be adopted."

As to the tendency to take the *status quo* structure of rights as given, this is often expressed as part of a greater, pragmatic need to accept background law so as to "get on with the efficiency analysis" of the new law, legal doctrine, or proposed policy under scrutiny. This quest to move forward is exemplified in Chicago Law and Economics by Coase (1960: 43) in the following: "A better approach would seem to be to start our analysis with *a situation approximating that which actually exists*, to examine the effects of a proposed policy change and to attempt to decide whether the new situation would be, in total better or worse than the original one" (emphasis added).[22] In a similar vein, proponents of Public Choice assert:

> The modified Paretian–Wicksellian framework implies that the social scientist *must be prepared to accept the status quo* when analysis indicates that tractable "solutions" to social problems are not possible. . . . He accepts what is for the simple reason that is where he starts.
> (Tollison 1972: 4–5, emphasis added)

> *There is an explicit prejudice in favor of previously existing rights*, not because this structure possesses some intrinsic ethical attributes, and not because change itself is undesirable, but for the much more elementary reason that only such a prejudice offers incentives for the emergence of voluntary negotiated settlements among the parties themselves.
> (Buchanan 1972: 452, emphasis added)

Undertaking an efficiency analysis following the contours outlined above necessitates "picking up a camera," so to speak, that inevitably frames the issue and thereby conditions the outcome. Donald Schön (1979: 264–65) has labeled this process "naming and framing," and describes the process and its effects as follows:

> Things are selected for attention and named in such a way as to fit the frame constructed for the situation. . . . Through the processes of naming and framing, the stories make . . . the normative leap from data to recommendations, from facts to values, from "is" to "ought." It is typical of diagnostic/descriptive stories such as these that they execute the normative leap in such a way as to make it seem graceful, compelling, even obvious.

In efficiency analysis (including that which transpires in a comparative institutional approach to law and economics), the parties of interest, the court, or the legal-economic analyst may all frame the issue differently with a propitious choice as to the level of analysis and selected background law. For example, in litigation involving, say, rent control, one could elect to focus on any one of several provisions in a rent control ordinance that allowed for rent increases; alternatively, they could elect to look at the entire ordinance as a whole (i.e., look at all of the provisions collectively that allowed for the same); or they could focus on rent control generally as a policy option.[23] The "level of analysis" deemed "appropriate" depends upon which level best supports one's argument as each attempts to press its respective claims.

The parties of interest, the courts, or the legal-economic analyst may all differ as to which level of analysis to employ and which background law is best to assess the efficiency of the proposed legal change. The important point is that once made, these antecedent choices drive the efficiency analysis. And therein lies the inherent tension within an approach that selectively culls out one law, doctrine, or policy, and places it against a selective legal relief. The tension stems from the desire to inform choice (through positive description) using an analysis that is normatively conditioned by both the selected level of analysis and the choice of background law. That is, the level at which the efficiency analysis is conducted and the propriety given to background law drives the results by making some elements of the analysis central and fundamental (and perhaps efficient) while others are pushed into the background. This tension is further complicated by the inherent circularity of the process.

Circularity problem

In using efficiency as a performance indicator to assess the impact of a new law, proposed policy, or an alternative legal doctrine to help inform choice, the circularity problem necessarily arises. In American Institutional Law and Economics it is recognized that rights (rules and legal doctrines as well) are rights because they are protected, they are not protected because they are rights. The circularity problem arises due to the fact that the law conditions the determination of what is efficient. Since efficiency is a function of rights, and not the other way around, it is circular and inappropriate to maintain that efficiency alone can determine rights. An outcome that is claimed to be efficient is efficient only with regard to the assumed initial structure of rights which is often part of what is at issue (Schmid 1989: 68–69). Just as costs, prices, outputs, wealth, and so on are derivative of a particular rights structure, so too then are cost minimization, value-of-output maximization, benefit–cost calculations, and wealth maximization.[24] Different specifications of rights will lead to different (and economically noncomparable) minimizing or maximizing valuations. Thus, as Samuels (1981: 154) asserts, "[t]o argue that wealth maximization [or any other efficiency criterion] can determine rights serves only to mask a choice of which interests to protect as rights."

Sector analysis

Finally, there are significant differences in the measurement of efficiency across the four sectors of the economy – private, public, communal, and open-access resource sectors. As Deborah Stone (1997) has pointed out, the measurement of efficiency in the public sector is marked with some very difficult issues; these same issues can be raised in the context of the communal and open-access resource sectors of the economy. What constitutes efficiency in each sector of the economy is predicated, in part, on: (i) who determines what is the correct output goal or program objective; (ii) how we value and compare multiple objectives; (iii) how different objectives or outputs benefit different constituencies or groups; (iv) how we count inputs that are simultaneously outputs to somebody else; (v) how we decide which of the many benefits/outputs of any input to count; and (vi) how we count the virtually unlimited opportunity costs of resources used as inputs (Stone 1997: 66). Stone argues that "to go beyond the vague [efficiency] slogans and apply the concept to a concrete policy choice requires making assumptions about who and what counts as important" (Stone 1997: 65). As Stone puts it:

> There are no correct answers to these questions to be found outside the political process. The answers built into supposedly technical analyses of efficiency are nothing more than political claims. By ordering different assumptions, sides in a conflict can portray their preferred outcomes as being efficient.
>
> (Stone 1997: 65)

Legal decisions or changes in law can be said to be efficient only from the point of view of the party whose interests are given effect through the identification and assignment of rights (Samuels 1981: 154). For those who advocate a comparative institutional approach, there is a recognition that there is much more to the character of economic life than vague references to efficiency; as Samuels has argued, "[f]or law to be preoccupied solely with economic maximization would rob law of life and of much of what makes for human meaning and significance" (Samuels 1981: 165).

As emphasized within American Institutional Law and Economics, in modern mixed-market economies, society is constantly redefining rights between competing sets of interests. Rights are in flux; moving among the private sector, the public sector, the communal sector, and the open-access resource sector. The inevitable result of legal change is that some will gain and some will lose. Since rights are continually being created and recreated, choices must be made against a legal relief that is constantly in flux. The normative selection of the level of analysis, together with the normative acceptance of prevailing background law, has implications for the assessment of efficiency and therefore developing legal-economic policy. Given the win–lose nature of legal-economic policy, a deeper understanding of the fundamental issues surrounding the quest for "efficient" legal change is garnered by making known the implications of the chosen level of analysis and the background law used in the analysis. Urging that legal analysis adopt efficiency as its dominant criterion, and that it accept the prevailing background law for "pragmatic reasons" or to "set the stage for voluntary agreements" without regard to the implications for the nature and character of economic life, takes much for granted.

Distributional equity

Rights determination is a normative activity with immediate consequences for both efficiency and distributional equity; the definition and assignment of rights determines which efficient allocation *and* which distribution of benefits and costs will carry the day. At the same time, the specification of rights, and the resulting efficient outcome, structure the future distribution of income, wealth, and power in society.[25] It has been argued that "most public policy decisions are usually even more concerned with distributional equity issues (namely, *who* gets the benefits and *who* pays the costs) than with efficiency issues (namely, how *large* are the benefits and costs)" (Wolf 1997: 30). As Jacob Viner (1960: 69) wrote: "Extensive government intervention has come about largely as a result of dissatisfaction with the prevailing distribution of income. . . . No modern people will have zeal for the free market unless it operates in a setting of 'distributive justice' with which they are tolerably content." Indeed, one could invert Posner's argument (quoted above in the section on Efficiency) and suggest that: Since distribution of resources is an important, although not always paramount social value, the burden, I suggest, is on the authors to present reasons why an efficiency standard that appears to impose unfair distributions on society should nonetheless be adopted.

Due to the non-uniqueness of efficiency, efficiency is inevitably bound up with the issue of distributional equity; as Samuels and Schmid (1981: 2) describe it, "the concept of efficiency as separate from distribution is false." "With no unique optimal use of resources and opportunities independent of rights identification and assignment, the legal system must select the [distributional] result to be pursued: the definition of the efficient solution is both the object and the subject of the legal system" (Samuels 1978: 106). The choice of rights, then, is ultimately an issue of distributional equity. Thus, to the extent possible, the distributional equity impacts consequent to a legal change should be made known.[26] But here too, just as with the antecedent normative premises that underlie efficiency analysis, so too are there antecedent normative premises as to the exact interpretation of what constitutes distributional equity. The concept can be interpreted in several ways. For instance, as Charles Wolf has made clear, it can be defined in the sense of equality of outcome or, perhaps, using equality of opportunity (with little or no regard for outcome). Or, distributional equity could be defined in terms of horizontal equity (treating equally situated people equally) or vertical equity (treating unequally situated people in appropriate unequal ways), or perhaps in terms of Marxian equity ("from each according to ability, to each according to need") (Wolf 1997: 28–30, 82–83).

In addition, there is the issue of the distribution of welfare over time. Consideration of intergenerational equity raises the question as to the current generation's responsibilities and obligations to future generations.[27] Choosing one method over another to assess the intergenerational impact carries with it the ethical implications of weighing the preferences and/or welfare of members of one generation *vis-à-vis* those of another generation. Consequently, a comparative institutional approach must be concerned not only with structuring institutions to help answer such questions as "Who is part of the 'community'?" but also assess the distributional impacts of the legal change on that so-defined community. In all this, Schmid (1987: 242–43) asserts that, when people's interests conflict, the call for distributional and/or intergenerational equity in the abstract is without meaning and will only obfuscate the real conflict and the ethical questions to be faced. It is the antecedent identification as to what constitutes distributional equity as a performance indicator that ultimately conditions the final outcome and tells us something about legal change and the character of economic life.

The impact on the rule of law / legal order / continuity

Legal change obviously alters the legal order. As Coase (1960 :19) has reminded us, in contemplating institutional change "uncertainty about the legal position itself" must be taken into account. The underlying rationale for the stated concern is that society needs a system of law that provides it a stable pattern of expectations. So structured, this allows individuals to plan their economic affairs (with respect to both production and consumption) with reasonable confidence so that they can know in advance the consequences of their choices. Society's quest for legal order and continuity can be understood at two different levels – identified by legal scholars as the *meta level* and the *object level* (Hampton 1994: 25–32). As with the other performance indicators of efficiency and equity, vague calls for continuity or legal order obfuscate the nature of the choice – the issue is which legal order and whose continuity should be preserved.

Meta level

The meta level is that which defines the system. The *rule of law* within the meta level is comprised of the system-defining laws and rules that give rise to the very definition of the legal system itself (Hampton 1994: 25–32). In terms of the comparative institutional approach, what transpires at the meta level is analogous to the various machinations that take place at the constitutional stage of choice or in framing a social contract. Consistent with the jurisprudential arguments set forth by H. L. A. Hart and others, the rule of law asserts that the authority and maintenance of the rule of law is accomplished under a shared set of principles that have their source in and derive their authority from the individuals in society – both the rulers and the ruled.

Individuals are the baseline, ultimate source of the legitimacy of the political/legal system and therefore are the ones to decide (acting individually or collectively) on continuing the system (and if so, under what form and structure).

The conventional expression of the rule of law carries with it the notion that government action should be controlled by known rules that prevent arbitrariness; in effect the rule of law embodies the requirement to make rule-governed reliability and predictability as pervasive as possible within the legal order.[28] A legal system is said to satisfy the requirements of the rule of law if the commands are: (1) clear and general (i.e., specific and independent of the status of the particular individuals or groups); (2) accessible, knowable, and prospective (i.e., be publically promulgated with all changes prospective) and (3) performable (i.e., there be a clear nexus between enacted law and real law so that individuals can exercise the latter without violating the former).[29] As described by Richard Flatman, the dominant concern of those scholars writing on the rule of law – such thinkers as Plato, Aristotle, Montesquieu, Hayek, Rawls, Fuller, and others, "has not been with the question whether or how much governance there should be, but," as stated by Flatman (1994: 302), "rather with preventing arbitrariness and other misuses of political authority and power."

The conventional notion notwithstanding, in response to the question – What is the rule of law? – the answer is still far from obvious. One response to that question, by George P. Fletcher (1996: 12), was "we are never quite sure what we mean by the rule of law;" a response consistent with Richard H. Fallon's (1997: 1) observation that "the precise meaning of the rule of law may be less clear today than ever before." Fallon (1997: 4–5) went on to say that "although agreement on these elements establishes the rule of law as a shared concept, many of the operative terms are vague." Wolfgang Friedmann has also argued that there is no one interpretation of the rule of law. On this point Friedmann has said that:

> [T]he rule of law means to one the absolute integrity of private property, to another the maintenance of private enterprise, free from state control and official regulation, and to another the preservation of the "right to work" against the power of the unions to determine conditions of labor. To some, the rule of law means a minimum of administrative power whereas to others it means, on the contrary, assurance by the state to all of minimum standards of living and security.
>
> (Friedmann 1972: 501)

At the meta level, with different conceptions of the rule of law come different manifestations of the legal order and corresponding calls for continuity. Fallon (1997: 10–24) has described four different types or conceptions of the rule of law. These include:

a. Historicist ideal type   Promotes the idea that the political legitimacy of law and adjudication lies in the historically understood meaning of past political decisions. That is, the legitimacy of law is founded in the fact that there is a clear and unambiguous nexus between law's substantive content and past, publically accountable acts by decision makers who are recognized under historically established norms as possessing legitimate law-making power. Under a Historicist ideal, in constitutional law, legal meaning should be fixed, as determinately as possible, either through "original understanding" or through the implied "intent of the Framers and ratifiers." As such, through originalist interpretation, judges are able to rule by (known) law rather than creating the law through adjudication. The Historicist ideal achieves democratic legitimacy by promoting democratic acceptability and accountability; in part, this is accomplished by eliminating judicial arbitrariness by subjecting judges (and ordinary citizens) to the law/rules/norms laid down by legislative law-making authorities prior to their application to particular cases.

b. Formalist ideal type   Requires that legal directives be generally and rationally comprehensible as mandating particular conduct or outcomes; the legal rules must be conceived as a clear prescription and exist prior to application; the Formalist ideal endorses known rules over loosely defined standards or multi-factor balancing tests. The emphasis is on form, not substance. The legal rules provide maximally effective guides to behavior and ensure that judges and other government officials are bound by laws; there must be clear lines of responsibility between the legislature and the judiciary. As a consequence, adherence to the formalist conception of the rule of law would enable both statutes and constitutional directives (when properly read) to yield clear, rule-like results, that is, appropriate conduct and/or legal outcomes.

c. Legal Process ideal type   Denies that law necessarily consists of rules that pre-exist occasions for their application. At the same time, with respect to the ongoing reconstruction of law, the Legal Process ideal seeks to explain how judicial reasoning (while not determined either by history or by known rules) enables courts to adapt legal norms to rapidly changing conditions. The Legal Process ideal needs to satisfy some limited requirements (briefly summarized here): (i) procedural fairness in the development and application of the law; (ii) a nexus between the notions of law and reasonableness; (iii) that rights and responsibilities be determined through reasoned elaboration; and (iv) governance by rational deliberation together with the requirement of judicial review. Thus, in maintaining a reasoned connection (through reasoned elaboration together with rational deliberation) between recognized legal norms and sources of authority and the outcome in particular cases, the Legal Process ideal provides a current, normative consensus as to both the nature of legal institutions and their choice-making processes; by bounding the domain of proper legal decision making, the Legal Process ideal validates legal decision making and legitimates the legal outcomes.

d. Substantive ideal type Implies that manifestations of the law – rules, doctrines, conventions of legal reasoning – are unintelligible as legal forms unless they are grounded in a substantive political theory (or legal theory) imbued with its own internal morality and/or norms of substantive justice. Thus, particular legal concepts derive their meaning either from substantive political morality or, alternatively, substantive political morality provides controlling principles of legal interpretation. Suffused with moral principles, the stated law then constitutes a moral, authoritative guide to social conduct; in effect, this turns the rule of law into a partisan ideal.

In the context of Law & Economics, individuals, groups of individuals, and public bodies all make allocative choices among alternative courses of action under different meta-level conceptions of the rule of law (and shifting meta conceptions of the rule of law), the result of which is to thereby undermine, to some extent, the "uncertainty in the legal position itself" for some, while preserving continuity for others.

Object level

More often than not, this "uncertainty in the legal position itself" is raised at the object level. The object level is the level at which laws are made by those in power, analogous to and consistent with that which takes place at both the institutional stage of choice and the economic impact stage of choice; it is the level at which the political/legal system structures the full suite of property rights, working rules, and legal doctrines. It is at this level where individuals most often jockey for position in the legal-economic-political arena by changing the law and promoting selected public policies. In their effort to enhance their individual or collective welfare they inevitably create uncertainty in the legal position itself. This is a difficult issue for any society. On the one hand, there are many reasons to maintain the rule of law at the object level so as to preserve "reasonably-backed expectations" which provides economic actors continuity and the ability to make allocative choices among alternative courses of action. On the other hand, for many reasons (especially due to changes in technology), legal change (changes in property rights, legal doctrines, and working rules) continues to occur producing an ever changing set of new expectations.[30] This, in turn, results in demands for a new legal order to accommodate the new set of reasonably-backed expectations and, once in place, new calls for continuity.

While it is often argued that legal change should be incremental and that order should be preserved, this obfuscates more than it enlightens. It neither addresses the issue at what level – the meta level or the object level – the incremental change should come; nor does it do anything to resolve the question of the rate of change. More importantly it bypasses the question as to whose interests are served under the existing legal order and whose will be served under a new meta-level conception of the rule of law or a new object-level property right regime. Consistent with the comparative institutional approach, the inclusion of the *Rule of Law/Legal Order/Continuity* as a performance indicator serves to help inform choice by making known the potential consequences of more versus less continuity (and for whom) brought on by altering the rule of law at the meta level or at the object level.

Freedom to/freedom from

As the core themes of American Institutional Law and Economics emphasize, in democratic societies, individuals and groups of individuals use government to alter the constitution, change legal doctrine, revise working rules, or change property rights in an effort to enhance their individual or collective welfare. While the freedom to do so is highly valued, so too is it highly nuanced. In certain instances the fundamental issue concerns "freedom from the State," while at other times the issue concerns "freedom within the State." Arguably, advocates of freedom from the State find themselves advocating either libertarian or anarchistic systems of government. More mainstream concerns (those focused on here) seem to center on the issues of "freedom within the State." In this context, one immediately confronts: (i) the paradox of freedom – that freedom of some must be limited or restrained in order to be enhanced for others; and (ii) the related issue of the reciprocal nature of freedom in "Alpha–Beta" disputes.

In addressing the paradox of freedom, it is important to note that freedom is neither created nor destroyed by the State; that is, the State, through legislative, judicial, and regulatory actions, changes the pattern of freedom that the previously existing legal relations governing society had allowed. It is in this sense that the very law, regulation, or judicial decision that may be said to have "created" freedom, is the same law, regulation, or judicial decision that "destroyed" freedom. Thus, while law is a *per se* infringement on freedom, it is at the same time a source of freedom. As Samuels stated (quoting John Bowning 1962):

> The relation is reciprocal, and although one part may be stressed over the other, from context to context, "the law cannot create rights," and therefore cannot create spheres of freedom, "without creating the corresponding obligations," which is to say, without limiting freedom: ". . . all laws creative of liberty, are, as far as they go, abrogative of liberty".
>
> (Samuels 1966: 169)

The freedom paradox manifests itself in many ways. As Viet D. Dinh (1999: 27) has reminded us: "[T]o mark the tercentenary of Harvard University in 1936, Professor John M. Maguire described the law as *the system of wise restraints that make men* free, a definition that is still used to confer the law degree on the university's graduates" (emphasis added). In addition to the paradox of freedom, the usefulness of freedom as a performance indicator raises yet another question, this one concerning the direction or flow of freedom. That is, when interests conflict, should Alpha be allowed to harm (impose uncompensated costs) onto Beta or should Beta be entitled to be free of Alpha's harm-causing actions? One's freedom is relative to: (i) the freedom of others; and (ii) the limitations imposed by both the prevailing legal relations governing society and non-legal factors (e.g., customs). Since virtually every law both restricts and enhances freedom (typically for different individuals or groups), the issue is never really freedom versus coercion; rather the issue centers on a question of whose freedom will prevail and who will be subject to the freedom of others. In the face of the "freedom to/freedom from" paradox, there is a natural tendency to offer up a joint maximand in an attempt to help unravel the paradox. For example, one may conclude that: "The problem then is, and has always been, how to *maximize* both freedom 'to' and freedom 'from'" (Phillips 1979: 72, emphasis added). Superficially, this may lay one's mind to rest – as might calling for "the greatest good for the greatest number." However, one must not forget what was learned from the French mathematician D'Alembert[31] and from each rereading of Garrett Hardin's *Tragedy of the Commons* (1968: 1244): "it is not possible to maximize for two (or more) variables at the same time."

This "freedom to/freedom from" conceptualization is perhaps better understood in the context of the four property right regimes – the private property rights, status rights, communal rights, and open-access resources. Such rights undergird the market, private, public, communal, and open-access resource sectors, respectively.[32] Each sector constitutes a different means for allocating society's scarce resources; concomitantly, each of these sectors represents a different system of social control. Within each sector a certain pattern of "coercion" is legitimated, thereby determining a freedom vector for Alpha, while at the same time legitimating the costs imposed on Beta. The legitimated freedom vector for Alpha (the set of rights, expectations, and freedoms) and the pattern of costs imposed on Beta are different, dependent on the sector selected to allocate society's scarce resources. Thus, when a society decides to set in place its preferred pattern of legal relations, the preferred bundle of private property rights, status rights, communal rights, open-access resources, it is making the combined choice of freedom and coercion. That is, in selecting the legal relations to govern society it sets in place: (i) which pattern of freedom shall be structured – who shall be allowed to impose uncompensated costs on whom within the market, public, communal, and open-access resource sectors; and (ii) which pattern of coercion shall be legitimated. Notwithstanding the assertions of Chicago Law and Economics, as well as Public Choice, one is not "free" in the market sector and "coerced" in the public sector.

Within each sector, for each Alpha–Beta conflict, a choice must still be made: Shall Alpha be allowed to impose a cost onto Beta (freedom to) or shall Beta be protected from Alpha's action (freedom from)? As Schmid

(1987: 242–43) has pointed out in his discussion of "freedom" as a performance indicator:

> The issue is one of whose freedom rather than freedom in the abstract. The great moral choice in any society is whose freedom counts when interests conflict in the face of scarcity. When people conflict, global freedom is without meaning and can only obfuscate the real conflict and the ethical question.

Macroeconomic indicators and inputs and output

Any comparative institutional approach that ignored macroeconomic performance indicators would be remiss. To the extent possible and when relevant, consequent a proposed legal change, the impact on employment rates, poverty rates, inflation, productivity, growth, fiscal deficits, trade deficits and any other macroeconomic variable that may be impacted should be incorporated into the analysis. However, just as with the other performance indicators, particular definitions of the macro-indicators or the particular definitions of the inputs and output used to assess performance will affect the assessment of the institutional impact.

For example, the institutionalized definition of what selectively constitutes: (i) *unemployment* – in particular, the number of monthly attempts at a job search that defines "unemployment" (as opposed to being "an out-of-the-workforce discouraged worker"); (ii) *poverty* – the threshold level of family-of-four-income that defines "being in poverty" (and thereby eligible to qualify for a stream of government benefits or programs); and (iii) *inflation* – the "current basket of goods" selected to calculate the CPI, the PPI or the GDP deflator that, in many instances, triggers certain built-in government/industry actions (for example, cost-of-living increases) all bear heavily on assessing the character of economic life. As a result, the aggregate macroeconomic impact – as measured by these collective macroeconomic performance indicators – is conditioned by the antecedent normative identification of their constituent elements. In addition, when economists advocate the maintenance of full employment or price stability, indeed, invoke or advocate the use of any macroeconomic indicator, as observed by Tibor Scitovsky (1950: 315) a half-century ago, "they [economists] can not disclaim responsibility for having made a value judgment on the ground that he was only interpreting the preferences of society as a whole. . . . In so arguing, he would make the implicit value judgment that the majority opinion fully represents and should determine society's preferences."

Moreover, the definitions of "inputs" and "output" – that is, what it is that one is to be efficient about – requires an antecedent normative specification as to what constitutes each. With respect to output categories, social output (the aggregate well-being of society), consumptive output (the value of goods from the consumer point of view), and productive output (the value of goods from the producer point of view) are three examples of the alternatives that are available. The value-laden choice of a particular definition of output as the maximand, which in effect is the choice of a particular social welfare function where many are possible, will ultimately drive the decision as to what constitutes the efficient allocation (Samuels 1978: 102–104).[33]

Some in Chicago Law and Economics and Neoinstitutional Law and Economics have broadened the conventional definition of commodities and resources (inputs) using the terms "effective commodities" and "effective resources."[34] As proffered by Erik Furubotn and Svetozar Pejovich (1974), an effective commodity is the physical commodity plus the associated property rights defining the commodity, including the rights to use and transfer the commodity; whereas an effective resource is the physical factor of production (land, labor or capital) plus the associated property rights to use and transfer the resource. This notion of "rights running with" commodities and resources is important from the vantage point of American Institutional Law and Economics as it gives further credence and deeper meaning to "institutional-ized markets."

Recall above, in American Institutional Law and Economics the market is institutionally niched in and complemented by government – the institution-alized market is not an alternative to government. The "effective-rights" component of inputs and output is a necessary element of any market with the "effective-rights" coming about through government and the power of government institutions.[35] The market, as system of social control, does not allocate resources apart and distinct from government. The allocation and distribution of effective commodities and effective resources through institu-tionalized markets are a function of government institutions and power structures which form and operate through them. Two simple examples illus-trate the significance and importance of the "effective-rights" component of inputs and output as it is the rights that are being exchanged on the market and at the core of the character of economic life.

First, what constitutes an automobile includes, among other things, the rights governing: (i) the very definition of an automobile (now including air bags and a catalytic converter together with severe legal sanctions for dis-connecting either); (ii) the government mandated standards and tests that govern automobile production; and (iii) the terms, conditions, and the enforcement of warranties. It is the government-structured definition, assign-ment, and enforcement of rights that run with the physical entity that form and shape the market for automobiles – it is not a question of an automobile market with government or without government. In a like manner, on the input side, what constitutes labor includes, among other things: (i) the rights governing child labor laws; (ii) occupational health and safety laws, and (iii) minimum wage laws. Again, it is not a question of a labor market with gov-ernment or without government. The market for automobiles, for labor, indeed all markets, are institutionalized markets complemented by govern-ment. The suggestion to use macroeconomic performance indicators within a comparative institutional approach to law and economics requires that the antecedent selective identification and definition of these indicators be made known, since the antecedent rights that run with a commodity or those that run with a factor of production – the very definition of inputs and output – say a lot about the character of economic life.

Ecological integrity

Garrett Hardin (1968) reminded us in his seminal article:

> If the word responsibility is to be used at all, I suggest that it be in the sense Charles Frankel uses it. "Responsibility," says this philosopher, "is the product of *definite social arrangements*." Notice that Frankel calls for social arrangements – *not propaganda* [emphasis added].

As society furthers its understanding about the workings of our natural systems, in an effort to assess the impact of legal change and public policy on our natural resources and environment, a performance indicator such as *ecological integrity* needs to be incorporated into the overall assessment of institutional change. In a mixed-market economy, individuals act in a multitude of ways that directly affect a nation's natural resource base (through rates of extraction) and its environment (through rates of depositing residuals back into the natural systems). There is no reason to believe that various policy initiatives and/or legal changes, including changes in property rights, working rules, and legal doctrines, will all impact our natural resources and the environment in the same manner and with the same intensity. In past decades, production and consumption residuals have been absorbed or assimilated with relatively few deleterious side-effects; similarly, many ecosystems have exhibited few disruptions from the extraction of the renewable and non-renewable resources utilized by the economy. However, more recently, the ability of nature to assimilate residuals from industrial production and consumption or recover from the mining or harvesting activities that accompany resource extraction has exceeded regional ecosystems' ability to support these activities. Under these circumstances, changes within the affected ecosystems dramatically alter or destroy the full suite of structures and functions these systems provide, thereby inevitably imposing costs onto society in both the short and the long term.

The idea of ecological integrity as a performance indicator is intended to convey the notion of congruence with ecological systems. In the simplest of terms it gets at the question: Do the legal-economic institutions and the policy initiatives and /or legal changes that emanate therefrom enhance or reduce a nation state's congruence with its ecological systems; that is, do they enhance or undermine the ecological integrity of the nation's natural environment? The principle of ecological integrity is derived from Karr's (1996) aspects of biotic impoverishment. The concept is defined by several indicators with each indicator providing one vector of assessment as to the impact of a particular activity.[36] Thus, if a society is contemplating the adoption of a policy initiative and/or a legal change (that necessitates altering property rights, working rules, or legal doctrines), one can use ecological integrity as a performance indicator to assess whether the contemplated legal change leaves a nation's political-economic system in greater or lesser congruence with its underlying ecological systems.

From a somewhat broader vantage point, individuals in society have options with respect to institutional design; inherent within an American Institutional Law and Economics – institutions matter. Consequently, institutions can be structured in an attempt to maintain the ecological integrity of a nation to various degrees. For example, institutionalized markets can be structured with few or no environmental/natural resource laws and regulations – under the euphemism of *laissez faire* markets. Alternatively, institutionalized markets may be joined with a host of environmental/natural resource laws and regulations that attempt, to the extent possible, to maintain the ecological integrity of a nation environment. Or, as is now occurring, whole new paradigms are being developed aimed at providing for new systems of social control – structured by the principles set forth under the headings of sustainable development, ecological economics, or industrial ecology.[37] Within a comparative institutional approach there exists a wide spectrum of possible remedies to ameliorate natural resource and environmental problems, which could involve: (i) amending or altering the constitution; (ii) adopting new legal doctrines, or specifying new working rules; or (iii) placing the rights to the natural resources or the residual-receiving environmental media (the air, land resources, or water), directly or implicitly, into one of the four property rights regimes outlined above. There are many policy options each of which involves different impacts on the ecological integrity of the environment. Inherent within a comparative institutional approach to law and economics is the need to describe the nature of the choices being contemplated and the consequences that follow. Inclusion of ecological integrity as a performance indicator does *not* argue for any one set of remedies – it argues for informed choice.

Conclusion

In contrast to the variety of legal movements and theories that have evolved in law, especially within the several approaches to Law & Economics, American Institutional Law and Economics draws no distinction between jurisprudential, legislative, bureaucratic, or regulatory treatments. All are seen as particular parts or manifestations of the interrelation of government and the economy, or of legal and economic processes. The goal of a comparative institutional approach is not normative judgment, but description. A viable approach to the study of the interrelations between economics and the law should be content with describing the full array of impacts of alternative institutions and legal arrangements, together with an articulation of whose interests will be served and at whose expense. Such analysis will not privilege one set of interests over others, but it will enable those who study and participate in the processes of the legal-economic arena to better understand these processes and their resulting effects on law and economy.

It may well be that this overtly positive, even agnostic approach to Law & Economics is discomforting to those who would seek refuge in determinate solutions to the questions of legal-economic policy. Some may be inclined to dismiss it on this ground. It may be that the six performance indicators set forth above may go far beyond the more limited intentions of those who prefer to narrowly focus on efficiency. Against this, Schmid (1994: 36–37) responds: "If [Institutional Law and Economics] has no dispositive answer to resolve policy arguments, what is it good for? It can identify many less than obvious sources of power in an economy so that people can know where their welfare comes from. It can raise the level of normative debate so that issues can be joined and people can live with tragic choices rather than ignoring and dismissing them."

Notes

1 On this point, see Posner (1987); and Minow (1987).
2 For a concise review of critical legal studies, feminist legal theory, law and literature, and critical race theory, see Gary Minda (1995); for a concise overview of the schools of thought comprising the field of Law & Economics, see Mercuro and Medema (1997 and 1995). The use of the ampersand in "Law & Economics" is intended to connote all four schools of thought contributing to the field.
3 The growth and maturation of Law & Economics is evidenced by the establishment of professional associations across the world including: (i) the American Law and Economics Association; (ii) the Canadian Law and Economics Association; (iii) the European Association of Law and Economics; (iv) the Mexican Association of Law and Economics; as well as (v) the New Zealand, and (vi) the Australian Associations of Law and Economics. In addition, there are a number of leading publications dedicated to publishing the scholarly contributions to the field, including several journals – the *American Law and Economics Review*; *Journal of Law and Economics*; *Journal of Legal Studies*; *Journal of Law, Economics & Organization*; *International Review of Law and Economics*; *European Journal of Law and Economics*; *Public Choice*; and *Constitutional Political Economy*. Beyond these journals, there are a wide variety of traditional law reviews that now regularly publish Law & Economics articles. In addition, there are four research annuals: the *Supreme Court Economic Review*; *New Horizons in Law and Economics*; *Research in Law and Economics*; and *The Economics of Legal Relationships*.
4 The reader should not be confused by the titles of American Institutional Law and Economics and Neoinstitutional Law and Economics. Neoinstitutional Law and Economics, like the other Chicago-oriented schools of thought within Law & Economics, actively distance themselves from the (American) institutionalists' perspective. For example, it is not unusual to see proponents of Neoinstitutional Law and Economics assert that "[Neoinstitutional law and economics] has little in common with the older Institutionalists, whose research extends back to the work of Commons and Veblen" (Drobak and Nye 1997: xv).
5 Bell, John F. (1967: 539–71). For concise overviews of institutional economics see Gordon (1964); Pribram (1983); and Spiegel (1971). Early contributions to the institutional approach

to study of the interrelations between law and economics include the work of Henry Carter Adams (1897) on economics and jurisprudence; Richard T. Ely (1914) on the relation of property and contract to the distribution of wealth; and, especially, John R. Commons (1924, 1925, 1934) on the legal foundations of the economic system. Important elements of the institutional approach to the study of law and economics can also be found in the work of Thorstein Veblen (1899, 1904); lawyer-economists Robert Lee Hale (1924, 1927, 1952); and Walton H. Hamilton (1932); and legal scholars Karl Llewellyn (1925); Jerome Frank (1930); and Roscoe Pound (1911a, 1911b, 1912).

6   Warren J. Samuels is Professor Emeritus and University Distinguished Professor, Department of Economics; A. Allan Schmid is University Distinguished Professor, Department of Agricultural Economics.

7   Samuels and Schmid's respective approaches are best understood as two complementary branches that differ only with respect to the relative emphasis given to "structure" and "conduct" *vis-à-vis* performance. The work of Schmid has tended to concentrate on the interdependence between (i) structure and (ii) performance, with an emphasis on empirical work that explores the economic impact of alternative legal structures. In contrast, Samuels' work has tended to concentrate on describing the interdependence between (i) the conduct and behavior of individuals and groups and (ii) legal-economic performance.

8   Others at Michigan State University who continue to contribute to this tradition are Harry Trebing (1976, 1989, 1993), whose works exhibit many of the same concerns as Robert Lee Hale with regard to the analysis of regulation and public utilities; and Robert A. Solo (1967, 1974, 1982), much of whose work focuses on monopoly regulation and institutional change. Former students of Samuels and Schmid who have gone on to focus their research on the relations between legal (or governmental) and economic processes, rather than the application of microeconomic theory to the law, include Steven G. Medema (1998, 1996b, 1996a, 1994, with Zerbe 1997) and Nicholas Mercuro (1989b; with Ryan 1984); writing together Mercuro and Medema (1997, 1995) and individually on topics including the Coase theorem; the policy implications of Coasean economics; the commonalities between the work of the institutionalists and the work of Coase; law, economics, and public policy; the comparative institutional approach to law and economics; schools of thought in Law & Economics; and the economic role of government in the history of economic thought.

9   Samuels (1981: 148–49), for one, has praised Posner for the usefulness of his analysis in once again bringing to the attention of economists and legal scholars alike how economic conditions affect the law, and conversely.

10   On this point, see Samuels (1971: 440; 1989: 1565); and also Schmid (1989: 67).

11   The notion of 'rights-taking behavior" is explored in Samuels and Mercuro (1984).

12   The need for a comparative institutional approach to legal-economic policy has long been recognized. Other proponents of a comparative institutional approach, coming from somewhat different perspectives, include Coase (1960); Demsetz (1969); Komesar (1981, 1994); Stewart (1987); and Shepsle and Weingast (1984).

13   A complete discussion of these three stages of choice is in Mercuro (1997: 72–80).

14   See also Komesar (1981, 1994); and Schmid (1987, 1994).

15   The incentives to move from anarchy to a social contract are described in McKenzie and Tullock (1978).

16   Examples as to how these four property right regimes have gained acceptance within the field are provided in Burger and Gochfeld's (1998) 30-year retrospective on Garrit Hardin's "Tragedy of the Commons"; see also Berkes et al. (1989); and Feeny (1990). For a detailed description of the the the distinction between common property and open-access resources, see Bromley (1991: 25–31).

17   The original formulation of status rights was provided by John H. Dales (1972: 152–54).

18   Kaldor–Hicks efficiency – the so-called compensation principle in economics – implies that society should adopt those legal changes that as a result of the change (i) income could have been redistributed after the change in the law so as to make everyone better off than before,

and also that (ii) it was not possible to improve welfare before the legal change took place simply by redistributing income. A straight-forward analysis is provided in Price (1977: 19–30), while a more detailed explanation is presented in Feldman (1980: 138–49).

19   It has been noted that in the absence of authoritative enforcement of the "group rules," the allocation of the resources under common property (*res communes*) may well degenerate into an open access (*res nullius*) state of overuse (Bromley 1991: 27).

20   See Garrett Hardin (1968).

21   This point is taken up by Komesar (1994: 5–7) and extended here to comport to Figure 12.1 of this chapter.

22   It should be noted that while Coase's concern for efficiency was expressed as a desire to minimize costs, including transaction costs and government-related costs, his notion of a comparative institutional approach to law and economics did not rely solely on efficiency.

23   Basically, what transpired in *Pennell v. City of San Jose* 108 S.Ct. 849 (1988) – the case deals with a rent-control ordinance adopted by the City of San Jose, California, in 1979 that included a so-called "tenant hardship provision." The Supreme Court was asked to determine whether the "harm to tenants" provision of this rent control ordinance constituted a taking of private property without just compensation under the Fifth and Fourteenth Amendments to the US Constitution. In 1979 the City of San Jose, California, enacted a rent control ordinance stipulating that a landlord may annually set a "reasonable rent" comprised of (a) an increase of as much as 8 percent, plus (b) an increment based on seven factors that are subject to review by the Mediation Hearing Officer. If a tenant objects to a greater than 8 percent increase in rent, a hearing is required before the hearing officer to determine whether the landlord's proposed increase is reasonable under the circumstances. Of the seven factors to be considered, the first six factors were described by the Court to be *objective* in that they were derived from: (1) the history of the premises; (2) the physical condition of the units; (3) any changes in the provided housing services; (4) the landlord's costs of providing an adequate rental unit (including cost of debt servicing); and (5) the prevailing status of the rental market for comparable housing. Application of the first six factors resulted in an objective determination of a reasonable rent increase. The seventh factor included in the ordinance was termed "the tenant hardship provision" which, in part, read as follows:

> In the case of a rent increase . . . which exceeds the standard set [in the ordinance], with respect to such excess and whether or not to allow same to be part of the increase allowed . . . the Hearing Officer shall consider the economic and financial hardship imposed on the present tenant(s) . . . If the Hearing Officer determines that the proposed increase constitutes an unreasonably severe financial or economic hardship . . . he may order that the excess of the increase . . . be disallowed.
>
> (*Pennell v. City of San Jose* 108 S.Ct. 849 (1988) at 854)

It was the potential denial of the incremental rent increase on the grounds of the tenant's financial hardship that was at issue in this case. Plaintiffs argued that the potential reduction (solely attributable to the application of the provision regarding the tenant's hardship), from what otherwise would have been a *reasonable* rent increase based on the other six specified *objective* factors, constituted a taking in that transferred the landlord's property to individual hardship tenants.

24   For a detailed examination of the determination of costs in this regard, see Samuels and Schmid (1997: 208–98).

25   Among others, Valerie Bunce (1983) in assessing the social inequality (in communist countries) includes the distribution of both income and power.

26   An example of trying to incorporate distributional impacts into legal-economic analysis is provided in Calabresi (1991).

27   An analysis of intergenerational equity as applied to environmental questions is provided in Lesser, Dodds and Zerbe, Jr. (1997).

28   See Roger Cotterrell (1989: 112–16, 144–49).

29 Fallon (1997: 8) provides five modern elements that constitute the rule of law. Lon L. Fuller (1964: 33–39) provides a similar list of eight criteria. See also Eskridge and Ferejohn (1994) and Sunstein (1996).
30 An interesting rule of law/legal order/continuity example is provided by the tensions created in altering property rights at the object level thereby raising the takings issue together with the response as manifested by the property rights movement (see Meltz 1995).
31 Formally presented in J. von Neumann and Oscar Morgenstern (1947: 11).
32 For the sake of brevity, I chose to focus on the economic impact stage of choice here, though much of this argument applies to choices at both the constitutional and institutional stage as well.
33 The value-laden nature of definitions of inputs and outputs is explored by Ragnar Frisch (1965: 1–10).
34 The use of the term "effective" for effective commodities was first used in Furubotn and Pejovich (1974: 1–9); Mercuro and Ryan (1984: 24) extended the concept to include factors of production.
35 This is not unlike Coase's (1960: 44) suggestion to think about what are traded on markets are, in fact, rights.
36 According to Karr, one can assess the degree to which a proposed activity or legal change is in congruence with the ecological systems by assessing the impact on each of the vectors described below:

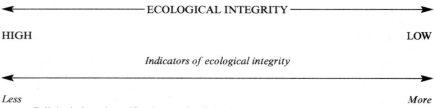

$\longleftarrow$ ———————————— ECOLOGICAL INTEGRITY ———————————— $\longrightarrow$

HIGH   LOW

Indicators of ecological integrity

$\longleftarrow$ ——— $\longrightarrow$

Less   *More*
   Soil depletion, desertification, and salinization
   Depletion of renewable resources
   Impacts associated with extraction of non-renewable resources
   Depletion and contamination of lakes, rivers, and aquifers
   Habitat destruction and fragmentation
   Loss of biodiversity
   Introduction of exotic species, pests, and diseases
   Alteration of biogeochemical cycling
   Human induced climate change
   Toxic chemical contamination

37 Sustainable development, industrial ecology, and ecological economics are explored, respectively, in Batie (1989); Allenby (1992); and Costanza (1996).

References

Adams, Henry C. (1897) "Economics and Jurisprudence," reprinted in Joseph Dorfman (ed.) *Two Essays By Henry Carter Adams: Relation of the State to Industrial Action and Economics and Jurisprudence*, New York: Augustus M. Kelley, 1969, 135–75.

Allenby, Brad R. (1992) "Achieving Sustainable Development Through Industrial Ecology," *International Environmental Affairs* 4, 1: 56–68.

Ayres, Clarence E. (1944) *The Theory of Economic Progress*, Chapel Hill, NC: University of North Carolina Press.

Batie, Sandra S. (1989) "Sustainable Development: Challenges to the Profession of Agricultural Economics," *American Journal of Agricultural Economics* 71 (December): 1083–101.

Bell, John F. (1967) "Institutional Economics," in *A History of Economic Thought*, New York: Ronald Press, 539–71.

Berkes, F. D. et al. (1989) "The Benefit of the Commons," *Nature* 34: 91–93.

Bowring, John (ed.) (1962) *The Works of Jeremy Bentham*, New York: Russell and Russell.

Bromley (1991) *Environment and the Economy: Property Rights and Policy*, Cambridge, MA: Blackwell.

Buchanan, James M. (1972) "Politics, Property and the Law: An Alternative Interpretation of *Miller et al. v Schoene*," *Journal of Law and Economics* 25: 439–52.

Buckingham, Walter S. (1958) *Theoretical Economic Systems: A Comparative Analysis*, New York: Ronald Press, 89–124.

Bunce, Valerie (1983) "Neither Equality Nor Efficiency: International and Domestic Inequalities in the Soviet Bloc," in Daniel N. Nelson (ed.) *Communism and the Politics of Inequality*, Lexington, MA: D. C. Heath, 5–34.

Burger, Joanna, and Michael Gochfeld (1998) "Tragedy of the Commons – 30 Years Later," *Environment* 40 (December): 4–13, 26, 27.

Calabresi, Guido (1991) "The Pointlessness of Pareto: Carrying Coase Further," *Yale Law Journal* 100: 1211–37.

Coase, Ronald H. (1960) "The Problem of Social Cost," *Journal of Law and Economics* 3: 1–44.

Commons, John R. (1924) *Legal Foundations of Capitalism*, New York: Macmillan. Reprinted, Clifton, NJ: Augustus M. Kelley, 1974.

—— (1925) "Law and Economics," *Yale Law Journal* 34: 371–82.

—— (1934) *Institutional Economics*, New York: Macmillan.

Costanza, Robert (1996) "Ecological Economics: Reintegrating the Study of Humans and Nature," *Ecological Applications* 6, 4: 978–90.

Cotterrell, Roger (1989) *The Politics of Jurisprudence*, London: Butterworths.

Dales, John H. (1972) "Rights and Economics," in Gene Wunderlich and W. L. Gibson, Jr. (eds) *Perspectives of Property*, University Park, PA: Institute for Research on Land and Water Resources, Pennsylvania State University, 149–55.

Demsetz, Harold (1969) "Information and Efficiency: Another Viewpoint," *Journal of Law and Economics* 12: 1–22.

Dinh, Viet. D. (1999) "What is the Law in Law & Development?" *Green Bag* 3: 19–27.

Drobak John N., and John V. C. Nye (eds) (1997) *The New Frontiers of the New Institutional Economics*, New York: Academic Press.

Ely, Richard T. (1914) *Property and Contract in Their Relation to the Distribution of Wealth*, 2 vols., New York: Macmillan.

Eskridge, William N., and John Ferejohn (1994) "Politics, Interpretation and the Rule of Law," in Ian Shapiro (ed.) *The Rule of Law*, New York: New York University Press, 265–94.

Fallon, Jr., Richard H. (1997) "'The Rule of Law' As a Concept in Constitutional Discourse," *Columbia Law Review* 97: 1–56.

Feeny, D. F., et al. (1990) "The Tragedy of the Commons: Twenty-Two Years Later," *Human Ecology* 18: 1–19.

Feldman, Allan M. (1980) *Welfare Economics and Social Choice Theory*, Boston, MA: Martinus Nijhoff Publishing.

Flatman, Richard (1994) "Liberalism and the Suspect Enterprise of Political Institutionalization: The Case of the Rule of Law," in Ian Shapiro (ed.) *The Rule of Law*, New York: New York University Press, 297–327.

Fletcher, George P. (1996) *Basic Concepts of Legal Thought*, New York: Oxford University Press.

Frank, Jerome (1930) *Law and the Modern Mind*, New York: Brentano's.

Friedmann, Wolfgang (1972) *Law in a Changing Society*, New York: Columbia University Press.

Frisch, Ragner (1965) *The Theory of Production*, Chicago, IL: Rand McNally.

Fuller, Lon L. (1964) *The Morality of Law*, New Haven, CN: Yale University Press.

Furubotn, Erik, and Svetozar Pejovich (1974) "Introduction: The New Property Rights Literature," in Erik Furubotn and Svetozar Pejovich (eds) *The Economics of Property Rights*, Cambridge, MA: Ballinger Publishing, 1–9.

Gordon, Robert A. (1964) *Institutional Economics*, Berkeley, CA: University of California Press.

Hale, Robert Lee (1924) "Economic Theory and the Statesman," in Rexford G. Tugwell (ed.) *The Trend of Economics*, New York: Knopf.

—— (1927) "Economics and the Law," in William F. Ogburn and Alexander A. Goldenweiser (eds.) *The Social Sciences and Their Interrelations*, Boston, MA: Houghton Mifflin.

—— (1952) *Freedom Through Law*, New York: Columbia University Press.

Hamilton, Walton H. (1932) "Property According to Locke," *Yale Law Journal* 41: 864–80.

Hampton, Jean (1994) "Democracy and the Rule of Law," in Ian Shapiro (ed.) *The Rule of Law*, New York: New York University, 13–44.

Hardin, Garrett (1968) "The Tragedy of the Commons," *Science* 162: 1243–48.

Hodgson, Geoffrey M. (1994) "Evolution, Theories of Economic," in Geoffrey M. Hodgson, Warren J. Samuels and Mark R. Tool (eds) *The Elgar Companion to Institutional and Evolutionary Economics*, Aldershot: Edward Elgar Publishing, 218–24.

Karr, J. R. (1996) "Ecological Integrity and Ecological Health Are Not the Same Thing," in P. C. Schulz (ed.) *Engineering within Ecological Constraints*, Washington, DC: National Academy Press.

Komesar, Neil K. (1981) "In Search of a General Approach to Legal Analysis: A Comparative Institutional Alternative," *Michigan Law Review* 79: 1350–92.

—— (1994) *Imperfect Alternatives: Choosing Institutions in Law, Economics, and Public Policy*, Chicago, IL: University of Chicago Press.

Lesser, Jonathan A., Daniel E. Dodds and Richard O. Zerbe, Jr. (1997) *Environmental Economics and Policy*, Reading, MA: Addison-Wesley, 341–83.

Llewellyn, Karl N. (1925) "The Effect of Legal Institutions upon Economics," *American Economic Review* 15: 655–83.

McKenzie, Richard, and Gordon Tullock (1978) "The Emergence of Social Order: Defining Behavioral Limits," in *Modern Political Economy*, New York: McGraw-Hill, 75–90.

Medema, Steven G. (1994) *Ronald H. Coase*, London and New York: Macmillan and St. Martin's Press.

—— (1996a) "Ronald Coase and American Institutionalism," *Research in the History of Economic Thought and Methodology* 14: 51–92.

—— (1996b) "Of Pangloss, Pigouvians, and Pragmatism: Ronald Coase and Social Cost Analysis," *Journal of the History of Economic Thought* 18: 96–114.

—— (1998) *Coasean Economics: Law and Economics and the New Institutional Economics*, Boston, MA: Kluwer Academic Publishers.

Medema, Steven G., Nicholas Mercuro and Warren J. Samuels (1997) "Institutional Law and Economics," in Boudewijn Bouckaert and Gerrit De Geest (eds) *Encyclopedia of Law and Economics*, Aldershot: Edward Elgar Publishing [http://encyclo.findlaw.com/lit/0520art.htm].

—— "Institutional Law and Economics," in Boudewijn Bouckaert and Gerrit De Geest (eds.), *Encyclopedia of Law and Economics*, Aldershot: Edward Elgar Publishing, 418–56.

Medema, Steven G. and Richard O. Zerbe, Jr. (1997) "The Coase Theorem," in Boudewijn Bouckaert and Gerrit De Geest (eds.) *Encyclopedia of Law and Economics*, Aldershot: Edward Elgar Publishing, 836–92.

Meltz, Robert (1995) "The Property Rights Issue," Congressional Research Service – Report for Congress, January 20, 1995: 1–22.

Mercuro, Nicholas (ed.) (1989a) *Law and Economics*, Boston, MA: Kluwer Academic Publishers.

—— (1989b) "Toward a Comparative Institutional Approach to the Study of Law and Economics," in Nicholas Mercuro (ed.) *Law and Economics*, Boston, MA: Kluwer Academic Publishers, 1–26.

—— (ed.) (1997) *Ecology, Law and Economics*, Lanham, MD: University Press of America.

Mercuro, Nicholas, and Steven G. Medema (1995) "Schools of Thought in Law and Economics: A Kuhnian Competition," in Robin Paul Malloy and Christopher K. Braun (eds) *Law and Economics: New and Critical Perspectives*, New York: Peter Lang, 65–126.

—— (1997) *Economics and the Law: From Posner to Postmodernism*, Princeton, NJ: Princeton University Press.

Mercuro, Nicholas, and Timothy P. Ryan (1984) *Law, Economics and Public Policy*, Greenwich, CT: JAI Press.

Mercuro, Nicholas, and Warren J. Samuels (1999) "A Retrospective Interpretive Essay on the Diverse Approaches to the Fundamental Interrelationships Between Government and Property," in Nicholas Mercuro and Warren J. Samuels (eds.) *Fundamental Interrelationships Between Government and Property*, Stamford, CT: JAI Press, 269–88.

Michelman, Frank I. (1980) "Constitutions, Statutes, and the Theory of Efficient Adjudication," *Journal of Legal Studies* 9: 431–61.

Minda, Gary (1995) *Postmodern Legal Movements: Law and Jurisprudence at Century's End*, New York: New York University Press.

Minow, Martha (1987) "Law Turning Outward," *Telos* 73 (Fall): 79–100.

Mitchell, Wesley C. (1914) "Human Behavior and Economics: A Survey of Recent Literature," *Quarterly Journal of Economics* 29: 1–47.

—— (1928) *Business Cycles: The Problem and Its Setting*, New York: National Bureau of Economic Research.

—— (1937) *The Backward Art of Spending Money and Other Essays*, New York: McGraw-Hill.

von Neumann, J., and Oscar Morgenstern (1947) *Theory of Games and Economic Behavior*, Princeton, NJ: Princeton University Press.

Phillips, Derek L. (1979) *Equality, Justice and Rectification*, New York: Academic Press.

Posner, Richard A. (1973) "Strict Liability: A Comment," *Journal of Legal Studies* 2: 205–21.

—— (1987) "The Decline of Law as an Autonomous Discipline: 1962–1987," *Harvard Law Review* 100 (February): 761–80.

Pound, Roscoe (1911a) "The Scope and Purpose of Sociological Jurisprudence, Part I," *Harvard Law Review* 24: 591–619.

—— (1911b) "The Scope and Purpose of Sociological Jurisprudence, Part II," *Harvard Law Review* 25: 140–68.

—— (1912) "The Scope and Purpose of Sociological Jurisprudence, Part III," *Harvard Law Review* 25: 489–516.

Pribram, Karl (1983) *A History of Economic Reasoning*, Baltimore, MD: Johns Hopkins University Press.

Price, Catherine M. (1977) *Welfare Economics in Theory and Practice*, London: Macmillan.

Samuels, Warren J. (1966) *The Classical Theory of Economic Policy*, Cleveland, OH: World.

—— (1971) "Interrelations Between Legal and Economic Processes," *Journal of Law and Economics* 14: 435–50.

—— (1972) "Ecosystem Policy and the Problem of Power," *Environmental Affairs* 2: 580–96.

—— (1974) "Commentary: An Economic Perspective on the Compensation Problem," *Wayne Law Review* 21: 113–34.

—— (1975) "Approaches to Legal-Economic Policy and Related Problems of Research," in Stuart Nagel (ed.) *Policy Studies and the Social Sciences*, Lexington, MA: Lexington Books, 65–73.

—— (1978) "Normative Premises in Regulatory Theory," *Journal of Post Keynesian Economics* 1: 100–14.

—— (1981) "Maximization of Wealth as Justice: An Essay on Posnerian Law and Economics as Policy Analysis," *Texas Law Review* 60: 147–72.

—— (1989) "The Legal-Economic Nexus," *George Washington Law Review* 57: 1556–78.

Samuels, Warren J., and Nicholas Mercuro (1979) "The Role and Resolution of the Compensation Principle in Society: Part One – The Role," *Research in Law and Economics* 1: 157–94.

—— (1984) "A Critique of Rent-Seeking Theory," in David C. Colander (ed.) *Neoclassical Political Economy: The Analysis of Rent-Seeking and DUP Activities*, Cambridge, MA: Ballinger Publishing, 55–70.

Samuels, Warren J., and A. Allan Schmid (1981) *Law and Economics: An Institutional Perspective*, Boston, MA: Martinus-Nijhoff Publishing.

—— (1997) "The Concept of Cost in Economics," in Warren J. Samuels, Steven G. Medema and A. Allan Schmid, *The Economy as a Process of Valuation*, Aldershot: Edward Elgar Publishing, 208–98.

Schmid, A. Allan (1987) *Property, Power, and Public Choice: An Inquiry into Law and Economics*, 2nd edn., New York: Praeger.

—— (1989) "Law and Economics: An Institutional Perspective," in Nicholas Mercuro (ed.) *Law and Economics*, Boston, MA: Kluwer Academic Publishers, 57–85.

—— (1994) "Institutional Law and Economics," *European Journal of Law and Economics* 1: 33–51.

—— (2000) "Notes on 'Overview of Socio-Economics,'" Association of American Law Schools, January 6, 2000 (on file).

Schön, Donald A. (1979) "Generative Metaphor: A Perspective on Problem-Setting in Social Policy," in Andrew Ortony (ed.) *Metaphor and Thought*, Cambridge: Cambridge University Press, 254–83.

Scitovsky, Tibor (1950) "The State of Welfare Economics," *American Economic Review* 41: 303–15.

Shepsle, Kenneth A., and Barry Weingast (1984) "Political Solutions to Market Problems," *American Political Science Review* 78: 417–34.

Solo, Robert A. (1967) *Economic Organization and Social Systems*, New York: Bobbs-Merrill.

—— (1974) *The Political Authority and the Market System*, Cincinnati, OH: South-Western.

—— (1982) *The Positive State*, Cincinnati, OH: South-Western.

Spiegel, Henry William (1971) *The Growth of Economic Thought*, Durham, NC: Duke University Press.

Stewart, Richard B. (1987) "Crisis in Tort Law? The Institutional Perspective," *University of Chicago Law Review* 54: 184–99.

Stone, Deborah (1997) *Policy Paradox: The Art of Political Decision Making*, New York: W. W. Norton.

Sunstein, Cass R. (1996) "Understanding (and Misunderstanding) the Rule of Law," in *Legal Reasoning and Political Conflict*, New York: Oxford University Press, 101–20.

Tollison, Robert D. (1972) "Chapter 1 – Involved Social Choice," in James M. Buchanan and Robert D. Tollison (eds) *Theory of Public Choice*, Ann Arbor, MI: University of Michigan Press, 3–7.

Trebing, Harry M. (ed.) (1976) *New Dimensions in Public Utility Pricing*, East Lansing, MI: Institute of Public Utilities, Michigan State University.

—— (1989) "Telecommunications Regulation – The Continuing Dilemma," in K. Nowotym, D. B. Smith and H. M. Trebing (eds) *Public Utility Regulation*, Boston, MA: Kluwer Academic Publishers, 120–22.

Trebing, Harry M., and Maurice Estabrooks (1993) "Telecommunications Policy in the Global Information Economy of the Nineties," in Rodney Stevenson, T. H. Oum and H. Oniki (eds) *International Perspectives on Telecommunications Policy*, Greenwich: CT: JAI Press, 17–37.

Veblen, Thorstein B. (1899) *Theory of the Leisure Class*, New York: Macmillan.

—— (1904) *The Theory of Business Enterprise*, New York: Charles Scribner's Sons.

—— (1923) *Absentee Ownership and Business Enterprise in Recent Times*, New York: B. W. Huebsch.

Viner, Jacob (1960) "The Intellectual History of Laissez Faire, *Journal of Law and Economics* 3 (October): 45–69.

Whalen, Charles J. (1996) "The Institutionalist Approach to Economics", in Fred Foldvary (ed.) *Beyond Neoclassical Economics: Heterodox Approaches to Economic Theory*, Aldershot: Edward Elgar Publishing.

Wolf, Charles, Jr. (1997) *Markets or Government: Choosing between Imperfect Alternatives*, Cambridge, MA: MIT Press.

13 On the changing nature of the public utility concept

A retrospective and prospective assessment

Harry M. Trebing

Introduction

Economic regulation has come under an increasingly heavy attack from a variety of sources during the past 30 years. This has resulted in the full deregulation of prices, earnings, and entry controls for airlines and motor carriers, and substantial deregulation of rail transport. In the traditional public utility industries, telecommunications, natural gas, and electricity, which are the primary focus of this chapter, there has been selective but growing deregulation. Where residual controls remain, they typically involve "light regulation," which focuses on transitional price ceilings, attempts to promote open network access, and concerns over the availability of service to low-income recipients and high-cost markets. This light regulation is a far cry from the comprehensive economic regulation that was traditionally embodied in the public utility concept.

The apparent acceptance of deregulation raises two fundamental questions. First, why have the public utility concept and economic regulation fallen into general disfavor? And second, does the concept still have validity and applicability for any portion of the public utility industries, and if so what changes or modifications in the regulatory format are required? In the search for answers, this chapter will consider the origin and development of the public utility concept and the associated framework of commission regulation, the assault on regulation at both the academic and applied levels, the consequent effects of deregulation, the deficiencies of transitional public policies, and finally, the applicability of the basic argument for economic regulation, as formulated by prominent public utility economists during the period 1927–61, to the emergent industry structures which now characterize these industries. The conceptual framework created by these economists serves as the institutionalist model of regulation that will be used to evaluate the potential contribution that the concept could make in the future.

Origin and development

The public utility concept emerged as the product of three factors: (1) public concern over the performance of the railroads as the nation's first large-scale industry; (2) the designation of selected types of enterprises as a "business affected with the public interest;" and (3) the widespread acceptance of the natural monopoly concept as the preferred method for achieving efficiency and equity goals in public utility industries.

Almost at the outset the railroad industry developed cost and service characteristics that were conducive to consumer exploitation and great public hostility. Consumers could be readily differentiated on the basis of type of service, geographic region, and the value of the commodities being shipped. At the same time the large common costs associated with the railroad's cost function could not be precisely assigned to each type of traffic on a cost causation basis. This led railroads to assess costs on the basis of ability to pay or the relative bargaining power of individual user groups. Price discrimination and cross-subsidization were the logical outcome. The problems of the railroads were further complicated by the general over-expansion of rail capacity, periodic episodes of cutthroat competition, and highly volatile earnings – all of which would eventually culminate in mergers and pooling arrangements. Remedial government intervention could choose between a number of options. These included public ownership, yardstick regulation (Windom Committee Report 1874), or the creation of an independent regulatory agency (Cullom Committee Report 1886). The latter was chosen and the Interstate Commerce Commission (ICC) was created in 1887. The ICC subsequently became the prototype for the wave of state regulatory commissions that followed. The first state commissions were established in Wisconsin and New York in 1907. Between 1907 and 1913, 29 states established commissions designated as railroad and public utility commissions. The rapid growth of federal regulation occurred in the New Deal period with the creation of the Federal Communications Commission (FCC), Securities and Exchange Commission (SEC), enlarged Federal Power Commission (FPC), and the Civil Aeronautics Board (CAB). These agencies became known as the fourth branch of government.

The second factor that shaped the public utility concept was the designation of a special category of private property as "a business affected with the public interest." In *Munn* v. *Illinois* (1877), the Supreme Court held that the state of Illinois could regulate the prices charged by grain elevators because the firms engaged in this activity had the ability to exploit consumers dependent on the service.[1] Accordingly, the owners of the elevators would have to submit to the controls imposed by the state in the exercise of its police power. At about the same time, technological advances created the telephone service (1876) and electricity supply (1882). It was an easy step for the concept of a business affected with the public interest to be applied to these new industries as well as to other public services.

In the years that followed, the Supreme Court reviewed a number of cases as the states sought to apply the concept to a number of other activities including the sale of insurance, the resale of theatre tickets, and the sale of ice. In redefining the applicability of the concept, the Court moved toward two fundamental tests: (1) the potential for exploitation or extortion, and (2) the degree to which the service could be construed as a necessity. The concept was last applied in the *Phillips Petroleum* case (1954), where it served to extend federal price regulation to the producers of natural gas making sales in the interstate market.[2]

The third factor was the general application of the theory of natural monopoly to public utility industries. While originally attributed to John Stuart Mill, AT&T was the first business to endorse the concept in 1910. AT&T construed the provision of terminal equipment on the customer's premises, inside wiring, and local loops, as well as all local and long-distance plant to be part of the natural monopoly. AT&T aggressively endorsed the natural monopoly argument until its breakup and the divestiture of local phone service in 1984. A natural monopoly was assumed to exist when one firm could supply an entire market at less cost than two or more firms. When the SEC restructured the holding company systems under the Public Utility Holding Company Act (1935), it sought to implement the natural monopoly concept by replacing holding company empires with independent, vertically integrated electric and gas utilities serving a specific geographic market.

From the interaction of these three factors, the public utility concept would come to be represented by a certificated monopoly supplier subject to the obligation to serve all comers with adequate service at just and reasonable rates. The same supplier would have the right to earn a fair return, but would not be guaranteed that return. It would have the power of eminent domain and a limited degree of freedom from intra-industry competition through the franchise and certification process. The federal and state commissions that exercised authority over these firms were assumed to embody the public interest theory of regulation. That is, the goal of regulation is to promote the general welfare.

Critical assault and regulatory retreat

The assault on the public utility concept and the independent regulatory commission has proceeded at two levels. The first is the critical academic literature that has accumulated since 1940. The second is the growth, after 1969, of broad-based public dissatisfaction with the performance of the regulated public utility industries. The second, it should be noted, was the major driving force promoting actual deregulation.

The first of the academic critics was Horace M. Gray, whose seminal paper, "The Passing of the Public Utility Concept" (1940), argued that grants of special privilege could not be reconciled with the public interest through public regulation. Instead, Gray believed that regulation had become a "haven of refuge for all aspiring monopolists who found it too difficult, too costly, or too precarious to secure and maintain monopoly by private action alone."[3] Incumbent firms, Gray observed, used regulation to constrain rivals and prevent price reductions in the Great Depression, while at the same time forestalling any interference with the property rights of the public utility. The concept, he believed, had become an obsolete institution, and as such it should be replaced with new forms of institutional inventiveness, such as public power projects, creative economic planning by government, and institutional competition.

The next challenge to public utility regulation came from the historical revisionists. Marver H. Bernstein (1955) introduced the capture theory of regulation by arguing that independent commissions would eventually become captives of the firms that they regulated.[4] Reform required a stronger politicization of the regulatory process to negate the influence of these firms. For Bernstein, this would require transferring the independent agencies to the executive branch of government. Gabriel Kolko (1962) was much less sanguine about the opportunities for reform. His interpretation of the history of regulation led him to conclude that regulation itself was the creation of those seeking to avoid competitive pressures.[5]

The historical revisionists were followed by a diverse collection of critics who built upon the alleged failure of the public interest theory of regulation. Sam Pelzman's theory of coalition building (1976) held that regulatory action was a response to special interests and that agency survival depended on building a coalition of political support.[6] Hence, regulators would be responsive to the needs of these interests and not to the general welfare. More significant and more rigorous was the challenge to regulation posed by public choice theorists. A salient feature of this criticism was the argument that the rent-seeking actions of special interest groups subverted government's ability to achieve public interest goals. The best way to avoid the rent-seeking problem would be to avoid establishing the government institutions that create rents. These institutions would include regulations and regulatory agencies that initiate the rent creation process. The solution would involve recourse to unregulated, competitive markets. As a group, all of these critics would vigorously oppose both the public utility concept and any attempt to improve the effectiveness of regulation by strengthening its resource base or redefining its authority. Such efforts would only worsen the problem.

While the previous critics focused on government's inability to achieve public interest goals through regulatory intervention, the neoclassical economists argued primarily that the performance of free markets would be far superior to economic regulation. Their argument was based on the following four points. First, deregulation would create market-driven incentives and new forms of supply that are superior to the regulated monopoly provision of service. Second, market power would not be sustainable after deregulation. Market concentration would be rapidly eroded by new entry, and for the first time consumers would be able to exercise free choice among competitive suppliers. Third, profits would serve to promote innovative entry and new technology so interim price ceilings designed to protect consumers during the transition period must be divorced from any regulatory oversight of earnings or profits. Fourth, any network economies inherent in public utility industries can be readily treated through requirements for open access and interconnection to facilitate the entry of new competitors. Open access was assumed to benefit all players since it would have the effect of increasing total traffic on the combined network. The neoclassical argument fostered the belief that deregulated market forces would put the most efficient industry structure in place with minimum government intervention.[7]

Paralleling the academic critique was the much more meaningful attack on the public utility concept that took place at the applied level after 1969. The year 1969 was pivotal. After that year total factor productivity in electricity began to fall and real prices began to increase due to cost increases, redundancy, and the failure of large nuclear generating units. At the same time, the field price of natural gas began to escalate rapidly and there was increasing evidence that gas was being diverted from the interstate market by major oil producers in anticipation of higher prices. This led to the curtailment of demand and rationing of gas supplies, followed by a period of oversupply and flagrant price discrimination between different classes of customers. In telecommunications, demands for new services, new supply options, and greater customer flexibility encountered stiff resistance from AT&T and the other telephone carriers.

In the face of increasing evidence of poor performance, there was a growing popular disenchantment with both utility management and the ability of regulators to protect consumer interests. Increasingly, consumer groups sought to promote pluralism in supply whenever possible as a solution to these problems. This was particularly evident in the case of large buyers who sought to secure price and service concessions from the utilities. This would require a departure from traditional cost of service regulation. Toward this end, big users employed trade associations, such as ELCON, to lobby state legislatures to introduce various forms of deregulation.

These strategies were complemented by new technologies in telecommunications that greatly increased network capacity and service options. In electricity, new technology centered on the combined cycle gas turbine that was quicker and easier to build, had lower capital costs, and was less vulnerable to the construction delays and environmental problems that plagued nuclear power and large fossil fuel generators.

These pressures for change began in telecommunications with the *Carterfone* case (1968),[8] the *MCI* case (1969),[9] and AT&T divestiture (1984), and culminated in the passage of the Telecommunications Act of 1996. In natural gas and electricity, the movement toward competitive supply began with the Public Utility Regulatory Policies Act (1978) and the Natural Gas Policy Act (1978), and culminated in the passage of the Energy Policy Act of 1992. The shift in public policy toward the promotion of competition at the federal level was now thought to be complete. Federal efforts were complemented by state actions. By late 1999, 21 state legislatures had enacted deregulation legislation affecting electricity. Comparable steps were taken at the state level to relax intrastate regulation of telephone carriers and natural gas suppliers.

Once it was recognized that regulation no longer constituted a source of support and that a new environment and new profit opportunities were taking shape, there was a major change in management culture in the public utility industries. At the prospect of being left as the supplier of last resort, management began to move aggressively to retain existing markets, capture new markets, participate in new technology, and, whenever possible, remove or drastically reduce all forms of regulatory intervention. This new set of managerial incentives would be a major driving force in transforming markets and promoting industry concentration in the wake of deregulation.

Effects of deregulation

As neoclassical economists had forecast, deregulation introduced a number of new institutions, new markets, and new players. For example, electricity and gas deregulation has led to the emergence of cogenerators, merchant generators, marketers, and spot and futures markets for electricity and gas trading. In telecommunications there has been a proliferation of deregulated marketers, resellers, new facility-based carriers, and niche market suppliers. Perhaps the most distinctive feature of telecommunications has been the convergence of telecommunication and computer technologies to create an information revolution and the proliferation of Internet service providers.

The most distinctive feature of deregulation, however, has been the massive move toward greater concentration at both the national and global levels. Industries that were once considered to be localized monopolies have been transformed into large regional, national, or transnational enterprises. It is less than coincidental that the decline in economic regulation has been matched by a parallel, substantial growth in industry concentration.

In domestic telecommunications, the seven original Regional Bell Holding Companies were reduced to four as Bell Atlantic acquired NYNEX; SBC acquired Ameritech (giving SBC one-third of the national market); and WorldCom acquired MCI and Sprint. AT&T and WorldCom would now control over 95 percent of the long distance market. Despite efforts to promote competition in local phone markets, the incumbent telephone companies still controlled 97 percent of that market in late 1999.

In global communications, AT&T/British Telecom created a joint venture to provide broadband service that would be five times greater than the closest rival, which was Global One, sponsored by Sprint, Deutsche Telekom, and France Telecom. The Vodaphone–AirTouch merger created the world's largest cellular carrier.

British experience was similar. Thirteen years after privatization, British Telecom still had 89 percent of the local market, and 78 percent of the national market. Mercury, the second largest rival, had only 2 percent of the local and 10 percent of the national market.

Electricity mergers have been equally impressive, as demonstrated by the following table listing the dollar value of pending and completed mergers by year:

Table 13.1 Value of pending and completed mergers

Year	$ (billions)
1994	8.9
1995	3.5
1996	0.0
1997	212.9
1998	47.4
1999	233.5

Source: Diane Moody, Director of Statistical Analysis, American Public Power Association.

These electricity mergers have been matched by cross-industry mergers as electric utilities acquired 22 natural gas companies and pipelines by late 1999.

To some extent this move toward greater concentration can be explained by the need to realize the network and coordination economies inherent in public utility industries. Network economies arise from economies of scale, pooled reserves, and economies of joint production. As a result, the incremental cost of adding new services falls as the size of the network increases. There are also concurrent gains in reliability and reserve margins as network size increases. Achieving these gains requires a minimum efficient size. The difficulty is that no one has been able to ascertain with any accuracy whether the merger movement represents a concerted effort to achieve these goals or merely reflects strategies to achieve market dominance.

The same thing can be said for coordination economies. These arise from the ability of a network to balance diverse usage patterns to achieve full utilization of plant and low unit costs. Achieving coordination economies requires a minimum market share so that diverse user patterns can be matched with a capital-intensive supply network. But again, it is difficult to determine whether the merger movement was driven primarily by the need to realize such gains. A more persuasive case can be made for the strategies directed toward achieving market dominance.

It should also be noted that these network characteristics bring with them two factors that facilitate strategies aimed at achieving market dominance. These are the existence of monopoly focal points that control access to the network and the ease with which customers can be differentiated on the basis of volume of use, time of use, and demand elasticity. The latter constitute the fundamental requirements for price discrimination and cross-subsidization.

With substantial deregulation the firm must deploy all of its resources, including pricing, marketing, and investment strategies, to contend with the threat of entry and the potential loss of market share, while at the same time moving aggressively to capture new markets. The firm can employ price to foreclose entry and retain existing customers. Examples of this practice include quoting a low standard offer and special contracts for existing customers. The firm can also employ price to migrate customers from one service to another simply by raising the price on individual services and offering discounts on bundled packages. Pricing can also shift the risk of new technology to basic service customers by underestimating the incremental cost of new technology and assigning more of that cost to basic service customers. Finally, the firm can seek to control price wars among rivals through price leadership and conscious parallelism.[10]

Market structure strategies have taken the form of acquisitions to reach new markets, acquisitions to reach foreign markets, acquisitions of privatized government enterprises, horizontal mergers, cross-industry mergers, collaborative alliances, and joint ventures. The interaction of pricing and market structure strategies goes a long way toward explaining the concentration movement previously discussed.

Growing concentration has resulted in the emergence of tight oligopoly in most of the public utility industries. Tight oligopoly exists when the four leading firms, combined, account for 60–100 percent of the output, barriers to entry persist, and substitutes are not readily available in all markets. It is clearly evident that market concentration has not rapidly disappeared as the proponents of competition had optimistically forecasted.

Impact of tight oligopoly

Tight oligopoly has produced two demonstrable benefits. The rate of technological innovation has accelerated rapidly in telecommunications. This is best demonstrated by the rivalry between AT&T (using broadband cable) and the regional Bell holding companies (using asymmetric digital subscriber lines) to serve the Internet market. But such cases of Schumpeterian rivalry are not spread consistently across the deregulated industries. Nor is there any basis for judging how long such conditions will prevail. A second benefit is the movement toward internal efficiency as demonstrated by reductions in the firm's work force. The unresolved problem is determining whether these reductions are demonstrable evidence of expense padding that has been removed through deregulation, or whether these reductions are really a denigration of quality of service and reliability.

There are at least eight cases that demonstrate the adverse effects of tight oligopoly. First, prices will not track costs, but rather will reflect market segmentation and the bargaining power of major players. This is illustrated by the percentage change in price for natural gas by class of service between 1984 and 1996. Prices at the wellhead (point of production) dropped 21 percent, prices at the city gate (point of delivery) dropped 17.7 percent, prices to industrial users dropped 23.5 percent, but prices for residential customers increased by 14.4 percent.[11] Similar evidence exists in telecommunications. For example, the Consumer Federation of America found that the average per minute rate for households using less than 30 minutes of calling per month tripled between 1997–99, while the rates for households with large calling volumes decreased.[12]

It can be argued that such differentials will be erased by competitive entry, but the evidence in electricity is far from encouraging. The largest marketer of electricity, Enron, has withdrawn from the residential markets in California, Rhode Island, and Massachusetts, citing low profit margins and low transitional prices. In November 1999, only 1.2 percent of California residential customers had moved to alternative, competitive suppliers. Consumer choice appears to vary substantially by class of customer.

Second, oligopolistic concentration gives the firm substantial discretionary power over prices, services, and investment. There is clear evidence that oligopolies will follow patterns of price leadership and conscious parallelism. For example, between 1991 and 1997, AT&T, MCI, and Sprint raised long-distance prices in lock step while access fees paid to local phone companies dropped substantially.[13] Concentration also gives the parent holding company a comparative advantage in the cost of capital by pooling lower risk utility services with higher risk competitive services. A competitive entrant could not match this advantage if that firm were only supplying the competitive service. Concentration also gives the parent holding company the financial capability for aggressive acquisitions. To illustrate, in 1998 AT&T had no share of the domestic cable TV industry. With the acquisition of TCI and Media One, it will have 60 percent of that industry.

Third, profit levels under oligopoly will be higher than those prevailing under competition or effective regulation. This can be shown by comparing price/earnings multiples and market-to-book ratios over time:

Table 13.2   Price/earnings multiples versus book ratios

| | Price/earnings multiple | | M/B ratio |
	1989	*1999*	*12 mos. ending 6/99*
Electricity	10.6	15.4	1.63
Combination			
Elec. & Gas	10.6	16.6	1.83
Telephone Cos.	17.5	27.9	4.94

Source: C. A. Turner *Utility Reports*, September 1999.

The traditional M/B ratio for public utilities under regulation was 1.05, but now these ratios are substantially higher for all utilities, ranging from 1.63 for electrics to 4.94 for telephone companies. Price/earnings multiples have also increased substantially over time.

Fourth, there will be a strong pressure for network design to be driven by the requirements of the large users and not by the infrastructure requirements of all classes of users. This redirection of resources may also be matched by an incentive to disinvest in services for low income customers and services for low profit markets. Under these conditions direct public subsidization will be required to correct the problems.

Fifth, there will be a redistribution of both income and the gains from technological advance whenever oligopolies maintain rigid prices in residential/small business markets while giving major price concessions to large users. Furthermore, there will be no incentive for an oligopolist to experiment with lower prices in residential markets or engage in a price war if demand in that market is perceived to be price inelastic.

Sixth, there will be both an incentive and an opportunity to shift costs to third parties. These costs will arise when the cherry picking of targeted customers raises the costs for residual customers, or when inadvertent energy flows along a transmission path pose low voltage problems for customers not directly involved in a bilateral transaction. Costs will also be shifted to third parties when the oligopsonist seeks to attract targeted customers by understating the cost of a technological upgrade for that customer group, while charging the balance of the cost of the upgrade to overhead costs to be borne by all customers. These discretionary actions would be minimized or eliminated under regulation or competition.

Seventh, oligopsony could have the effect of reducing reserve margins and denigrating reliability. Under traditional rate base regulation there was an incentive to carry sufficient reserve margins, but there is no incentive for a major merchant generator to provide sufficient reserves for an entire system in the absence of direct regulation. As evidence, the traditional reserve margin for electricity generation has been 15 percent, but forecasts for the year 2002 indicate that such margins may drop to 2–3 percent for much of the nation.

Eighth, tight oligopolies will have a strong incentive to engage in political activity to support the goals of the firm. They will have far greater resources than consumer groups when it comes to dealing with state legislatures. This is best illustrated by the successful effort of California utilities to defeat Proposition Nine in 1998. The utilities and their supporters spent $40 million to defeat a consumer initiative that would have adversely affected stranded cost recovery. Consumer groups spent $1.1 million. Under traditional regulation the entire utility expenditure would have been charged against shareholders. Absent regulation, no such adjustment will be made. The consequences of greater political involvement by large firms have been set forth by Robert Reich.[14] Reich noted that large combinations can influence public opinion; can achieve federal tax breaks, promote subsidies, and secure favorable administrative decisions. They can also effectively oppose litigation that gets in the way and impose a form of censorship on dissent. Conversely, the large oligopsony can be employed by government to achieve political goals. This has been demonstrated by Edward Comor in his discussion of the application of new telecommunications technology to achieve global acceptance of US free trade policies.[15]

The inadequacy of transitional public policies

The conflict between deregulation and the growth of concentration focuses attention on the adequacy of interim public policies designed to protect consumers while stimulating competition. Price caps, mandatory interconnection, and functional restructuring suffer from significant shortcomings. Price caps or ceiling prices impose only the weakest constraint on cross-subsidization while they do nothing to address oligopolistic pricing strategies. Price leadership, limit entry pricing, tie-in sales, and umbrella pricing will continue without interference. Furthermore, by severing the connection between prices and profit levels, one of the critical tests of the existence of oligopoly is foreclosed. Regulators are denied the ability to ascertain whether the pricing practices of the firm have been able to sustain abnormally high profits over time.

The FCC has mandated open access and interconnection for the local exchange carriers, but without successful results. As noted earlier, local carriers still retain more than 97 percent of the market. It is becoming increasingly evident that open access will be achieved on the basis of negotiation between large players in the local and long distance markets. The Bells want access to the long-distance market and AT&T, MCI-WorldCom-Sprint want access to the final customer. Any agreement between giants will reflect their perception of the net benefits to be derived. It is difficult to believe that this process will achieve a socially optimal infrastructure.

In electricity, control of the networks is a focal point for exercising market power. The Federal Energy Regulatory Commission (FERC) has sought to promote the voluntary creation of regional transmission organizations that would possess some degree of independence, but without requiring mandatory structural separation of the grid from the parent holding company.[16] As a result, FERC will have to proceed case-by-case to detect manipulative behavior on the part of incumbent players. This will be a major challenge since the stakes are so large.

At the same time, public policy has shifted much of the responsibility for service to primary and secondary markets. This has resulted in a phenomenal growth in the trading of electricity as a commodity between deregulated marketers. It is estimated that a megawatt hour may be traded ten times before it reaches the final customer. As a consequence there has been great price volatility, and an increased premium for risk which adds to the price of electricity. While no definitive studies of the impact of trading on retail power prices have been made to date, some observers in 1999 believed that power prices on an hourly basis for both peak and off-peak sales have increased by 30 percent.

A question can also be raised about the impact of deregulation on the search for renewable power sources. At present, renewable power from wind, biomass, solar, and other sources is more costly than fossil fuels if social costs are ignored. Market pressures will force generators to choose less expensive sources of power over more expensive but less polluting sources. Public policy can impose requirements to label "clean power" or it can mandate that a portion of power come from renewable sources. But these steps will only be successful if consumers are willing to pay a premium for such energy. Public policy can also levy a tax to fund renewable power development. But each of these measures represents a very imperfect solution to a potentially significant form of market failure.

A final note should be made with respect to the feasibility of forming procurement aggregators to protect retail customers. This option has been applauded by the proponents of deregulation. The assumption is that the aggregator will exercise countervailing power to protect residential customers. But if the aggregator represents both residential and large industrial buyers, the same problems of interclass discrimination still remain. If the aggregator represents only residential customers, then it will be burdened by the poor load factors of residential customers and eventually will end up paying as much as the stand alone cost of residential power.

Of course, proponents of deregulation always argue that antitrust is a remedial step for addressing monopoly practices. This overlooks the fact that antitrust has done little to challenge tight oligopoly. Furthermore, the budgets of the US Department of Justice and the Federal Trade Commission peaked in 1977. It is optimistic to believe that antitrust will grow to fill the gap produced by deregulation.

Revisiting the public utility concept: a purposeful option for reform

The rapid growth in industry concentration, together with the serious deficiencies in current public policies, strongly suggests that the real world differs sharply from the vision of an unfettered free market economy promoted by the champions of deregulation. This dichotomy between vision and reality can have profound consequences for the general welfare. Public utilities are network industries that are an integral part of society's infrastructure. This infrastructure, in turn, serves as a platform for promoting growth in productivity and gains in real income. It cannot be assumed that oligopolistic market structures will automatically culminate in the realization of an optimal infrastructure, the realization of all network and coordination economies, or the distribution of these gains to all sectors of the economy.

Other options for public policy must be considered. The first step would involve a reexamination of the quintessential features of the original public utility concept as it was set forth by those academic proponents who championed public utility regulation during the period 1923–61. This was the golden age of involvement by institutional economists in matters pertaining to public utility regulation. The principal contributors included Martin G. Glaeser, James C. Bonbright, John Maurice Clark, Eli W. Clemens, C. Emery Troxel, and John Bauer. A synopsis of their perception of particular topics should permit a better appreciation of the reform measures needed to address current industry problems and policy shortcomings.

With respect to the rationale for regulation, Clark (1939) noted that neither the essential nature of the service nor the theory of natural monopoly is sufficient to designate an industry as susceptible to government regulation. Clark stated that the concept of natural monopoly fails to consider a number of those businesses affected with the public interest. A more comprehensive justification for regulation is "afforded by the theory advanced by Professor Tugwell: that of consumers' disadvantage . . . The essential fact seems to be that the nature of the business is such that competition, for one reason or another, does not afford the protections to buyers and sellers that it is supposed to afford . . ."[17] Significantly, Clark also noted that "a public interest of this sort need not apply to an entire industry but to only certain relations or functions."[18] Clark stated that natural monopoly may exist with a clear potential for exploiting the consumer, but there are also other areas or functions where regulation is justified on the grounds of consumer protection.

Bonbright (1961) held a similar view. He noted that price control alone was not sufficient to confer public utility status. Bonbright emphasized that the primary purpose of regulation must be the protection of the public in the role of consumer rather than in the role of producer or taxpayer. In effect, a public utility is any enterprise subject to price regulation of a type designed primarily to protect consumers. "What must justify public utility regulation is the necessity of regulation and not merely the necessity of the product."[19]

On the question of industry structure and the sustainability of competition, Glaeser (1957) believed that public utility functions were a distinct sector positioned between traditional public sector functions and private markets. He believed that competition would not be sustainable in the public utility sector, that monopoly was the preferred organizational form, and that oligopoly could emerge in the transitional zone between public utility functions and competitive markets. Clark doubted that ruinous cutthroat competition would emerge between public utilities despite high fixed costs, implying conscious parallelism. Troxel (1947) also believed that firms would be hesitant to engage in retaliatory price cutting in the absence of significant unused capacity, but would rather a live-and-let-live policy. Interestingly, Clark dismissed the effectiveness of potential competition as a constraint on market power. About 50 years before the theory of contestable markets, Clark noted that potential competition "is a slow and wasteful check, especially where the new plant has to be large and expensive . . . in order to have a fair chance of success . . . ."[20] Continuing, he stated that "it is inherently impossible to have an industry effectively governed by potential competition alone."[21]

On the question of price discrimination, there was agreement among the institutionalists as to the incentive to discriminate and the need to constrain such practices. As Glaeser (1927) noted, customer segmentation leads to a differential class price that permits the monopolist to "invade what might otherwise be . . . a consumer's surplus,"[22] but the offsetting advantage would be the sale of increments of supply of different prices, thereby covering costs but contributing to a better overall utilization of plant. When excess profits appeared, Glaeser argued that the prices on all units should be reduced and output expanded. Troxel was equally concerned with the evolving structure of differentiated prices. He viewed pricing that reflected different demand elasticities as essentially discriminatory: "when private managers control price changes, cost economies of plant operation are translated primarily into price reductions for the large buyers or the new buyers . . . inelastic demand . . . receive(s) no price reductions at all . . ."[23] Bonbright argued that the firm would seldom be under sufficient competitive pressure to make general rate reductions. He believed that there would be no incentive, in the absence of regulation, to make rate reductions conform to cost-of-service standards.

While all of these institutional economists agreed on the importance of the connection between prices and earnings, Bonbright and Glaeser extended the discussion by introducing an intermediate step that tied the expected revenue contribution to the class of customer. Bonbright held that rate base/rate-of-return regulation should be used to determine total revenue requirements, and marginal cost pricing should be used for rate design, but that class rate standards should be introduced to determine the proper revenue contribution assessed to each class or group of customers. The class rate standard would reflect an apportionment of total costs on the basis of differential relationships rather than absolute cost by service. Glaeser developed the alternative justifiable expenditures theory that could be used to complement Bonbright's class rate standards. It would establish the direct (or avoidable) cost for each class and then assign the common/joint costs to each class on the basis of the relative benefits derived from joint development. For each service, its relative benefit would be equal to the difference between its stand alone cost and its direct cost. Where joint economies were large, the gains for that service would be large. Conversely, where the gains were small or non-existent, the assignment of common and joint costs would be negligible. The Glaeser approach would permit captive markets to share in the gains from expansion and diversification, assuming that they made use of common plant.[24]

With respect to regulatory governance and organization, Clemens, like the others, accepted the public interest theory of regulation. Clemens (1950) noted that the interests of the public transcend those of the individual. Private interests must yield to a greater public interest, and the firm accordingly accepts a unique set of obligations and rights which differentiate it from other enterprises.

Bonbright and others sought to preserve the integrity of public interest regulation, focusing on the need to create an industry structure that was amenable to effective regulation. This meant constraining the abuses inherent in the holding company systems, combination companies, and diversification into non-utility activities. These tactics, according to Bonbright, were conducive to waste, inefficiency, and financial manipulation. The solution involved extending regulation to the holding company, discouraging the formation of holding companies that could not demonstrate engineering and economic gains through improved performance, and the divestment of non-utility enterprises.

John Bauer (1950) held similar views regarding an optimal utility structure. Integration and consolidation would be promoted only to achieve economies of operation. Toward this goal, Bauer believed that commissions should be turned into positive planning agencies. Giving the commissions appropriate powers and duties, raising the professional status of staff and commissioners, and providing adequate financing would improve regulatory planning. With these resources, commissions could focus on improving all phases of regulation, including integrating utility properties and operations whenever justified by economies of scale. This planning process, he noted, would be greatly strengthened by broader public participation because consumers had been under-represented in the past.

To summarize, the public utility concept implemented by public interest regulation was the centerpiece of these institutional economists writing in the period 1923–61. We will call this the "institutionalist model of regulation." The overriding rationale for government intervention was the achievement of a degree of consumer protection that would not be provided by imperfectly competitive markets. Furthermore, the interrelationship between cost and demand characteristics created an incentive to engage in pricing and organizational strategies that required cost-based pricing within the context of overall control of revenue requirements. These economists also sought to implement regulation within a political-economic structure that was most conducive to its success. Achieving these objectives would require commissions to incorporate an industry-wide responsibility for planning.

An application of the institutionalist model

The future of the public utility concept is closely tied to acceptance, at least in principle, of the institutionalist model. If across-the-board deregulation programs eventually succeed, then the concept will be little more than an apologetic for the subsidization of selected services. These would include premium payments for a default supplier, subsidies for low income customers, and payments to assure service in high cost markets. But if the earlier discussion in this chapter is correct and the movement toward greater concentration creates new opportunities for the exercise of market power, then the institutionalist model will have renewed applicability. The model will also gain strength with the growing recognition of the multi-dimensional nature of market failure in these industries and the inability of existing public policies to contend with these failures.

This chapter will demonstrate how the institutionalist model could be applied in the current industry setting. This will also show how sharply it contrasts with current thinking. Electricity, natural gas, and telecommunications will be considered in terms of the need to balance direct regulation of the network function concurrently with the promotion of competition where appropriate and the installation of necessary consumer safeguards. Broader questions of market power and consumer and environmental protection will also be treated.

In electricity supply, the network would include the transmission grid, the distribution system, and all ancillary services involving either the monopoly supply or joint production of these services. To realize inherent network and coordination economies (as envisioned by Glaeser and Bonbright), these functions must be totally independent of the rest of the industry. The networks would have common carrier status (an obligation to serve all comers), independent financing, independent management, and rates set by regulation on a cost-of-service basis. An independent network would have a strong incentive to maximize the use of that network and, because of regulatory oversight, no opportunity to restrict capacity or restrict access at monopoly focal points. An independent transmission network would be free to expand to achieve its most efficient size. It is possible that three transmission grids could cover virtually all of the US with a few minor exceptions. Because the network would be fully independent of holding company control, it could be expanded without the requirement that a parent utility also be given expanded authority. Pricing on the network could incorporate the Glaeser model so that each customer class would pay a cost on the basis of its relative benefits received rather than usage during a peak period.

The major advantage of an expanded common carrier network would be the opportunity to increase the number of competitive generators and the number of competitive marketers. At the retail level consumers would have a greater choice among generators and marketers, or they would have the option of negotiating for direct purchases if they were a large user. If residential consumers chose to select an aggregator to bargain on their behalf, that aggregator would now have the advantage of being able to deal with a much larger array of suppliers. Another advantage of a large comprehensive grid would be the ability to mitigate price volatility. The greater the number of potential suppliers, the less the opportunity for a price fly-up during critical periods.

The network would, of course, be under full regulation. This would extend beyond setting prices to establish reserve margins. At the retail level regulation could still have a role, even in cases where state legislation mandated removal of price controls. Deregulated marketers could be certificated and conditions imposed regarding reliability of service and adequacy of reserve margins. If the marketer failed to meet these standards, then there could be a provision to recapture the certificate and award it to another supplier. It is to be hoped that new options for retail distribution of power could be explored, including the municipal marketing of electricity.

In natural gas supply, the same principles could be applied by separating the network from the provision of gas inputs and final retail sales of gas to consumers. The network would include gathering lines, transmission pipelines, storage facilities, and distribution systems. The pipeline could be integrated into a fully independent common carrier network, including gathering lines and storage capability. Again, pipeline costing could be designed along the lines of the Glaeser approach to set the revenue contributions by each class of customer. At the distribution level customers could choose between direct dealings with natural gas producers, relying on the local utility for full service, recourse to an aggregator, independent marketer, or municipalization of the system. In each case separation of the network from those trading on the network would be critical. State commissions could impose service reliability standards on all entities serving retail customers.

As in the case of electricity, there are always cases where a restructured system could be gamed. However, gaming under the institutionalist model would be far more difficult than in the current industry setting. Nevertheless, problems can be envisioned. For example, it is possible that the large deregulated marketer could purchase substantial amounts of pipeline capacity and control significant gas supplies. This marketer would require the purchase of bundled service that included both transport and gas as a commodity. Any retail customer seeking more capacity would have to purchase the bundled package, which would mean buying both transport and the commodity at inflated prices. This would circumvent the regulator's attempt to fix pipeline rates because these prices would be included as part of a high-cost total package. One way to handle this problem would be to require mandatory unbundling. A second approach would be to expand the network to such a degree that the market power of an individual entity would be negated. It should be noted that expanding the network would also tend to diminish the market power of natural gas producers (typically major oil companies) who could hold substantial proved reserves on a per field basis. By expanding the network, buyers would have access to many more producing fields.

In telecommunications, the distinction between networks and those using the network is much more complicated since all of the major carriers are actively seeking to provide end-to-end bundled packages for a full range of voice, data, video, and Internet services. Eventually, this could mean no more than three or four such systems would prevail and the political pressure which these systems could bring to bear would be so great that network separation would be impossible. However, this would not foreclose regulators from taking major steps toward network separation. The New York Commission moved in this direction in January 1995 by separating the local network from the provision of competitive services for the Frontier Corporation. In 1999, the Pennsylvania Commission moved to separate the local distribution plant from those who would market services on that plant. Similar conditions could be imposed as AT&T acquires cable companies, as AT&T and British

Telecom promote joint ventures, as regional Bell systems seek to enter the long distance market, and as consortia of telecommunications carriers form to plan transoceanic networks. Again, this would tend to mitigate the oligopoly power of the integrated firm and its ability to exploit monopoly focal points. Hopefully this separation would also serve to stimulate experiments with new institutional forms designed to protect residential and small business customers. This could include the introduction of municipal aggregators who could buy phone, cable, broadband, and Internet service for their customers. Thus, a structure that differentiates between the network and the deregulated user could serve as a basis for experimentation with new forms of consumer protection.

Finally, the institutionalist model would endeavor to promote industry-specific planning in order to consider the general factors that are an integral part of consumer protection. This type of planning could address the availability of service by class of customer throughout the relevant market. In addition to the traditional issues of assuring available service to low income customers and thin markets, attention should be given to the widest diffusion of network benefits since the network is, in principle, a common resource to be enjoyed by everyone. Also, J. M. Clark (1939) argued that a good system of public control must be democratic, powerful, and adaptable. Based on these criteria, Clark sought to introduce incentives into the process to divert management away from subverting regulation and toward the goal of improving efficiency. For the network, this could include incentive adjustments to the rate of return. But it should also include, as Clark noted, a penalty for not modernizing by reducing the value of the assets in light of the existence of a more efficient substitute. At the same time, Clark believed that management should be prevented from foisting "excessive extravagances" on consumers in the guise of improvements. This is particularly relevant in contemporary telecommunications.

A second major area that can be uniquely addressed through regulatory planning involves the definition and measurement of market power. Neoclassical economics would define market power as restricting output to raise price above marginal cost or above a competitive market price. Indeed, this is the definition adopted by FERC in the application of the Herfindahl–Hirschman Index.[25] However, as Clemens has shown, price discrimination in public utilities actually expands total output and can, if properly employed, be used to satisfy a number of the criteria associated with competitive equilibria. In the real world, there is ample evidence that market power can be exercised at a number of levels relating to market structure and pricing policies, gaming existing institutional arrangements, and service differentiation. Confronting these strategies will require regulation to greatly expand its reporting requirements. These will require data on price leadership patterns, changes in the cost of inputs, more sophisticated measures of market concentration, and, perhaps most important, more refined criteria for judging mergers, acquisitions, and joint ventures. The permissive merger policies of

the past should give way to a new set of criteria requiring: (1) a demonstration that there are demonstrable efficiency gains from such actions; (2) an
analysis of how these gains will be distributed between the firm and consumers over time; and (3) conclusive proof that these gains can only be
achieved through merger, acquisition, or joint venture.

If such steps can be taken, significant progress will have been made toward
rehabilitating the public utility concept and implementing the institutionalist
model of regulation.

Notes

1   *Munn* v. *Illinois*, 94 US 113 (1877).
2   *Phillips Petroleum Co.* v. *Wisconsin*, 347 US 632 (1954).
3   H. M. Gray (1940: 9). In 1975, I invited Horace Gray to reexamine his earlier work and
    reassess public utility regulation. Gray was still unsympathetic to regulation, but he called
    for an even stronger application of *Munn* v. *Illinois* to reassert the primacy of the public
    interest. He wrote:

    > We now face a radically different situation that compels us to restate, in much stronger
    > terms, the proposition of Lord Hale (as embodied in *Munn* v. *Illinois*). The conditions
    > of production and the necessities of the people, in our modern industrial and urbanized
    > society, require a more positive assertion of public interest. Public power must be superi-
    > or and responsible; private power must be demoted from principalship to agency. This
    > shift of power-relations need not disturb the private property rights of owners, nor their
    > right to receive a reasonable compensation for the use of their capital. It would relate
    > solely to management, and in this area government would make the broad policy deci-
    > sions while private management would carry out the purely administrative functions..
    >
    > See Gray (1976: 9)

4   M. H. Bernstein (1955). For his later reassessment of regulation, see Bernstein (1972).
5   G. Kolko (1965). Also note the rejoinder by R.W. Harbeson (1967).
6   S. Peltzman (1976).
7   For a comprehensive evaluation of market-oriented critics of government intervention, see
    W. J. Samuels (1992, Vol. 2).
8   *Carterfone Device in Message Toll Telephone Lines*, 13 FCC 2d. 420 (1968).
9   *MCI Communications Corp.* v. *American Telephone & Telegraph Co.*, 18 FCC 2d 953 (1969).
10 For a further discussion of pricing strategies, see H. M. Trebing (1999: 427–29). Also see H.
    M. Trebing (1997: 29–40).
11 R. Barua and G. Crandall. "Natural Gas Price Trends Since Deregulation," presentation at
    National Consumer Law Center Annual Conference, Washington, DC, February 27–28,
    1997. Data presented in Table 1. Large users would argue that an increase in residential rates
    is appropriate since this class of user contributes significantly to the peak. This argument
    reinforces the straight-fixed-variable (SFV) costing methodology that assigns all fixed invest-
    ment costs to peak users. However, there are alternative methods for assigning these costs.
    One option is described in the institutionalist model cited at Note 24. It should also be noted
    that SFV assigns these costs to residential customers whose demand is the most price inelas-
    tic.
12 Initial Comments of Consumer Federation of America, Consumers Union, and the Texas
    Office of Public Utility Counsel, Before the Federal Communications Commission, *In the
    Matter of Low-Volume Long-Distance Users*, CC Docket No. 99–249, September 21, 1999.
13 *Trends in Long Distance Rates and Exchange Access Charges*. Data and chart compiled by
    Bell South Corporation.
14 R. B. Reich (2000: 56).

15 E. A. Comor (1998: Ch. 8).
16 Federal Energy Regulatory Commission, *Regional Transmission Organizations*, Docket No. RM99-2-000, Order No. 2000, issued December 20, 1999.
17 J. M. Clark (1939: 178).
18 J. M. Clark (1939: 179).
19 J. C. Bonbright (1961: 9).
20 J. M. Clark (1923: 444).
21 J. M. Clark (1923: 445).
22 M. G. Glaeser (1927: 627).
23 C. E. Troxel (1947: 592).
24 The Glaeser methodology is developed at length in M. G. Glaeser (1939), beginning at p. 259.
25 For FERC use of the Herfindahl–Hirschman Index, see: FERC *Order 592* (1996), and FERC's *Notice of Proposed Rulemaking on Revised Merger Filing Requirements* (1998). FERC defines market power as the ability to hold price at more than 5 percent above the actual or estimated market price.

References

Bauer, J. (1950) *Transforming Public Utility Regulation*, New York: Harper and Bros.
Bernstein, M. H. (1955) *Regulating Business by Independent Commission*, Princeton, NJ: Princeton University Press.
—— (1972) "Independent Regulatory Agencies: A Perspective on Their Reform," in W. J. Samuels and H. M. Trebing (eds) *A Critique of Administrative Regulation of Public Utilities*, East Lansing, MI: Michigan State University Press.
Bonbright, J. C. (1961) *Principles of Public Utility Rates*, New York: Columbia University Press.
Clark, J. M. (1923) *Studies in the Economics of Overhead Costs*, Chicago, IL: Chicago University Press.
—— (1939) *Social Control of Business*, 2nd edn., New York: McGraw-Hill.
Clemens, E. W. (1950) *Economics and Public Utilities*, New York: Appleton-Century-Crofts.
Comor, E. A. (1998) *Communication, Commerce and Power: The Political Economy of America and the Direct Broadcast Satellite, 1960–2000*, New York: St. Martin's Press.
Glaeser, M. G. (1927) *Outlines of Public Utility Economics*, New York: The Macmillan Co.
—— (1939) "Those TVA Joint Costs," *Public Utilities Fortnightly*, August 31.
—— (1957) *Public Utilities in American Capitalism*, New York: Macmillan.
Gray, H. M. (1940) "The Passing of the Public Utility Concept" in *Journal of Land & Public Utility Economics* (February).
—— (1976) "The Sharing of Economic Power in Public Utility Industries," in W. Sichel (ed.) *Salvaging Public Utility Regulation*, Lexington, MA: Lexington Books, D. C. Heath.
Harbeson, R. W. (1967) "Railroads and Regulation, 1877–1916: Conspiracy or Public Interest?" *Journal of Economic History* (June).
Kolko, G. (1965) *Railroads and Regulation, 1877–1916*, Princeton NJ: Princeton University Press.
Peltzman, S. (1976) "Toward a More General Theory of Regulation," *Journal of Law and Economics* (August).

Reich, R. B. (2000) "AOL-Time Warner's Kingly Prerogative," *The American Prospect*, Cambridge, MA: The American Prospect, February 14.

Samuels, W. J. (1992) *Essays on the Economic Role of Government, vol. 2: Applications*, London: Macmillan Press.

Trebing, H. M. (1997) "Emerging Market Strategies and Options for Regulatory Reform in Public Utility Industries," in W. H. Melody (ed.) *Telecom Reform: Principles, Policies and Regulatory Practices*, Lyngby: Technical University of Denmark.

—— (1999) "New Challenges for the Consumer Movement in an Era of Utility Deregulation," *Quarterly Bulletin* 19, 4, Columbus: National Regulatory Research Institute.

Troxel, C. E. (1947) *Economics of Public Utilities*, New York: Rinehart.

Part IV

Aspects of institutional and Post Keynesian economics

14 The institutional economics of Nobel Prize winners

A. Allan Schmid*

I have bedeviled Ph.D. candidates during their preliminary oral exams by asking them to name five institutional economists who have won the Nobel Prize. Can there be five in this sometimes marginalized part of economics? Some come up with the names of Douglass North and Ronald Coase because they are relatively recent winners and founders of the new International Society for New Institutional Economics. But five? I shall argue here that there are more than five, and many more who utilize and advance portions of institutional economics theory. To make this argument I shall have to select the components of what constitutes institutional economics, and since there is no official version, it is a personal selection. My claim is not that everyone cited here is an institutionalist, but rather that good economists find it useful to embrace some of its various elements. By putting them all together, I hope to demonstrate that there is a unified body of theory that constitutes institutional economics.

Institutional economics has been condemned for being critical but offering no theory for a research program. I do not want to use the Nobelists in an *ex cathedra* role arguing that if they said it, it must be good. I merely want to demonstrate that respected practitioners use institutional theory to do good economics. Part of the assertion that institutional economics has no theory is a quarrel over what constitutes theory. One answer is to ask rhetorically, that if the Nobelists are not doing theory, what are they doing? More seriously, we must first address the question of what is theory. If propositions to be called theory must be deterministic deductions about constrained maximization, then few institutional propositions can use the term. But if one simply means the specification of a set of variables and relationships among them, then much of what the Nobelists and others do is theory. In the words of Simon Kuznets (1977: 4), "by a theory we mean a statement of testable relations among empirically identifiable factors, such relations and factors having been found relatively invariant under diverse conditions in time and space." He defines his research program: "to draw some suggestions from the empirical record about the deter-

* Warren Samuels has once more given me the benefit of his critical review. For this and years of friendship, I thank him. Thanks also to David Reisman and Steven Medema for their review.

mining factors, as guides to the further study of the data and particularly to the directions in which testable theoretical analysis must be pursued."

For James Buchanan (1968: 1): "Explanation is the primary function of theory." It may also be the basis for specific conditional forecasts of the type, if A, then B. But he is more interested in what he calls "inferential predictions," which reveal the logical structure of an economy and that take the form "A tends to equal B." Examples are: "Prices will equal cost; wage rates for similar workers will be equalized; factors of production will earn their marginal product." He is less interested in theory which assumes the institutional-organizational structure such as pure competition, but rather he proposes that the economist's "task includes the derivation of the institutional order itself from the set of elementary behavioral hypotheses with which he commences. In this manner, genuine institutional economics becomes a significant and an important part of fundamental economic theory" (Buchanan 1968: 3). Here he sets his task and defines "institutional economics." So for him a competitive order is not something to be assumed, but something to be predicted.

In this chapter I shall first discuss the unit of observation in institutional economics. Next institutions are defined and related to individuals and organizations. Research programs that emphasize impact versus change analysis are then contrasted. This is followed by a theoretical construct which relates situation (attributes of goods) to alternative institutions (structures) to predict performance. As noted, a theory includes variables and relationships. We need more than prices and quantities – the universe of commodities. Institutional economics might better be called institutional and behavioral economics for its utilization of behavioral variables. A section outlines the behavioral regularities featured by the Nobelists. Other sections feature variables describing the content of coordinating signals and communications, technology, and the incorporation of time and expectations. Any economic model or story specifies expected relationships among its variables. These are grouped below into relationships involving feedback, learning, and evolution which features a non-marginal and non-equilibrium economics. The chapter concludes with how institutional economics avoids the value circularity problem.

Institutional theory is used to understand how alternative institutional structures direct the human interdependencies created by different preferences and different kinds of goods to obtain different substantive performance outcomes. The institutional structure may be formal or informal (habits and culture) and implemented at the constitutional, organizational or individual level. Institutional theory is also used to understand institutional change and evolution.

The transaction as the unit of observation

Our existence in a world of scarcity creates an interdependence among actors which institutions must sort out to provide order. Coase emphasizes the reciprocal nature of externality problems. He argued that it is selective perception to say that A harms B rather than B harms A. The machinery of the candy maker surely harms the physician upstairs, but if the physician demands quiet, there is harm and extra expense for the candy maker. Coase argues that "what are traded on the market are not, as is often supposed by economists, physical entities, but the rights to perform certain actions, and the rights which individuals possess are established by the legal system" (Coase 1992: 717). Study of the price system independent of institutions is impossible. Because of transaction costs "the rights which individuals possess, with their duties and privileges, will be, to a large extent, what the law determines" and can't be contracted around. Taking the transaction as the unit of observation makes the dual character of rights clear. Property rights necessarily involve a holder of an opportunity and others who are subject to that opportunity. Uncompensated losses are inevitable. This transactional view avoids the confusion contained in the oft-cited conflict between the individual and government. As Arrow puts it: "The demands of society sound like a formidable and crushing burden, but of course behind social rules are always other individual people . . ." (Arrow 1974: 27). The transactional view reveals externalities to be ubiquitous and inevitably active. If there is order, there will be some collective understanding (government) that necessarily chooses whose interests count. As North (1997a: 3) says: "Put bluntly there is no such thing as laissez faire – that means anarchy somewhat akin to what we have been observing in Russia." An institutional economics explicitly focuses on the parties to a transaction rather than only on the prices that result. It is institutions that link transacting individuals.

Individuals, organizations and institutions

Theory begins with transacting individuals or aggregates thereof. If these transactions are structured by institutions, just what are they? North defines them as "the formal rules (constitutions, statute and common law, regulations, etc.), the informal constraints (norms of behavior, conventions, and internally imposed rules of conduct), and the enforcement characteristics of each." He further elaborates, "Institutions exist to structure human interaction in a world of uncertainty." "Without institutions there would be no order, no society, no economy, and no polity" (North 1998: 2). Coase defines economics as the study of "the working of social institutions which bind the economic system together: firms, markets for goods and services, labour markets, capital markets, the banking system, international trade, and so on" (Coase 1977: 487).

Institutionalists emphasize that individuals shape institutions and institutions shape individuals. North makes a distinction between organizations and institutions, where "institutions are the rules of the game; organizations are the players." He has in mind groups of people with a common objective working to obtain a formal institutional change – for example, new legislation. Simon observes that most economic activity is not individual, but in organizations (firms) with some kind of hierarchical structure. These firms make their own internal rules for their members/employees which function much like a government. Coase explains the firm as the answer to transaction costs in market contracting among separate individuals. Simon (1957: 199) says: "It is only because individual human beings are limited in knowledge, foresight, skill, and time that organizations are useful investments for the achievement of human purpose."

Hayek (1982: 148) observes that "[s]ince agents are only able to initiate social action by drawing upon social rules (which do not of course determine exactly what they do), their actions are simultaneously individually motivated and socially sanctioned." "A catallaxy is thus the special kind of spontaneous order produced by the market through people acting within the rules of the law of property, tort and contract" (109). Arrow (1994: 8) is referring to institutions when he observes that "social variables, not attached to particular individuals, are essential in studying the economy or any other social system and that, in particular, knowledge and technical information have an irremovable social component, of increasing importance." (He had earlier referred to professors who are interchangeable in many courses, which implies the role of position.) "Limitations on individualistic methodology appear very strongly when considering the role of information . . ." (Arrow 1994: 2). We can speak of individual actors but they are embedded in institutions, some of which predated the actor and some of which the present actors themselves created.

Institutions act both as constraints on action and as the context in which values (preferences) are learned. In the first case, North speaks sometimes of constraints with institutions acting as incentive structures (changing the flow of benefits and costs) and sometimes of institutions and ideology shaping preferences and world views. Arrow, speaking of evaluating social choice institutions, is aware that "if individual values can themselves be affected by the method of social choice, it becomes much more difficult to learn what is meant by one method's being preferable to another" (Arrow 1963: 8). Robert Solow (1992: 272) argues that: "Pretty clearly, economic behavior depends on the nature of social institutions (and on culturally determined attitudes and beliefs or, better still, on these attitudes and beliefs as filtered through social institutions)."

Institutional economics is about relationships which distribute opportunities. These can usefully be expressed as rights. Coase says: "Economists commonly assume that what is traded on the market is a physical entity, an ounce of gold, a ton of coal. But, as lawyers know, what are traded on the market are bundles of rights, rights to perform certain actions. Trade, the dominant activity in the economic system, its amount and character, consequently depend on what rights and duties individuals and organizations are deemed to possess" (Coase 1988a: 656). It is institutions that determine who has what opportunities to trade.

This discussion of individuals, organizations, and institutions already begins to identify variables and relationships constituting institutional economics, and in the sections to follow this will be made more explicit. But before that we will distinguish research programs that study the *impact* of alternative institutions in the past and predictions of future impacts *if* they were changed, and programs that explain past institutional *change* or the political rules that might facilitate a certain kind of change in the future.

Impact and change analysis

Impact theories support a research program which produces information useful to citizens and policy makers on the different consequences of alternative institutions if they were to be implemented. They might also explain what institutions are responsible for current economic conditions. Simon (1978b: 6) contrasts structural and qualitative analysis versus predictive, equilibrium analysis. Examples: "Not 'how much flood insurance will a man buy?' but 'what are the structural conditions that make buying insurance rational or attractive?' Not 'at what levels will wages be fixed?' but 'when will work be performed under an employment contract rather than a sales contract?'" He sees economics moving to "a much more qualitative institutional analysis, in which discrete structural alternatives are compared." In the case of informal institutions which evolve from the aggregation of individual choices, one can only speak of explaining what institutions are responsible for current performance. This is not easy since these are the things that appear to be the natural order of things and people may not be aware of their functioning.

What sort of research program does Solow suggest? What does he want from analysis? Not forecasting. "It is rather the uncovering of mechanisms that cause the economic system to malfunction in significant ways, and then the analysis of kinds of policy measures, directions of policy even if not exact doses, that are potentially therapeutic" (Solow 1989: 37).

The research program of Coase is primarily in terms of the impact of legal alternatives, that is, the impact of law upon the economic system. "Economists cannot be expected to pronounce on the detailed arrangements of the legal system, but we may be able to contribute something to our understanding of how the legal system affects the economic system and thus to the development of those general principles which should govern the delimitation of rights" (Coase 1988a: 656).

The most overarching research program would require: "A theory of economic performance through time [that] would entail an integration of theories of institutional change, demographic change, and change in the stock of knowledge" (North 1998).

Theories of institutional change, in contrast to impact theory, support a research program to explain the past paths of change and, in the case of formal institutions, to suggest how alternative political rules for making economic rules affect the working rules that might emerge in the future. A research program addressing change in *informal* cultural institutions emphasizes the learning process. North asks: "How comparable is the learning embodied in intentional choice to the selection mechanisms in evolutionary theory? The latter are not informed by the beliefs about the eventual consequences; the former, erroneous though it may be, is driven by perceptions of downstream consequences." A research program is suggested by North's statement that "the origins of some norms, including those embedded in religious beliefs may have had their ultimate source in basic features of primitive agriculture with diverse climatic, soil, and product characteristics imposing organizational imperatives on the players" (North 1997: 5). North suggests that "[w]e need to understand a great deal more about the cumulative learning of a society. The learning process appears to be a function of (i) the way in which a given belief structure filters the information derived from experiences and (ii) the different experiences confronting individuals and societies at different times" (North 1994: 364). Arrow also points to the learning process and says, "An important task of economic analysis today, in conjunction with recent work in psychology and in computer science, is to know better how we come to acquire knowledge and form beliefs and how we act and can act on that knowledge" (Arrow 1989: 22).

A research program addressing *formal* institutional change embodied in law must address competing interests and the rules for making rules. The changes in informal learning noted above are behind the formation of interests. People's perceptions of opportunities that might be better achieved with a change in the working rules drive change. North (with Knight) frames a research program when he observes that

> people are motivated to create institutional forms that will maximize their individual utility. In seeking to do so they will create institutions that lower the transaction costs of those relationships. The degree to which these resulting institutions will actually minimize these costs is, in large part, a function of the competitive pressure exerted by the relevant political and economic markets.
>
> (Knight and North 1997: 214–15)

Here we see a convergence of themes by North and Coase. North says: "Institutions are not necessarily or even usually created to be socially efficient; rather they, or at least the formal rules, are created to serve the interests of those with bargaining power to create new rules" (North 1994: 360–61). This bargaining power is channeled by the political rules for making economic rules. North suggests that "[a] theory of institutional change must embody a theory of the political process as an integral part since it is the polity that specifies and enforces the formal rules" (North 1998). A similar theme in found in Buchanan, who developed a research program in constitutional economics. (More on this below.) Buchanan conceives of a political process in which the individual is envisaging the range of public projects that is likely to be adopted over some future time period, and then deciding on a constitutional fiscal rule as to the taxation system. An institutional economics research program would give citizens information to help make this decision. For Buchanan, "politics is not a process of fact finding or identification of truth but rather of conflict resolution between individuals" (Sandmo 1990: 52; see also Reisman 1990).

Situation, structure, and performance

The construction of any theory whether formal or informal involves a specification of a dependent variable, independent variables, and the expected relationships. The dependent variable is frequently some measure of the performance of an economy. In institutional economics, performance is measured in substantive terms which will be explained below. As noted above, for an impact research program the dependent variable is who gets what, and the explanatory variables are some interaction between the character of goods creating interdependence and the alternative institutional structures. For a change research program, workaday institutions become the dependent variable, and the interaction of alternative constitutional political institutions and the character of goods and groups are the independent variables shaping what workaday institutions emerge. Note that the character of goods variables are common to both impact and change analysis.

Situation and structure

In institutional economics theory, the character of goods and the character of people matter. In North's work he refers to technology, organizational imperatives, and the characteristics of the polity. General purpose goods such as the infamous "widgets" will not do. Simplistic description of how people think will not do (to be explored in a separate section below). First, the character of goods influences the substance of how one person's actions affect another (an aspect of the transaction perspective). North observes that institutions "are different for different industries at a moment of time and change with changes in the above characteristics over time" (North 1997: 3). The situational character of the good involved in a transaction interacts with alternative institutional structures to produce different performances in impact analysis. Similarly, a change in technology alters the character of goods and with the old institution may produce a different result than formerly. This leads to efforts by some groups to reassert the old results with a new institution and efforts by others to keep the new performance or enhance or better take advantage of it. Thus a theory of institutional change can be built.

Some of the most relevant situational variables are goods with incompatible uses, high exclusion costs, marginal cost of another user equals zero, increasing returns, and various kinds of transaction and information costs. Various Nobelists have focused on one or more of these characteristics. Every economist understands the basic facts of resource scarcity and the role of ownership rights in determining who may use and exchange a resource and who cannot. This will be referred to here as goods with incompatible use so that if one person has the opportunity, others do not. This characteristic may be true for both commodities and behaviors. One case will illustrate. Vickrey observes:

> To a very large extent the attributes of social states that are of interest to political, ethical, and social man are indivisible or at least interdependent, to an extent that is at least less true of the mere economic wants. One man's desire for freedom to propagate ideas may run directly counter to another's desire for protection against the intrusion of unwelcome thoughts in a manner that is quite a different matter from the competition for the allocation of resources between satisfying the material wants of two or more individuals.
>
> (Vickrey 1994: 49)

This transactional view is consistent with Coase's view of reciprocal externalities noted above.

An adequate theory should suggest what institutional structures direct the interdependence created by each situation. In the case of *incompatible use goods*, it is straightforward. We speak of ownership by one party versus another. This is involved in land tenure, environmental regulation, opportunities in the radio-magnetic spectrum, the right to contribute to political candidates, labor law, etcetera. Economics has placed much emphasis on gains from trade. The institutionalists ask who has what to trade. Coase says: "It makes little sense for economists to discuss the process of exchange without specifying the institutional setting within which trading takes place, since this affects the incentives to produce and the costs of transacting" (Coase 1992: 718). "The legal system will have a profound effect on the working of the economic system and may in certain respects be said to control it" (1992, 717–18). Others include informal institutions as well.

Goods that are characterized by the *cost of another user being zero* ($MC = 0$) once it is produced have been much studied by James Buchanan. A "pure public good" has zero "distribution costs" (Buchanan 1968). The Nobelists have quite different structural prescriptions for these goods. Buchanan advocates charging different prices to different people with different valuations. Samuelson (1969: 122) derisively calls this policy "interpersonal 'Robin-Hood pricings'." The institutionalists find that no characteristic of a good dictates policy because that requires choosing whose interests count. The prices that people face are as much a part of their real income as is an annual wage. A pricing rule functions as a property right.

Goods whose cost functions exhibit *increasing returns* are much studied.

Vickrey observes that, "[a]s soon as production takes place with durable capital facilities that must be adapted to the needs of an individual firm there may no longer be an effective market for these facilities and a cost of their use during any particular period must be determined by other means" (Vickrey 1994: 198). He adds, "More serious problems arise in the increasingly widespread cases of joint production of several distinguishable products or services." He observes that taxes to subsidize the difference between marginal and average cost are also distorting. A subsidy gives no incentive for management to be efficient. So, he endorses the Ramsey inverse pricing rule, "which says that the margin of price over marginal cost as a percentage of the price shall be inversely proportional to the elasticity of demand" (209). This is supposed to be the least distorting because it affects quantities the least. Institutionalists ask by what principle can we put more of the cost on those with the most inelastic demands, for example, the person who has to fly home for a death in the family? Where there are several products from the same overhead, a more general formulation is one that states that prices shall be such that consumption of the various services would be decreased by a uniform percentage from that which would have been consumed if price had been set at marginal cost and demand had been a linear extrapolation from the neighborhood of the "second-best" point (209–10).

Vickrey examines the possibility that land rents and congestion charges can finance the subsidy. This raises another distributive question of who owns the rents from infrastructure. Coase (1946) objects to marginal cost pricing cum government tax subsidy on income distributional grounds, but ignores that multi-part pricing is inherently an income distribution matter (see Medema 1994). Koopmans called attention to the non-linearities that flow from increasing returns to scale and that bring with them "different problems of institutional frameworks conducive to best allocation" (Koopmans 1974: 265).

Goods which are associated with high *transaction costs* attract increasing attention as a result of the theoretical work of Coase. "A large part of what we think of as economic activity is designed to accomplish what high transaction costs would otherwise prevent or to reduce transaction costs so that individuals can freely negotiate and we can take advantage of that diffused knowledge of which Hayek has told us" (Coase 1992: 716). The alternative structures of hierarchy within firms and of markets are contrasted in terms of reducing transaction costs. North identifies a broader range of institutions that lower the "cost of measuring the valuable attribute of what is being exchanged" (North 1990: 27). He studied the history of the role of medieval trade fairs, ritual, religion, standard weights and measures, as well as third party enforcement and interpretation of necessarily incomplete contracts.

Information costs create many interdependencies. Just one sort is illustrated here, namely that of *fundamental uncertainty* to which no probability can be attached. Many future prices and production functions cannot be predicted and business persons are faced with making decisions without the microeconomic data featured in the text books. Malinvaud (1983) emphasizes profitability as a determinant of investment, but he also emphasizes that the precise meaning of profitability is unclear whenever the future is unclear. The formation and evolution of a firm or other organization cannot be understood as an optimization process when the materials for optimization are not known. Firms form images and conjectures of the future, and the sharing of these has much do to with investment cycles. Leontief (1976) notes that prices can't help much in the formation of expectations of alternative futures. Arrow suggests that the formation of our image of the future is not without sense and reason, "but we are subject to the necessity of oversimplification and to biases built into us. We can effectively use only part of the knowledge that is or could be available to us. But even if we used all we could, our prevision would be deficient because so much can happen that will necessarily be a total surprise" (Arrow 1989: 21).

In Klein's Wharton Econometric Forecasting Model, he found that expectation variables performed better than objective variables. Human cognition matters. "Careful direct measurements of expectations may help in prediction, and if Hyman's results can be extended they can be included on a self generating basis" (Klein 1997: 296). Expectation variables are also important for Coase. "It should be noted that accounting records merely disclose figures relating to past operations. Business decisions depend on estimates of the future" (Coase 1938: 108). Costs and receipts cannot be expressed unambiguously in money terms since courses of action may have advantages which are not monetary in character, because of the existence of uncertainty and because of differences in the point of time at which payments are made and receipts obtained. Myrdal's (1939) early theoretical work on macroeconomics emphasized the role of expectations and how that affected business cycles.

Turning again to structures, impact analysis can be done on alternative institutional structures whether they were explicitly chosen in governmental processes or evolved non-deliberatively from the aggregation of individual practices. For example, the pricing of MC = 0 goods may be the result of a regulatory policy or grow out of business practice and custom. North (1990) describes the history of broad institutional changes that made it possible to trade at a distance with strangers. Some of these were government created and others were changes in informal business practice. The structure of evolutionary processes evolves and has performance consequences.

Structure of formal institutional change

Change analysis can be done where institutions are the dependent variable. For formal institutions, one independent variable is the rules for making rules, that is, the constitutional level. Voting rules (e.g., the shift to universal suffrage and abolition of property requirements) explain some of the differences in formal economic working rules over time. Of course, these structural changes in voting rules themselves must be explained and this may have to do with ideological learning to be explored below. North (1990: 48) observes, "political rules in place lead to economic rules, though the causality runs both ways." "In equilibrium, a given structure of property rights (and their enforcement) will be consistent with a particular set of political rules (and their enforcement)." North argues that "formal political rules, like formal economic rules, are designed to facilitate exchange . . ." (1990: 51). Buchanan and Tullock (1962) have researched the consequences of vote-trading and logrolling.

The role of alternative formal political structures in institutional change is clear. But, what is meant by speaking of the structure wherein the informal institutions form and evolve?

Structure of informal institutional change

A "structure" describes how people are related. We are related in evolutionary processes as much as we are related in political processes. We may not explicitly make the rules for this process, but there are structures nevertheless which evolve and have performance consequences. Hayek was noted for his inquiry into evolutionary processes. "Human groups have been selected for the effects of their habitual practices, effects of which the individuals were not and could not be aware. Customs are mostly group properties, beneficial only if they are common properties of its individual members but referring to reciprocal action" (Hayek 1984: 319). He gives the example of language. "All the paradigms of culturally evolved institutions, morals, exchange, and money refer to such practices whose benefits transcend the individuals who practice them in the particular instances." "Such practices can lead to the formation of orderly structures far exceeding the perception of those whose actions produce them." Hayek argued for the superiority of the informal, unplanned economic institutions that emerged from this informal, unplanned process relative to the more formal political process. The idea that one could do better than "spontaneous order", he called our "fatal conceit." Many institutional theorists object to this, but that is another topic to be taken up in the final section of the chapter below.

Others refer to evolutionary structures. "Social institutions are not chosen, they evolve. No doubt this evolution is subject to selective pressure" (Solow 1992: 272). Buchanan recognizes the role of social learning:

> Individuals must abide by behavioral standards which dictate adherence to law, respect for property and personal rights, fulfillment of contractual agreements, standards which may not, in specific instances, be consistent with objectively measurable economic self-interest. Absent such standards as these, markets will fail even when there are no imperfections of the sort that have attracted the attention of the welfare theorists.
>
> (Buchanan 1979: 210–11)

R. Selten (1991) distinguishes mutation, changes in gene frequencies, cultural transmission, and individual learning, and stresses different time dimensions. North (1994: 362) observes that "[l]earning entails developing a structure by which to interpret the varied signals received by the senses." Part of the structure is genetic, part the result of experience; part physical environment, and part cultural. Categories evolve to organize perceptions. "The capacity to generalize from the particular to the general and to use analogy is a part of this redescription process" (363). This is a source of creative thinking, ideology and belief. "Ideologies are shared frameworks of mental models . . . ." "Institutions are the external (to the mind) mechanisms individuals create to structure and order the environment." Further discussion of evolutionary processes can be found below, when some of the primary relationships among institutional variables are spelled out.

Performance

Institutional economics focuses on substantive performance rather than labeling the result, whatever it is, in abstractions of efficiency and maximization of total production. By substantive I refer to who gets what. Whose ox is gored and whose is fat. Institutional theory is designed to provide information to each person to guide their choice of institutional alternatives to further their self-interest as they see it. Buchanan (1987: 243) suggests that "[e]conomists should cease proffering policy advice as if they were employed by a benevolent despot, and they should look to the structure within which political decisions are made." Buchanan does not construct a welfare economics to calculate economic efficiency, but rather offers institutional alternatives which he hopes will be rather universally adopted in the political process.

Comparative institutional analysis is at the heart of the institutional research program addressing the impact of public laws and organizational formats. "Economic policy", says Coase, "involves a choice among social institutions," with different outcomes (Coase 1988b: 28). I wish I could find a lot of quotations from Nobelists illustrating that their theory and research programs were stated in substantive terms. Perhaps the closest is Kuznets, who was committed to gathering historical data on economic performance. Part of what Coase derisively calls "blackboard economics" reflects thinking in terms of substantive outcomes. He observes that "somehow we don't study the real flow of goods and services. I've always said that the economists invented the widget. They introduced it because it doesn't mean anything" (Coase 1999: 8). This penchant for real flow of goods and services may reflect Coase's early training in business accounting. This accounting approach was also preferred by Hicks, who said he would rather be known as an accountant than for his welfare theory (Klamer 1989). This is also implied in Simon's urging that economists get out of their "armchairs" and study business practices and results in such terms as "average ratio of the salaries of managers to the salaries of their immediate subordinates" (Simon 1978a: 497). Coase

(1999: 4) is critical of much of law and economics, which has prided itself for its ability to provide efficiency criteria for judging alternative laws and procedures. He wants more attention to "the effects of the legal system on the economic system. That is to say, what people have done is to use economics to study the legal system rather than discuss how changes of the law affect the actual way the economic system operates."

The issue is nicely illustrated by the interdependence created by increasing returns discussed above. Vickrey's applied work includes pricing policy for the New York subway. After discussing the usual efficiency theory that argues for marginal cost pricing with the shortfall in revenues being financed by taxes, he observes that taxes to subsidize the difference between marginal and average cost are also distorting (Vickrey 1994: 209). He goes further towards an institutional research program when he acknowledges "the distributional problem of how the fare structure or the alternative sources of revenue will affect the distribution of income among the population of the city. Fourth is the political problem of the degree to which the fare structure is acceptable to riders and taxpayers . . ." (277–78). "Any actual fare structure will reflect a compromise among revenue, mechanical, political, distributional, ecological, and utilization considerations." (So much for straightforward efficiency criteria.) He comes out for higher fares for rush-hour trips over congested routes, but realizes that the shortfall in revenue has to be made up by subsidy, which he thinks can be raised by raising some "appropriate taxes."

Coase makes a distributional objection to marginal cost pricing – "there is a redistribution of income in favour of consumers of goods produced under conditions of decreasing costs" (Coase 1946: 176).

Leontief was speaking of substantive performance when he argued that "a planning process should start out not with the formulation of what theoretical economists refer to as the general 'objective function,' but with elaboration of alternative scenarios each presenting in concrete, non-technical terms one of the several possible future states of the economy" (Leontief 1976: 34). He illustrates: "A friend invites me for dinner in a first-class restaurant and asks that I supply him with a general description of my tastes so that he could order the food in advance. Unable to describe my – or anyone else's – tastes in general terms, I prefer to see the menu and then select, without hesitation, the combination of dishes that I like" (33). What analysis has to offer is not a way to maximize, but rather a spelling out of alternatives for choice. The latter allows a debate over preferences and whose preferences count rather than this being assumed away. "Public discussion and democratic choice among the available alternatives will be possible only if each of them is presented in concrete tangible details rather than in such summary terms as the per capita GNP, the average rate of unemployment, or the annual rate of growth of the 'implicit price deflator'" (Leontief 1976: 35).

Distributional performance is of major interest to institutional theorists. This is illustrated by Meade (1993: 8), who notes three forms of redistributive policy. The first two involve redistribution of unearned income from property: (1) "Property-Owning-Democracy" operates through "measures devised to increase the widespread and more equally distributed ownership of private wealth and so of the income received from holdings of wealth." (2) "Social Ownership of Property" arranges "for a considerable proportion of what would have been privately owned wealth to pass into ownership of the State; and the income accruing from such property can be distributed in some forms of social benefit payable to the generality of citizens without regard to their individual earnings from work." (3) "Welfare state method . . . converts income from pay into income unrelated to pay by raising the rate of tax on existing incomes and using the revenue to pay out to the generality of the citizens social benefits of one kind or another . . . ."

The acknowledgment of competing interests and conflict is illustrated by Kuznets' observations of the failure of many poor countries to take advantage of new technologies. New institutions to realize technological potential are not automatic, "the difficulty of making the institutional and ideological transformations needed to convert the new large potential of modern technology into economic growth in the relatively short period since the late eighteenth century limited the spread of the system." "Moreover, obstacles to such transformations were, and still are being, imposed on the less developed countries by the policies of the developed countries" (Kuznets 1973: 250).

Behavioral regularities as part of situation

The way institutions work is not only a function of the characteristics of goods, but also the characteristics of people. Some theory has made the simplifying assumption that consumers have well-formed, stable preference maps and are rationally calculating the choices that follow from putting prices to these maps. Ditto for firms putting production functions and prices of inputs and outputs together. But this will not do for institutional and behavioral economics. The importance of behavioral regularities deserves a separate treatment here. One of the key set of variables is related to bounded rationality, a term coined by Herbert Simon. The human mind has limited information processing capacity and simply cannot calculate all human actions. "The theory of bounded rationality does not permit all one's theorems to flow from a few *a priori* truths. Fixing the postulates of such a theory requires close, almost microscopic, study of how human beings actually behave" (Simon 1992: 266). Humans accommodate to their limited information processing capacity by quickly fitting impressions into boxes with behavior attached. Simon refers to standard operating procedures, rules of thumb, and so on. Simon acknowledges that "[t]he principal forerunner of a behavioral theory of the firm is the tradition usually called Institutionalism." "Commons' ideas . . . provided me with many insights in my initial studies of organizational decision making" (Simon 1979: 499).

Coase goes even further. "There is no reason to suppose that most human beings are engaged in maximizing anything unless it be unhappiness, and even this with incomplete success" (Coase 1988b: 4). He suggests that analysts try to understand "learning rules" and "the way in which we translate experience into expectations" (130).

Norms of behavior get formed from conscious reason, but also from the unconscious reinforcement of experiential feedback. Solow says, "I do not know how such norms get established, historically speaking, but once established they draw their force from shared values and social approbation and disapprobation, not from calculation" (Solow 1990: 49). "We do things because they are the right thing to do, not because we have reckoned all the consequences" (43). Arrow notes that "we are subject to the necessity of oversimplification and to biases built into us. We can effectively use only part of the knowledge that is or could be available to us. But even if we used all we could, our prevision would be deficient because so much can happen that will necessarily be a total surprise" (Arrow 1989: 21). "Economic agents do not and indeed cannot perform all the calculations demanded by the theory. To anticipate prices rationally, they have in effect to understand a correct model of the economy and use it to project future prices . . ." (20). This voids the supposed advantage of prices as reducing the amount of information needed for decisions.

The evolution of preferences is an empirical matter. Arrow argues that, "There is nothing in economic theory which specifies that tastes remain unchanged . . ." (Arrow 1986a: 321). North (1990: 84) observes that "changing relative prices play some role in changes in taste." Preferences are learned and resources can be devoted to their change as well as fulfilling them.

Maurice Allais says: "I think that men are motivated by their interests, their prejudices, their passions, and that logic, even scientific, really has no hold over what they do" (Allais 1992: 21). "Whether dealing with theoretical economic analysis or applied economics, consideration of human psychology has always appeared fundamental to me" (22). Experience and experiments have shown many times that people make inconsistent choices between probability weighted outcomes. This has become known as the Allais Paradox. Allais himself says, "this paradox is only apparent, and is the reflection of a fundamental aspect of reality: the preference for security in the neighborhood of certainty" (Allais 1979: 441). He did applied work for the Algerian Office of Mining Research, where the problem was to make "a reasonable compromise between the mathematical expectation of the gains that might be expected and the probability of ruin" (451). Mining exploration is like "a lottery with the tickets costing several hundred million and prizes of several hundred billion francs . . ." (451). If you could explore long enough, you could get your money back handsomely, but ran the risk of ruin before. Allais observes a subjective distortion of objective probabilities. For example, "a gain whose monetary value may be ten times that of another may be only worth twice as much, or even less, in psychological terms" (Allais 1979: 47). "It would be wrong to consider a game as psychologically attractive if the mathematical expectation of the monetary values involved is positive" (50).

Arrow (1982) also questions the neoclassical attempt to handle uncertainty by attaching subjective probability and use of the Bayesian probability calculus. Agents do not typically make decisions consistent with this approach. North discusses the role of ideology filling the gaps in uncertainty. Knight and North (1997) approvingly quote Hutchins, who says that to understand cognition one observes that "culture, context and history . . . are fundamental aspects of human cognition and cannot be comfortably integrated into a perspective that privileges abstract properties of isolated individual minds" (Hutchins 1995: 354). The basic task is one of "locating cognitive activity in context, where context is not a fixed set of surrounding conditions but a wider dynamical process of which the cognition of an individual is only a part" (Hutchins 1995: xiii). By doing so, we can "show that human cognition is not just influenced by culture and society, but that it is in a very fundamental sense a cultural and social process" (xiv). Institutional theory in relating alternative institutional structures to situations of interdependence takes people as it finds them. The theory is open to the possibility that the analyst's objective calculation of advantage is not the basis for actual behavior.

Symbols, signals and communication

Institutions link transacting parties and it is communication that provides the linkage. The content of this communication provides an important set of variables for institutional theory at least since Commons. Among the relevant variables are prices, quantities, administrative orders, sanctions, and observations of others. Simon notes: "The usual argument for markets, as in the well-known 1945 paper of von Hayek, is that they simplify the decision process by reducing the need of each actor to know what the other actors are doing or what situations confront them" (Simon 1991: 39). "Prices perform their informational function when they are known or reasonably predictable. Uncertain prices produced by unpredictable shifts in a system reduce the ability of actors to respond rationally" (40). Systems in equilibrium with perfect knowledge have little relevance for issues of economic organization. "Coordination by adjustment of quantities is probably a far more important mechanism from a day-to-day standpoint, and in many circumstances will do a better job of allocation than coordination by prices" (40). "Quantities of goods sold and inventories, not prices, provide the information for coordinating these systems. The Leontief input–output models, with exogenous vectors of final demands, are examples . . ." (40). Simon observes that "the assertion that markets permit each firm to do its business with little knowledge of its partners is a fiction" (41). A great deal of detailed information is exchanged. "In construction, in heavy industry, in manufacturing involving high technology, and in other areas, contracting partners carry on communication at a level comparable to the levels observed between departments of a firm" (41).

Use of prices and markets is not costless. This was Coase's fundamental insight. He suggested that "the distinguishing mark of the firm is the supersession of the price mechanism" (Coase 1937: 389). Coase hypothesizes that a firm (organization) will emerge where a series of short-term market contracts would be unsatisfactory. The entrepreneur can make a single general employment contract, and then tune it over time with commands as the environment changes. Coase says: "A firm, therefore, consists of the system of relationships which comes into existence when the direction of resources is dependent on an entrepreneur" (393).

For Coase, the structural problem is to discover price among a large number of factor owners under changing conditions. The firm emerges if it economizes on transaction costs. The role of transaction costs for North is somewhat different. His emphasis is on the historic problem of how to facilitate trade among strangers at a distance. This is largely an assurance problem even if price is discovered (North 1993). He found that both formal enforcement of property rights and informal evolution of norms of behavior played a role. Wallis and North have calculated a time series of transaction costs and found them constantly increasing (Wallis and North 1986). They include marketing and legal costs. This suggests that transaction costs are not something simply to be eliminated, but are deliberately created to provide information and direct coordination.

Simon provides still another perspective on transaction costs and organizations. The successful organization creates a culture of learned habit and loyalty wherein calculation of individual advantage is suspended in favor of firm goals. He is critical of the Coasian research program.

> The idea behind these ideas is that a proper explanation of an economic phenomenon will reduce it to maximizing behavior of parties who are engaged in contracting . . . . The terms of the contract will be influenced by the access of the parties to information, by the costs of negotiating, and by the opportunities for cheating. Access to information, negotiation costs, and opportunities for cheating are most often treated as exogenous variables that do not themselves need to be explained . . . they even introduce a sort of bounded rationality into the behavior, with the exogeneity of the limits of rationality allowing the theory to remain within the magical domains of utility and profit maximization.
>
> (Simon 1991: 26)

"All phenomena are to be explained by translating them into (or deriving them from) market transactions based on negotiated contracts . . ." (26). While the theory is compatible with neoclassical theory, "it does greatly multiply the number of auxiliary exogenous assumptions that are needed for the theory to work" (27).

Coase recognizes that the firm can reduce some transaction costs, but can also create new problems in their place as it grows (Coase 1937: 394–95). The entrepreneur is thus balancing the costs of internal communication with the costs of market coordination. Alternative forms of internal organization constitute a major research program for Simon. He applies his bounded rationality conception to the problem of choosing organizational structure. Large firms have no single entrepreneur with perfect information on the pay-offs to organizational alternatives within the firm. Shall the firm organize by regions, functions, products, etcetera? The structure within the firm affects performance as does the alternative of hierarchy or market. Top management is negotiating among themselves and is dependent on information flows within the firm to assess organizational as well as production alternatives.

Technology

The study of technology and its role in economic development is an old institutional research program, at least since Veblen. But it took Robert Solow to bring it into mainstream economics with a formal model showing that technological development will be a fundamental ingredient in economic growth. Solow puzzled over the small part of growth attributable to capital measured in dollars. A dollar invested in an old machine is simply not the same as a dollar invested in a new improved one. So he came up with the idea of "embodiment." Technology is embodied in new capital equipment. "Therefore, the effectiveness of innovation in increasing output would be paced by the rate of gross investment" (Solow 1988: 315). Formal models demand numerical data but we have no way to summarize real capital goods in an aggregate number. Institutionalists were content to work with what they had and assembled stories of individual technologies and their impact. But others would not recognize the role of technology unless they had a theory that would utilize available numbers such as Solow's rate of gross investment and a story linking it to the quality and size of the capital stock. Solow says this makes common sense, but, in practice, Denison found this had no explanatory value. In retrospect, Solow said:

> To be faithful to my own methodological precepts, however, I should remind you that other interpretations are also possible. For example, it could be the case that some countries are better able to exploit the common pool of technological progress than others, for reasons that have nothing to do with the rate of capital formation; but in exactly those technologically progressive countries investment is most profitable, so naturally the rate of investment is higher. Or else rapid technical progress [and] high investment could both be the result of some third factor, like the presence of conditions that encourage entrepreneurial activity. High investment and fast technical progress will then go together.
>
> (315)

A growth model with capital measured in terms of the rate of gross invest-ment has no institutional content. But when you speak of how one country is better able to exploit the common pool of technological progress than others, you are talking institutions.

Arrow observes that technology is not only embodied in machines, but in people's heads. Arrow quotes Veblen approvingly:

> Veblen did not deny that the capital goods are more significant in modern economies, but, "the commonplace knowledge of ways and means, the accumulated experience of mankind, is still transmitted in and by the body of the community at large; but, for practical purposes, the advanced "state of the industrial arts" has enabled the owners of the goods to corner the wisdom of the ancients and the accumulated experience of the race.
>
> (Arrow 1994: 6)

Arrow articulates institutional theory with its emphasis on distribution. Arrow notes that Hayek (1948: Ch. 4) emphasizes the dispersed and tacit nature of knowledge but that he used this in his argument for the weakness of central planning, which got in the way of his "understanding of the genera-tion of knowledge" (Arrow 1994: 6). "Hayek tends to minimize the role of scientific knowledge and does not really discuss technological knowledge at all, a good deal of which is transmittable to others" (6). Arrow calls this "reproducible knowledge."

Institutions are more explicit independent variables in explaining *techno-logical change* itself. Arrow says knowledge is acquired by observing nature and others. "Technical and other knowledge exists in social form: books or universities . . ." (Arrow 1994: 7). With regard to scientific research agendas, institutional theory also adds formal and informal institutions variables to the usual cost–benefit analyses of pay-offs to different lines of research. There are fads in research as there are in consumer goods, not to mention the formal public institutions involved in how research is financed. Without attention to beliefs and ideology it would be hard to explain the investment in space research or one medical problem versus another (North 1997). Kuznets proposed a research program conceptualizing a time pattern, a life-cycle model of a major innovation in which the time sequence of effects could be outlined. (Kuznets 1972: 450). This would require a discussion of the causes and sources of technological innovation.

Arrow notes that various models emphasize the *diffusion of technology*. Diffusion involves cognition and framing, and is much more than objective calculations of net returns by entrepreneurs. Theory also addresses the adjustments complementary to technological change. Kuznets says,

> here we are concerned with requirements that involve changes in insti-tutions, and in the responses of participants in the production

process – changes needed to provide the proper institutional channels and forms for the new technology and to supply the workers and entrepreneurs to man it. These changes are called for because the old institutional channels are geared to an older technology and are not suitable for the new . . .

(Kuznets 1972: 440)

Kuznets emphasizes the potential for positive and negative effects of technology. "This implies that the elimination of these effects lies in the province of the social structure" (450).

Time and expectations

Time is of the essence in institutional theory. A time subscript is often specified for many variables. It is implicit in the discussions above of preference, technology, and institutional change. It is central to decisions made now in expectation of the future. Adjustments are not instantaneous. Time defines historical research. North (1994: 359–60), in arguing that institutions matter, observes that "[t]ime as it relates to economic and societal change is the dimension in which the learning process of human beings shapes the way institutions evolve." "The learning embodied in individuals, groups, and societies . . . is cumulative through time and passed on intergenerationally by the culture of a society." The role of time in institutional theory is perhaps best understood as the relationships among the variables outlined above are specified. This is our next topic.

Relationships among variables

Theory suggests the relationship between and among the variables identified above. In formal models, relationships are specified in expected signs on the variables, whether the variables are related linearly or as complex systems with feedback, path dependence, and lags. Other relationships are specified as causal and the expected order in time. Equivalents of these relationships are also present in informal models and stories. Some systems exhibit deterministic equilibrium characteristics. Institutional economics emphasizes the many systems which are evolving and emergent.

The "Situation, Structure, Performance" framework outlined above is one way to specify relationships among the variables noted here. Situation refers to a collection of variables that describe attributes of goods which create human interdependence that is given order by institutional structures. Situation also includes attributes of people, especially the way the brain works. The framework specifies different dependent and independent variables depending on whether the question is one of impact or change. Different independent variables are specified for formal and informal institutional change. The theory explicitly recognizes opportunities for cooperation and for conflict among different interests. Performance and whose interests count is, importantly, a matter of how institutions give order to interdependencies.

Institutional theory takes the root of the word economics seriously in emphasizing general interdependence. Myrdal (1956: 16) states:

> The underlying fact is the existence of such an interdependence between all the factors in a social system that any change in any one of the factors will cause changes in the others; these secondary changes are generally of a nature to support the initial change; through a process of interactions, where change in one factor continuously will be supported by reactions of the other factors, the whole system will have been given momentum to move in the direction of the primary change, though much further.

Arrow has been honored for his general equilibrium theory. In his own assessment of his contributions, he says that the main implication of this formal modeling is to demonstrate general interdependence. The importance of proving the possible existence of general equilibrium is in "recognizing that a particular economic change will have remote repercussions that may be more significant than the initial change" (Breit and Spencer 1995: 54).

The relationship specified among the variables in an institutional model is that of an open-ended process rather than an equilibrium. Koopmans (1974: 328) argues that "the notion of a process does not presuppose the approach to an equilibrium." "In a world of continuing but only dimly foreseeable change in technology and in preferences, the notion of equilibrium disappears, but that of an adjustment process remains." On the consumer side, he regards preferences as changeable. Hayek rejects equilibrium theory and gives emphasis to problems of information. Hayek in latter writings came close to the idea of the individual as both producer and product of institutions.

The above introduces the general specification of relationships among variables. More detail can be seen if we focus on three processes: (1) feedback, learning, and evolution; (2) reaction functions; and (3) non-marginal relationships.

Feedback, learning and evolution

When a pendulum is set in motion it eventually returns to its original equilibrium and resting place. The forces which act upon it are unchanged by anything the pendulum can do. For short run impact analysis, preferences are taken as given. Take for example the case of a high exclusion cost good. Institutional theory suggests that the amount of the payments/contributions to its production is a function of alternative institutions (market and government tax including sanctions). Other relevant variables with a positive sign are social capital and group solidarity. The size of the group has a negative sign. Preferences for the good are taken as given, as is the technology which makes the cost of exclusion high. The short run impact analysis predicts the amount of contributions if the institution is changed from a market to a tax. It predicts the number of free riders and the number of unwilling riders (people who pay more than what the product is worth to them.)

But in the longer run change analysis, preferences and technology can change. The pendulum can feed back on the forces that set it in motion. There can be a feedback from the performance which will cause people to work to change the institution again. A new technology can change high exclusion cost broadcast TV into low exclusion cost cable or satellite TV, for example. Some of the effort to change formal institutions is conscious of predicted results. The evolution of informal institutions such as social capital and habits of contribution to social causes can occur without any explicit understanding of the eventual result. North (1998: 6) argues that "[t]he inspiration for a dynamic model must come from some variant of evolutionary reasoning." He asks an empirical question: "How comparable is the learning embodied in intentional choice to the selection mechanism in evolutionary theory? The latter are not informed by beliefs about the eventual consequences; the former, erroneous though it may be, is driven by perceptions of downstream consequences" (13).

Institutional change theory is marked by institutions being both a dependent and independent variable (overdetermination). North observes that "[t]he process of change results from a continuous change in that reality which results in changing the perceptions which in turn induce the players to modify or alter the structure which in turn leads to changes in that reality – an ongoing process." He sees this in evolutionary terms. "This institutional framework has evolved over many generations, reflecting, as Hayek reminds us, the trial and error process which has sorted out those behavioral patterns that have worked from those that have failed" (North 1997a: 11). But of course, failure depends, in part, on where you want to go and who gets to decide. A dynamic is created when:

> The perceptions of political and economic entrepreneurs change reflecting ubiquitous competition amongst organizations with changes in relative prices, other new information leading such entrepreneurs, given their beliefs and the constraints imposed by the existing scaffold (not to mention the standard economic constraints) to modify or alter institutions to improve their competitive positions. The result is to alter the "REALITY" of the economic system which in turn will lead to altered perceptions and BELIEFS of the system which in turn will lead to further INSTITUTIONAL change in an endless process of societal change.
>
> (11)

Learning is one way to describe altered perceptions and beliefs. The environment is always feeding back on the actors and reinforcing certain behaviors and extinguishing others. "Learning entails developing a structure by which to interpret the varied signals received by the senses" (North 1994:

362). Learning turns the human pendulum into a destroyer of equilibrium. "Statements about disequilibrium, in Hayek's view, are necessarily empirical statements 'about how experience creates knowledge,' and an assertion to a tendency toward equilibrium is an empirical not a logical proposition" (Langlois 1991: 130). Institutional theory is open to non-equilibrating evolutionary processes.

One of the dominant relationships among variables is given by path dependence. "Path dependence means that the degrees of freedom that policy makers possess to alter the direction of economies are constrained by the institutional matrix and the belief systems of the players." North says, "What constrains the choices of the players is a belief system reflecting the past – the cultural heritage of a society – and its gradual alteration reflecting the current experiences as filtered (and therefore interpreted) by that belief system" (North 1997: 229).

One evolving relationship among variables can be specified as cumulative and circular causation, already briefly referred to above. Myrdal (1994) observed that African-Americans had a set of behaviors that resulted in low incomes which fed back and reinforced the previous behaviors. For example, low savings lead to low investments in education and low incomes, making it again hard to save. These behaviors in turn contributed to racial prejudice and helped whites rationalize habits and institutions of discrimination. Myrdal generalized this relationship among variables where an initial change in an independent variable impacts a dependent variable, and then the dependent variable feeds back on the formerly independent variable, causing it to change further in the direction of its original movement. Circularity is at the heart of cumulativeness, for if A caused B, but B had no feedback to A, then once the force of A is exhausted there would be equilibrium. But with feedback, the system is open-ended and evolves. It can be a vicious downward spiral or a positive process of economic growth. An example of the latter is when economies of scale lower prices and expand the market which feeds back allowing still further economies of scale to be implemented (or the profits thereof perhaps invested in technology development, creating still further economies of scale) (Myrdal 1968: Vol. III, App. 2).

North extends Myrdal's concept to what is now known as path dependence and applies it to understand institutional change such as the Northwest Ordinance in the US. "The increasing-returns characteristics stemmed from the fact that the structure of property rights, inheritance laws, and political decision rules in the territories was derived from the act and in turn spawned organizations and (political and economic entrepreneurs) who induced marginal alterations in the act downstream" (North 1990: 98).

Reaction functions

One kind of feedback process that links institutional variables is the reaction function. Part of the situation environment which an actor evaluates is formed by the choices of others. For example, the demand function facing a firm may not be given determining marginal revenue but is influenced by other firms' reactions to the firm's price and output decisions. "Game theory addresses itself to the 'outguessing' problem that arises whenever an economic actor takes into account possible reactions to his own decisions of the other actors" (Simon 1979: 505). The main product "has been to demonstrate quite clearly that it is virtually impossible to define an unambiguous criterion of rationality for this class of situations . . ." (505–506). Simon (1978b: 9) elaborates by saying: "For situations where the rationality of an action depends upon what others (who are also striving to be rational) do again, no consensus has been reached as to what constitutes optimal behavior. This is one of the reasons I have elsewhere called imperfect competition 'the permanent and ineradicable scandal of economic theory.'" He finds "rational expectation" models lacking and says a better term would be "consistent expectations" (10). Too much effort has been given "to find substantive criteria broad enough to extend the concept of rationality beyond the boundaries of static optimization under certainty" (10). He, of course, would prefer attention to how decisions are made rather than what decisions are made. Arrow (1986b) makes this same point and asks how to be rational in an irrational world, and concludes that rationality is not the property of the individual alone, but is an institutional phenomenon.

The reaction function depends in part on learning. North (1998: 12) is critical of game theory because it lacks a description of the players' reasoning processes, that is, how they learn. But he says there is something deeper than learning. This involves belief in theories in the face of uncertainty (nothing already existing to learn). Probability distributions do not seem relevant in this case. Still, "human beings do construct theories all the time in conditions of pure uncertainty" (12). We may call these myths, taboos, prejudices, and simply half-baked ideas. North suggests that the central question is: "How and why they do develop theories in the face of pure uncertainty" (13). Klein (1997: 293) echos this thought when he notes that "[t]he missing link is an explanation of the generating process of the expectations themselves."

A non-marginal and non-linear economics

In general, institutions change slowly. Yet, occasionally, there are big changes, or failure to make a big change results in no change in performance. Myrdal conceptualized the process of development as a social system with six categories: output and incomes; conditions of production; levels of consumption; attitudes toward life and work (North calls it beliefs); institutions; and policies. He investigated when a change in one of the categories would cause a change in the others, in the same direction or not (Reynolds 1974: 1868). The possibility of upward movement was not assured. To overcome negative feedback may require a "big push" on several parts of the system (non-marginal change). Myrdal (1968: 1899) observed that "underdeveloped countries cannot rely on a 'gradualist' approach." Further, "functional relationships of the interacting variables are not linear" (1875).

Non-marginal situations are commonplace. Simon was particularly interested in non-marginal changes such as environmental disturbances so large that the classical solutions are not an adequate approximation. Buchanan objects to Pigovian policy of equating social and private marginal cost because he argues that the value placed on the clean air by the housewife cannot be known objectively since she can't be given a competitively marginal choice to trade off money and air – she can only adjust to the non-marginal quantity available to all. "Smoke damage cannot be even remotely approximated by the estimated outlays that would be necessary to produce air 'cleanliness.'" "Clean air cannot be exchanged or traded among separate persons" (Buchanan 1969: 72).

A marginal change is often defined as one with no income effects. But many challenges to existing institutions do have income effects. For example, when considering the impact of a particular environmental interest group being declared the owner of a resource use opportunity, a difference between willingness to pay and willingness to sell is observed. The resource bulks so large in the wealth of the parties that there is an income effect.

Value circularity and welfare economics

In discussing the situation, structure and performance relationships above it was emphasized that performance was measured in substantive terms of who gets what rather than in some summary abstraction such as maximizing total output or efficiency or Pareto-optimality. Institutional theory provides no internal, independent criteria to label one set of institutions generally better than another. This must be worked out in the political process as interests contend to be the one that counts. Coase has been cited above for some of his contributions to institutional theory. There is one sense in which he is very neoclassical. He would allocate property rights so that the value of production is maximized.[1] But Simon notes a value circularity problem here. "The institutional, political decision cannot be made on the basis of market criteria, since until it has been made, the domain of applicability of the market criteria has not been defined" (Simon 1982: 4). "Economic choices take place in an environment of political institutions and not vice versa" (4). Rights affect prices so that using existing prices to compare alternative institutions is circular. Economics and law (politics) form a nexus and economics is no independent judge of correct politics.

Buchanan expresses a related point. The set of contracts that will emerge depends on the institutional structure of society. This

> suggests only that any allocation of resources that is to be classified as 'efficient' depends necessarily on the institutional structure within which

resource utilization-valuation decisions are made. This implication creates no difficulty for the subjectivist-contractarian who does not acknowledge the uniqueness of the resource allocation that is properly classified to be efficient.

(Buchanan 1984: 157)

A hallmark of institutional theory is that efficiency is relative to the starting place of who is a buyer and who a seller of interdependent opportunities.

Buchanan (1984) recommends that the economist see himself as someone who proposes policy changes in the form of hypotheses to be subjected to the empirical test of political approval. Many institutional theorists would agree though disagree on the rules for approval. Arrow (1963: 119) dismisses unanimity as the ideal criterion of choice by observing that "under such a rule, the status quo is a highly privileged alternative." (It would seem to run foul of his non-dictatorship criterion.) Institutional theory recognizes conflicts of interest and investigates how institutions allocate power so that one interest or another counts. Arrow does not speak of power, but it is implicit when he refuses to privilege the *status quo*. Paul Samuelson also has dismissed Pareto-optimality in a critique of Richard Musgrave: "He tacitly lapses into the cardinal sin of the narrow 'new welfare' economists: 'If you can't get (or even define!) that maximum of a social welfare function, settle for Pareto-optimality,' as if that were second-best or even 99th best" (Samuelson 1969: 105).

Evolutionary models have been emphasized above. What do they imply about optimality? Some try to read into evolution a kind of legitimation for whatever exists – only the best institutions survive. This is not the implication of institutional theory. Paul Samuelson (1978: 174) argues that various maximization concepts such as "[f]itness are redundant ways of describing the positivistic fact that Nature's cookie sometimes crumbles in such a way as to make certain patterns recurrent and viable, while certain other patterns are only transiently persistent." "The present analysis seems to emerge with a debunking indictment of the claims for maximizing and teleological constructs in biology, evolution, sociobiology, and imperialist-economics . . ." (182). He quotes R. Lewontin with approval: "'The concept of adaptation implies that there is a preexistent form, problem or ideal to which things are fitted by a dynamical process.' The word 'preexistent' can be made to lack force in this argument" (182). This view is consistent with the evolutionary interdependence relationships specified above, in which neither individual, institutions, nor technology is prior.

Neither is there any implied legitimacy to be derived from observing that a particular institution serves a particular function. Food production institutions may be necessary for survival. But Simon reasons that this does not legitimate any particular institution, "when the system is complex and its environment continually changing . . . there is no assurance that the system's momentary position will lie anywhere near a point of equilibrium, whether local or global. Hence, all that can be concluded from a functional argument is that certain characteristics (the satisfaction of certain functional requirements in a particular way) are consistent with the survival and further development of the system, not that these same requirements could not be satisfied in some other way" (Simon 1978b: 4).

It is tempting to try to go from observable facts to policy decisions without the mess of working out value conflicts in the political process. Many would like to have a welfare economics that could instruct the political process. One such attempt is contingent valuation of non-marketed goods which hopes to discover the real demand curve even if markets cannot elicit it. Arrow asserts that "[t]he demand curve should not be considered as some kind of 'reality' to which we should hope to aspire. . . . demand curves themselves are problematic" (Arrow 1986: 181). The value that is elicited is affected by the vehicle for elicitation. "It is a fact that WTP (willingness to pay) depends on who gets the 'P', and on what that means" (183). He finds nothing remarkable in the fact that "taxing according to one principle, like use permits, gives a different result entirely than putting a general price, for example a bonus tax, on the public at large . . ." (184). He notes that willingness to pay is very skewed with a few having high values, implying the appropriateness of benefit taxation. Practitioners want to design vehicles that will not bias the findings. He asks: "What, even ideally do we mean by accuracy? What is the reference? What is the reality to which we refer?" (184):

> All the concepts of marginalism, are counterfactual statements. They are statements comparing something to what would be true if it were not so. "If you produce one unit less," or statements of that kind – "if your income was one unit higher." There is a certain impalpable air of alternatives that are not being realized in some sense. Sometimes very occasionally, nature will supply you with that experiment . . . but in general there is a problem of this nature, and I don't have any answer to it.
>
> (185)

Other institutionalists have an answer to a slightly different question – the reference point is always moving/learning/creating and is itself a matter of institutional choice. Institutional theory then provides no general answer to the question of which institution is best. It does try to warrant an association between an institution which serves one interest group better than another.

Conclusion

The point of this chapter is not to argue that all of the Nobelists cited are institutionalists. Some have described themselves as such and others have not. Many who have been cited as supporting a key ingredient of institutional theory do not support all of them and, in fact, may reject some. The point is not even to make an *ex cathedra* argument that if a Nobel Prize winner says something, it must be true. One point is simply to note that reputable economists use institutional concepts. This review makes it harder to dismiss institutional economics as something practiced by a few at the margin of the profession. But most important, the point is to pull together what is otherwise seen as a set of disparate unconnected concepts into what begins to look like an integrated paradigm that can be used to address a wide variety of questions. North says he is searching for "an analytical framework" comparable to general equilibrium theory in its ability to organize our thoughts. I believe it is amongst us.

The institutional economics theory which emerges from this selection from the Nobelists is based on the best understanding we have of how the brain works, including bounded rationality and learning of preferences. It includes both deliberative, calculated choice and non-deliberative actions and habit. It is an economics marked by non-equilibrium, non-marginal, and non-linear relationships of evolution, and concern for feedback loops and learning over time. It is characterized by cumulative causation, adjustment processes, and path dependence. The basic unit of observation is the transaction. The communications among the parties not only include prices, but also other signals including quantities, orders, and persuasion. It addresses expectations, especially those widely shared in the face of fundamental uncertainty. The transaction view exposes the reciprocal and ubiquitous character of externalities. A situation, structure, and performance paradigm unites the study of both institutional impact and change. The variables describing the characteristics of goods and groups create human interdependence, which affects the impact of alternative workaday institutions as well as the process of institutional change. These variables include incompatibility, exclusion costs, economies of scale, marginal cost of another user being zero, and others. Institutional economics avoids the value circularity problem and does not foreclose the political and cultural working out of whose interests count. By recognizing that efficiency is not unique, but is derived from a particular set of institutions, the application of institutional theory promises to inform different groups of how their interests will be substantively served. If the reader now says that all of this has been incorporated into mainstream economics, then the mainstream has become institutional economics. If not, then there is work still to be done in the tradition of the man for whom this *festschrift* is organized.

Note

1   For more comparisons of Coase and other institutionalists, see Medema (1996).

References

Allais, M. (1979) "The So-Called Allais Paradox and Rational Decisions Under Uncertainty," in M. Allais and O. Hagen (eds) *Expected Utility Hypotheses and the Allais Paradox*, Dordrecht: D. Reidel Publishing.

—— (1992) "The Passion for Research," in M. Szenberg (ed.) *Eminent Economists: Their Life Philosophies*, Cambridge: Cambridge University Press, 17–41.

Arrow, K. J. (1963) *Social Choice and Individual Values*, 2nd edn., New Haven, CT: Yale University Press.

—— (1974) *The Limits of Organization*, New York: W. W. Norton.

—— (1982) "Risk Perception in Psychology and Economics," *Economic Inquiry* 20, 1: 1–9.

—— (1986a) "Comments by Professor Kenneth Arrow," in R. G. Cummings et al. (eds) *Valuing Environmental Goods*, Totowa, NJ: Rowman and Allanheld.

—— (1986b) "Rationality of Self and Others in an Economic System," *Journal of Business* 59, 4: S385–99.

—— (1989) In Sichel, W. (ed.) *The State of Economic Science: Views of Six Nobel Laureates*, Kalamazoo, MI: Upjohn Institute for Employment Research.

—— (1994) "Methodological Individualism and Social Knowledge," *American Economic Review* 84, 2: 1–9.

Breit, W., and R. W. Spencer (eds) (1995) *Lives of the Laureates: Thirteen Nobel Economists*, 3rd edn., Cambridge, MA: MIT Press.

Buchanan, J. M. (1968) *The Demand and Supply of Public Goods*, Chicago, IL: Rand McNally.

—— (1969) *Cost and Choice*, Chicago, IL: Markham.

—— (1979) *What Should Economists Do?* Indianapolis, IN: Liberty Press.

—— (1984) "Rights, Efficiency and Exchange: The Irrelevance of Transaction Costs," in *Liberty, Market and State*, Brighton: Wheatsheaf Books, 153–68.

—— (1987) *Economics: Between Predictive Science and Moral Philosophy*, College Station, TX: Texas A & M University Press.

Buchanan, J. M., and G. Tullock (1962) *The Calculus of Consent*, Ann Arbor, MI: University of Michigan Press.

Coase, R. (1937) "The Nature of the Firm," *Economica* n.s. 4: 386–405.

—— (1938) "Business Organization and the Accountant," *The Accountant* (October–December).

—— (1946) "The Marginal Cost Controversy," *Economica* n.s. 14: 169–82.

—— (1977) "Economics and Contiguous Disciplines," in M. Perlman (ed.) *Organization and Retrieval of Economic Knowledge*, Boulder, CO: Westview.

—— (1988a) "Blackmail," *Virginia Law Review* 74: 655–76.

—— (1988b) *The Firm, the Market, and the Law*, Chicago, IL: University of Chicago Press.

—— (1992) "The Institutional Structure of Production," *American Economic Review* 82, 4: 713–19.

—— (1999) "Special Interview with Ronald Coase," *ISNIE Newletter* (International Society for New Institutional Economics) 2 (Spring): 3–10.

Hayek, F. (1948) *Individualism and the Economic Order*, Chicago, IL: University of Chicago Press.

—— (1973) *Law, Legislation, and Liberty*, London: Routledge and Kegan Paul.

—— (1984) "The Origins and Effects of Our Morals: A Problem for Science," in C. Nishiyama and K. R. Leube (eds) *The Essence of Hayek*, Stanford, KY: Hoover Institution Press, 318–30.

Hutchins, E. (1995) *Cognition in the Wild*, Cambridge, MA: MIT Press.

Klamer, A. (1989) "An Accountant Among Economists: Conversation with Sir John Hicks," *Journal of Economic Perspectives* 3 (Fall): 167–80.

Klein, L. R. (1997) "Anticipation Variables in Macroeconomic Models," in E. Marwah (ed.) *Selected Papers of Lawrence R. Klein: Theoretical Reflections and Econometric Applications*, Singapore: World Scientific Publishing.

Knight, J., and D. North (1997) "Explaining Economic Change: The Interplay Between Cognition and Institutions," *Legal Theory* 3: 211–26.

Koopmans, T. C. (1974) "Is the Theory of Competitive Equilibrium With It?' *American Economic Review* 64 (September): 325–29.

Kuznets, S. (1972) "Innovations and Adjustments in Economic Growth," *Swedish Journal of Economics* 74, 4: 431–51.

—— (1973) "Modern Economic Growth: Findings and Reflections," *American Economic Review* 63, 3: 247–58.

—— (1977) "Two Centuries of Economic Growth: Reflections on U.S.," *American Economic Review* 67, 1: 1–14.

Langlois, R. N. (1991) "Knowledge and Rationality in the Austrian School: An Analytic Survey," in J. C. Wood and R. N. Woods (eds) *Friedrich A. Hayek: Critical Assessments*, Vol. IV, London: Routledge, 118–40.

Leontief, W. (1976) *The Economic System in an Age of Discontinuity*, New York: New York University Press.

Malinvaud, E. (1983) "Notes on Growth Theory with Imperfectly Flexible Prices," in J.-P. Fitoussi (ed.) *Modern Macroeconomic Theory*, Oxford: Basil Blackwell.

Meade, J. E. (1993) *Liberty, Equality and Efficiency*, London: Macmillan.

Medema, S. G. (1994) *Ronald H. Coase*, New York: St. Martins.

—— (1996) "Ronald Coase and American Institutionalism," *Research in the History of Economic Thought and Methodology* 14: 15–92.

Myrdal, G. (1939) *Monetary Equilibrium*, London: W. Hodge.

—— (1944) *An American Dilemma: The Negro Problem and Modern Democracy*, New York: Harper.

—— (1956) *An International Economy*, New York: Harper and Brothers.

—— (1968) *Asian Drama: An Inquiry Into the Poverty of Nations*, New York: Pantheon.

North, D. (1990) *Institutions, Institutional Change and Economic Performance*, Cambridge: Cambridge University Press.

—— (1993) "Institutions and Credible Commitment," *Journal of Institutional and Theoretical Economics* 149, 1: 11–22.

—— (1994) "Economic Performance Through Time," *American Economic Review* 84, 3: 359–68.

—— (1997a) "The Process of Economic Change," Working Paper No. 128, Helsinki: World Institute for Development Economics Research.

—— (1997b) "Towards a Theory of Economic Change," unpublished paper distributed at the first conference of the International Society for the New Institutional Economics, St. Louis.

—— (1997c) "Some Fundamental Puzzles in Economic History/Development," in W. B. Arthur, S. N. Durlauf and D. A. Lane (eds) *The Economy as an Evolving Complex System II*, Reading, MA: Addison-Wesley, 223–37.

—— (1998) "Economic Performance Through Time: The Limits to Knowledge," in J. Traub (ed.) *Fundamental Limits to Knowledge in Economics*, New York: Oxford University Press.

Reisman, D. A. (1990) *The Political Economy of James Buchanan*, Basingstoke: Macmillan.

Reynolds, L. G. (1974) "Gunnar Myrdal's Contribution to Economics, 1940–1970," *Swedish Journal of Economics* 76, 4: 479–97.

Samuelson, P. A. (1969) "Pure Theory of Public Expenditure and Taxation," in J. Margolis and H. Guitton (eds) *Public Economics: An Analysis of Public Production and Consumption and Their Relations to the Private Sector*, London: St. Martin's Press, 98–123.

—— (1978) "Maximizing and Biology," *Economic Inquiry* 26 (April): 171–83.

Sandmo, A. (1990) "Buchanan on Political Economy: A Review Article," *Journal of Economic Literature* 28 (March): 50–65.

Selten, R. (1991) "Evolution, Learning, and Economic Behavior," *Games and Economic Behavior* 3: 3–24.

Simon, H. A. (1957) *Models of Man*, New York: Wiley.

—— (1978a) "On How to Decide What to Do," *Bell Journal of Economics* 9 (Autumn): 494–507.

—— (1978b) "Rationality as a Process and as a Product of Thought," *American Economic Review* 68, 2: 1–16.

—— (1979) "Rational Decision Making in Business Organizations," *American Economic Review* 69, 4: 493–513.

—— (1982) *Models of Bounded Rationality*, Cambridge, MA: MIT Press.

—— (1991) "Organizations and Markets," *Journal of Economic Perspectives* 5, 2: 25–44.

—— (1992) "Living in Interdisciplinary Space," in M. Szenberg (ed.) *Eminent Economists: Their Life Philosophies*, Cambridge: Cambridge University Press, 261–69.

Solow, R. M. (1988) "Growth Theory and After," *American Economic Review* 78, 3: 307–17.

—— (1989) In W. Sichel (ed.) *The State of Economic Science: Views of Six Nobel Laureates*, Kalamazoo, MI: Upjohn Institute for Employment Research.

—— (1990) *The Labor Market as a Social Institution*, Cambridge: Basil Blackwell.

—— (1992) "Notes on Coping," in M. Szenberg (ed.) *Eminent Economists: Their Life Philosophies*, Cambridge: Cambridge University Press, 270–74.

Vickrey, W. (1994) "Some Objections to Marginal-Cost Pricing," in R. Arnott et al. (eds) *Public Economics*, Cambridge: Cambridge University Press.

Wallis, J. and North, D. (1986) "Measuring the Transaction Sector in the American Economy," in S. L. Engerman and R. E. Gallman (eds) *Long-term Factors in American Economic Growth*, Chicago, IL: University of Chicago Press, 95–148.

15 J. Fagg Foster's theory of instrumental value*

Marc R. Tool

> The determination of what ought to be is a constant part of what is.
>
> (J. F. Foster)

Introduction

Foster's development of the instrumental theory of value, an explanation of the criterion of judgment in all scientific social inquiry, is one of his most original and important, if not revolutionary, contributions. Foster's perception of social (and economic) inquiry indicates that the initiation, formulation, and application of warranted knowledge requires that judgments continuously be made concerning the selection of topic, the choice of data, the logical ordering of data, and the plausibility, pertinence, and explanatory capacity of causal hypotheses. Since there can be no choosing among alternatives, no making of judgments in scientific inquiry, unless a warranted criterion of judgment is employed, *all social inquiry logically and continuously requires the employment of an applicable standard of judgment.*

We shall argue here that Foster's instrumental theory of inquiry itself incorporates the criterion that enables the making of choices in any scientific inquiry process. Any such criterion of choice must itself be derived from, and remain compatible with, other distinguishing analytical aspects of instrumentally warranted inquiry.

Such warranted inquiry, argues Foster, employs the instrumental logic of science in identifying value; it does not, for example, employ deductivistic apriorisms or non-experiential certitudes generated otherwise than through

* This chapter appears as Chapter 4 in Marc R. Tool, *Value Theory and Economic Progress: The Institutional Economics of J. Fagg Foster*, Boston, MA, Dordrecht and London: Kluwer Academic Publishers (2000).

the logic of scientific inquiry. Value analysis is an integral and essential element in all scientific inquiry. It is a continuing element *inside* warranted inquiry, not a unique antecedent *outside* of inquiry. In the history of economic thought, economic analysts have offered an array of affirmations of what "goodness" is, *none* of which, in Foster's view, can be validated through recourse to the logic of scientific inquiry. He writes:

> The ancient Greeks sought to analyze their economy in the light of "justice"; the Canonists explained economic intercourse on the basis of "God's will"; the mercantilists used "national honor" as the sum end of economic analysis; physiocratic doctrine explained the "natural order" of the economic world; classical theory showed the working of "human nature" toward the establishment of the "natural order;" neoclassical theory explained how "happiness," maximum "utility," and "equilibrium" were attained through the functions of the current economy.
>
> (Foster (1942) 1981: 894)

None of the above characterizations is derived from, or warranted by, the logic of scientific inquiry. Indeed, each is incompatible with what Foster perceives as scientific inquiry. He argues that the logic of scientific economic inquiry, in contrast, permits one to provide a functional analysis and characterization of the process of generating real income.

> People have always been engaged in activities contributory to sustaining human life in its total[ity]. . . . The total existential function of human beings is what is meant – no mystic, self-contained entity is . . . connoted] in the word *life* as used here. Human life *means* functioning as a human being; it is the function that is life, not an expression of life. . . . Human life in this sense can be handled logically as part of the total inclusive continuum. . . . In the logical sense, life has no "ends" in the ultimate. Ultimates are, from the logical view . . . [inadmissible in warranted inquiry]; life is a continuum, any item in which has meaning in terms of the other items with which each is causally related, and in no other terms can any item be said to have logical meaning.
>
> (Foster (1942) 1981: 894 (emphasis in original))

Foster affirms the non-availability of ultimates in the logic of scientific inquiry. He locates value, in contrast, within the existential reality of the social process and the economic function embodied therein:

> Economics is concerned with that aspect of human experience called making a living – the production and distribution of goods and services. What, then, is value in the economic sense? . . . [I]t cannot exist as a separate entity. It must exist . . . [in the existential evidences] in the continuum that is the economy, and the run of the facts therein is a

technological process. No imaginary situation ever produced one nail, or delivered one letter, or composed one song. The existential economic realities can be considered logically only in terms of their interconnectedness. And there is where value makes sense. Consider any item, either in the present situation or in the projection of the present situation: Does it add to the function that is called economic? If so, it has economic value; if not, it does not have economic value. Economic value is the degree of technological efficiency. It is as simple as that. This is, and always has been, the actual, functioning theory of value. People have always acted upon it in their economic functions, not forgetting that ritualistic functions are frequently confused with economic functions. In the actual provision of the means to function as a human being, each item in the process has value in proportion as it implements that provision. That is the logical meaning of economic value; that is the *only* real meaning of economic value that permits logical treatment in economic analysis and upon which a science of economics may be built.

> (Foster (1942) 1981: 895 (emphasis in original))

As Abraham Kaplan observes, all social inquiry is purposive: "what we call 'facts' all involve an element of value. For purposes are embedded in all our meanings, and every purpose determines a value. Discourse, even the most theoretical and abstract, is a segment of purposive behavior" (Kaplan 1961: 35). Inquiry is addressed to a query about, or condition in, the social process that has generated doubt about present understandings, behaviors or outcomes. The undertaking of any effort to explain the origins and impact of an initiating question or observed condition must generate reflective effort to determine "what goes on here" and by implication, "what ought to go on here." The normative dimension of inquiry reflects this purposiveness. A criterion of judgment, a theory of value, is necessarily implied in the pursuit of purpose to change "what is" into "what ought to be."

It is commonplace and routine to employ an implicit criterion in social inquiry in distinguishing between social purposes that are evidentially warranted, and those that are not so warranted. On the one hand, the pursuit of social inquiry, for example, that: (a) explains and extends our understanding of causal connections in behavioral and conceptual contexts; (b) pushes out the frontiers of warranted knowledge and enhances our capacities for comprehension of observed behavioral phenomena; and/or (c) recommends adjustments in the current problematic institutional structure to assure and augment productive performance and contribution, are all viewed here as being constructive, that is, serving instrumental purposes. Implicit is a necessarily continuing concern for the community's well-being and continuity. On the other hand, the pursuit of social inquiry, for example, that: (a) reaffirms antecedently acquired, but unexamined and unappraised, beliefs; (b) reinforces the status and discretion of existing economic and social power systems; or (c) provides apologia for sustaining the *status quo*, are all normatively viewed as being actually or potentially destructive, that is, serving invidious purposes.

The intent here is to re-emphasize that since all inquiry is and must be purposive, the character of inquiry pursued *inherently* has normative elements and implications. Foster's value theory should be understood, then, as providing a warranted criterion of judgment in social inquiry that distinguishes between constructive and destructive purposes. This value theory is derived through scientific social inquiry; its character reflects its standing as an existential scientific generality; it plays a critical and continuing role in such social inquiry; its application guides judgments of social policy.

To present and develop Foster's value theory herein we address the following topics: (a) value theory and economic analysis; (b) instrumental value theory: locus; (c) instrumental value theory: sources; (d) instrumental value theory: substance; and (e) instrumental value theory: implications.

Value theory and economic analysis

Foster offers a largely unique theory of value reflecting and extending the theoretical contributions, especially of John Dewey, Thorstein B. Veblen, and Clarence E. Ayres. This value theory, Foster argues, is a necessarily integral and essential element of all scientific economic and social theory. Inquiries into public policy, then, if they are to be credible, robust, substantive and directive, must employ the methodology of scientific inquiry. In the application of instrumental value theory to the construction of public policy options, the choosing of pertinent and constructive institutional adjustments must be analyzed and guided by the continuing employment of pragmatic instrumentalism. All such inquiry, then, is value-laden.

The following encompassing analytical affirmations of fact, as offered by Foster, provide an introductory overview of the critical linkages between value theory and economic analysis. He is, in effect, redefining the nature and significance of inquiry in economics.

Economic inquiry

Foster insists that "economics is and always has been concerned with the process of providing the means of human life and experience." "It is the continuing task of economists . . . to explain it, to make it understandable to the community so that the community may proceed to a solution of its economic problems." But, as a social science, economics "is concerned primarily with the institutional aspects of the social order, not with the physical-engineering aspects, except as the latter bear on the former. . . . Economics is . . . concerned with [institutions] . . . the prescribed patterns of human relations, patterns of correlated activities and attitudes, among groups of persons who are organized for the purpose of carrying on the process of providing the means of human life and experience" (Foster (1949) 1981: 899–900).

Economic problems

The community supports inquiry in economics because "it is and always has been confronted by real economic problems" and has presumed that extended inquiry might contribute to their understanding and amelioration. The significance of inquiry, then, for Foster

> lies in its applicability to the solution of real problems. Our conception of what constitutes significance and importance . . . remains fixed on the possibility of solving real problems confronting real people, and we concede significance to any inquiry in any field only on the basis of that possibility. A problem arises when that process ceases to be carried forward at the level of efficiency indicated by the current state of the industrial arts. It becomes an economic problem when that failure is caused by the failure of any one, or several, of those patterns to contribute to the economic process or when any institutional arrangement interferes with its on-going. . . . An economic problem appears [then] when disrapport arises between two or more patterns of human activities that are supposed to be correlated toward the effective continuation of the productive process.
>
> (1949/1981: 900–901)

For Foster, then, "economic problems are situations of instrumental dislocation. [I]t follows that answers to economic problems must take the form of institutional judgments – modifications of prescribed patterns of human relations looking toward the instrumentally effective correlation of those organizational patterns with each other and with the non-institutional aspects of the economic process." The identification of an economic problem is clearly, then, a "recognition of a discrepancy between 'what is' and 'what ought to be', between 'what goes on here' and 'what ought to go on here'. Problem solving would destroy that discrepancy" (1949/1981: 900–901).

Institutional change

"If the dictum that 'whatever is, is right' holds true, then most certainly there could be no such thing as an economic problem." Trying to sustain the *status quo* at a time when the community is confronted, for example, with maldistribution of income, invidious discrimination or underutilization of available resources, is unproductive labor. "[T]he community finds repeatedly that the economic process does not go forward at the level of efficiency that the non-institutional factors indicate is available. [T]he economic general theory must be the theory of institutional adjustment. Otherwise, economic theory can have no significance insofar as significance is a function of problem solving." And no scholar or advisor has successfully argued the contrary. "Since the physical circumstances that converge to bring on an economic problem remain just what they are, there can be no way of resolving the problem except to adjust the institutional structure so as to bring the two phases [physical, social] into instrumental rapport" (Foster (1949) 1981: 901).

Value theory

So long as there are persons with reflective capacity and social concern, "there is no way, short of forceful destruction, to *prevent* recognition of a discrepancy between 'what is' and 'what ought to be' in terms of instrumental efficiency of the economic process. [T]he problematic situation is a matter of factual circumstances the human incidences of which *cannot* be escaped except by 'making up our account' with those physical circumstances. This requires adjusting the relevant institutional structures so as to remove the inefficiency; there is no other way to remove the human incidences that comprise the compulsions toward adjustment" (1949/1981: 902, emphasis added). It follows, then, that:

> A criterion of judgment independent of any particular institutional structure is necessary if an economic problem is ever to be recognized . . . the substance of that criterion is the instrumental efficiency of the economic process. [S]ince 'what ought to be' in economic affairs is nothing less than the application of a theory of value, and since no economic problem can be conceived or resolved without some comprehension of 'what ought to be'. . . significant economic analysis necessarily involves the application of the theory of value. This is the simple and apparent relationship between value theory and economic analysis.
>
> (Foster (1949) 1981: 902)

> [T]o say that an economic problem exists is to say that part of that structure, that particular pattern of human relationships, has ceased or failed to provide for the effective participation of its members. In so saying, we are necessarily in the position of asserting that the instrumental efficiency of the economic process is the criterion of judgment in terms of which, and only in terms of which, we may resolve economic problems.
>
> (Foster (1949) 1981: 905)

Instrumental value theory ɪ: locus

The continuing existential universe in which value theory is developed and utilized is perceived by Foster to be the encompassing social process. This social process is the locus of Foster's value theory. This process is a universally continuing phenomenon of interaction of structure and function under the deliberate, normative, and continuing discretionary guidance of members of the social order. Instrumental value theory, then, is grounded in the *actual experience continuum of human agents* encompassing the following loci of interest and concern: the social setting compels a genuine recognition of the physical and emotional status of the community. The physical setting provides the context in which identified problems are exhibited in particular places and times where the well-being of actual individuals and communities is actually being directly determined. The cultural setting fosters recognition that all those affected by problems are themselves products of lifelong behavioral conditioning. The conceptual setting provides the source from which analyses, beliefs, and convictions acquired over long periods are brought into evaluative consideration. The judgmental setting reminds all inquirers that choice making pervades the whole of human experience and that all such choice making *compels* recourse to criteria of choice.

Institutions are structural stipulations organizing the behavior, and often the thinking, of members of the human community. In Foster's view, institutions are prescribed or proscribed patterns of correlated behavior and attitudes directed to the performance of one or another social function. Institutional structures that have demonstrably failed adequately to provide for the community's well-being must become the objects of inquiry and perhaps revision or abandonment, if the continuity of the community is to be assured and its efficiency in applying warranted knowledge is to be enhanced.

Inquiry categories of *social functions* that comprise most of the social process, as viewed by Foster, would particularly include, among others, the following continuing areas of major human interest and concern:

1. The provision of the means of life and experience.
2. The determination and administration of public policy.
3. The development in the young of the capacity to think critically and coherently.
4. The creation and communication of warranted knowledge.
5. The creation and equitable distribution of real and money income.
6. The provision of public health and safety.
7. These and other major loci of social functions are developed in, and given effect through, organizing and coordinating institutional structures. Such structures are the vehicles through which intellect and judgment guide the conduct and performance of functions comprising the social process.

Mal- or non-performance of these functions in institutions on which the community depends creates problems of disjunction, disrapport, disintegration, and/or recourse to invidious distinctions. Solutions to institutional problems require, obviously, changes in institutional structure. The theory of instrumental value, when employed, provides the criterion identifying the determinants of problems in and among these functional areas of human activity. Note that all references to utilitious concepts are abandoned as intrusive and irrelevant in the identification and resolution of instrumentally defined human problems.

Instrumental value theory II: sources

Although over the last 100 years or so a large number of scholars have formulated, continued, and extended the inquiry discipline of institutional economics, we focus here on three scholars whose contributions were particularly significant in the development of Foster's perspective on the normative aspects of his theory of economic progress: Thorstein Veblen, John Dewey, and Clarence Ayres.

Thorstein B. Veblen

Veblen was generally perceived as someone well outside of the general culture of intellectuals in the late nineteenth and early twentieth centuries. As Foster views him:

> Veblen was never really able to become a part of American culture, he never understood the idiom. This gave him both advantages and disadvantages. He was influenced by Spencer's sociology, by Hume, Kant, and Darwin. As always he took what he could use and discarded the rest. Dewey and Veblen took from each other. From about 1921 there was a different tenor in Veblen. But he . . . discloses only the most rudimentary beginnings of his general theory.
>
> (Foster 1974 (LN) AmCont: 2)

Foster was intimately familiar with the Veblenian literature; indeed he once remarked that institutionalists, following his own practice, should reread the Veblenian library every few years. More particularly, it seems evident that Veblen's *Theory of the Leisure Class* (1899), *The Instinct of Workmanship* (1914), and *The Place of Science in Modern Civilization* (1919b) were the most important sources of insights for Foster in developing his scientific mode of social inquiry that encompassesd his theory of instrumental value. In addition, he often alludes illustratively to Veblen's *The Nature of Peace* (1917), as an indicator of the predictive significance of Veblen's analyses.

Foster surveys and assesses the contributions and limitations of Veblen's work in institutional thought in various places, but most directly, perhaps, in his course entitled "The American Contribution to Economic Thought." Both the contributions and the limitations are instructive in understanding instrumental value theory in institutional economics. But perhaps the most significant contribution for Foster is Veblen's fundamental distinction "between the 'institutional' and the 'technological' aspects of the economy" (Foster (1943) 1981: 926). This Veblenian distinction or dichotomy is the initial and primary construct on which Foster's scientific theory of instrumental value is built. This dichotomy between science and non-science in social inquiry is a profound and significant undergirding construct for contemporary institutionalist analyses of social value and its applications.

Somewhat ironically, however, Foster observes that Veblen himself was theoretically blocked by the value problem. He made judgments about institutional structure; he acknowledged the fact of, and sought to explain the determinants of, economic change. But he did not develop a theory of value rooted in his basic commitment to a scientific approach to inquiry. He was blocked by his "basic mistake . . . that institutions are a result of unconscious habituation" not of deliberate selection (Foster 1974 (LN) AmCont: 4). Veblen frequently disclaimed that he was generating and applying social value theory. He insisted that about tastes, "there is no disputing" (1919b/1961: 29); that "in making use of the term 'invidious', it may perhaps be unnecessary to remark that there is no intention to extol or deprecate, or to commend or deplore any of the phenomena which the word is used to characterize" (1899/1934: 34); that in discussion of the leisure class, "'right' and 'wrong' are of course here used without conveying any reflection as to what ought or ought not to be"(ibid.: 207). But Veblen "doth protest too much". Disclaimers notwithstanding, Veblen was an inveterate "judger" of social and economic conduct and institutions. As Foster observes, Veblen was blocked by the value problem; he seemingly never escaped the contradiction of his own making. He disclaimed use of normative criteria while he was, in fact, offering normative assessments.

Veblen, despite his blockage, was extensively and consistently engaged in evaluation. "He was applying value theory in distinguishing between institutions that exhibit 'compatibility or incompatibility with the effective evolutionary process.' He distinguishes between institutions that are 'imbecile' and those that are not . . . Veblen's inquiry is purposive; it is value laden" (Tool 1986: 34–35).

The Veblenian dichotomy

Some years ago, the present author, prompted by a long period of working and writing in the Foster tradition, attempted more fully to identify the Veblenian dichotomy as a normative premise. I here draw upon that analysis (Tool 1986: 36–37):

In *Leisure Class* we are offered this descriptive statement: "Institutions – the economic structure – may be roughly distinguished into two classes or categories, according as they serve one or the other of two divergent purposes of economic life. . . . they are institutions of acquisition or of production. . . . they are pecuniary or industrial institutions. . . . they are institutions serving either the invidious or the non-invidious economic interest" (Veblen (1899) 1934: 208). Veblen used the term "*invidious*" to describe a "comparison of persons with a view to rating and grading them in respect of relative worth or value" (Tool 1986: 34, emphasis in original).

But the forms or versions of the distinction extend well beyond the three mentioned above. Indeed, the distinction appears in all of Veblen's published works in one form or another; it was for him a *general* principle. Note the following diverse additional examples:

salesmanship	vs.	workmanship [(1914) 1946: 216ff.]
business	vs.	industry [(1904) 1932: 20ff.]
ceremonial	vs.	technological [(1915) 1964: 26ff.]
ownership	vs.	production [(1923) 1964: 65ff.]
free income	vs.	tangible performance [(1919a) 1946: 63ff.]
vested interests	vs.	common man [(1919a)1946: 85ff. & 159ff.]
sabotage	vs.	community serviceability [(1917) 1945: 167ff.]
pecuniary employment	vs.	industrial employment [(1904) 1932: 313ff.]
invidious emulation	vs.	technological efficiency [(1899) 1934: *passim*]
conscientious withdrawal of efficiency	vs.	inordinately productive enterprise [(1921) 1965: Chs. 1 and 2]
competitive advertising	vs.	valuable information and guidance [(1904) 1932: 57]
business prosperity	vs.	industrial efficiency [(1904) 1932: 178ff.]

"And the foregoing does not exhaust the list. Entries in the left-hand column refer to individuals, behaviors or institutions that are different in kind from those in the right-hand column; the distinction is a dichotomy" (Tool, 1986: 37.) As I argued earlier:

The normative use, by Veblen, of this set of distinctions can hardly be in doubt. "The interest of the community at large demands industrial efficiency and serviceability of the product, while the business interest of the concerns as such demands vendibility of the product" (1904/1932: 157–58). It is scarcely morally colorless to contend that "all business sagacity" in the final analysis "reduces itself . . . to a judicious use of sabotage." "Captains of industry" through owners' discretion give "authoritative permission" and "authoritative limitation" to the industrial process. It is Veblen's lament that such authority is not used with "an eye single" to produce the "largest and most serviceable output of goods and services, or to the most economical use of the country's material resources and man-power, regardless of pecuniary consequences." "The volume and serviceability of the output must wait unreservedly on the very particular pecuniary question of what quantity and what degree of serviceability will yield the largest net return in terms of price" (1917/1945: 168–69).

Veblen characterizes a "vested interest" as a "prescriptive right to get something for nothing" (1919a/1946: 162). He sees the objective of competitive advertising as the establishment of "differential monopolies resting on popular conviction" which are of "slight if any immediate service to the community" (1904/1932: 57–58). Can these observations be considered devoid of normative content? Obviously not.

(Tool 1986: 37)

Accordingly, disclaimers notwithstanding, Veblen was engaged in normative inquiry. Foster identifies his problem. Veblen perceived and articulated the continuing (indeed, inescapable) need to judge institutions with applicable criteria, but was never able to formulate a theory of value that would provide a continuing criterion that itself was drawn from the warranted inquiry process. Foster, as we have seen, is able to provide the warrantable value theory that continuing discretionary involvment in the social order requires. Value is instrumental efficiency, as Foster has cogently and persuasively affirmed.

Foster's views of Veblen's contributions

Veblenian economics is the only [approach to] . . . economics that is peculiar to America. Americans [tend to] talk ismatically and generally act instrumentally.

(Foster 1974 (LN) AmCont: 5)

(a) [Veblen's] distinction between technology and institutions, [was misunderstood]. Critics said [that] since he was not going toward any ism he was not going anywhere; he was directionless and meaningless. But Veblen recognized that the identification of direction cannot be stated validly in terms of institutional structure. That is, the criterion of judgment cannot be in terms of institutional structure. To Veblen, an ism exists as an idea, and it is a useful structure as identifying a pattern of ideas in reference to a theory of value. He noted that these patterns were accepted as natural, but they were not so.

(Foster 1974 (LN) AmCont: 4)

(b) Veblen realized that given data must be taken from technology (state of industrial arts), but he didn't go far enough . . . [He did not] distinguish between instrumental and ceremonial [functions of] institutions. Veblen knew of no way to determine the validity of an institution, implying that technology is valid and institutions invalid. But all institutions are partially valid, and there is a criterion of judgment for evaluating them. That is what makes social science significant. Without a criterion there is no significance.

(Foster 1974 (LN) AmCont: 5)

What Veblen started is the development of a theory of institutions, of which economics is one phase. We have been devoid of a general theory; Veblen gives us a chance to work toward one. He does away with ismatic criteria for the judgment of direction. Ayres works from Veblen with what he calls a technological theory of value.

(Foster 1974 (LN) AmCont: 5)

John Dewey

Foster, in fashioning his instrumental theory of inquiry, draws heavily on the philosophical contributions of John Dewey, perhaps the most prominent and productive philosopher in the United States in the twentieth century. Of Dewey's work, *Logic: The Theory of Inquiry* (1938) and *Theory of Valuation* (1939) are clearly the most relevant and significant for Foster. But Dewey was an extraordinarily productive scholar; several other publications were also important sources: for example *Human Nature and Conduct* (1922), *Experience and Nature* (1925), *The Public and Its Problems* (1927), and *Problems of Men* (1946).

Foster, in a paper written in 1942, is attempting to clarify the meaning of the term value: All economists use the word, and this fact would lead one to suppose that value is subject to definition, or at least carries a constant core of meaning sufficiently peculiar to allow independent identification. A great many theories of how value arises and how it is to be measured clamor for attention, but the meaning of what it is that arises and what it is that is to be measured is seemingly assumed. This arouses suspicion. Perhaps value has been used to designate no particular concept – but [our inquiry discloses the contrary].

(Foster (1942) 1981: 872)

Foster draws on Dewey to reset the analytical context:

For the existing state of discussion shows not only that there is a great difference of opinion about the proper theoretical interpretation to be put upon the facts, which might be a healthy sign of progress, but also that there is great disagreement as to what the facts are to which theory applies, and indeed whether there are any facts to which a theory of value can apply. For a survey of the current literature of the subject discloses that views on the subject range from the belief, at one extreme, that so-called 'values' are but emotional epithets or mere ejaculations, to the belief, at the other extreme, that a priori necessary standardized, rational values are the principles upon which art, science, and morals depend for their validity.

(Dewey 1939; quoted in Foster (1942) 1981: 872)

Foster's conception of value is not derived from either extreme. Drawing on Dewey, he develops instead a logically acceptable and empirically demonstrable theory of social value.

> John Dewey comes into the picture because of a failure on the part of the economists. They have failed to produce a theory of value which does not violate every requisite of scientific reflection and explanation; this despite the fact that all economic theory has, of necessity, to do with value in some connotation or other. This side of nihilism, some concept of value is a necessity in dealing with any problem at all. But this is not to say that value must be an occult, all-pervading "something" that is *inherent* in any object or event. The failure by the economists to produce an acceptable theory of value has led to [a] "lament for economics" by those who recognize the inadequacy of orthodox theory. And these persons' failure to continue on to a positive reappraisal of economics results in the meaninglessness and doubt of nihilism. The character of that reappraisal is most maturely stated by John Dewey.
>
> (1942/1981: 872–73, emphasis in original)

Foster explains why social value theory is such a forbidding area of inquiry for economists to address:

> The problem of value . . . is very difficult to handle in 'economic' terms. Its difficulty does not derive from complexity, but from novelty. It is new in its full realization, if indeed it is yet fully realized. The new is always difficult, and particularly so if it replaces old concepts or habits, and very much so if the new cannot be handled in terms habitually used in handling what it replaces. There is an "inalienable and ineradicable framework of conception which is not of our own making, but given to us ready-made by society – a whole apparatus of concepts and categories within which and by means of which all our individual thinking, however daring and original, is compelled to move" (Cornford 1912: 45). The "apparatus of concepts" requisite to handling the problem is at hand, but it is so new in the field of economics that much blundering is occurring and is to be expected. Even an economist of the caliber of J. M. Keynes, with his . . . [awesome] erudition, fails to see his key problem, although he does realize the inadequacy of his habitual "apparatus of concepts."
>
> (1942/1981: 873)

Scientists in any field, Foster contends, must concern themselves with ethical implications of their work and any social opportunities or responsibilities arising therefrom. A scientist (social or physical) must become aware of the "widening circle of consequences" generated by, and emerging from, his/her inquiry and policy recommendations. As Dewey observed: "Just as the validity of a proposition in discourse, or of conceptual material generally, cannot be determined short of the consequences to which its functional use gives rise, so the sufficient warrant of a judgment as a claimant to knowledge (in its eulogistic sense) cannot be determined apart from connection with a widening circle of consequences" (1938: 490).

But the outcomes that derive from "the continuum of the widening circle of consequences" of inquiry are, of course, social as well as physical. Foster explains:

> In a very real sense, scientists determine the social environment. Technological development which is continuous with inventions in "pure" science . . . is the most obviously changing aspect of man's environment. And it is this changing which, "at bottom" gives rise to the inadequacy of institutional arrangements instituted on the basis of former technological situations. . . . "[T]he notion of the complete separation of science from the social environment is a fallacy which encourages irresponsibility on the part of scientists regarding the social consequences of their work."
>
> (Dewey 1938: 489; Foster (1942) 1981: 875)

Dewey would agree with Foster that:

> [T]he recognition by scientists of their social responsibility would not render to logic all the plain and fancy superstitions. The results of the development of physical science are, in large measure, not in the hands of scientists . . . They are the result of all the items in the panorama of organized human relations. That is why "science is an important part of education, not because it satisfies curiosity, but because intelligent citizenship is no longer possible unless we understand the place of science in the everyday life of everybody."
>
> (Hogben 1937: 55; quoted by Foster (1942) 1981: 877)

Foster shares Dewey's view that technological change "is the chief determining condition of social relationships and, to a large extent, of actual cultural values in every advanced industrial people, while they have reacted intensively into the lives of all 'backward' people. Moreover, only an arbitrary, or else purely conventional point of view . . . can rule out such consequences as these from the scope of science itself" (Foster (1942) 1981: 876).

Clarence E. Ayres

Fagg Foster studied formally and informally with Clarence E. Ayres for a decade and a half from 1931 to 1946; he wrote his doctoral dissertation under Ayres's supervision; he remained a good friend and professional colleague until the death of Ayres in 1972. Ultimately, in some areas, Foster even reversed the roles of teacher and student. Ayres seems to have had as great an impact on Foster's professional development and maturation as any other scholar. Accordingly, Foster's perception of Ayres's work reflects this long interactive association. Perhaps Ayres's most important contributions for Foster were his *Theory of Economic Progress* (1944, 1962, 1978) and his *Toward a Reasonable Society* (1961).

"Veblen left his general theory at the stage of 'making up one's account' with the material conditions that converge to bring it [institutional] (adjustment) on" (Foster 1946: 96). But how is this "accounting" to occur? A clarification of the concepts of "institutional" and "technological" and their relationship, was undertaken by Ayres. Indeed, Ayres is extending, in two directions, Foster's early-on perception of a theory of institutional adjustment.

The first of these extensions concerns the theory of value, "the theory of that in terms of which the account may be drawn" (Foster 1946: 97). Ayres recasts the Veblenian distinction between the technological and institutional aspects of institutional performance in the economy. Drawing on more recent material than was available to Veblen, Ayres explains:

> For every man the real and valid judgments of economic value are those he makes between purchases, judgments of value in use as economists once said, tested and verified by the way things work in the continuous effort of existence. It is to this test that all economic values are in fact submitted, those of public policy affecting the industrial system as a whole no less than those of private life. For every individual and for the community the criterion of value is the continuation of the life-process – keeping the machines running. That is what we have in fact been doing throughout the ages, and that is what we must continue to do and do continually better – technologically better – if we are to continue and exceed the achievements of the past.
>
> (Ayres 1944: 230; quoted in Foster 1946: 97)

Ayres is affirming "the run of the physical facts" and, says Foster:

> [I]t is obvious that any criterion of value in terms of which action is taken which contravenes the continuity of the economic process thereby cancels all human action, including the action taken under those terms. It is proposed, then that economic estimation be made directly in terms of the criterion which the run of the facts dictates. Professor Ayres views the character of that dictation much as the curvature of a lens is dictated by its function in the process in which it plays a part. The problem posed by any disrapport between the lens grinder's predilections concerning proper concavity or convexity on the one hand and the dictation of the facts on the other hand can be resolved only by an adjustment of the predilections. In this sense Professor Ayres points out that the locus of economic value is in the economic process, not in predilections drawing warrant from any other source.
>
> (Foster 1946: 98)

Something of this same conception of value is implicit in most of Veblen's work, and he tacitly applies it in almost all of his discussions. But his view of science as being motivated by 'idle curiosity' blocked any logical way to a theory of value drawn in terms dictated by the run of the facts . . . [I]f science is valid only as an exercise in idle curiosity, although its content is dictated by the run of the facts, there is no way to base the validity of science itself in the sort of mental processes with which it examines and explains the facts.

(Foster 1946: 98–99)

A second area in which Ayres extends the Veblenian theory of institutional adjustment, in Foster's view, has to do with what Ayres calls "the power of ideas." Some reading Veblen "got the impression that institutional adjustments, being changes in the 'settled habits of thought common to the generality of men' are altogether a matter of unconsciously modified habituation." Some have drawn the conclusion "that changes in structural institutions are exclusively unreasoned change in habits." Ayres, drawing on his concept of "the power of ideas," argues that "ideas are the immediate point of departure for adjustments in structural institutions, that is, in the prescribed relations of a group of people organized for definite purposes" (Foster 1946: 99).

Indeed, Ayres "points out . . . [that] two kinds of ideas are involved":

On the one hand, conceptual formulations based on the authority of personalities serve toward maintaining the existing rules of the game. On the other hand, ideas arising as conceptual formulations of the material economic process serve toward changing the rules of the game as the material conditions of the economic process change. Either way, the pattern of ideas is the immediate prescription of the pattern of human relations, and any change in the former is the immediate prescription of a change in the latter. Professor Ayres's contribution at this point is that the causal potency of an idea based on the authority of personalities is a function of the coercive power of those personalities whereas the causal potency of an idea based on the run of the facts in causal terms is a function of the correctness of the idea.

The former, Professor Ayres identifies as non-causal or metaphysical; the latter, he identifies as science. Metaphysical ideas have no potency in themselves; the source of their potency is exterior to the ideas. Scientific ideas are potent as such. Then it is the interplay of these two forces that determines the pattern of any adjustment. Professor Ayres concludes that there is no way, short of total destruction, in which metaphysics can prevent the encroachment, however gradual, of science as a way of understanding and therefore specifying the patterns of human relationships. And the reason for this is that the inherently developmental character of science means that it constantly proliferates beyond its immediate boundaries. As a way of explanation, science encroaches upon new areas and therefore specifies the trespassed area.

(Foster 1946: 100–101)

Instrumental value theory III: substance

Foster's theory of instrumental efficiency

Because of its incisiveness, and given its comparative brevity, we present here Foster's summarized conception of the institutionalists' instrumental efficiency theory of social value as he drafted it for his students. That it draws on his precursors, Veblen, Dewey, and Ayres, will become evident: We consider in sequence: (a) value in process; (b) condition versus direction; and (c) measurement.

Value in process

Foster explains:

> Since truth lies or is identifiable only in continuity, and since the only continuity which is not self-contained, and therefore not tautological, is the evidentially determined (scientific) progression of human devices, then the true criterion of judgment must be identified in terms of that process. And the kind of thinking which characterizes it in conjugate correspondence with that process must be the kind of thinking which can bring into view the referent in question.
>
> The notion that *any* theory of value can be applied even though only one is in fact applicable, is a paradox. It is not that others are applied; it is rather that we try to apply others. The apparent paradox is resolved by discerning correctly the relationship between the facts ("what is") to "what ought to be." That relationship is as follows: the activity of judging alternatives (which necessarily involves the application of value theory) is one of the most obtrusive facts in the continuum of events, and that activity connects the present and the future through the efforts to resolve problems, and thus the choosing among alternatives, and thus the determination of the course of events, etc., etc. Judgment is the connecting link between the present and the future.
>
> (Foster 1950 (LN) Value: 2 (emphasis in original))

Foster affirms instrumental value:

> Already we have seen that the concept of value must be in terms of process because the *whole* of our experience has been with process. We have seen, also, that to be a true concept, it must display the attribute we call continuity. Therefore, a true concept of value must be in

correspondence with the evidential facts of continual process. But the only identifiable continuum in our whole social experience is the progressive causally-determined sequence of events we call the social process. And so it is in that process itself that we can correctly identify the locus of value. But even yet, the character of the identification which we seek is not in view because the locus of value (Ayres's terminus) does not identify its character and because that locus, the social process, may be and is gauged in two ways: (a) direction, (b) condition.

(Foster 1950 (LN) Value: 2 (emphasis in original))

Condition versus direction

"Direction" may be and is used in the sense that judgments may be and are made with reference to whether the process is toward or away from a particular pattern of invidious differentiation, a particular institutional structure, a structure within which the process goes on. But in this instance, the structure must have its validity outside and irrespective of the character of the process which goes on within it. And, to attain such a separate identification, the institutional structure must in fact be determined independently of the remainder of the process. But all of the facts of history and of common experience prove beyond any . . . doubt that the character of the process and the structural institutions are not independent of each other; they are causally related, although separately identifiable, phases or aspects of the same process.

(Foster 1950 (LN) Value: 2–3)

Not only is the "direction" concept of the criterion of judgment invalid because the referent for direction cannot be separately established in fact, but also that criterion is devoid of truth because its referent is discontinuous. Nothing is better established in human history than the fact that the institutional structure itself constantly changes, and not only the remainder of the process. And so we shall have to discard "direction" as value.

(Foster 1950 (LN) Value: 3)

"Condition," in the sense of how efficiently the social process is proceeding, is the other way to gauge the process. But here again the referent we seek for the term 'value' is not yet specifically identified. For 'condition' also can be conceived in two ways. First, it can be thought of as a degree of efficiency in maintaining or attaining a particular pattern of invidious differentiation, a particular institutional structure. But this concept displays all of the defects of the "direction" concept; it is, in fact, fundamentally the same idea. Thus the condition of efficiency alone does not end our quest for a true identification of value.

(Foster 1950 (LN) Value: 3)

The second way in which "condition" can be conceived is instrumental in character. The social process can be judged in terms of how efficiently the non-invidious function is being carried on. But . . . it is this very aspect of the social process which we have identified as the continuum which does not change in character, but only in degree and in quantity. . . . [A]lso . . . it is this function that is continuous – inescapably so. This concept of value, like the ceremonial concept of efficiency, is applicable to the whole or any part of the social process at any time or over any period of time. But it differs from the other in that its referent remains the same – it is continuous. It has real and uninterrupted continuity. Its referential content at any time and in reference to any item is continuous with all that has gone before and with all that exists concurrently, and what succeeds that content can be conceived only as causally continuous with it. It has uninterrupted continuity and it has unexceptional applicability throughout the universe of its application.

(Foster 1950 (LN) Value: 3)

Measurement

The application or employment of the instrumental efficiency criterion of value is neither obvious nor automatic. What *theory of valuation* accompanies the instrumental theory of value? Is it possible numerically to measure more or less efficiency in the scientific sense? In the orthodox neoclassical general theory and tradition, the referent for value is utility. Since units of utility, "utils," defy both identification and measurement, price became and remains the surrogate measure of utility. The theory of price determination comprises the only orthodox theory of valuation. It permits the use of numerical calculations of price movements and therewith by imputation, the determination of greater or lesser utility, that is, value. One could assume, then, that utilitious satisfaction varies inversely with price for consumers and directly with price for producers. Recourse to mathematics to "explain" price determination provides the allusion of factual certainty for the analysis offered.

For institutionalists, there can be no scientific credibility for the orthodox theory of valuation. But an institutionalist view of the theory of valuation remains to be considered. Foster asks, "How do you know what is more or less [instrumentally] efficient?" A concept of more or less efficiency would appear to be necessary. He responds: "in science, there is no common unit of measurement for efficiency . . . comprised of different items, events, and/or objects" (1948 (CN) Value: 362). The efficiency of a combustion engine is not measured in the same way as that of a telescope. Efficiency relates to differing functions and the adequacy of performance thereof.

In instrumental social inquiry, then, there is no singular theory of valuation; "there is no unit of measurement of social value" (363). "Every problem specifies the units of measurement; the facts of the problem specify the theory of valuation applicable to it. It is from those facts, and reference to relationships of those facts, that that unit becomes available or not available" (362). For example: the instrumental efficiency of the function of teaching children to think critically and clearly about substantive social issues would be measured differently from the instrumental efficiency of the function of achieving full and meaningful employment.

Foster's concluding value affirmation:

> This concept of the criterion of judgment satisfies all of the requisites of truth; it is true. Value is instrumental efficiency. It is as simple as that. Fundamentally, social value cannot be anything else, because with anything else the very process being judged ceases to be, and thus all worth in it and of it ceases to be; continuity becomes a meaningless sound, and truth is a lie.
>
> (Foster 1950 (LN) Value: 3)

Characterizing attributes of Foster's value theory

Following are some hallmark and derivative characterizations of Foster's theory of instrumental value, the criterion of judgment in social analysis. Foster did not fashion the following attributes in the form presented here; they are induced and deduced from Foster's general normative position. But they are, I believe, logically credible and empirically grounded characterizations that are helpful in understanding how the processual and evidential instrumental value principle identifies problematic conditions and determinants and guides the fashioning of corrective institutional adjustments.

Pancultural, not parochial

Foster's instrumental value theory incorporates a conception of scientifically warranted knowledge that is universal in social analysis generally. Social inquiry is addressed to the causal determinants of breakdowns in the social structure. This inclusive theory of inquiry is not delimited by time, by place or by culture. The principles of instrumental value theory are continuously pertinent, warranted by scientific generation and validation, and are panculturally applicable. With continued warranted inquiry, the defining principles of this inquiry mode must be expected to be revised in consequence of that inquiry, but the substantive methodological content and problem-solving relevance will continue indefinitely, even if in modified form. Science is a continuously emergent and universal way of generating and employing warranted knowledge. The data change; the problems change; the hypotheses change; the institutional policy formats change; the scope of institutional applications change; the consequential impacts change; the loci of discretion over policy change. But Foster's basic causal inquiry model of social valuation should be thought of as a continuing analytical construct that remains itself a potential object of inquiry.

The degree of success in instrumental institutional problem solving will, of course, vary over time and place. But the instrumental value principle is as pertinent in Washington as in London, in Tokyo as in Delhi. However, a considerable degree of intellectual freedom must exist in relevant private or public bodies if there are to be any pertinent proposals for modification of institutions in search of more instrumentally efficient operations. Accordingly, instrumental value theory is not the intellectual property of any one national or cultural group. But its continued development does depend, as indicated, upon permissive, if not supportive, governance structure that facilitates and supports warranted inquiry and its institutional applications.

Degrees, not directions

Foster's instrumental value theory addresses degrees and/or levels of instrumentalness in appraising institutional structure. It has no directional constant in the sense of installing and/or implementing otherwise warranted (ceremonial, invidious, coercive) institutional adjustments. It has no teleological "drivers" (e.g., natural laws) that inherently shape the direction and implementation of institutional adjustments. It offers no ideological institutional recipes – capitalism, communism, fascism – to serve as all-purpose, all encompassing, institutional solutions for problems confronted. Indeed, these isms have proven to be theoretical and behavioral cul-de-sacs. They do not and cannot guide a processual economy in any constructive direction. The instrumental theory of value does require knowledge about and assessment of the condition and performance of existing structure. One may ask: does the proposed institutional adjustment create conditions that are less invidious and/or are more instrumental in the performance of a social function? Do the changes envisioned enhance the mechanisms of democratic governance?

Continuous, not episodic

Foster's instrumental value theory is processual and continuous in form and substance. For inquirers, value analysis is always "on the way;" its "arrivals" are tentative and provisional. Its relevance and applicability must be determined anew in every particular problematic context. This normative inquiry mode then has no *a priori* beginning and no preconceived end in view except for enabling continual provisional assessments generated by inductive, deductive, and/or hypothetical inferences about institutional structure and performance.

Episodic inquiry, in contrast, rests on an anterior and unexamined use of an analyzing and organizing conceptual frame whose character is determined and established prior to and/or outside the conduct of inquiry itself. An episodic presumption implies inquiry movement through an *a priori* succession of preconceived stages or sequence. These stages shape and delimit the structure of inquiry. For example, the data may be developed and sorted with reference to the anterior function of reinforcing the *status quo*. Experience is guided and shaped by the process of making and assessing consequences of institutional adjustments. Instrumental inquiry is cumulatively developmental of warranted knowledge and its application, as institutional adjustments, to problematic areas of political economy.

Evidential, not conjectural

Foster's instrumental value theory is grounded in existential and experiential phenomena, evidentially affirmed. The quest is to seek, through inquiry, to establish conjugate correspondence between theory and fact. Evidentially grounded theory does explain what it purports to explain. To confirm this accounting, one must demonstrate logically and empirically that the explanation offered and the institutional adjustment proposed are grounded in the perceived run of pertinent evidences, both as to cause and to consequence. There is no place in instrumental value theory for idle conjectures, ungrounded speculations or positivist affirmations. It is a continuing task to secure pertinent facts and theoretical accounts which demonstrably explain what they purport to explain.

Conjectures, then, are not stand-ins for hypotheses. The latter are the major creative dimension of all warranted inquiry. The significance of hypotheses derives from their contribution to the ordering of data, the defining of focus, and the offering of causal accounts. They provide for social inquiry addressed, for example, to real problems of income generation, growth in warranted knowledge, and equitable distribution of money and real income. Conjectures, on the other hand, are speculative guesses not necessarily based on warranted knowledge. They may well be suppositions that consist of inferences drawn from false, non-existent or inadequate data. It is not inconceivable that a surmise, guess or conjecture may, through inquiry, ultimately become a relevant and purposive hypothesis or be validated as a construct capable of being included in scientific social inquiry. But this, surely, is an infrequent outcome. Conjectures, generally, are devoid of context placement, evidential grounding, and explanatory capacity. Conjectures, *per se*, are not capable of being integrated into processual instrumental analysis of observed phenomena.

Instrumental value theory III: implications

Choice and habit

Foster's instrumental value theory, in application, relies on both choice and habit. Habits are conservative. They represent an acquired disposition to think or behave in a particular way. They fortuitously preserve judgments, canons, and tenets of conduct made earlier in response to then pertinent concerns. Habits order our lives and provide predictability. They are critical attributes of learned behavior and critical reflection. Habits, by permitting one to economize on time and effort, are an essential precondition for choice making. The role of instrumental value theory is continuously to provide for a running appraisal of habits even as they are indulged and exhibited, often uncritically and routinely. Habits are critical in inquiry and in problem solving. They represent previously found solutions to problems. By economizing on inquiry efforts, they enhance the probable intellectual focus on problems that do currently exist. Habits are stabilizers; they may be simple or complex. But they are imbedded in institutions. In economies, most of the structural fabric consists of habits, routines, established patterns, concerning the creation of goods, the marketing of goods, and defining roles each plays in the economic process. Skills become habitual; speech patterns become habitual; inquiry modes become habitual; responses to external stimuli may well be habitual. But a habit does not create a habit. A habit does not attain significance merely in consequence of it offering a familiar response; the consequences it invokes must continuously be appraised; habits do not provide criteria of appraisal.

Choices are pivotal. Habits may not preclude the application of criteria of appraisal, but the construction of choice requires the employment of some criterion of choice. Value premises are essential in choosing among options or patterns of conduct. One cannot select among two or more options without some standard, some criterion, some value premise that indicates what ought to be. When we contend that prevailing habits produce unacceptable consequences we are evaluating conduct with an appraiser's eye on what "better" conduct might be. Choice making formally, but minimally, permits the choosing among two or more options. But choice making, employing the instrumental value principle, does direct that social choices non-invidiously enhance social reconstruction, solve economic problems, and/or restore instrumental functions of existing institutions.

Problem solving

Foster's instrumental value theory, in sum, functions to direct the resolution of institutional problems. Indeed, one cannot even define a social or economic problem without engaging in normative assessments of institutional behavior. Solving problems requires institutional change; a directed modification of the structural fabric that has become non-functional, non-instrumental or invidious in some significant operations or impact. Problem solving means adjusting or modifying institutional patterns in pursuit of a more productive, less invidious, and/or more technically efficient institutional fabric.

Problems originate and appear, then, as disjunctions, malfunctions, and/or disrapport in the institutional structure that organizes the social and economic processes. The perception of a disjunctive gap occurs between what is going on and what ought to go on. For discernible reasons, instrumental functions have been abandoned, precluded, rejected, reduced, impaired or ignored. Ceremonial functions may have become dominant, pervasive, and destructive: The economy may confront problematic conditions of inflation or deflation, impeded growth or stagnation, structural and/or cyclical unemployment, technical retardation or misdirection, environmental destruction and/or invidious discrimination, skewed distribution of income and product, and other impediments in the provision of the means of life and experience.

Accordingly, it is Foster's instrumental value principle that provides for an economic problem to be identified and resolved through instrumental reasoning. The solution of problems, then, requires the continuing adjustment of institutions to enhance their instrumental functioning and to diminish the invidious or ceremonial impairments of one or another instrumental function in the social process.

References

Ayres, Clarence E. (1944) *Theory of Economic Progress*, Chapel Hill, NC: University of North Carolina.

—— (1961) *Toward a Reasonable Society*, Austin, TX: University of Texas Press.

Cornford, Frances M. (1912) *From Religion to Philosophy*, London: Edward Arnold.

Dewey, John (1922) *Human Nature and Conduct*, New York: Henry Holt.

—— (1925) *Experience and Nature*, Chicago, IL: Open Court.

—— (1927, 1946) *The Public and Its Problems*, Chicago, IL: Gateway Books.

—— (1938) *Logic: The Theory of Inquiry*, New York: Holt, Rinehart and Winston.

—— (1939) *Theory of Valuation*, Chicago, IL: University of Chicago Press.

—— (1946) *Problems of Men*, New York: Philosophical Library.

Foster, J. Fagg (1942, 1981) "John Dewey and Economic Value," *Journal of Economic Issues* 15: 871–897.

—— (1946) *Theoretical Foundations of Government Ownership in a Capitalist Economy*, Ph.D. Dissertation, University of Texas (unpublished).

—— (1948) Lecture Notes (LN), "Value and Its Determinants" [recorded and transcribed].

—— (1949, 1981) "The Relation between the Theory of Value and Economic Analysis," *Journal of Economic Issues* 15: 899–905.

—— (1950) Lecture Notes (LN), "Value and Its Determinants."

—— (1974) Lecture Notes (LN), "American Contributions to Economic Thought."

Hogben, Lancelot (1937) *Retreat from Reason*, New York: Random House.

Kaplan, Abraham (1961) *The New World of Philosophy*, New York: Random House.

Veblen, Thorstein (1899) *The Theory of the Leisure Class*, New York: Modern Library, 1934.

—— (1904) *The Theory of Business Enterprise*, New York: Charles Scribner's Sons, 1932.

—— (1914) *The Instinct of Workmanship*, New York: The Viking Press, 1946.

—— (1919a) *The Vested Interests*, New York: The Viking Press, 1946.

—— (1919b) *The Place of Science in Modern Civilization*, New York: Russell and Russell, 1961.

—— (1921) *The Engineers and the Price System*, New York: Augustus M. Kelley, 1965.

—— (1923) *Absentee Ownership*, New York: Augustus M. Kelley, 1964.

16 Monetary policy in the twenty-first century in the light of the debate between Chartalism and Monetarism

Paul Davidson

Since Aristotle's time, as Schumpeter (1954: 288) noted, there have been two views regarding the nature of money in a money-using market oriented entrepreneurial economy: the Chartalist view and the Monetarist (or Metallist) view. The latter assumes that the institution of money evolved from barter relationships where producible goods always traded for other producible goods. Ultimately, in this Monetarist view one commodity (normally a metal) became the embodiment of the other goods traded for any specific good. Thus, behind the Monetarist conceptualization of money is the idea that money merely represents the trading of one specific producible commodity for all other producible commodities. From this there develops the idea that the use of such a (producible) commodity-based money is more efficient than direct barter for it avoids what Clower called "the double coincidence of wants."

According to Schumpeter (1954: 56), Plato can be considered the "first known sponsor" of the second "fundamental" theory of money – an anti-Monetarist theory that we now call Chartalism. For Plato, money comes into being once a society organizes itself along continuous market lines. Social custom, *supported by social behavior and/or legislation*, gives money its unique importance in a system where, as Clower (1965) noted, "goods trade for money and money trades for goods, but goods do not trade directly for goods."

The Monetarist versus Chartalist distinct conceptual streams can be traced through the centuries-old development of economic thought. For example, in the nineteenth century this difference of views involved the debate between the currency school and the banking school. Nevertheless, the vast majority of economists over the years have either explicitly or implicitly accepted the Monetarism vision of money at the back of their minds. Certainly the most famous economists of the eighteenth and nineteenth centuries – Adam Smith and Karl Marx – both accepted the Monetarist view as did Petty, Locke, and Mill. Followers of the Chartalist view since Plato – with one exception – are far less well known. To today's generation of economists, perhaps the only recognizable Chartalists are John Law, Georg Fredrick Knapp, and John Maynard Keynes.

Most economists recognize that the Monetarist vision of money involves the conceptual idea of a barter exchange of a producible good for an ultimately commodity backed money. The meaning of Chartalism, however, is far less clear. In fact, Schumpeter defines the Chartalist view as merely the negative of the Monetarist conception (where Schumpeter equates Metallism with Monetarism). This negative connotation is designed to immediately put the impartial observer off the idea that Chartalism is a "good" or "proper" view. One purpose of this chapter is to provide a better perspective.

Monetarism and neutral money

The Monetarist vision of money as an efficient evolution of a barter system to avoid the double coincidence of wants has imbedded in it the belief in the neutrality of money. In his vision of money, the foremost Monetarist of our times, Milton Friedman (1974: 27) explains,

> we have accepted the quantity-theory presumption, and have thought it supported by the evidence we examined, that changes in the quantity of money as such *in the long run* have a negligible effect on real income, so that nonmonetary forces are 'all that matter' for changes in real income over the decades and money 'does not matter'. On the other hand, we have regarded the quantity of money, plus the other variables (including real income itself) that affect k as essentially 'all that matter' for the long-run determination of nominal income.

In other words, money is presumed to be neutral – at least in the long run. "For shorter periods of time" than the long run, Friedman (1974: 27) acknowledged that changes in the quantity of money could affect real income as people *adapted* their expectations to the equilibrium outcome. When what Tobin called Mach II Monetarism was developed by Lucas by adding rational expectations to Friedman's old Monetarism vision, however, Lucas closed the loop and assured that money would be neutral in both the short run and the long run.

Hence, if we follow Schumpeter's guide that Chartalism is the negative of Monetarism then Chartalism must argue that money is never neutral either in the short run or the long run. One obvious question immediately arises: how can Chartalists be so sure of the non-neutrality of money even in the long run? After all, in the long run we will all be dead and, therefore, we cannot produce empirical evidence culled from the human experience to statistically prove that, in the long run, money is still not neutral.

Knapp, Keynes and the law

Keynes endorsed the Knapp vision of Chartalism when he wrote: "And the Age of Chartalist or State Money was reached when the State claimed the right to declare what thing should answer as money to the current money-of-account – when it claimed the right not only to enforce the dictionary but also to write the dictionary. To-day all civilised money is, *beyond the possibility of dispute*, Chartalist" (Keynes 1930, Vol. I: 4–5 (emphasis added)). Earlier Knapp (1924: 1) had declared: "Money is a creature of law. A theory of money must therefore deal with legal history." Keynes (1930: 3) associated the concept of "money itself [with] that by delivery of which debt-contracts and price-contracts are *discharged*." In other words, the concept of money is inevitably tied to the civil law of contracts. Moreover, Keynes declared "Something which is used merely as a convenient medium of exchange on the spot may approach to being Money, inasmuch as it may represent a means of holding General Purchasing Power. But if this is all, we have scarcely emerged from the stage of Barter" (Keynes 1930: 3).

Accordingly, there is an obvious distinction between Keynes's vision of money as a Chartalist thing and Friedman's view of money as "a temporary abode of purchasing power", that is, a means of holding generalized purchasing power for a relatively short period of calendar time while one decides on how to spend completely one's permanent income stream. Clearly, the Friedman vision has scarcely emerged from a "the stage of Barter" view alluded to by Keynes in the aforecited quote.

The Chartalist emphasis on the legal history of money and the legal discharge of contracts, on the other hand, may suggest a narrower focus than Friedman's anything that is a "temporary abode of purchasing power" since the emphasis on law may suggest that only legal tender is considered money. Keynes, however, expanded that legal strait-jacket vision of money when he noted that "the State may exercise its chartalist prerogative to declare" that a private debt can become money. Keynes noted: "At the cost of not conforming entirely with (1930) current usage I propose to include . . . not only money which itself is legal tender but also money which the State or the Central Bank undertakes to accept as payment to itself or in exchange for legal tender money" (Keynes 1930: 6). Thus whatever the State accepts in payment of taxes by the private sector also comes under the rubric of Chartalist money. This wider Chartalist view means that even if the State or the domestic banking system is not the (monopoly?) issuer of that thing which the State accepts in payment of taxes, that thing *is* the money of the nation.[1]

Under Keynes's Chartalist vision, rejecting the neutrality axiom does not require assuming that agents suffer from a money illusion. It only means that "money is not neutral" (Keynes 1973: 411); money matters in both the short run and the long run in affecting the equilibrium level of employment and real outputs, as long as entrepreneurs and other owners of the factors of production use State enforced nominal contracts to organize a preponderance of production and exchange activities. As Keynes put it:

> "The theory which I desiderate would deal . . . with an economy in which money plays a part of its own and affects motives and decisions, and is,

in short, one of the operative factors in the situation, so that the course of events cannot be predicted in either the long period or in the short, without a knowledge of the behavior of money between the first state and the last. And it is this which we ought to mean when we speak of a monetary economy.

(Keynes 1973: 408–409)

Once we recognize that money is a real phenomenon, that money matters, then neutrality must be rejected. It then follows that it is the nominal rate of interest that affects real output and that the concept of a real rate of interest is a meaningless *ex ante* variable.[2]

Arrow and Hahn (1971: 356–57) implicitly recognized the importance of this Chartalist vision of non-neutral money in the development of any "serious monetary theory" when they wrote:

> The terms in which contracts are made matter. In particular, if money is the goods in terms of which contracts are made, then the prices of goods in terms of money are of special significance. This is not the case if we consider an economy without a past or future. . . . *If a serious monetary theory* comes to be written, the fact that contracts are made in terms of money will be of considerable importance [italics added].

Moreover Arrow and Hahn demonstrate (1971: 361) that if contracts are made in terms of money (so that money affects real decisions) in an economy moving along in calendar time with a past and a future, then *all existence theorems are jeopardized*. The existence of money contracts – a characteristic of the world in which we live – implies that there need never exist, in the long run or the short run, any rational expectations equilibrium or general equilibrium market clearing price vector.

What type of an economy system is "irrational" enough to use money contracts that fix prices and are enforceable only in nominal terms?

A fundamental axiom of neoclassical theory is the neutrality of money. Hence, economic agents in a neoclassical world are presumed to make decisions solely based on "real" valuations; they do not suffer from any "money illusion." Thus in a neoclassical world, all contracts should be made in real terms and are always enforceable in real terms.

The economy in which we live, on the other hand, utilizes money contracts – not real contracts – to seal production and exchange agreements among self-interested individuals. The ubiquitous use of money contracts has always presented a dilemma to neoclassical theory. Logically consistent neoclassical theorists must view the universal use of money contracts by modern economies as irrational, since such agreements fixing payments in nominal terms over a period of calendar time (i.e., the short run) can impede the self-interest optimizing pursuit of real incomes by economic decision makers. Hence, mainstream economists tend to explain the existence of money contracts by using non-economic reasons such as social customs, invisible handshakes, etcetera – societal institutional constraints which limit price signaling and hence limit adjustments for the optimal use of resources to the long run. For Post Keynesians, on the other hand, *binding* nominal contractual commitments are a sensible method for dealing with true uncertainty regarding future outcomes whenever economic activities span a long duration of calendar time.

In order to understand why there is this fundamental difference in viewpoints regarding the use of money contracts, one must distinguish between a money-using entrepreneur economy and a cooperative (barter) economy.[3] A *cooperative economy* is defined as one where production is organized such that each input owner is rewarded for its real contribution to the process by a predetermined share of the aggregate physical output produced. Examples of cooperative economic systems include monasteries, nunneries, prisons, or even an Israeli kibbutz. In each of these cooperative economies, a central authority or a predetermined set of rules governs both the production and payments in terms of real goods distributed to the inputs. There is never any involuntary unemployment of monks, nuns, prisoners, or workers on a kibbutz. Say's Law prevails. This is the world of neoclassical analysis.

An *entrepreneur economy*, on the other hand, is a system that has two distinctly different characteristics. First, production is organized by "a class of entrepreneurs who hire the factors of production for money and look to their recoupment from selling the output for money" (Keynes 1979: 77). Second, there is no automatic mechanism which guarantees that all the money paid out to inputs in the production process will be spent on the products of industry. Hence entrepreneurs can never be sure that they can recoup all the money costs of production. As Keynes (1979: 78) pointed out "it is obvious on these definitions that it is in an entrepreneur economy that we actually live to-day." In an entrepreneur economy, by definition, Say's Law cannot be applicable.

In our entrepreneur economy, market-oriented managers of business firms organize the production process on a forward-money contract basis, that is, they hire inputs and purchase raw materials for the production process by entering into contractual agreements to pay money sums for delivery of specific materials and services at exact future dates. These managers of production processes expect to recoup these money outlays by selling the resulting output for money on either a spot or forward contracting basis. When we speak of "the bottom line" in our economy, we are essentially indicating that entrepreneurs are motivated by pursuing cash inflows from sales that will equal or exceed the money outflows spent on production costs.

In an entrepreneurial economic system, the earning of income (as defined by Keynes[4]) is directly associated with the existence of these money contracts which permit entrepreneurs to "control" both the sequencing of inputs into production activities and the net cash outflows of firms. These contractual money payments give the recipient claims on the products of industry.[5]

Although Keynes defined the economy that we lived in on the basis of the use of monetary contracts for hire and sale, this definition does not *per se* explain the existence and ubiquitous use of this human institution. In order to provide an explanation for the widespread use of money contracts, we must delve into how entrepreneurs make decisions, and recognize the difference between risk and uncertainty – a difference which is essential to Keynes's analysis of involuntary unemployment.

Information, decisions, and uncertainty

Mainstream perspectives involving uncertainty presume that expectations are based on either (i) a statistical analysis of past data, with market signals providing information about objective probabilities, or on (ii) a subjective perception of these probabilities founded on the axioms of expected utility theory, especially the ordering axiom. In the mainstream perspective *probabilistic risk and uncertainty are synonymous*, while the ordering axiom rules out uncertainty in deterministic expected utility models.

Post Keynesians (Davidson 1978; 1982–83) have developed a different perspective about uncertainty, where existing objective probability distributions are not the basis for comprehending real world behavior under uncertainty. According to this Post Keynesian analysis, there are many important situations where "true" uncertainty exists regarding future consequences of today's choices. In these cases of true uncertainty, today's decision makers believe that no expenditure of current resources can provide reliable statistical or intuitive clues regarding future outcomes of today's decisions. In other words, the future cannot be reliably estimated from existing data (what orthodox economists call information).

Given this Post Keynesian perspective on uncertainty, decision makers may, in an uncertain environment, either avoid choosing between alternatives that commit the use of real resources because they "haven't got a clue" about the future, *or* follow their "animal spirits" for positive action for the use of real resources in a "damn the torpedoes, full speed ahead" approach. This Post Keynesian perspective on uncertainty provides a more general theory explaining long-run decisions regarding liquidity demands and investment decisions, the existence of long period underemployment equilibrium, the long-run non-neutrality of money, and the unique and important role Keynes assigned to nominal contracts, and especially the money wage contract.

Keynesian uncertainty, money, and explicit money contracts

Individuals in the real world must decide whether past experience provides a useful guide to the future. Should one presume that economic processes are uniform and consistent over time so that forthcoming events are predetermined, either by ergodic stochastic processes or at least by specified and completely ordered prospects? Can the agent completely dismiss any fear of tragic uninsurable error during the time between choice and outcome? Does the agent believe he or she can make actuarially certain estimates about the future or does the agent recognize he/she is ignorant regarding the future? No rule can be specified in advance regarding how individuals decide whether they are in an objective, a subjective, or a true uncertainty environment. Their perception of the environment that they are in, however, will make a difference to their behavior.

Keynes laid great stress on the distinction between uncertainty and probability, especially in relation to decisions involving the accumulation of wealth and the possession of liquidity. The essence of his *General Theory* involves liquidity preferences and animal spirits dominating real expenditure choices. Money plays a unique role in "ruling the roost" among all assets (Keynes 1936: 223) and it is non-neutral in both the short and long run (Keynes 1973a: 408–11). These claims, as Keynes made clear in his 1937 restatement (Keynes 1973b: 112, 114) of where he saw his general theory "most clearly departing from previous theory," rested on the clear distinction between the "probability calculus" and conditions of uncertainty when "there is no scientific basis to form any calculable probability whatever. We simply do not know."

Liquidity

Liquidity and animal spirits are the driving forces behind Keynes's analysis of long-period underemployment equilibrium, even in a world of instantaneously flexible spot prices and pure competition (i.e., marginal cost pricing). Neither objective nor subjective probabilities suffice to understand the role of non-neutral money and monetary policy in Keynes's underemployment equilibrium analysis.

It is not surprising, therefore, that unemployment still plagues today's global-oriented economies, since most economists still formulate policy guidelines that are only applicable to a limited domain where agents choose "as if" they had specific and completely ordered knowledge about the future outcomes of their actions. Politicians (or as Keynes called them "madmen in authority") are, in this era of instant communications, "distilling their frenzy from some academic scribbler" whose student acts as a policy advisor to the Prime Minister or the Head of the Council of Economic Advisors, etcetera.

In Davidson (1978, 1982, 1988), I have shown that the existence of the societal institution of legally enforceable forward contracts denominated in nominal (not real!) terms creates a monetary environment that is not neutral, even in the long run. Tobin (1985: 108–109) has written that the existence of money "has always been an awkward problem for neoclassical general equilibrium theory . . . [and] the alleged neutrality of money. . . . The application of this neutrality proposition to actual real world monetary policies is a prime example of the fallacy of misplaced concreteness." Tobin then associates Keynes's rejection of the money neutrality presumption with Keynes's emphasis on "the essential unpredictability, even in a probabilistic sense," of the future (Tobin 1985: 112–13).

Legal contractual arrangements permit agents to protect themselves to some extent against the unpredictable consequences of current decisions to commit real resources towards production and investment activities of long duration. Legal enforcement of fixed money contracts permits each party in a contract to have sensible expectations that if the other party does not fulfill its contractual obligation, the injured party is entitled to just compensation and hence will not suffer a pecuniary loss. In an entrepreneurial money-using economy it is the lack of liquidity, rather than real resources, that can cascade into a case of insolvency that ultimately causes death by bankruptcy of economic decision makers (in the short run as well as the long run).

The social institution of money and the law of fixed money contracts enables entrepreneurs and households to form sensible expectations regarding cash flows (but not necessarily real outcomes) over time and hence cope with the otherwise unknowable future and avoid the problems of illiquidity and insolvency. Contractual obligations fixed in nominal terms provide assurance to the contracting parties that despite uncertainty, they can at least determine future consequences in terms of cash flows and therefore hopefully avoid death by illiquidity. Entering into fixed purchase and hiring contracts of long duration limits nominal liabilities to what the entrepreneur believes his or her liquidity position (often buttressed by credit commitments from a banker) can survive. Entrepreneurs feeling the animal urge to action in the face of uncertainty will not make any significant decisions involving real resource commitments until they are sure of their liquidity position, so that they can meet their contractual (transaction demand) cash outlays. Fixed forward money contracts allow entrepreneurs (and households) to find an efficient sequence for the use of and payment for resources in time-consuming production and exchange processes.

Money, in an entrepreneur economy, is defined as the *means of contractual settlement*. This implies that in the Post Keynesian monetary theory, the civil law of contracts determines what is money in any law-abiding society.[6] The possession of money, or any liquid asset[7] (Davidson 1982: 34), provides liquidity. Liquidity is defined as the ability to meet one's nominal contractual obligations when they come due. In an uncertain world where liabilities are specified in terms of money, the holding of money is a valuable choice (Keynes 1936: 236–37). Further, the banking system's ability to create "real bills" to provide the liquidity to finance increases in real production flows is an essential expansionary element in the operation of a (non-neutral) money production economy. If tight money policies prevent some entrepreneurs from obtaining sufficient additional bank money commitments at reasonable pecuniary costs, when managers (in the aggregate) wish to expand their production flows (and the liquidity preference of the public is unchanged), then some entrepreneurs will not be able to meet their potential additional contractual payroll and materials-purchase obligations before the additional output is produced and then profitably sold. Accordingly, without the creation of additional bank money, entrepreneurs will not be willing to sign additional hiring and material supply contracts and long-run employment growth is stymied, even when entrepreneurs feel that future effective demand is sufficient to warrant expansion. A shortage of money can hold up the expansion of real output, despite expected profits!

Liquid assets also provide a safe haven for not committing one's monetary claims on resources when the threat of uncertainty becomes great, as in Keynes's discussion of precautionary and speculative motives. Keynes claimed (1936: 237n) that the attribute of liquidity is only associated with durables that possess "essential properties so that they are neither readily produced by labor in the private sector nor easily substitutable, *for liquidity purposes*, with goods produced by labor."

When agents' fear of the uncertain future increases their aggregate demand for "waiting" (even in the long run), agents will divert their earned income claims from the purchase of the current products of industry to demanding additional liquidity. Consequently, effective demand for labor in the private sector declines. Only in an unpredictable (nonergodic) environment does it make sense to defer expenditures in this way, as opposed to spending all one's earnings on the various products of industry being traded in free markets.

This liquidity argument may appear to be similar to the view of general equilibrium theorists like Grandmont and Laroque (1976), who stress an option demand for money. However, in their model and many others, money has an option value only because of very unrealistic assumptions elsewhere in the model. For example, Grandmont and Laroque (1976) assume that (a) all producible goods are non-storable; (b) no financial system exists, which means no borrowing and no spot markets for reselling securities; and (c) fiat money is the only durable and hence the only possible store of value which can be carried over to the future. Of course, if durable producible and productive goods existed (as they do in the real world) and outcomes associated with holding producible durables were completely orderable, flexible spot and forward prices would reflect the multi-period consumption plans of individuals and no "optimizing" agent would hold fiat money as a store of value. Say's Law would be applicable, and the nominal quantity of money would be neutral. Hence Grandmont and Laroque can achieve "temporary" Keynesian equilibrium via an option demand for money to hold over time only under the most vacuous circumstances. By contrast, Keynes allowed the demand to hold money as a long-run store of value to coexist with the existence of productive durables.

Another modern approach to liquidity is that of Kreps, whose analysis of "waiting" (1988: 142) presumes that at some earlier future date each agent will receive "information about which state prevails" at a later future pay-off date. Accordingly, waiting to receive information is only a short-run phenomenon; long-run waiting behavior is not optimal in the Kreps analysis – *unless the information is never received!* The option to wait is normally associated with a "preference for flexibility" until sufficient information is obtained. Although Kreps does not draw this implication, his framework implies that if agents never receive the needed information and thus remain in a state of true uncertainty, they will wait forever.

Keynes (1936: 210), on the other hand, insisted that decisions not to buy products – to save – did "*not* necessitate a decision to have dinner or to buy a pair of boots a week hence or a year hence or to consume any specified thing at any specified date. . . . It is not a substitution of future consumption demand for current consumption demand – it is a net diminution of such demand." In other words, neither Kreps's waiting option nor the Grandmont and Laroque option demand for money explains Keynes's argument that there may be no intertemporal substitution. In the long run, people may still want to stay liquid and hence a long run unemployment equilibrium can exist.

This argument has empirical support. Danziger et al. (1982–83: 210) analyzed microdata on consumption and incomes of the elderly and have shown that "the elderly do not dissave to finance their consumption at retirement . . . they spend less on consumption goods and services (save significantly more) than the non-elderly at all levels of income. Moreover, the oldest of the elderly save the most at given levels of income." These facts suggest that as life becomes more truly uncertain as one ages, the elderly "wait" more without making a decision to spend their earned claims on resources. This behavior is irrational according to the life-cycle hypothesis, inconsistent with Grandmont–Laroque option demand for waiting, and not compatible with Kreps's "waiting" – unless one is willing to admit that even in the long run "information about which state will prevail" may not exist, and these economic decisions are made under a state of Keynesian uncertainty.

Probabilistic analysis of waiting and option value recognizes only a need to postpone spending over time. However, only Keynesian uncertainty provides a basis for a long-run demand for liquidity and the possibility of long-run underemployment equilibrium

Conclusions

The fundamental building blocks of Post Keynesian monetary theory are: (1) the non-neutrality of money; (2) the existence of nonergodic uncertainty in some important decision-making aspects of economic life; and (3) the denial of the ubiquitousness of the gross substitution axiom. One way that humans have coped with having to make decisions where pay-offs will occur in the unforeseen and possibly unforeseeable future is via the development of the law of contracts by civilized societies,[8] and the use of money as a Chartalist means of discharging contracts.

Keynes's revolutionary analysis, where money is never neutral and liquidity matters, is a general theory of an economy where the complete unpredictability of the future may have important economic consequences. By contrast, neoclassical optimization requires restrictive fundamental postulates regarding uncertainty and hence expectations regarding future consequences that Keynes's analysis does not. The analyst must therefore choose which system is more relevant for analyzing the economic problem under study.

For many routine decisions, assuming the uniformity and consistency of nature over time (that is, assuming ergodicity) may be, by the definition of routine, a useful simplification for handling the problem at hand. For problems involving investment and liquidity decisions where large unforeseeable changes over long periods of calendar time cannot be ruled out, a Keynesian uncertainty model is more applicable. To presume a universe of discoverable regularities which can be expected to continue into the future and where the neutrality of money is therefore central (Lucas 1981: 561) will provide a misleading analogy for developing macropolicies for monetary, production economies whenever money really matters and affects production decisions in the real economy.

Economists should be careful not to claim more for their discipline than they can deliver. The belief that in "*some* circumstances" the world is probabilistic (Lucas and Sargent 1981: xi–xii), or that future prospects can be completely ordered, will tend to lead to the argument that individuals in free markets either will not make persistent errors or will tend to know better than the government how to judge the future. Basing general rules on these particular assumptions can result in disastrous policy advice for governmental officials facing situations where many economic decision makers feel unable to draw conclusions about the future from the past.

If, however, economists can recognize and identify when these (nonergodic) economic conditions of true uncertainty are likely to be prevalent, government can play a role in improving the economic performance of markets. Economists should strive to design institutional devices which can produce legal constraints on the infinite universe of events which could otherwise occur as the economic process moves through historical time. For example, governments can set up financial safety nets to prevent, or at least offset, disastrous consequences that might occur, and also provide monetary incentives to encourage individuals to take civilized actions which are determined by democratic processes to be in the social interests (Davidson and Davidson 1988). Where private institutions do not exist, or need buttressing against the winds of true uncertainty, government should develop economic institutions which attempt to reduce uncertainties by limiting the possible consequences of private actions to those that are compatible with full employment and reasonable price stability.

Keynes distinguished an entrepreneurial, money-using economy from a classical non-monetary, real exchange system. The latter is a "special case" of a *general theory* where the imposition of three restrictive classical axioms is required to assure that instantaneously flexible prices assure full employment (and, in modern classical models, assures consistent expectations of all economic agents). The requisite classical axioms are: (a) money is always neutral (at least in the long run); (b) the future can be (statistically) reliably predicted using past and current (relative) price signals and hence expectations of all participants are "correct"[9] at least in the long run (the ergodic axiom[10]) and (c) everything is a substitute for everything else (the gross substitution axiom).

In contrast, an *entrepreneurial economy* is a market oriented system where people use money and contracts to deal with an uncertain future. In this truly uncertain world, people "do not know what is going to happen and they know they do not know. . . . As in history" (Hicks 1977: vii). In terms of stochastic models, this concept of uncertainty means that agents *know* that past and current market (price) signals do not provide a statistically reliable basis for making probability statements regarding future outcomes. The ergodic axiom therefore cannot be used to explain behavior underlying decisions (e.g., investment) where agents believe the future is uncertain rather than just risky.

Lucas (1977: 15) has argued that "in the cases of uncertainty [i.e., nonergodic conditions] economic reasoning will be of no value." Keynes (1937a), on the other hand, argued that his effective demand reasoning dealt specifically with an uncertain (nonergodic) environment[11] rather than merely a risky economic system.

In nonergodic conditions, there is great utility in organizing production and exchange activities via time-duration money contracts that limit liabilities to nominal sums. In such a monetary-entrepreneurial economy, firms and households are concerned not just with their real income but also with their cash flows. No matter how unpredictable (nonergodic) the "real" future is, agents can avoid the pain of bankruptcy as long as cash inflow exceeds outflow. The use of non-indexed nominal contracts to organize economic activities, allows firms and households to gain control of cash flows in an uncertain environment. Models of optimizing agents that produce "correct" and consistent expectations of future real flows may be an idealized objective, but it is nigh impossible to achieve in the real world as Robert Burns recognized when he wrote "the best laid schemes o'mice an' men gang aft agley." Controlling nominal cash flows by using money contracts to avoid illiquidity and ultimately bankruptcy, however, is an attainable and useful objective and is, therefore, the basis of most expenditure decisions in an entrepreneurial economy – as the businessman's "put-down" of the classical academic economist, "They have never had to meet a payroll," clearly suggests.

In a monetary economy, it is sensible for entrepreneurs to enter into monetary forward contracts for the hire of labor and other factor inputs. As long as entrepreneurs have, or can contractually arrange to obtain, the necessary liquidity (cash holdings plus net cash inflows) to meet contractual cash-outflow obligations *as they come due*, they need not fear an uncertain "real" future. Liquidity, therefore, affects entrepreneurial decisions to produce real output and hire workers. In an entrepreneurial economy, it is cash-flow conditions that determine production and employment-hiring decisions.

Money is *never* neutral in either the short or long period as long as entrepreneurs continue to organize production with a myriad of overlapping and concomitant money contracts.[12] In an entrepreneurial system, neither the ergodic axiom nor the neutral money axiom applies. Any model built on the microfoundation of ergodicity and neutral money provides a misleading explanation of important economic expenditure decision making and hence can provide dangerous policy implications for the real economy.

Notes

1 One example where government does not control the issuance of money in its economy is Panama where US Federal Reserve Notes circulate as legal tender and any bank accounts that are immediately convertible at a fixed price into US Federal Reserve Notes are accepted by the State in payment of taxes. In Argentina, a currency board issues pesos endogenously as it receives US dollars from private sector transactors. A historical example would be the era of wildcat banking between 1835 and the Civil War.

2 Keynes (1936: 142) believed that the "real rate of interest" concept of Irving Fisher was a logical confusion. In a monetary economy moving through calendar time towards an uncertain (statistically unpredictable) future there is no such thing as a forward looking real rate of interest. In an entrepreneur economy the only objective for a firm is to end the production process by liquidating its working capital in order to end up with more money than it started with (Keynes 1979: 82). Moreover, money has an impact on the real sector in both the short and long run. Thus, money is a real phenomenon.

This is just the reverse of what classical theory and modern mainstream theory teaches us. In orthodox macro theory the rate of interest is a real (technologically determined) factor while money (at least in the long run for both Friedman and Tobin) does not affect the real output flow. This reversal of the importance or the significance of money and interest rates for real and monetary phenomena between orthodox and Keynes's theory is the result of Keynes's rejection of a neoclassical universal truth – the axiom of neutral money.

3 The distinction between a cooperative economy and an entrepreneur economy was developed by Keynes in an early draft of *The General Theory* (see Keynes 1979: 76–83).

4 One should remind the reader that in some economic discourse, the term "income" is not only associated with current output, but also with a welfare aspect as measured by the current services available to the community. Since some services available to the community in any period will flow from pre-existing durables, the use of the "income" term in its welfare garb is not compatible with the use of income as the value of current output, except if all the goods produced are always non-durable.

5 Since the term "income" is associated with contributions to the production of current output in the economy, therefore aggregate income is equal to the money receipts arising from the contractual sale of services and current products. (Profits occupy a sort of halfway house – since they are not directly determined by factor-hire contracts. Instead they are the residual due to the difference between the contractually determined receipts on the sale of products and the contractual costs of the hired factors of production.)

Income-in-kind payments should be conceived of as the combination of two separate contractual transactions, namely money income payments to factor owners from the employer, with a simultaneous purchase commitment of goods by the factor owner to the employer.

6 In the first page of text in his *Treatise on Money* (Keynes 1930: 3), Keynes reminds us that money comes into existence is association with contracts!

7 A liquid asset is one that is resalable for money on a well-organized, orderly spot market.

8 The abolition of slavery makes the enforcement of real contracts for human labor illegal. Accordingly, civilized society has decided not to permit "real contracting," no matter how efficient it can be proved to be in neoclassical economics.

9 Mutually correct expectations of entrepreneurs and workers are the basis of both Phelps's and LNJ's concept of equilibrium.

10 In non-stochastic models, the ordering axiom plays the same role as the ergodic axiom (Davidson 1991: 134; Hicks 1979: 113, 115).

11 Although Keynes never used the term "ergodic," Keynes's (1937b: 308) criticism of Tinbergen's "method" is that the economic system in which we live is not stationary, and non-stationarity is a sufficient condition for nonergodicity.

12 Any economy that abandons the use of money contracts must revert to some form of a completely centralized cooperative system with very primitive production processes (e.g., as in a nunnery or kibbutz).

References

Arrow, K. S., and F . H. Hahn (1971) *General Competitive Analysis*, San Francisco, CA: Holden-Day.

Clower, R. W. (1965) "The Keynesian Revolution: A Theoretical Appraisal, " in *The Theory of Interest Rates*, ed. by F. H. Hahn and F. P. R. Brechling, London: Macmillan.

Danziger, S., J. vander Gaag, E. Smolensky and M. Taussig (1978) "The Life Cycle Hypothesis and The Consumption Behavior of the Elderly," *Journal of Post Keynesian Economics* 5.

Davidson, P. (1978) *Money and the Real World*, 2nd edn., London: Macmillan.

—— (1982–83) "Rational Expectations: A Fallacious Foundation for Studying Crucial Decision-making Processes," *Journal of Post Keynesian Economics* 5.

—— (1988) "A Technical Definition of Uncertainty and the Long-Run Non-neutrality of Money," *Cambridge Journal of Economics* 12.

Grandmont, J.-M. and G. Laroque (1976) "On Temporary Keynesian Equilibrium," *Review of Economic Studies* 43.

Knapp, F. G. (1924) *The State Theory of Money*, London: Macmillan.

Keynes, J. M. (1930) *A Treatise on Money*, London: Macmillan .

—— (1936) *The General Theory of Employment, Interest and Money*, New York: Harcourt.

—— (1973a) *The Collected Writings of John Maynard Keynes*, Vol. 13, ed. by D. Moggridge, London: Macmillan.

—— (1973b) *The Collected Writings of John Maynard Keynes*, Vol. 14, ed. by D. Moggridge, London: Macmillan.

—— (1979) *The Collected Writings of John Maynard Keynes*, Vol. 29, ed. by D. Moggridge, London: Macmillan.

Kreps, D. M. (1988) *Notes on the Theory of Choice*, Boulder, CO: Westview Press.

Schumpeter, J. A. (1954) *History of Economic Analysis*, New York: Oxford University Press.

Tobin, J. (1985) "Theoretical Issues in Macroeconomics," in *Issues in Contemporary Macroeconomic and Distribution*, ed. by G. R. Feiwel, Albany, NY: State University of New York Press.

17 1935 where we were – where we are 2000

Robert Solo

Life is the great vehicle that carries us through time. In observing the passing landscape from our particular space on the deck of that great vehicle, we come to know what we know of the world. It is a complex journey that for each one of us moves simultaneously on a diversity of paths. In this chapter I recount a voyage of learning and encounter, of observation and discovery, of disenchantment and dissent, in traversing the spaces of thought on economics qua discipline, in the formulation and experience of economic policy, in confrontation with and learning from encounters with economic realities. I offer it not as an account of what I did, but only of what I saw and learned of economics in the doing.

I was surely very fortunate in those who taught me my trade. My first course in economics was in 1935 at the University of Pennsylvania during the first two years of my undergraduate studies there. My instructor was Allan Young who, as Chief Economist for the Federal Reserve Board, would establish the Survey Research Center at the University of Michigan. My tutors at Harvard were Edward H. Chamberlin and Kenneth Galbraith. There, under John Williams, I discovered the magic of money and the amazing powers of the banking system. There, under Edward Mason, I discovered the "Great" corporation, a quasi-political entity detached from the prerogatives of ownership, as the persona of the modern industrial economy, and the varieties of industrial organizations in relation to the law and the role of the state. There under Ed Chamberlin and Paul Sweezy, I was seduced by pure theory in those days of arithmetic and geometric model making. There, through my contact with Joseph Schumpeter, I was led to comprehend the impact on the economy of a technological innovation as it fulfills its potential in the long cycles of growth and development. Through the air I breathed at Harvard, but perhaps especially through Ray Walsh, I discovered Marx and Marxism, and encountered the baby Bolsheviks of the Young Communist League playing at conspiracy.

It was during my junior and senior years (1936–38) at Harvard that I truly became an economist. This "becoming an economist" had far more to do with a new and awakened awareness than with any new knowledge I might have acquired: which is to say that I discovered the economy, not simply as a circumstance and environment lived in and adapted to, but as an object to be viewed apart from workaday experience, shaped by a complex of forces, with a past, with a history, with a destiny, an object to be dissected, analyzed, comprehended, and possibly controlled. Such certainly was the case with respect to the phenomenon called the Great Depression.

For those of us who were born into it, who knew nothing of what went before it, this Great Depression that had shaken, and was shaking, the very foundations of capitalism seemed the natural and normal state of affairs and the context of our aspirations. My father was a "businessman." So was my mother. I observed and even shared in their ugly, ferocious struggle to stay afloat and to seize upon and climb the ladder of affluence in a snarling world of dog eat dog. Unemployment, the muttered "brother can you spare a dime?", and the bread lines were as familiar to me as my morning coffee. But only at Harvard did I discover the depression as an integral and autonomous phenomenon controlling the destiny of the world; again, an object apart to be analyzed, dissected, comprehended, and possibly controlled.

I came to know my economics very, very well. I will say quite immodestly that I have yet to meet anyone whose grasp of the core theory (what the physicists would call the fundamental equations within the frame of which their research is carried on) is as deep as mine. It is precisely because I am secure in my understanding of that which underlies the theory and discipline of economics that I have been willing and able to judge it, critique it, and reject it.

Thomas Kuhn called this defining framework of any science its 'paradigm'. The economics paradigm conceives a universe of individual entrepreneurs exercising the powers of private ownership competing in, and in turn being controlled by, a system of freely moving price. This image is postulated as the essence of economic reality.

The times through which we move in this essay are of continuous and radical change, change in the structure and character of society, change in the character and structure of the economy. What does not change, what is constant throughout, is this selfsame neoclassical paradigm framing the research output of the discipline and taught and inculcated into the thought of generation after generation of hapless, helpless students. The "neoclassical paradigm" was the same then as it is now; indeed, the same as it was in the far-off days of Adam Smith and Ricardo. This amazing durability of the paradigm, unchanged, though the universe to which it ostensibly refers changes fundamentally, confirms Kuhn's characterization of the nature of the paradigm in science. And we will observe in what follows defensive tactics, conscious and unconscious, on the part of its adepts, in fending off the threat of change.

One might have supposed that the highly creative research findings and analytic realizations made during the 1930s would have upset and overturned the established economics paradigm. We knew and no one challenged as a fact that the giant corporate organization had replaced the individual entrepreneur as the key persona of the American industrial economy. Kenneth Boulding called it the organizational revolution. That and its implications contradicted a fundamental assumption of neoclassical theory. And we knew from the work of Berle and Means that among these corporate entities ownership (by share holders) was separated from control, eliminating the motivational force on which the established theory depends. All good reasons to reject and replace the paradigm. We knew all that, but the paradigm was not rejected, not even challenged.

The very precise and entirely logical work of Edward H. Chamberlin in his "The Theory of Monopolistic Competition" and of Joan Robinson and her "Imperfect Competition", both confirmed by commonplace observation, demonstrated that even when individual entrepreneurs who own and control their business compete in a free market, their competition is likely of another order than that postulated by the paradigm. Another good reason to challenge and change the paradigm! But the paradigm was not challenged or changed.

Years later while I was studying at the London School of Economics, a raging George Stigler came to London in a ferocious campaign directed specifically against the theory of monopolistic competition. Listening to him I understood that the disregard of the implications of the organizational revolution and of the separation of ownership from control and of monopolistic and imperfect competition was not simply a matter of inertia and indifference. For here, from the University of Chicago, was George Stigler playing the role of the ideological enforcer, seeking to thrust monopolistic competition (as later he did with Galbraith's idea of countervailing power) outside the zone of consideration. But why? Because to recognize monopolistic competition as an element of analysis would introduce an ineradicable uncertainty into the paradigm with its pretensions to the status of "science" and would eliminate its moral imperative equating free competition with perfect efficiency.

But in those days the greatest threat to the established paradigm existed in the seeming endless masses of the unemployed consequent upon the long continuing depression; Say's Law, expressing perfectly the logic of the established theory, denies that such a condition could possibly exist. Yet it did exist, and the paradigm offered policy makers no avenue of escape. Along comes the Keynesian theory, which offers an avenue of escape.

They called it the Keynesian revolution. It was touted as the new paradigm. We all, certainly myself, accepted it as that. It was no revolution. In retrospect it appears as a transitory and rootless attachment that saved the neoclassical paradigm and the traditional liberal ideology from the wrath of society, but did not displace, replace or in any way change the neoclassical paradigm. True, it did offer an explanation and a solution to the problem of mass unemployment, but one that for a long time had been urged by despised amateurs in the underground of thought, and one that Herr Hitler and Marshall Goering understood very well and applied with great success in Nazi

Germany: namely that with fixed or "rigid" prices, a decline in aggregate demand (total spending) will reduce output and generate mass unemployment: but where the unemployed can be re-employed by restoring the level of aggregate demand through incremental spending by the state. Such was the long and the short of Keynesian theory. The acceptance of that simple formula should have challenged and forced if not the displacement, then at least a critical restructuring of the neoclassical paradigm. It is a monument to the inability of the academic mind to see the obvious, that it did not do so. Consider.

Most of us learned (and taught) Keynesian economics via Samuelson's *Principles*. Samuelson's text conceives of the (same, single) economy as to be understood from two points of view. The *Micro* describes its internal operations, and the *Macro* allegedly describes that same economy from the outside, so to speak, as a function of aggregates.

But Samuelson himself and the hundreds of thousands of those who taught with or learned from his book failed to see that his micro and his macro could not possibly be facets of the same economy. The two were absolutely incommensurable. The micro operated through and could not function without free moving price. The macro required and would not operate without fixed or rigid prices. These were two different and distinct forms of economic organization. The micro was at one with the nonclassical paradigm. The price-behavior of the macro was to be observed in the corporate industrial sector, in a system that must be explained by other principles entirely.

Harvard in the late thirties was an exciting community close to the center of a virtual social revolution. Intellectuals there and, indeed, throughout the country, myself among them, were so caught up in the American social dynamic as to be quite unaware of, even stone blind to, a colossal tragedy that had already taken hold in Europe and Asia, and that would soon threaten our very civilization. When I graduated from college in 1938, I took a $500 inheritance and shipped off on the *Isle de France* to spend the next three months biking through Europe. There I encountered the Nazis, there I saw the face of Fascism: discoveries that, for years, would set me apart from my peers at home. I went there as a pacifist and an isolationist. I had written an honors thesis on the economics of embargo imposed to keep America out of any European entanglement. I went as a pacifist and isolationist, I came back knowing there would be a war, that there had to be a war, and the sooner the better. Later, when I worked in Washington, it was this discovery, this awareness, this realization, this commitment that set me apart from a New Deal host, indifferent or blind to events, even as the whole of Europe fell into the Nazi maw.

It was in 1936 that John Maynard Keynes published *The General Theory of Employment, Interest and Money*. It made a great stir. In 1937–38 the best of my peers and professors were scrabbling to understand it, which is not easy to do for, though its message is simple enough, its reasoning is diffuse and obscure. Its great success confirms Solo's Social Law, that institutionalized bodies of thought and ideologies (like the paradigm) are protected by walls that will withstand all the storms of experienced contradiction and all the assaults of reason coming from the outside. They are to be breached only through the tactic of the Trojan Horse. Here Keynes, the preeminent British economist of his time, played the role of the Trojan Horse. It was his defection (not his arguments) that breached the walls and opened the possibility of change.

At the time, junior members of the Harvard faculty published a symposium purporting to explain *The General Theory* and its implications for public policy. One of its authors, Richard Gilbert, was brought down to Washington to organize The Division of Industrial Economics as the staff of Harry Hopkins in the Department of Commerce. It was a small agency consisting initially of seven senior and five junior members. I came at its beginning as one of the juniors. Its task was to provide Keynesian guidance for the planning and implementation of a full employment policy. Such policy was based on the proposition that there existed a great gap, permanent or recurrent, between the spontaneously generated level of aggregate spending and that required for full employment. The task, then, was to forecast the size of that gap and to propose the level of incremental public (or induced private) spending required to fill it.

How to finance a massive increase in public spending in order to fill the full employment gap, where such spending must be an addition to, not a net diversion from, the income–expenditure flow. My Keynesian colleagues favored public borrowing to finance such incremental public spending. Foreseeing the problems implicit in a cumulating public debt, I took a different position and argued for, and have frequently published in favor of, the use of funds created as "interest-free debt" through the Federal Reserve Board.

The Division of Industrial Economics never succeeded in guiding or promoting a public action geared to, let alone achieving, a condition of full employment. Swept aside by events in Europe, it was finally absorbed into the war agencies. On my own, I published a monograph, *Industrial Capacity in the United States*, which served as the reference for industrial planning throughout the war. I devised a system for the continuous monitoring of excess industrial capacity as an aid to the planning of capital investment throughout the war. I devised a basis for estimating the magnitude of strategic imports. I was probably the first to propose that the practice of assigning priorities be replaced by a system of direct material allocation. I ended my work in wartime Washington as economic advisor to the American Executive Secretary of the Combined (British American) Raw Materials Board.

One lesson I learned from this experience in government was the practical irrelevance of the established economics paradigm to any of the problems we faced.

After Pearl Harbor I served as an officer in the US Navy at advanced bases in the Pacific. Demobilized in 1945, from 1946 until 1949, I studied at the London School of Economics, reading economics under Lord Robbins and philosophy under Karl Popper.

Karl Popper, a positivist philosopher, was generally acknowledged as the great man, so to speak, as the "king" in the philosophy of science. In his view the statements of science must be constantly submitted to the test of prediction, and a statement in science can be accepted as tentatively true only inasmuch as its has been so tested and has not yet failed any test of prediction. Hence, mathematics was the language proper to science because it is the appropriate instrument for testing through prediction. Eventually, in their extension into new spheres of application or investigation, all such theories or statements will fail the test of prediction, revealing their fallibility or imperfection and forcing their discard, thrusting back to the science, the task of formulating a more encompassing theory and a higher law.

How did all this relate to the neoclassical paradigm in ecoomics? First that economics was not a science and could never be a science in Popper's meaning of the term, not because of the character of economic theory, but because of the universe to which the economic statement relates. There can be, and there are, no general statements in economics that could not have at any time been falsified through a specific failure of prediction, simply because general statements about society (including statistical laws and probabilities) are always a "sometimes thing" at once true here and false there, true today and false tomorrow.

Then how can one rationally establish the credibility and acceptability of a particular theory or statement? Only as an act of judgment, hopefully based on an assessment of the evidence pro and con, including a record of predictions, and, certainly, through the direct observation of function and practice. That, in the dissertation I wrote, was my message to economists.

Which leads to another question. Mathematics is the appropriate instrument of prediction, but economics and the social sciences cannot be refuted through experimental prediction. And where credibility must be established through a judgment based on the direct observation of function and practice, mathematics is the worst of possible languages. Then why, since the 1930s, has economics been translated into and virtually encompassed by the language of mathematics?

Because it makes economics looks like physics? – though it excludes qualitative data relative to rational judgment, and stands in the way of the direct observation of function and practice. Because as a secret language confined to an elite, it shuts off outside observation and critical evaluation of the operation of economics and the meaning of its statement? You can read more about this in a book *The Philosophy of Science and Economics* that I published in 1997.

My message to economists was, alas, not appreciated by or acceptable to Lord Robbins and his ilk. So I returned to the States to take my degree at

Cornell University where I wrote on the economics and politics of research and development: a new, hitherto unconsidered variable for the systematic production of innovations. I will spare you the details of my subsequent academic and extra-academic career, with its many defeats and occasional victories; save to note that our "Spartan Group" at Michigan State, including Warren Samuels, Harry Trebing, Allan Schmid, James Shaffer, Stephen Woodbury, and myself constituted, in the midst of an unsympathetic economics department, virtually a Michigan State School critical of the paradigm and seeking to transcend its boundaries. Our voice, in that score, weak as it was, was still perhaps the strongest in the world.

The word "liberalism" has very different but coexisting meanings. Classical liberalism in British parlance is to be associated with the established economic paradigm, assuming and idealizing an economy of individual entrepreneurs freely interacting in a price-competitive market. It is anti-state, anti-monopoly, with its emphasis on privacy, private rights, and private property. Milton Friedman could, I suppose, be considered a classical liberal.

When I returned to the United States in 1949, liberalism and the liberal had come to possess a very different meaning. It was associated with the American Left, in turn identified with Keynesian monetary policy and the responsibility of the state for the level of employment, the full welfare agenda and social reforms of the New Deal. Call it New Deal liberalism.

New Deal liberals saw an activist Federal state as necessary and, in their experience, as beneficent. That state had mobilized our forces to pursue and destroy the Axis powers. That state was our proper instrument of Keynesian full employment planning. It became our guarantor against the vicissitudes of old age, ill health, and natural disaster. It was our protector against exploitation by corporate monopolies. To that end, under the banner of the New Deal ideology, the Supreme Court opened gates that had been tightly closed for more than half a century for positive action by the Federal state, and the state had launched the most intensive, extensive anti-trust prosecutions ever undertaken. It safeguarded for the first time our bank deposits and guaranteed the viability of the banking system. It uplifted a battered agriculture and imposed a floor on key commodity prices. In so doing it accelerated investment in agriculture and set in motion the most rapid rise in the productivity of American agriculture on record. It began the process of pollution control and the cleanup of the massive dumps of industrial wastes whose poisons were and are upseeping the earth.

For the New Deal liberal, the highest priority attached to the achievement of full employment, individual opportunity in the workplace, and the absolute and relative rise in the real income of working men and women. To that end legislation introduced minimum wages. Legislation outlawed discrimination in the workplace on grounds of race, religion, and gender. New doors to education were opened as in the establishment of a junior college network. In its GI Bill of Rights, New Deal liberalism gave higher education in the United States a boost without precedent. Taxation was made more progressive with new impositions on corporate profits. Under the aegis and protection of the state, industrial trade unionism was nurtured and a powerful trade union movement was established that was expected to spearhead the drive for higher real wages and improved working conditions, and also to provide solid support for the continuation and development of New Deal liberalism.

New Deal liberalism was pragmatically protectionist, to enable the state effectively to control market conditions, maintain full employment, and to raise the income and better the life of the working stiff. For that reason the Roosevelt Administration killed the "gold standard", which was then a primary support for international free trade.

New Deal liberalism was never without its enemies. I remember with a sense of wonder the ferocious boundless hatred of some of the rich for FDR. The old religion with the neoclassical economics paradigm as its bible, with its pure faith in the beneficence of market competition and its message of *laisser-faire* remained solidly entrenched, centered at the University of Chicago with Milton Friedman as its prophet, George Stigler, scourge of the heretics, at his right hand, and his disciples systematically sown over the length and breadth of the land.

We have spoken of the state under New Deal liberalism as interventionist, we have spoken of its Keynesian planning. This intervention and planning, however, was of a quite particular sort. It was normally an offset to problems spontaneously generated in the market or in society. Which is to say that it was responsive rather than purposeful and geared to the achievement of some grand design. And it normally took the form of dollar payments to individuals, corporations or institutions, or was simply fed into the aggregate expenditure stream, that is, it threw money at the problems and hoped they would go away. The neoclassical paradigm remained intact, accepted but ignored in the piecemeal and pragmatic, problem-responsive evolution of New Deal policy.

What I have described as New Deal liberalism was not a point of view and policy unique to the United States. Rather in its essential elements it was shared with all of postwar Western capitalism. And in the years following the end of World War II, at least the countries of Western Europe acted in concert in their implementation of Keynesian planning. And the two decades following the end of World War II, where that common policy and practice prevailed, are remembered as "golden years" for the United States, Western Europe, and Japan with low unemployment and rates of economic growth without precedent. Why then was this eminently successful policy abandoned? Why did it fail even as it succeeded? What happened to the point of view and outlook behind it?

New Deal liberalism was weakened by the changes in the character of organized labor. Rising affluence eliminated solidarity-based ties of shared desperation. A margin of workers joined the moneyed classes in their outrage at what the State was taking out and their indifference as to what the State was putting in. Labor ceased to be an object of public compassion and, in the public's eyes, became another hard-fisted interest group out for self-advantage. Recurrent waves of anti-Communism cast a shadow on labor's leadership. Trade union corruption and the infiltration of a criminal element were a source of general disenchantment. The new immigrants from Asia and Latin America relied upon to fill the depleted ranks were without a trade union tradition. With mass defections and the Southward flight of industry, the large and powerful union movement became small and weak. So that by the time Ronald Reagan chose to break the air controllers' union there was virtually no resistance nor any effective protest. And Bill Clinton with the Democrats most blithely trampled the demands and interests of organized labor both with NAFTA and as champion of a global economy.

I shall not speculate here on the other reasons for the decline and repudiation of New Deal liberalism, but decline it did. And by the time George Dukakis ran as the Democratic candidate for President and Reagan ruled the White House, to call a politician a liberal was something between a curse and an indictment. With the election of Bill Clinton, and during the years of his Administration, another sort of liberalism had come into fashion.

When I went overseas to do my bit in World War II, I departed from an America which was profoundly racist, deeply riven and divided by ethnic and religious prejudice. The black was a non-person. Neighborhoods, lodgings, clubs, corporations, whole industries were restricted, with Catholics, ethnics, and especially Jews excluded. Universities and medical schools had their admission quotas. The professoriate was a closed corporation. I came home to another chemistry of social relations. The war against the Nazis, with the horror and infinite ugliness of racism exposed by the holocaust, had changed things. The black stood upright, the Jew was no longer ashamed. Racism was in disgrace. Barriers were still there, but the sentiments that sustained them had radically changed.

And the barriers came down. Under the impetus of Constitutional reinterpretation, legislation, electoral choice, personal behavior, group, and institutional pressure, the barriers came down. New avenues of opportunity and of intercourse were opened. The movement took on its own momentum, its own credo, its own ideology, its own organizations, its own crazies. It was the nexus of a new liberalism; quite removed from New Deal liberalism, unrelated to the economy or economic betterment or income distribution or income inequality and equity or depression and employment, but focused on liberation: black liberation, women's liberation, gay liberation, lesbian liberation. It was the "Liberation Liberalism" of Bill and Hillary Clinton. Beyond the demand for equal treatment and equal opportunity, the new liberalism has moved onto dangerous and controversial territory in demanding preferential treatment and affirmative action. This has been tied to the feverish re-embrace of the old orthodoxy, a resurgent commitment to the Book, that is to say to a fanatic faith in neoclassical theory, now purified and restated in the impenetrable language of mathematics, far more rigid and emptier than was the economics of Alfred Marshall, shades of Malthus and Adam Smith. Its message is simple enough. Free trade. Balance the budget. Dismantle the Federal State. The Clinton Administration has followed these commands to the letter. Indeed, regulation and control of the economy has virtually vanished except as an appendage to, and an instrument of, corporate interests.

Thus the paradigm survives intact in spite of all its contradictions and failures. One reason for this is that we lack any alternative. There is an old political adage, that in the electoral process you can't beat someone with no one. Here also, you can't beat this paradigm with no paradigm. The fact is that the discipline needs, as its common reference, an encompassing theory that can serve as its framework, as its paradigm. Its nay-sayers, doubters, and critics have failed to formulate a theory and approach that might reasonably serve as an alternative to the neoclassical paradigm, competing with it on what they call the market place of ideas.

I tried to advance such an alternative paradigm when I published *Economic Organizations and Social Systems* in 1967. The book will be reissued in the spring of 2000 by the University of Michigan Press, again in a bid to serve as such an alternative. Take a look to envision it as an element in a more open and encompassing base for an economic (or a socioeconomic) curriculum to come.

And now, at the very edge of the millennium, I realize myself (I confess, to my surprise) amidst revolutionary change, with an unprecedented social and economic system unlike anything ever experienced before, with the computer in cyber space overturning our lives, with a global economy for the moment centered, it would seem, in the Wall Street Bull Market. Warren Samuels and myself are privileged to see at least the beginning of a new episode in the great adventure.

Appendix to Chapter 10

Barley Price Expectation Data
1822 - 1846

YEAR	jvill	hvill	shanb	tbuxt	tavel	rhanb	rpryo	ebuxt	apryo	Act. P
1822	28.0	29.0	25.0	33.0	27.5	23.5	28.0	0.0	0.0	30.0
1823	35.0	36.0	27.0	41.0	41.0	35.0	32.0	0.0	0.0	36.0
1824	35.0	37.0	35.0	38.0	36.0	35.0	34.0	0.0	0.0	49.0
1825	50.0	56.0	44.0	50.0	47.0	46.0	54.0	0.0	0.0	41.0
1826	40.0	32.0	39.0	32.0	39.0	36.0	38.0	0.0	0.0	39.0
1827	28.0	39.0	32.0	32.0	39.0	32.0	30.0	0.0	0.0	33.0
1828	30.0	45.0	36.0	45.0	42.0	34.0	40.0	0.0	0.0	42.0
1829	33.0	31.0	34.0	34.0	36.5	36.0	35.0	0.0	0.0	36.0
1830	29.0	27.0	27.0	37.0	35.0	33.0	38.0	0.0	0.0	42.0
1831	40.0	36.0	38.0	34.0	39.0	38.0	36.0	0.0	0.0	37.0
1832	33.5	36.0	35.5	33.0	40.0	35.5	30.0	0.0	0.0	33.0
1833	35.5	31.0	39.0	36.0	37.0	37.5	35.0	0.0	0.0	31.0
1834	32.0	28.0	35.0	32.0	38.0	37.0	35.0	0.0	0.0	28.0
1835	33.0	28.0	0.0	36.0	37.0	32.0	31.0	34.0	0.0	33.0
1836	31.0	29.0	0.0	36.0	0.0	34.0	36.0	34.0	0.0	39.0
1837	0.0	39.0	0.0	34.0	0.0	35.0	36.0	31.0	32.0	34.5
1838	0.0	33.5	0.0	32.0	0.0	32.5	34.0	33.0	33.0	49.0
1839	0.0	40.0	0.0	43.0	0.0	45.0	0.0	39.0	39.0	46.0
1840	0.0	40.0	0.0	40.0	0.0	38.0	0.0	38.0	39.0	38.0
1841	0.0	39.0	0.0	36.0	0.0	37.0	0.0	35.0	38.0	32.0
1842	0.0	31.5	0.0	30.0	0.0	32.0	0.0	31.0	33.0	32.0
1843	0.0	32.0	0.0	36.0	0.0	33.0	0.0	34.0	36.5	37.0
1844	0.0	37.0	0.0	0.0	0.0	37.5	0.0	38.0	41.0	36.0
1845	0.0	35.0	0.0	0.0	0.0	39.0	0.0	38.0	36.0	37.0
1846	0.0	0.0	0.0	0.0	0.0	51.0	0.0	48.0	49.0	61.0
MEAN	34.2	35.3	34.3	36.4	38.1	36.2	35.4	36.1	37.7	38.1
S.ERR.P	5.5	6.3	5.2	4.8	4.1	5.2	5.6	4.4	4.7	7.1

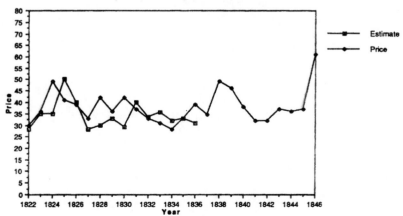

J. Vill Barley Price Estimate Vs. Actual Price

H. Vill Barley Price Estimate Vs. Actual Price

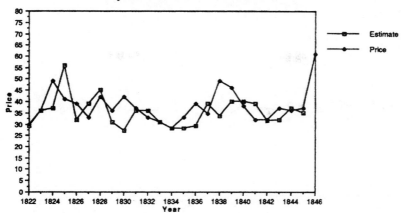

S. Hanb Barley Price Estimate Vs. Actual Price

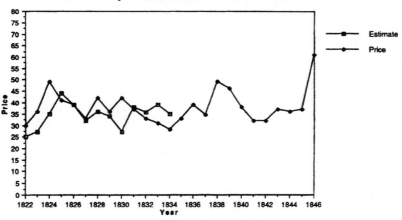

T. Buxt Barley Price Estimate Vs. Actual Price

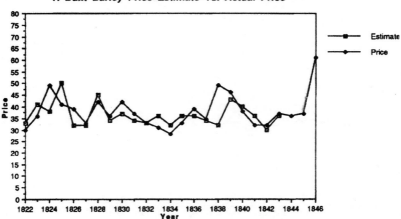

T. Avel Barley Price Estimate Vs. Actual Price

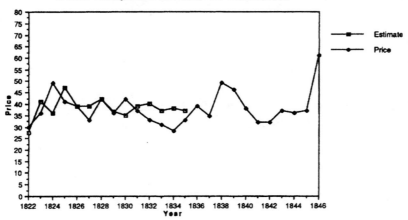

R. Hanb Barley Price Estimate Vs. Actual Price

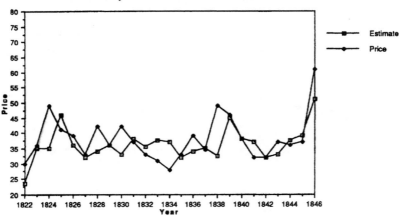

R. Pryo Barley Price Estimate Vs. Actual Price

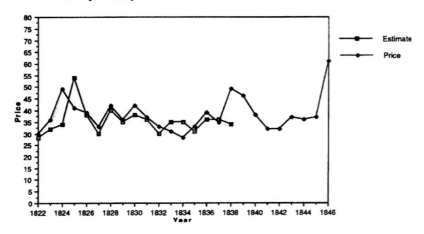

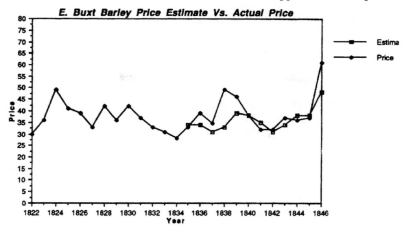

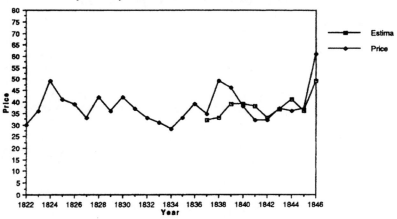

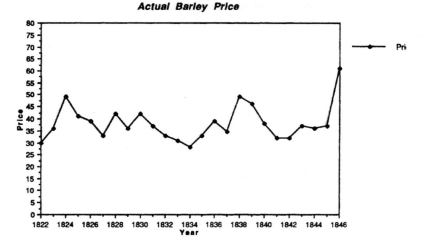

Hops Price Expectation Data
1822 - 1846

YEAR	jvill	hvill	shanb	tbuxt	tavel	rhanb	rpryo	ebuxt	apryo	Act. P
1822	84	76	95	75	105	84	84	0	0	84
1823	210	200	180	240	340	273	300	0	0	260
1824	80	210	140	400	205	160	155	0	0	152
1825	400	348	280	100	410	498	700	0	0	370
1826	110	95	130	160	220	126	120	0	0	100
1827	105	140	120	112	220	126	160	0	0	120
1828	84	60	115	160	150	84	95	0	0	120
1829	240	168	240	140	270	175	224	0	0	168
1830	189	147	130	100	210	202	200	0	0	220
1831	200	160	119	110	210	120	200	0	0	132
1832	102	110	115	105	145	118	112	0	0	189
1833	135	90	118	240	114	135	118	0	0	140
1834	150	140	155	105	278	231	224	0	0	126
1835	80	126	0	100	136	118	112	120	0	112
1836	85	89	0	100	0	90	100	90	0	126
1837	0	120	0	140	0	105	105	95	150	110
1838	0	180	0	95	0	130	160	135	150	132
1839	0	90	0	300	0	90	0	85	70	98
1840	0	320	0	160	0	340	0	360	355	336
1841	0	140	0	120	0	147	0	130	110	160
1842	0	140	0	147	0	120	0	112	147	110
1843	0	150	0	0	0	165	0	168	189	170
1844	0	210	0	0	0	205	0	190	230	174
1845	0	157	0	0	0	168	0	147	150	164
1846	0	0	0	0	0	105	0	105	108	105
MEAN	150.3	152.8	149.0	145.9	215.2	164.6	186.4	144.8	165.9	159.1
S.ERR.P	84.5	67.7	52.0	82.7	83.9	90.8	140.5	71.6	75.6	69.6

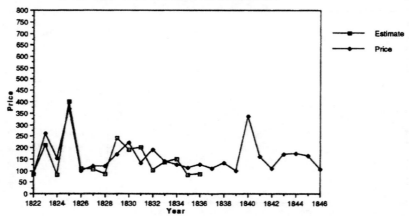

J. Vill Hops Price Estimate Vs. Actual Price

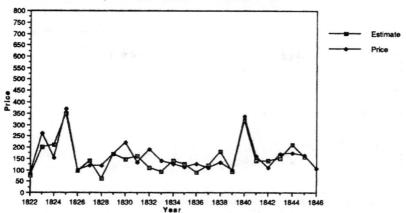

H. Vill Hops Price Estimate Vs. Actual Price

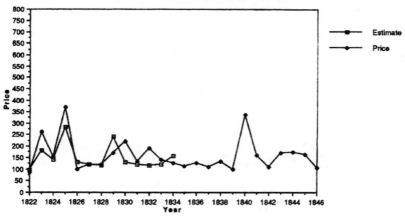

S. Hanb Hops Price Estimate Vs. Actual Price

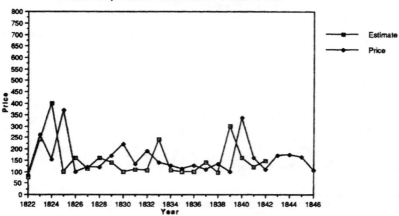

T. Buxt Hops Price Estimate Vs. Actual Price

T. Avel Hops Price Estimate Vs. Actual Price

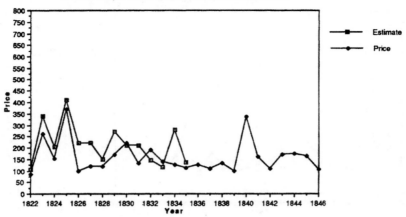

E. Buxt Hops Price Estimate Vs. Actual Price

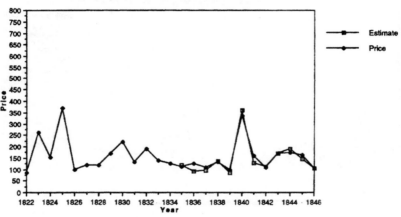

R. Hanb Hops Price Estimate Vs. Actual Price

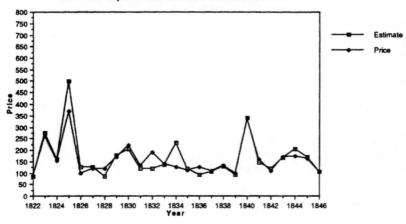

R. Pryo Hops Price Estimate Vs. Actual Price

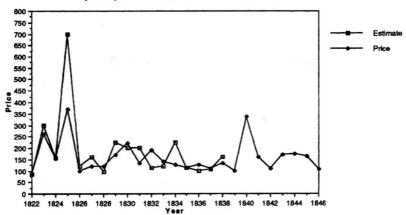

A. Pryo Hops Price Estimate Vs. Actual price

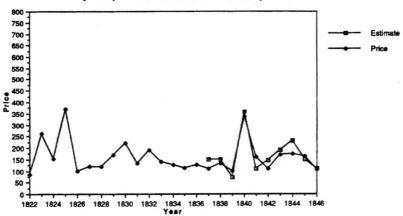

Actual Hops Price

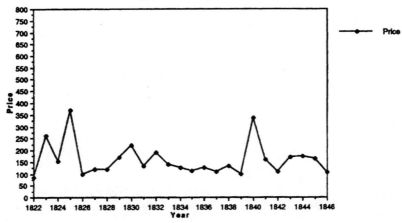

Index